THE NATURAL HISTORY OF MAN

A Woman of the Tuda Race

THE NATURAL HISTORY OF MAN;

COMPRISING

INQUIRIES INTO THE MODIFYING INFLUENCE OF PHYSICAL AND MORAL AGENCIES ON THE DIFFERENT TRIBES OF THE HUMAN FAMILY.

BY

JAMES COWLES PRICHARD, M.D. F.R.S. M.R.I.A.

Fourth Edition, Edited and Enlarged by

EDWIN NORRIS,

IN TWO VOLUMES

Vol. II.

GYAN

Published by

Gyan Publishing House
5, Ansari Road
Daryaganj, New Delhi-110002
Phone: 011-47034999, 9811692060
E-mail: books@gyanbooks.com

Distribution Network
gyanbooks.com
India, USA, Canada, UK, Australia, France

ISBN : 978-81-212-6661-1 (Set)
ISBN : 978-81-212-6675-8 (PB)
First Published, 1855

2nd Impression 2022

Printed at: Gyan Press, Delhi.

THE NATURAL HISTORY OF MAN (VOL. II)
Author: JAMES COWLES PRICHARD

THE

NATURAL HISTORY

OF

MAN;

COMPRISING

INQUIRIES INTO THE MODIFYING INFLUENCE OF PHYSICAL AND MORAL AGENCIES ON THE DIFFERENT TRIBES OF THE HUMAN FAMILY.

BY

JAMES COWLES PRICHARD, M.D. F.R.S. M.R.I.A.

PRESIDENT OF THE ETHNOLOGICAL SOCIETY,
CORRESPONDING MEMBER OF THE NATIONAL INSTITUTE,
AND OF THE ROYAL ACADEMY OF MEDICINE, AND OF THE STATISTICAL SOCIETY, OF FRANCE,
MEMBER OF THE AMERICAN PHILOSOPHICAL SOCIETY; ETC.

Fourth Edition, Edited and Enlarged by

EDWIN NORRIS,

OF THE ROYAL ASIATIC SOCIETY OF GREAT BRITAIN AND IRELAND.

ILLUSTRATED WITH SIXTY TWO COLOURED PLATES ENGRAVED ON STEEL, AND ONE HUNDRED ENGRAVINGS ON WOOD.

IN TWO VOLUMES.

VOL. II.

1855.

CONTENTS.

BOOK II.

DIVISION INTO GROUPS.

CHAPTER XVI. (*continued.*)

CHAPTER XVII.

CHAPTER XVIII.

CHAPTER XIX.

CHAPTER XX.

CHAPTER XXI.

CHAPTER XXII.

BOOK III.

CONCLUSIONS.

CHAPTER I.

CHAPTER II.

CHAPTER III.

CHAPTER IV.

CHAPTER V.

CHAPTER VI.

NATURAL HISTORY OF MAN.

BOOK II.

CHAPTER XVI.

OF THE SAABIAN OR LESSER SOUTH AFRICAN RACE, INCLUDING THE HOTTENTOTS AND THE BUSHMEN.

THE people called by Europeans Hottentots and Bushmen are said to have among themselves the national appellation of Saabs or Saaps. Quaiquæ is another name which belongs to them generally, and one syllable of this doubtless plural word seems to enter into the epithets of particular tribes of Hottentots, as Namaaqua, Gonaaqua. The origin of the word Hottentot is uncertain; it is probably a corruption of Houteniqua, the name of a particular tribe now extinct, or, at least, unknown. Dampier wrote the name of these people Hodmadods, instead of Hottentots. There was a tribe formerly termed Sonquas, and the Bushmen were termed in some old accounts Sonqua Hottentots.

The Hottentots are a most singular race of people; they are the primeval inhabitants of a country which, in its aspect and in all its productions, is equally singular, and displays phenomena, both in the animal and vegetable kingdoms, not elsewhere seen. The region of the world which it most nearly resembles, in all organised productions as well as in the dryness of its soil, is the great island of Australia. The high plain of Central Africa terminates to the southward in the plateau of the Gariep or Orange River, and hence the surface of the land declines towards the southern coast, not subsiding by a gentle and unbroken slope, or sinking precipitately by a sudden fall, but, like almost all the other table-lands which extend through the interior of great continents, by successive steps, or by a series of terrasses, each lower than the other, and all separated from each other by long elevated ridges, becoming in some parts high mountain-chains, which run like transverse walls almost across the south of Africa, from east to west.* The longest and the most elevated of them may be considered as the southern boundary of the plateau or domain of the Gariep. It bears in different parts the names of Nieuwbergen, Sneuwbergen, and Winterberg, and under the last name attains the height of 6000 feet. To the southward of this chain the dry and barren plains of the Great Karroo extend, though seventy or eighty miles in breadth, and are bounded farther south by the Zwarteberg, another transverse chain, which becomes the northern wall of a second terrass of lower level, and narrower than the Karroo. This longitudinal valley is the Lange-Kloof. The last range towards the south is formed by the Zwellendam, Outeniqua, and Zitzikamma Mountains, which cut off a littoral terrass, still of considerable elevation, stretching east and west from Algoa Bay to the Stormy Cape, and facing, like a great bulwark, the ocean of the Southern Pole. The interior of these regions consists, in many parts, of arid plains; there are also fertile valleys and fine pasture-grounds, and, in other parts, forests of consider-

* I have abstracted this short survey of the geographical direction of South Africa from Ritter's admirable outline in the "Erdkunde," adding many particulars from the excellent description of Mr. Bunbury, given in his "Journey to the Country of the Damaras." This traveller has evidently described from his own observation, and he appears not to have read the description given in the Erdkunde; yet he confirms the luminous views of the great geographer Ritter in almost every particular, and fills up his outline by additional observations.

able extent. In the deeper valleys are the channels of numerous streams, many of which are dry during a part of the year. The great river-system of the plateau is the Gariep, which in its length and direction has been compared to the Senegal. Unlike the other rivers of Africa, it scarcely fertilises its banks, which consist of bare and barren hills, surrounded by plains of yellow sand. South Africa is the region of a most peculiar vegetation, abounding in beautiful heaths and proteaceæ, aloës, euphorbias, and innumerable flowering shrubs, which, in their general forms, though not by identity of species, bear, as De Candolle and others have observed, a striking resemblance to the botany of Tasmania. In the same region are produced the multitudinous tribes of hoofed quadrupeds, of springbocks, nilghaus, and antelopes of various kinds, of giraffes and buffaloes, zebras and quaggas,—created, as it would appear, since elsewhere they exist not, to wander over the same vast level wildernesses with the ostrich, the winged camel of the desert. Such is the native country of the Saabian race; it resembles in some of its physical conditions the high plains of Central Asia, and its inhabitants, in many points of their bodily organisation, bear a corresponding analogy to the Mongoles of Great Tartary. The original Hottentots were herdsmen: they followed their flocks, clothed in sheepskins, roaming from place to place, and beguiling their movements with a monotonous but plaintive song. Their wealth consisted in their herds and in the simple utensils which they carried on their pack-oxen, and their temporary dwellings were huts composed of the boughs of trees and mats. Other tribes, less fortunate from the first, lived wholly in the woods, upon the scanty sustenance which chance brought within their grasp. Without cattle, their only art was that of shooting with poisoned arrows animals which they could not surprise by their natural craft and their almost supernatural quickness in the chase. The Bushmen were the outcasts of the more quiet and inactive herdsmen. They were robbers—their hand was against every man, and they suffered reciprocally the injuries which they inflicted.

There are few skulls belonging to this race in European collections. The cranium of a Bushman female has been described by Blumenbach, and another by Cuvier. Dr. Knox, who has seen the people in their native country, assures us that the face of the Hottentot resembles that of the Kalmuc, excepting in the greater thickness of the lips; and he sets them down as a branch of the Mongolian race. The width of the orbits, their distance from each other, the large size of the occipital foramen, are points in which the Hottentots resemble the northern Asiatics, and even the Esquimaux. The annexed outline represents the cranium of a Bushman, in which, however, the jaw projects more than in any other skulls of the same race.

Fig. 76.

Skull of a Bushman.

Mr. Barrow first described this people with accuracy. He says, "The Hottentots are well proportioned, erect, of delicate and effeminate make, not muscular; their joints and extremities small; their face generally ugly, but different in different families, some having the nose remarkably flat, others considerably raised. Their eyes are of a deep chesnut colour, long and narrow, distinct from each other, the inner angle being rounded, as in the Chinese, to whom the Hottentot bears a striking resemblance. The cheek-bones are high and prominent, and, with the narrow-pointed chin, form nearly a triangle. Their teeth are very white."

The Bushmen are thus described by the missionary Adulph Bonatz:—"These people," he says, "are of small stature and dirty yellow colour; their countenance is repulsive,—a prominent forehead, small, deeply-seated and roguish eyes, a much depressed nose, and thick projecting

Female of the Bushman Race.

Woman & Child of the Bushman Race

lips, are their characteristic features. Their constitution is so much injured by their dissolute habits and the constant smoking of durha, that both old and young look wrinkled and decrepid; nevertheless, they are fond of ornament, and decorate their ears, arms, and legs with beads, iron, copper, or brass rings; the women also stain their faces

FIG. 77.

Hottentot Female.

red, or paint them wholly or in part. Their only clothing, by day or night, is a mantle of sheep-skin thrown over their bodies, which they term a kaross. The dwelling of the Bushman is a low hut, or a circular cavity, on the open plain, in which he creeps at night with his wife and children, and which, though it shelters him from the wind, leaves him exposed to the rain. They had formerly their habitation among the rocks, in which are still seen rude figures of horses, oxen, or serpents. Many of them still live, like wild beasts, in their rocky retreats, to which they return with joy after escaping from the service of the colonists. I have never seen these fugitives otherwise occupied than with their bows and arrows; the bows are small, the arrows are barbed, and steeped in a potent poison, of a resinous appearance, distilled from the leaves of an indigenous tree. These they prefer to fire-arms, as weapons that make no report. On their return from the chase they feast till they become drowsy, and hunger only rouses them to renewed exertion. In seasons of scarcity they devour wild roots, ants' eggs, locusts, and snakes. As enemies, the Bushmen are not to be despised. Their language seems to consist of snapping, hissing, grunting sounds, all of them nasal."

Erroneous notions have long ago been entertained respecting the origin of the Bushmen, and their relation to the pastoral Hottentots. It is now possible to correct these mistakes, and I shall, for that purpose, enter into some details on the subject, and bring some facts to bear upon it which tend to elucidate the ethnology of Southern Africa, and, perhaps, to suggest useful inquiries respecting the origin of some nations in other parts of the world.

It has been supposed that the Bushmen are a race of people distinct from the Hottentots. This opinion was founded on the difference of their manners, on the supposed untameable character of the Bushmen, and, most of all, on the fact that the Hottentots do not understand the language of the Bushmen.

Others, who suppose the two nations to be of one stock, imagine that the hordes of Bushmen owe their existence to the hardships which were inflicted by the European colonists of South Africa on the Hottentots. The herdsmen of that race are supposed to have been plundered by the Dutch settlers near the Cape, and, after losing their cattle and all their property, to have been driven into the wilderness to subsist on such food as they could acquire by the chase and the rude arts of the most abject savages.

Neither of these opinions is well founded, as it has been fully proved by the researches of an able and well-informed traveller, who has made a long abode in South Africa, and was engaged by the Colonial Government to undertake a long journey of investigation in the interior of Hottentot- and Kafirland. From Dr. Andrew Smith's accurate information we are convinced that the Bushmen are of the same race as the Hottentots, and originally spoke the same language. They have been separated, however, from the pastoral Hottentots from a very distant period, and do not owe their destitute condition to the robberies inflicted on their forefathers by European colonists, though their numbers have been augmented from time to time by the resort of outcasts from various conquered and reduced tribes to the wandering hordes in their vicinity. It appears extremely probable from Dr. Andrew Smith's researches, that the Bushmen existed in separate hordes in Southern Africa from a period even long antecedent to the arrival of the first colonists of the Cape.

The earliest notice of the Bushmen that is known occurs in the narrative of an expedition to the country of the Amaquas, undertaken in the year 1685 by the Dutch governor of the colony, Simon van der Stell.* In this narrative an account was given of a people whose description exactly coincides with that of the present Bushmen. They were termed Sonquas, and lived in the immediate vicinity of the Amaqua Hottentots: they are said to have been robbers. "They carried," says the writer of this relation, "bows and arrows, and assagays, possessed no cattle, and subsisted on wild honey and the game which they shot. Their abodes, or rather places of wandering, were along a stream which flowed from the Gricqua mountains, falling into the Olifant river. On inquiry," continues the narrator, "we learned that *Sonqua* signifies the same as *pauper* does in Europe, and that each tribe of Hottentots had their own Sonquas, whom they employed to give notice of

---

* "Diary of a Journey made by the Governor Simon van der Stell to the Country of the Amaquas in the year 1685," translated from the Dutch by W. L. von Buschenroder, Esq. (South African Quarterly Journal, Cape Town, 1820.)

approaching strangers. These Sonquas never plunder from the kraals of the people in whose service they are, but they rob others, and that as well in time of peace as in time of war. They possess nothing besides what they obtain by depredation."

I have been assured by Dr. Andrew Smith, who has not yet given to the world a full account of the results of his extensive observations on South Africa, that almost every tribe of people who have submitted themselves to social laws, who recognise the rights of property and reciprocal social duties, and have thereby acquired some wealth, and have formed themselves into a respectable caste, are surrounded by hordes of vagabonds and outcasts from their own community, or have them in their vicinity; that these hordes are ever gathering accessions from the predatory parties of neighbouring tribes, or even of more distant bodies of people. Their haunts are in the wilderness, and in the fastnesses of mountains and forests, and become the resort of all who from crimes and destitution are obliged to retire and hide themselves from the abodes of the more industrious, and honest, and thriving of the community. Such are the Bushmen of the Hottentot race.* But a similar condition in society produces similar results in regard to other races; and the Kafirs have their Bushmen as well as the Hottentots. But the people known to the Cape colonists are merely the outcast Hottentots. There are likewise vagabonds belonging to the Bechuana nation, who are called by the latter people Balalas. The wild outcasts who are scattered over the Kalahaie desert are known by the title of Bakalahaie. These, like the Balala, consist of the paupers and outcasts from different nations

---

* One of the most recent travellers in South Africa, F. Galton, Esq., says—"Two African tribes never live close up to a common frontier: they are always fighting and robbing, and therefore a broad border-land is essential; and in these border-lands, so far as I have seen, the Bushmen and other outcasts live." (Journal of the Royal Geographical Society, 1852, p. 148).—Ed.

and the neighbourhood. "They all stand," as Dr. A. Smith assures me, "in the same relation to the Kafirs as the Bushmen to the Hottentots."

We may here mention that the Amakosah or Kosa Kafirs had formerly under their dominion a servile tribe of the same description, well known under the name of Fingoes. A detailed account of this race was sent to the Royal Geographical Society by Captain Alexander, from which the following particulars are taken :—

When Major-General Sir B. D'Urban crossed the Kei in the Kafir war of 1835, and entered Hintza's country, he found a numerous population of Fingoes living in a state of abject slavery under the Amakosah Kafirs. They amounted to 17,000 souls. The whole body of this servile race were emancipated by the English from their cruel bondage, and settled in a state of freedom on lands which were given them between the Lower Keiskamma and the Great Fish River.

The name Fingoes implies wanderers, beggars, or outcasts. They belong to various scattered tribes of the Kafir race, and have the language of the Amakosah. The following are the names of the tribes of Fingoes and of their chiefs :—1. Umslambisa, chieftain of the Amaslubi. 2. Matomela, of the Amakelidwani. 3. Iokwene, of the Amazisi. 4. Umkwenkwezi, of the Amabili. 5. Ucwana, of the Amagobizembi. 6. Uhlïso, of the Amasekuneni. 7. Umkwali, of the Abaswawo. 8. Unomtshatsho, of the Amantozake. 9. Umkuzangwe, of the Abayimani.

The Fingoes are darker and shorter than the Amakosah, but are said to be as active and even braver than "the sons of Kahabi;" six Fingoes being able to fight and overcome twelve Kosahs similarly armed. The men of the Fingoes have woolly hair, round noses, thickish lips, straight and muscular limbs, and average five feet eight inches in height. Their dress consists of a dressed ox-hide, worn with the hair inwards, rude sandals on their feet, a skin-sheath, like the other tribes; their ornaments are bead ear-rings, tufts of jackals' tails on their heads, bead-necklaces, generally blue and white, brass rings on their arms, and a belt of small rings, strung on leather, round their waists. The women wear small turbans of skin or cloth, not to defend the head from the sun, but to enable them better to carry burdens; a petticoat of hide, a skin breast-cover ornamented with beads; and some of them wear the Kafir female-kaross or mantle of hide, from which depends behind a flap covered with brass buttons. Beneath the petticoat is worn a small triangular apron, ornamented with beads; they also wear bead-necklaces and brass bracelets. The children are carried behind wrapped in the kaross.

The Fingoes are in general good-natured people. The men labour in the fields as well as the women, and in this respect are unlike the Kafirs, among whom the principal attention of the men is devoted to the cattle. The huts of the Fingoes are hemispheres of boughs covered with grass; their food, curdled milk and millet. In war they carry bundles of assagays, or javelins, and a large oval shield of ox-hide, over which they can just look. At night in the field they get close together; and they cover themselves with their shields when they sleep. At present they dread fire-arms.*

The fact of a tribe of people in a better condition, and looking upon themselves as of higher caste and dignity, having in its vicinity hordes of a lower state, a sort of *mlechchhas*, or *a* "*mixed multitude*," descended probably from refugees and outcasts, and more or less mingled with foreigners and vagabonds from various quarters, is a thing likely to have occurred in other parts of the world besides South Africa, and the supposition of its existence may tend to explain many phenomena in history or ethnology. In India, for example, it cannot be doubted that many a tribe of obscure origin living beyond the limits or on the outskirts of civilised communities, owes its existence, in a

* "Ten Years in South Africa," by Lieut. J. W. D. Moodie, Lond. 1835.

great part at least, to the shelter which woods, and fastnesses, and mountainous tracts afford, from time to time, to persons whose character and habits of life are such as to unfit them for the observation of laws, and for submission to regal and priestly ordinances. Many writers on Indian history have attributed this origin to the Bhíls and Gonds, and other tribes of the mountains, who display but slight differences in physical character and language from the people of the plains. The hypothesis that all such tribes are aborigines of the mountainous parts of India has been perhaps taken up in some instances hastily, and in others extended too far, though it is not unlikely that some of the mountains and wildernesses of the Dekhan may contain descendants of an ancient population, which was at least the original nucleus of the hordes of barbarians who now dwell there, and among whom the languages of the plains are still spoken, though with dialectic differences. It is probable that there was always in Egypt a large population of mixed races besides the pure castes of the Egyptian stock; and we thus are enabled to account for many varieties of statement in ancient descriptions of the Egyptians, and in the physical traits of mummies, while the national type, as represented by paintings and sculptures, was strikingly uniform. In Europe it is difficult to determine how far the same observations may serve to account for certain national relations. The Lappes seem to bear a similar relation to the Finns and their vicinity, as the Bushmen to the present Hottentots. They appear to have been a wild and predatory tribe who sought the desert, like the Arabian Bedouins, while the Finns cultivated the soil like the industrious Fellahs. Between the meagre and small Bedouins and the comparatively stout and athletic Fellahs of the same race, a greater difference of bulk and stature exists than that of the Bushmen and Hottentots; and the Lappes and Finns perhaps differ from each other still more in this respect.*

* Many instances may be remembered in ancient history in which tribes

Another phenomenon deserving of notice, and interesting in a general point of view, is the change of language or the difference of speech between the Bushmen and the Hottentots.

The language of the Bushmen is merely a dialect of the Hottentot idiom, spoken by all of that race. This is the decided testimony of all late travellers, though the differences of words collected in vocabularies are so great as to have given rise at one period to a different opinion. The people of some hordes speak much like the Namaaquas, others use the same words with a different pronunciation; a third party, as we are assured by Dr. Andrew Smith, vary their speech designedly by affecting a singular mode of utterance, and adopt new words with the intent of rendering their ideas unintelligible to all but the members of their own community. For this last custom a peculiar name exists, which is—" cuze cat." This is considered as greatly advantageous to the tribe in assisting concealment of their exploits and designs.* The modified dialect is more or less

---

of people, who were probably of kindred origin with their masters, have been reduced and kept in a state of vassalage for many generations, and treated with the greatest cruelty. The Helots of the Spartans are said to have been the enslaved people of Messenia, who themselves were akin to the Lacedæmonians. At all events they were Greeks, and belonged to the same family. In like manner, the people who are termed by St. Jerome and Ammianus, Limigantes, appear to have been a servile race under the ancient Sarmatæ. It is related by historians, that having been armed for the defence of their country against the Goths, they became aware of their strength and greater numbers, and, after gaining a victory over foreign enemies, expelled their masters. It is about this period, or soon after, that the names of Sarmatæ and Iazyges disappear from history, and that of the Slaves, or Slavonians, is for the first time heard.[1]

* A similar custom is prevalent among the Circassians:—" When they set out on a plundering expedition, they use particular languages known only to themselves. The two most usual jargons employed by them are called Shakobshe and Farshipse: the former seems to be original, for it has

---

[1] Ammian. Marcell. lib. xvii. 12. See several other writers cited in the " Ancient Universal History," vol. xvi. p. 133. It seems that the ruling caste among the Sarmatæ, who were expelled, were named Arcarogantes, and the slaves Limigantes.

understood by the population belonging to each Bushman tribe, but not to the Hottentots, or those who know only the common language of the race. That clapping noise occasioned by the various motions of the tongue, which is characteristic of the Hottentot language, is particularly of frequent occurrence among the Bushmen, who often use it so incessantly as to make it appear that they give utterance to a jargon consisting of an uninterrupted succession of claps. The dialects of the Bushmen thus modified are not generally intelligible to the Hottentots, though it is observed, on the other hand, that such Bushmen as live on friendly terms with the Hottentots in their neighbourhood, and associate with them, acquire such a modification of utterance that their language is perfectly understood.

The fact that a savage nation is thus known to modify its speech purposely for the sake of becoming unintelligible to its neighbours, is by no means unimportant in regard to the history of languages. It is impossible to say how many of the apparently original diversities of human speech may have derived their commencement from a similar cause, and from the voluntary adoption of a new jargon by some small separated community. The clapping articulation of the Hottentots may have originated wholly from this habit.

The present abodes of the Bushmen are scattered through the whole of the extensive plains lying between the northern boundary of the colony, the Kamiesberg range of mountains, and the Orange River. In former times they were more widely spread, and are said to have occupied many districts now far within the boundaries of

no analogy with Circassian......... The Farshipse is made up by adding the syllable *ri* to the syllables of Circassian words" (Klaproth, "Voyage au Mont Caucase," vol. i. p. 381, Paris, 1823). The last-mentioned jargon is like what our schoolboys term gibberish, by which they occasionally endeavour to hide their doings from their teachers or less knowing schoolfellows. Among the examples given by Klaproth are—*Iriari* for *Ia*, the hand; *Jarikeri* for *Jake*, the beard; *Tarikhurimari* for *Takhuma*, the ear. ED.

the colony, as the barren districts between the Olifant and Groene Rivers and the Great Karroo, as well as the country on the Camptoes River. The population is thinly spread, especially at particular seasons of the year, or when the supply of game is scanty. In situations where nature is liberal of productions readily applicable to the support of life, small communities exist; where food is scanty or water defective, it is rare to find more than one or two families in the same place. Little intercourse exists betweeen them, except when self-defence, or an occasional combination in some marauding expedition undertaken in the hope of booty, brings them into contact; and some mischief is apprehended by the colonists when it is known that many Bushmen have formed their kraals in the same neighbourhood.

They are constantly roving about from one place to another in quest of a precarious subsistence. Hence they bestow but little labour on their temporary dwellings. They erect a shelter of bushes for the night, or rest under mats suspended on poles, or dig holes in the ground, into which they creep. Their clothing is principally a kaross, or loose mantle of sheep-skin, which is a garment by day and a covering by night. They carefully besmear their skin with fat as a protection against the parching effect of the heat and wind, and, like other savages, they are fond of ornamenting their hair, and ears, and bodies, with beads and buttons, shells and teeth, and other barbaric decorations.

In physical characters the Bushmen differ little from the Hottentots in general. Dr. Andrew Smith declares that they are certainly not inferior in stature to the other Hottentots. Among the latter there are individuals of very puny growth, and those travellers who have given us the most striking descriptions of the Bushmen were probably less acquainted than this intelligent writer with the other Hottentot tribes. We are told by Mr. Leslie, who has described the Bushmen of the Orange River, that, small in stature as the Hottentot race is, they are in that quarter less than elsewhere. He adds that they seldom exceed five feet. This, however, indicates no great difference,—or, at least, not more than may well be attributed to scanty sustenance, beginning from childhood and continuing through many generations. We are assured by Mr. Bunbury, who had better opportunities than most travellers for observation, that the Hottentots are a very diminutive race. He declares that the majority of those in the Cape corps, at least of the new levies, are *under five feet* in height, and by no means strong. Their hands and feet are small and delicate, in which particular they differ remarkably from the Negoes.

The perceptive faculties of the Bushmen are wonderfully acute. Like the nomadic nations of High Asia, whom they resemble in the manner of their existence and in the general contour of their cranium, they discern objects with the naked eye from a distance at which Europeans can only read by means of the telescope. In situations where the eye is unavailable, says Dr. Smith, it is wonderful with what certainty and readiness the ear directs them to an object; and again, when distance renders sound inaudible, the eye operates with a precision and power which a person who has never witnessed the like would scarcely be disposed to credit.

Like other savages, the Bushmen are cruel and revengeful. The desire of revenge is one of the strongest of their passions; it urges them to the most barbarous acts; they commit the most frightful outrages under the impulse of momentary irritation, as well as in the gratification of long-fostered malice. The eagerness for vengeance is so urgent as to render them indifferent on whom they wreak it, provided the sufferer be of the same country as the offender, and they make the innocent suffer for the guilty. Dr. Andrew Smith assures us that he has seen their cruelty and revenge exercised on their own relatives with as much rancour as on strangers; and several instances have come within his knowledge in which parents destroyed their own children, and even boasted of their cruelty towards their own offspring, and were praised for it by their companions. The passion of anger has amazing influence over them: it incites them to frequent murders. A total want of forethought is one of their characteristics, and the prospects of to-morrow, or of the time to come, seldom occupy their minds.

Although the wild tribes of the Hottentot race display ferocity and all the other vices of savage life, yet we have abundant proof that these people are not insusceptible of the blessings of civilisation and Christianity. No uncultivated people appear to have received the instructions of the Moravian missionaries more readily than the Hottentots, or to have been more fully reclaimed and Christianised. In one of my former works I have taken pains to collect the most authentic accounts of their change of condition, and to compare it with that of other nations who in later times have received the blessing of conversion to the Christian religion.

OF THE GREAT SOUTH AFRICAN RACE.

I now proceed to the family of nations which I propose to designate as the Great South African race, and I shall endeavour to lay before my readers a brief survey of its principal branches, with an account of the countries inhabited by them in different parts of the African continent. They will be described under the following heads:—

1. The nations in the western parts of South Africa within the so-termed empire of the Mani-kongo.

2. The tribes of Kafirland, or South-eastern Africa, comprising all those nations who are known to speak the Kosa and the Sichuana languages.

3. The nations of the Mosambique coast and the adjacent inland countries.

4. The nations of the coast of Zanzibar and Ajan, including the Suaheli.

I shall commence with the western nations, who were first known to Europeans.

Our earliest accounts of the western parts of South Africa are derived from the Portuguese, who discovered and founded colonies on the coast during the fifteenth century. The country was termed by the geographers of that time, Southern Ethiopia. The first Portuguese ship is said to have made its appearance in the River Zaire, under the command of Diego Caba, in 1484. The adjacent country was described by Lopez, who resided in it several years, and whose account was drawn up and published by Pigafetta.* If we may believe the uniform representations of these writers, all the native races inhabiting the western side of Africa, from the equator to Cape Negro, were, at the era of their discovery, subject to a great empire, the sovereign of which, termed the Mani-kongo, held under his dominion all the countries between Loango in the north and Loanda in the south, inclusive. This empire is said to have been entire at the arrival of the Portuguese, but it became soon after that era dismembered, the governors of particular provinces assuming the rank of independent chieftains, or *manis;* and the province of Kongo, which was situated in the middle, between the north and south, remaining alone in subjection to the sovereign and his descendants.

The Portuguese regarded all the inhabitants of the region comprehended in the real or pretended empire of the Mani-kongo as forming but one people or race. They all spoke a common language, which was, however, divided into many dialects, but these dialects, according to the accounts transmitted by the Portuguese writers, differed not more widely than does the language of Lisbon from that of Madrid.

* "Descriptio Regni Congiani," in the "Vera Descriptio Regni Africani, quod tam ab incolis quam Lusitanis Congia appellatur, per Philippum Pigafettam, olim ex Edoardi Lopez acroamatis linguâ Italicâ excerpta, nunc Latino sermone donata ab Aug. C. Reinio," folio, Francof. 1698.

According to Ritter, the domain of the Mani-kongo consists of a triple terrass of mountain-lands, situated in successively declining levels, by which the high plateau of Southern Africa is gradually lowered towards the ocean. The highest terrass is bounded towards the lower country, on the west, by the lofty chains of the Serras de Cristal, de Sal, and de Prata. All these chains run from north to south, and, like the parallel ranges of the Alleghany mountains, they are all intersected by the excavated channels of those rivers which flow through them from the interior upland towards the Atlantic. Such is the direction given to the course of these rivers in the old chart of Lopez; the modern maps of the country are frequently erroneous in giving to the mountain-chains a direction parallel to that of the rivers.

On the lowest of these terrasses—that is, on the littoral plain, sandy, and intersected by numerous water-courses—is a region of torrid heat and pestilential climate, covered with morasses, and abounding in reptiles and wild beasts.

Very different from that above described is the middle region, which the Kongos themselves regard as a terrestrial paradise. It is extremely populous, and well cultivated, enjoys a temperate and delightful climate, and comprehends all the most fertile provinces of the empire of Kongo.

The most populous part of the empire is the celebrated and luxuriant Bamba, which is termed by Cavazzi "la chiave e lo scudo, la spada e la defesa del rè." Although forming but a sixth part of the Kongoan realm, it is said to have furnished an army of 400,000 warriors. "In the territory of the Ambriz," according to a recent traveller, "and in the neighbouring provinces, the country presents a succession of beautiful and picturesque landscapes, swelling into undulations, with gentle eminences crowned by thickets and clumps of trees, and divided by fertile valleys or deep ravines, which are covered with the luxuriant vegetation of the tropical climate. In other parts are barren hills, bleak and arid tracts, partially covered with detached rocks and masses of granite, displaying a striking contrast to the densely-wooded tracts through which the River Zaire pursues its course."*

The Portuguese had free access only to the littoral region of Kongo. Here the Roman Catholic religion was introduced at first by Portuguese ecclesiastics, and was afterwards propagated by the first and second missions of the Jesuits in 1539 and 1613, and subsequently by Franciscans. With the exception of Sogno, a district of the middle region, the progress of Christianity was confined to the lower or littoral provinces, among which was situated the mission of Loanda; San Salvador was the centre of Portuguese influence, and the chief seat of proselytism.

The high plain in the interior, towards the great inland plateau, was the region over which the celebrated Jagas, or Giagas, wandered, represented by the writers who describe them as tribes of nomadic warriors of fierce and cruel habits, delighting in blood and carnage, of whose inroads the settled inhabitants of Kongo were in continual dread. According to the representation of these people drawn by the old Portuguese writers, they in many respects resembled, and they may perhaps be considered as prototypes of the present Kafir tribes, the Amakosah, Amazulah, Amatemba, and other barbarians of Eastern Kafirland. The Jagas, under the command of their terrible chieftain Zimbo, made their first attack on the province of Batta in 1542, and in the following years they poured themselves in an overwhelming torrent upon the whole kingdom of Kongo. They were not expelled till after a war of four years in duration, and then with the assistance of the Portuguese. In 1569 the same people are said to have been completely

* "Observations on the Natives of the Three Kingdoms of Ambriz, Ambrizette, and Musula, southward of the River Congo, South Africa," by W. F. Daniell, Esq. M.R.C.S.: read before the Ethnological Society of London, November 12, 1847.

routed on the eastern coast, near Mombas, after having laid waste the whole region of Monomotapa. The Jagas are uniformly described as wandering, barbarous hordes, without knowledge of agriculture, and without fixed dwellings, who cut down forests for the fortification of their camps, burnt all the towns and villages, killed their enemies, and devoured the bodies of the slain. Under their queen Zingha, who is said to have established among them *a code of laws* for the regulation of their sanguinary warfare, many tribes of Jagas settled themselves in the conquered countries.

Mr. Daniell says that he has seen many Jagas. They now live in parts of Kongo, and speak with facility the Kongo language, which is a sort of "Lingua Franca" among the natives of the neighbouring countries. He supposed their own peculiar idiom to be a dialect of this language. Their physical characters are those of the Kafirs: their complexion, like that of the Kafirs, is a dark brown, partaking of a red tinge.

A curious account of the Giagas, or Jagas, was given by Andrew Battel, a native of Essex, who sailed from England in 1589, was captured by the Portuguese, and resided in Angola and the neighbouring countries eighteen years. His narrative was published by Purchas. He says: "These Giagas are the greatest canibals and maneaters that bee in the world, for they feed chiefly on man's flesh." Battel, however, was glad to make his escape from his captivity in Kongo to the camp of the Giagas. He says: "The town of these people is very great, and is so overgrowne with oleeander-trees, cedars, and palmes, that the streets are darkened with them." It seems that the Jagas were not, like the modern Kafirs, destitute of religious worship, for, says Battel, "in the middle of the towne there is an image, which is as bigge as a man, and standeth twelve foot high, and at the feet of the image there is a circle of elephants' teeth pitched in the ground. Upon these teeth stand great store of dead men's skulls, which are killed in the warres, and offered to this image. They use to pour palm-wine at his feet, and kill goats and pour their blood at his feet. This image is called Quesango, and the people have a great belief in him, and swear by him, and doe believe when they are sick that Quesango is offended with them. In many places of this town there were little images, and there was great store of elephants' teeth piled." "There were in the camp of the Giagas twelve captains: their generall, a man of great courage, warreth all by enchantment, and taketh the devil's counsel in all his exploits. The great Giaga Calando hath his hair very long, embroidered with many knots full of Bamba shells. His body is carved and cut with sundry workes, and every day anointed with the fat of men. He weareth a piece of copper crosse his nose two inches long, and in his ears also. His body is painted red and white. He hath twenty or thirty wives, which follow him when he goeth abroad, and when he drinketh they kneel down and clap their hands and sing." "The women are very fruitful, but enjoy none of their children, for as soon as the woman is delivered of her childe, it is presently buried *quicke*, so that there is not one child brought up in this generation, but when then they take a town they keep the boys and girls of twelve or thirteen years old as their own children."

The name of Jaga, denoting warlike nomades, is now a title of honourable distinction, and is claimed as the exclusive right of the Cassangas, a powerful tribe, who live to the eastward of the kingdom of Kongo. It is in the territory of the Cassangas, according to the information obtained by Mr. Bowdich, that the most remote fairs, or trading resorts, frequented by the Portuguese from Angola and Kongo, are held. Attempts have been made to penetrate from the country of the Cassangas farther into the interior, and to open, if possible, a communication with Mosambique on the eastern coast. A Mulatto traveller, sent from Cassanga, after a journey of two months, is said to have reached the capital of a tribe termed Múlúa, a large town laid out in regular streets, where fifteen or twenty Negroes are sacrificed every day. From the Múlúas the Cassangas receive in barter the copper which they sell to the Portuguese. The Cassangas have for their northern neighbours the Cachingas, and the Domges on the east, who maintain a communication with the Portuguese at Mombas. The Mexicongos, or Kongos of the interior, describe the Hocanguas as a powerful tribe, beyond whom are the dominions of the Amaluca, a nation of the interior, whose name indicates an affinity to the Kafir Amazulu and Amakosah.

It seems that the Jagas are no longer a formidable people; they appear never to have survived the defeat which they sustained not many years after their invasion of Kongo. They are still known as a distinct people, scattered in some of the higher districts to the east of Kongo.

Physical Characters of the People of Kongo.

From the great diversity of climate and local situation in the different provinces of the domain of Mani-kongo, we might be prepared to look for variety in the physical characters of the people, and this is what all travellers declare to exist in a most striking degree. Their complexion is said by Lopez and Cavazzi to differ considerably, some being of a dark brown colour, while others are of an olive, and some of a blackish red: all travellers are agreed in ascribing to the people of Kongo this variety, both in colour and in the form of their features.*

This variation in physical character cannot be fully explained on the hypothesis which attributes it to intermixture of races. There are indeed various tribes in the countries connected with Kongo, and these tribes, as we

* Professor Smith informs us, that a chieftain at Malambo, and many of his retinue, had noble countenances, with more of the Arab than of the Negro character.

shall have occasion to notice, are more or less mixed and blended in the actual population of some of the provinces; but the tribes alluded to are themselves, for the most part, and as far as we know without exception, merely branches of the same great nation. The differences of dialect noticed among them are but slight, and such as would tend to prove them to be one people. There is but one race foreign to the aborigines of South Africa, with whom it can be imagined with any degree of probability that the tribes of Kongo can have been intermixed: I mean the Portuguese. The Portuguese have had for some centuries settlements in this region, and in some parts have been intimately connected with the native inhabitants; but the Portuguese colonists have been by far too few in number to produce any impression on the stock of people inhabiting the great empire of Kongo. We are assured that, in fact, there are very few mulattoes among the inhabitants of the country; and it is well known that the Portuguese colonisation has been nearly confined to Angola.

The limits of the country occupied by the kindred nations of this part of Africa are not exactly known. The distance from Cape Lopez to Cape Negro is about 300 leagues; but it is probable that the natives of the country to the northward of Cape Lopez are of the same race. To the southward of Cape Negro are the people of Benguela, who are said to speak a different idiom from that of Kongo; but whether this is a distinct language, or only differs as a dialect from the speech of Angola, we have no certain information. There are many different nations, long separate and physically distinguished from each other, within the limits above defined; but they are, according to testimony which I shall cite, all branches of one race. We have obtained much new and valuable information as to the languages of the tribes and their mutual distinctions, both physical and moral, from a very intelligent traveller, Mr. W. Daniell, a medical man, who resided two years in different parts of the Kongoese country. The following notices are taken, partly from a memoir presented by this gentleman to the Ethnological Society of London, but principally from information which the author has kindly communicated to myself personally. The following sketch gives the relative position of different countries and races.

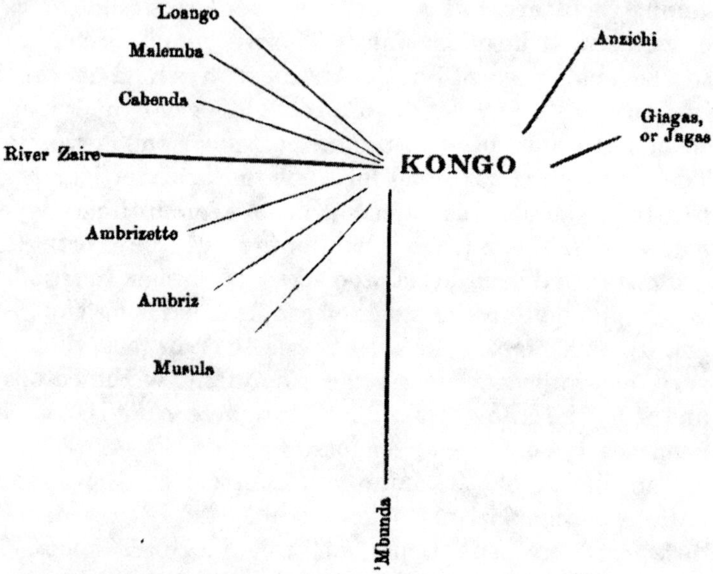

Loango, the northern country, has been described by Proyart, who says that one dialect,—we may presume one race,—extends through it and the other provinces to the northward of the Zaire. This includes Kakongo and Malemba, as well as Cabenda or Angoy, which is inhabited by a particular tribe, who differ from all the other nations in physical characters.

To the southward of the Zaire is the proper country of the Kongos, who have a different language from that of Loango; the difference is only dialectical. Kongo is divided into numerous provinces, among which are Bamba, Sogno, &c. Included in the limits of Bamba are the districts of Ambrizette, Ambriz, and Musula, among the natives of which Mr. Daniell chiefly resided.

Angola lies to the southward of the river Danda, and

extends from 8° 30″ to 16° S. lat. In Angola is Loando San Paoli, the capital of the Portuguese possessions in Africa.

The language of Angola is termed the Ambunda, 'Mbunda, or Bunda language; and the people are called by Mr. Daniell the Bundas. The Bunda or Angolan language was studied by the Portuguese missionaries, and a grammar and dictionary of it have been published, written by Father Cannecattim.

The Anzichi or Antziki are a people of the interior behind Loango. Their relation to the native tribes of the empire has hitherto been only conjectured. Mr. Daniell thus describes the people of Kongo proper.

"The characteristics of the primitive Kongoese are a dark or jet-black colour of the skin or complexion, crisp woolly hair, large black eyes, and a countenance of small features, having, but in a moderate degree, the Negro peculiarity of thick lips, a flat expanded nose, and a low depressed forehead, with that placidity of mien, or harmonious softness and quietude of expression, which gives a pensive or somewhat melancholy look. Something almost analogous to the subdued air of dejection that pervades the physiognomy of the Eboes and other tribes to the northward of the equator, may be recognised among the natives of Kongo. This peculiarity, however, is relieved by the bright and lively lustre of the eye when they are animated by any unusual emotion. Their stature and development of frame, as compared with the tribes of Northern Africa, present a rather diminutive and effeminate appearance; nor have they that aspect of dignity and symmetrical rotundity of form, blended with a firm muscular organisation, so commonly observed among the northern races, while the inferiority of their intellectual endowments is decided and manifest."

Mr. Daniell informs us afterwards that this description applies more particularly to the people of low maritime districts. He says,—"It must be considered that this description is only applicable within a limited sphere, and must be qualified before it can be applied to the people of the same race who inhabit the hilly regions adjoining Embomma, or those villages situated above the first and second falls of the river Zaire. "Here," he says, "the dark hue and the rough dirty aspect of the skin become less conspicuous, and in their place we observe a more delicate cutaneous tegument, comprising the different gradations of yellow, bronze, and deep-brown tints. The countenance in many instances, especially among the females, assumes a more interesting and pleasing character from the softened expression of the features, which is heightened in effect by the display of the feelings, more open and unreserved than the repressed and vindictive passions predominant among the Negro tribes who reside amid the swamps near the embouchure of the Kongo. The physical traits, in combination with an air of inferior intelligence and a corresponding outline of form, reveal a line of demarcation between various tribes of a common origin, inhabiting the banks of the same river, but severed from one another only by the peculiar endemic agencies of situation, temperature, and elevation of soil."

Mr. Daniell has given me the following notes on the differences observable between the several nations of the Kongo empire:—

Of the People of Ambriz.—Ambriz is the name of a province which formerly constituted a part of the principality of Bamba, one of the seven kingdoms or great states included in the ancient empire of the Mani-Kongo. Ambriz was distinguished by the name of Quitungo. In the confusion and anarchy which succeeded the dismemberment of the empire, the Portuguese subdued Ambriz, but were afterwards expelled by the natives. Ambriz and Ambrizette, which were used as distinctive epithets of provinces or states, are originally the names of the chief rivers which flow through these countries. Musula is a third province, and they are all within the limits of Bamba.

"The inhabitants of both Ambriz and Musula," as Mr. Daniell informs me, "are closely allied in physical structure and language, and other peculiarities, to the tribes resident on the banks of the river Zaire, and within the kingdom of Kongo." Yet they have some peculiarities which may be attributed to intermixture with the various hordes of people in the interior who from time to time have descended the channel of the river Ambriz. Compared with the people of Ambrizette, or the natives of the town and bay of Yuma, the natives of Ambriz are said by Mr. Daniell to have no distinguishing marks. "Their skin is of various colours. They are of a mixed character between the Negro and the Kafir, and have the peculiarities of both to a certain extent. Their features are far from agreeable, and are not so pleasing as are those of the people of Loango and other tribes farther northward. The hues of the skin most commonly met with are yellow, brownish-yellow, reddish-black, which is very common, and jet-black. They are comparatively of short stature."

Cabendas, or People of Angoy.—The Cabendas are the only race on the south-west coast of Africa who leave their country and enter into the service of strangers, like the Kroomen of North Africa. They man the launches and the ships of Europeans; they sail in boats, from Loanda as far north as Loango or Malemba, coasting the land all the way: the Portuguese implicitly trust them, and send their merchandise without any white men. The greatest peculiarity in their organisation is, that they are of much lighter colour than any other tribe—the predominant hue of their skins being of a moderate yellow, varying into a darker tint. It is a very curious circumstance, that the Kongo people to the southward are of a jet black, and the Loango people to the northward equally so, while the Cabendas are so different in colour as to be distinguished from most of the tribes in south-western Africa. The English do not trust them so much as the Kroomen; they have among the English a character for roguery.

There are generally three classes of chiefs under one king in this part of Africa. They are—

1. Mambookas, or governors of towns.

2. Mongroys, or king's councillors, who also possess some authority.

3. The Mafukas, or custom-officers, whose duty is to receive the customs for the monarch; they are among the chiefs who attend the king's council.

On the Kongo the term Chenoo is given in the place of Mambooka to the chieftains or governors. The governments in this part of Africa are not so despotic as those in the north; the power of the kings is much restricted; they are controlled by a council composed of the higher class of chiefs. In Ambriz the king reigns only a limited number of years: he is elected from amid the highest class of chiefs, and his tenure of power will in some degree depend upon the state of the seasons: for instance, if during the rainy season little or no rain falls—a very common occurrence—the country becomes parched, and a famine frequently ensues: if this occurs often, the king becomes unpopular, and is deposed. The greatest popularity that a king can obtain in Ambriz is from a heavy rainy season. When a king is once elected he is never permitted to visit the sea-shore, or live within sight of the ocean. The great distinction or prerogative of the king of Ambriz is, that he is allowed to wear shoes, which no one else is permitted to do in his dominions. In Cabenda, the wearing of European trousers, on the contrary, is a disqualification for any one aspiring to the dignity of a king.

The Anzichi, or Bowman Tribes.—The Anzichi are a race of people resident in the country behind the Cabendas, to the north-east of the river Kongo.* "They are readily distinguished from the Kongos by the much lighter colour of their skin, the complexion of the Anzichi being of a

* Lopez places the Anzigues beyond the kingdom of Loango, viz. to the eastward of Loango.

dark brown or bronze, and by their features, which have more of the European character. The most decisive marks, however, are four or five cicatrised incisions, extending from the zygomatic arch to the angle of the mouth on both sides of the face. Their cheek-bones also project, and the face has not the rotundity which is striking in the Ambriz Negroes, but it is thin and elongated. They are cannibals from choice, eating human flesh,—not from necessity, but from preference. They kill their parents and relatives, never suffering them to live beyond a certain age. The Anzichi are not more distinguished by anything than by their malevolent disposition. They are perpetually embroiled in hostilities with the people of Ambriz, whose huts they frequently burn down."

I find frequent notices of this race in the old accounts of Kongo, which agree very well with Mr. Daniell's statement.* For two or three hundred years they have been forgotten. They are described by Lopez, who, after speaking of the people of Loango, says :—

"Ulterius habitant alii populi, Anzigues dicti, incredibilis feritatis, se invicem enim devorant, ita ut ne amicis et propinquis quidem parcatur, quorum postea describimus historiam."

"Beyond the former are the dwellings of the people termed Anzigues, of incredible ferocity, for they eat one another, not abstaining from friends or relations," &c.

He afterwards terms them "Anziqui, reliquas omnes nationes barbaras, quæ humanis vescuntur carnibus, feritate superantes." He says, "They do not only eat their enemies slain in battle, but their nearest relations and friends. They have public shambles, where human limbs are exposed to be sold instead of beef or other meat : they make a display of their loyalty by offering themselves to be killed and eaten at the banquets of their kings. Their

* Mr. Daniell observes that there are two sorts of cannibalism in Africa: one, he says, is from choice, the other from necessity. The cannibalism of the Anzichi is of the former kind.

arms are a light bow and arrows, and an axe with a short handle (assagay)."*

According to Lopez, the country of the Anzichi, or Anzichani, was on the upper course of the river Zaire. There are many islands on this river inhabited by the Anzichi.

'Mbundas, or the People of Angola.—"The people of Angola greatly resemble those of Ambriz, but are," as Mr. Daniell has observed, "of a lighter colour. In this respect they differ much from the nations of the interior, who are of a jet-black. The skin of the natives near the coast, from the greater care and more frequent ablutions practised, is generally of a finer texture. They do not appear to have any distinguishing marks on their countenances, like those of the Anzichi. There seems to be more uniformity in the features of the natives of Angola,—perhaps from there being less admixture of various tribes.

"The Loango people are almost all of them of a beautiful jet-black or brownish-black colour. They seem to be endowed with a superior organisation to the tribes in this portion of Africa. They are a very lively and animated people, especially the females, who may be considered as the most beautiful Africans on the west coast. Their beauty is proverbial among European travellers; their features are symmetrical and feminine, and have more of the European than of the Negro type. The males are taller, and of a more manly organisation than that of the people of Kongo."

OF KAFIRLAND AND THE KAFIR TRIBES SOUTHWARD OF THE PARALLEL OF DELAGOA BAY.

The warlike nomadic tribes who inhabit or wander in the plains of Southern Africa, and more especially in the eastern parts, have long been known to Europeans by the name of Kafirs. This epithet was given first by the Arab

* "Vera Descriptio Regni Africani," before quoted.

voyagers, who so termed all savage nations, and all nations unconverted to Islam; from the Arabs it was adopted by the Portuguese and Dutch, and it became a general appellation. But the Dutch long used this name in a vague sense, and included nearly all the uncivilised nations of South Africa. Accordingly we find Caffraria, in the old maps of Africa, as in that of Dapper,* comprising nearly all the southern part of the continent. Not only the region of the Kafirs, but that of the Hottentots also, comes within its limits. In later times the eastern people have been termed Kafirs, to the exclusion of the Hottentots, and the separation between them has been so fully carried out, that even some qualities which they have in common have been overlooked.

When the name of Kafirs was first used in a strictly national sense, it was appropriated to one tribe of people, the Amakosah or Kosa Kafirs, who were the nearest neighbours of the colonists, and lived beyond the Keiskamma river. It was afterwards extended to several other tribes who resembled the Kosas, and spoke the same language. Lastly, it was more recently made to comprehend the Bechuanas in the interior, and a variety of nations in the inland country, who from time to time have become known to the English colonists. All these people speak the Sichuana language, which, though differing from the Amakosah speech, is only another dialect of the same mother tongue. At present, therefore, the name of Kafirs must be considered as including, together with a number of tribes living most to the east, and nearer to the coast, who speak the dialect of the Amakosah, all those tribes of the interior who speak the Sichuana language.

---

* "Description de l'Afrique, par D. O. Dapper, traduit du Flamand," folio, Amsterdam, 1686.

From this old work of Dapper's, which is now very scarce, and of which I have only the French translation, now scarcely met with, many compilers have taken a great deal of their matter. Dapper is a principal authority with the writers of the Old Universal History in what relates to Africa.

But though this name as a national and distinctive one is confined to the tribes above described, it must be observed that the nations far to the northward of them speak dialects which belong to the same family of languages. This was first, as I believe, observed by Lichtenstein, the celebrated traveller, whose history of his journeys in South Africa, and description of the country and its inhabitants, are universally known. Lichtenstein, deriving his information partly from personal experience, and in part from the accounts afforded him by others, came to the conclusion that the same race of people and the same family of languages were spread far into the interior, and at the same time to a very great distance towards the north, far beyond the limits of the proper Kafirs.*

The people of the Mozambique coast, who belong to this family of nations, differ considerably from the tribes commonly termed Kafirs. The coast of Mozambique is that part of the sea-border of Eastern Africa which is washed by the channel separating Madagascar from the Continent. In this tract are Malemba and Quiloa, places celebrated in the history of Portuguese trade and colonisation, as well as the more important settlement of Senna on the river Zambesi. To the southward of this coast is the river Inhambane, and the territory named from it, which belongs to the Portuguese. Delagoa Bay, however, may be considered as forming the division between Mozambique and Kafirland.

Kafirland or Caffraria is, then, the country to the southward of Delagoa Bay, and reaches on the coast to the river

* The researches of Dr. Krapf, and the vocabularies of Dr. Peters, prove the correctness of this observation: they even go further, and appear to unite all the eastern nations, from the Equator to the Cape Colony, in one great family. The features, customs, and languages of these differ mutually no more than the Sichuana from the Amakosah. Future researches will determine whether or not this observation is to be extended throughout the southern continent: it may certainly be predicated of the tribes on the west coast.—Ed.

Jan Tzatzoe

Kafir of the Amakosah Tribe

London & New York. H. Baillière [illegible]

Keiskamma, or, according to recent arrangement, to the Kei. It extends, in some parts, across the whole African continent. But in this wide acceptation of the term we must consider it as divided into two great regions, viz. the Maritime or Eastern, and the Western or Inland Kafirland. The former is the country of the Amakosah Kafirs, and the tribes who are closely allied to them in language and manners; the latter is the region of the Bechuanas, and all those tribes who agree with them in speaking the Sichuana dialect or the idiom of Litakú.

To these two principal divisions of the Kafirs, we must add, with reference to the present state of our knowledge of this race, a third subdivision intended to include the natives of the coast of Natal, and the country immediately bordering on Delagoa Bay. These people differ from the nomadic Kafirs in many respects. I shall term them for distinction Paralian Kafirs.

The Kafirs, speaking generally, recede considerably in features and the shape of the head from the prognathous races; and by persons who form their opinion from these traits alone, they have been classed with Europeans or with Arabs. Nothing, however, can be farther from the truth than the idea entertained by some that they are of Arabian origin. They are woolly-headed, and some tribes of them are black, and display the general characters of the Negro, though not so strongly marked as in the natives of Guinea. Even in the same tribes who generally are considered as receding most from the Negro character, and are undoubtedly of the Kafir race, individuals are seen who would be immediately pronounced to be Negroes, if found in any part of Europe. The plate adjoining displays an exemplification of this remark. On the other hand, the figure given in the text (see over) exhibits a form of features extremely different. It is the portrait of a Kosa Kafir taken by Mr. Daniels.

The Kafirs, upon the whole, are a very superior people when compared with the destitute savages who occupy the insulated hamlets of central Negroland. It is yet unknown from what quarter they have derived the rudiments of art which exist among them, and the improvement of moral and intellectual character which they have obtained.

FIG. 78.

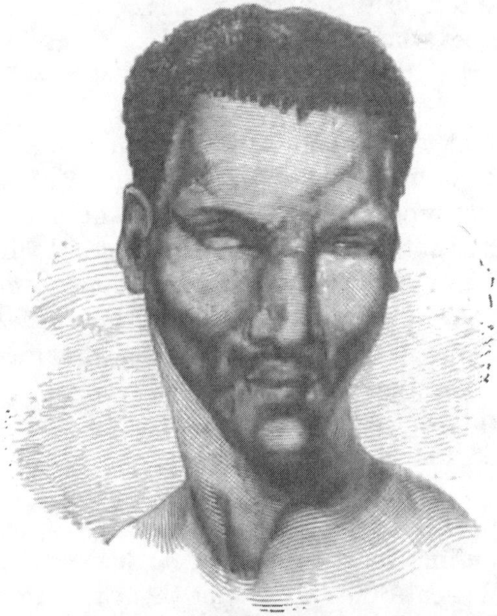

Kosa Kafir.

One trait certainly directs us to a foreign source,—they practise universally the rite of circumcision, though they have no account of the origin of this custom. It is probable that its practice is a relic of ancient African customs, of which the Egyptians, as it is well known, partook in remote ages. The Kafirs are associated together in large communities under chiefs, or kings; differing in this respect from the more savage class of African nations who live in insulated hamlets. They are semi-nomadic, although living in towns of considerable size and population resembling camps, which they occasionally move. Their clothing is scanty,—the men wear mantles, and the females a more complete covering of tanned skins.

The Kafirs have considerable herds of cattle: they practise agriculture, have fields and gardens, cultivate maize, millet, kidney-beans, and water-melons; make bread and beer; and manufacture earthenware out of sand and clay baked in fire. They are acquainted with the use of iron and copper, and have the art of working these metals, and of manufacturing articles of use and ornament.

The Kafirs are not, as some have thought, destitute of religion. They believe in a Supreme Being, to whom they give the appellation of Uhlunga, the "Supreme," and frequently the Hottentot name, Utika, or "Beautiful." They also believe in the immortality of the soul, but have no idea of a state of rewards and punishments. They have some notion of Providence, and pray for success in war and in hunting expeditions. They believe in the attendance of the souls of their deceased relatives, and occasionally invoke their aid. They conceive thunder to proceed from the agency of the Deity; and, if a person has been killed by lightning, say that Uhlunga has been among them. On such occasions, they sometimes remove from the spot, and offer a heifer or an ox in sacrifice.

They have some superstitions resembling those connected with the brute worship and consecration of animals prevalent among the Egyptians. If a person has been killed by an elephant, they offer a sacrifice, apparently to appease the demon supposed to have actuated the animal. Sometimes they imagine that a shuluga, or spirit, resides in a particular ox, and propitiate it by prayers when going on hunting expeditions.

I shall now, in the first place, describe the Eastern Kafirs, including the Amakosah and the people who speak their language.

1. *The Eastern Kafirs.*—The Eastern Kafirs consist of four principal nations:—the Amakosah or Kosa Kafirs, the Amatemba or Tambookies, the Amaponda or Mambookies, and the Amazulu or Zulus. The following

particulars are collected from Mr. Steedman's account of these nations :—

1. The Amakosah, who were formerly the subjects of Hintza, extended from the colony to the mouth of the Bashee river. The subordinate chiefs of this nation were the sons of Islambia, the sons of Gaika, Pato, Kama, Kongo, Enon, Duchani, Botuman, and Phundis. The whole numbers of the Amakosah nation were estimated in 1835 at 150,000 souls.

A tradition prevailed among the Amakosahs in reference to their origin, that the first great chief came out of a cave called U'Daluve, Dala being a word which they use for the Creator. This cave they describe as being situated to the eastward, from whence the sun issues every morning to warm and enlighten the world. They say that they came from the north under a chief named Togul, and first settled on the Kei river, where they purchased lands with herds of cattle, from the Gonaaqua Hottentots, the former inhabitants of the country. This migration is said to have happened 150 years ago.

2. The Amatemba tribes form the second grand division, commonly called Tambookies. They dwell near the Bashee river, and extend inland as far as the Karroo desert. They also inhabit the country to the northward and westward of the Amakosah. Their Umkumkani, or chieftain, who died in 1830, was Vapani. Mangwa and Tabo are the subordinate chiefs of this division, and, as they are in alliance with Hintza, the power of the Amatemba is really very small.

3. The third division are the Amaponda tribes, called Mambookies, whose territories extend from the Bashee to the river Umsikalia, about thirty miles beyond the St. John, or Umzimboobo river. Their Umkumkani is Fako, a very powerful chief, a man of talent, and much dreaded by the surrounding tribes.

4. The fourth and last division is the Amazulu or Zulu tribes, who dwell near Natal, between the Um-

zimboobo River and Delagoa Bay, along the coast, and inland as far as the source of the Orange River, bordering on the Bechuana country. These are divided into two branches, one near Natal, under their chief Dingau, successor to Chaka, and the other under Matacatzee, who resides far inland.

The Amazulu are a warlike nomadic people, who have conquered and extirpated the former inhabitants of the country to the southward of Delagoa Bay. They formed a barbaric kingdom of great extent, strikingly contrasted with the patriarchal sway prevalent among other tribes of the same race. They are a fine handsome people, said to be superior in stature and in beauty to all the other branches of the Kafir race. Captain Owen terms them "fine Negroes, tall, robust, and warlike; in their manners open, frank, and pleasing, with an air of independence in their carriage."

Under the protection of Fako is a tribe of Fingoes. The Fingoes are descendants of various wandering tribes, a vast number of whom are scattered through Kafirland. They are considered by the Kafirs as a very inferior race of people, having no chief of their own.*

2. *The Inland Kafirs, or Bechuanas.*—The inland Kafirs are separated from the Amakosah and the tribes already enumerated, by a chain of mountains. They inhabit the interior of Southern Africa, 300 miles to the northward of the Orange River, and are known to extend to a vast distance towards the east and north. Their limits in these directions are not ascertained, and it is probable that they extend far beyond the tropic of Capricorn. The Batclapis are the most southern nation of this race. They speak the Sichuana language, which is cognate with the idiom of the Amakosah; and the designation of Bechuanas may be considered as belonging to all the nations who speak that variety of the Kafir language.

* "Wanderings and Adventures in the Interior of Southern Africa." By H. Steedman. London, 1845.

The Bechuana tribes are described as superior to the Amakosah in arts and civilisation. They inhabit large towns and well-built houses, cultivate the ground, and lay up stores. In their physiognomy, they rise a degree above the Amakosah; their complexion is of a brighter brown; their features more like the European, and often beautiful.

North-eastward from the country of the Batzegurs, the most southern of the Bechuana tribes, along the elevated part which limits the basin of the Gariep, the improvement in the inhabitants increases. In the country of the Tammahas, Mr. Campbell saw fields of corn several hundred acres in extent, near the town of Mashow, which contains 10,000 people. Among the Murútsi, 160 geographical miles north-east by east of Litaku, he was surprised by the appearance of great progress in arts and industry. The Murútsi cultivate sugar and tobacco; manufacture razors and knives of iron, almost steel; build their houses with masonry, and ornament them with pillars and mouldings.

Beyond the Murútsi, towards the north-east, are the Macquaina, a numerous people, surpassing the Murútsi in wealth and numbers. The Murútsi obtain from the Macquaina beads, the money of the country, which are obtained by the latter people from the Mullaquam, or cleared in commerce from the Mahalasely, a great nation situated to the north-east of the Macquaina. The Mahalasely, as well as their neighbours, the Mateebeylai, are of brown complexion, and have long hair. They wear clothes, ride on elephants, climb into their houses, "and are gods." This last expression is usually applied to Europeans, with whom the Mahalasely are placed upon a level. All the nations from the Murútsi to the Mahalasely have the art of mitigating the virulence of small-pox by inoculating between the eyes.

According to Mr. Archbell, a Wesleyan Missionary, to whom we owe a grammar of the Sichuana language, the Damaras on the western coast of Africa speak a dialect of the Sichuana, and must, therefore, be considered as Bechuanas. Mr. Archbell is said to have visited their country twice, viz. once at Waalvisch Bay, and again by way of Great Namaaqualand; and as he was well acquainted with the language, his testimony may be regarded as trustworthy.*

We have, however, a different account of the Damaras from Captain J. E. Alexander, who undertook an expedition for the express purpose of exploring their country and visiting the people, under the authority of Sir B. D'Urban. The Damaras inhabit the country between the twenty-first and twenty-fourth parallel. According to Captain Alexander, there are two nations called Damaras. They differ from each other nearly in the same way as the Hottentots and Bushmen. The Damaras of the Plains are very rich in cattle, and for the possession of them have to wage frequent wars with the Namaaquas, who are their neighbours to the southward, and live between them and the Orange River. The Hill Damaras have, like the Bushmen, no cattle, but subsist by hunting and on *roots.* The Damaras of the Plains extend from the Swakop north and east; the Hill Damaras, from Kuisip for a considerable distance south and east.

With regard to their physical characters, Captain Alexander assures us that both nations are negroes; that is, they are blacks, with woolly hair, small round noses, and thickish lips. The Damaras of the Plains, from their superior living, are much more robust than those of the hills. Many of the former live as slaves among the Namaaquas.

The huts of both nations are conical, and built of stakes driven into the ground. The Damaras of the Plains wattle them, plaster them with clay, and cover them with hides. The Hill Damaras bring the stakes to a point at the top, and cover them with bushes.

The Damaras of the Plains are circumcised, and extract the two front teeth of the lower jaw. They are almost entirely naked, men and women wearing only a sort of skin

* Boyce's Preface to Archbell's "Grammar of the Sichuana Language."

kilt about the waist, reaching to the knees. In war the men have a plume of ostrich-feathers on the head, a leopard- or lion-skin thrown over the shoulders, besides the usual kilt and sandals. Their arms are bows and arrows, and a stabbing assagay or javelin, made entirely of iron.

The account given by Captain Alexander of the language of the Damaras differs from that of Mr. Archbell. He says, the Damaras of the Plains speak a language peculiar to themselves, of which he has got a vocabulary. It is much to be regretted that this vocabulary is not published, as it would afford an opportunity of comparing the idiom of these people with the Sichuana. He adds, "that the Hill Damaras speak the clicking Namaaqua language." Yet it would appear that the two nations are regarded by the Namaaquas as one race, since they are designated by them under the same name. "The Namaaquas call the whole nation of Damaras," says Captain Alexander, "Dam-âp,* and distinguish the Hill Damaras by the name of Humi (hill) or Hau (dung, that is, vile) Dam-âp. The Pastoral Damaras call themselves Om-otoronto-rondú, or Oke-temba-kachi-hîqui." This seems to be a Kafir word.

It appears from this account probable that the Hill Damaras are, like other outcast tribes, a mixed people. They sometimes live together with the Namaaquas, or inhabit the same tracts, and they are apparently more or less intermingled with them. The Namaaquas carry on bloody wars with the Damaras of the Plains.

Near the Kei-kuruh River, Captain Alexander found occasional traces of Haiji Aibib, the Namaaqua deity. Along a pile of stones lay a few branches, the offerings of wayfarers. Under the pile dwells Haiji Aibib, a person

* This termination is, without a doubt, the ordinary Namaaqua personal suffix, which is written *aup* or *aub* by the missionaries; the labial consonant restricting it to the masculine. The word Dam is not known to us as Namaaqua; it may be the native appellation, which however, appears to be Herero in the Scripture translations mentioned in the next note.—ED.

feared by the Namaaquas, but of whose appearance and power they have no distinct idea. "The only trace of religion I found among the Boschmans (between the Hill Damaras and the Namaaquas), was at a pool of water, near the Tans mountain, where, before they dug for water, they presented an arrow, or a piece of skin or flesh, to a large red man with a white head, who is supposed to inhabit the place, repeating a prayer for success in the chase." The people are, according to Captain Alexander, anxious for missionaries: the women in particular said, "Send us teachers for ourselves and our children." It does not appear clear whether this relation applies to the Hill Damaras, or to the Hottentots, or Namaaquas, who live in the same tracts.*

3. *Kafir Tribes of the Coast near Delagoa Bay.*—The natives of the sea-coast near Delagoa Bay, and reaching from Dundas River to Inhambane, nearly under the tropic, are tribes resembling each other in physical characters and manners. A vocabulary of the dialect spoken near Delagoa Bay was first collected by White, by means of which it was discovered that these people are of the Kafir race. The observation was made by Lichtenstein, and it has been confirmed by Captain Owen. According to Owen, all the people on this coast, as far northward as the Inhambane, speak a dialect intelligible to the Amakosah.

The hordes of native people on the coast of Natal have been conquered by the Zulus. They were partly expelled from their country, and in part admitted by the conquerors among themselves. They are described as inferior to the Nomadic Kafirs in stature, a less powerful and energetic people, and more similar to ordinary Negroes. They have been termed Kafirs of a degenerate sort,† though originally

* The publication of several Scripture narratives in the Damara language by the Rhenish missionaries, demonstrates the correctness of Mr. Archbell's statement. The language is a Kafir dialect. See Bleek de nominum generibus linguarum Africæ Australis, note 19, page 6.—Ed.

† White, Owen, and others.

of the same stock. The Fingoes above mentioned are said to be chiefly vanquished people of this region, reduced to a sort of slavery by the Amazulu warriors. Dampier described the native people of the coast of Natal, long before the Zulu conquest, as Negroes of a jet-black colour.

Physical Characters of the Kafirs.

In the 317th and 318th pages of the "Natural History of Man," I have collected the most authentic description of the Kafir nations in general. I shall now add some particulars referring to the different subdivisions of the race.

In the first place, I must remark that the Eastern Kafirs, taking the Amakosah for an example of them, display considerable varieties of feature and complexion. Individuals of the pure Kosa breed approximate in colour and in physiognomy to the ordinary Negro.*

The complexion of the majority is, however, of a lighter hue, and much redder. By some the Kafirs are reckoned among red rather than among black races of mankind; and a late American traveller declares that they resemble the so-termed Indians of the American continent. The adjoining coloured plate, taken from a drawing, of the accuracy of which I am assured by Dr. Andrew Smith, may serve to exemplify the complexion general among the Amakosah, and it will also exemplify a type of features strikingly different from that of the Guinea Negro, and prevalent among this nation.

It must be observed, that however their features and colour may vary, their woolly hair associates them with the African races. However, their hair, as Captain Owen assures us, is often intermediate in character between that of the Negro and the European. The cranium, as I have elsewhere shown, makes a great approach towards the European form.

The Bechuana tribes in the interior rise still higher

---

* The portrait of Tzatzoe, a well-known Kafir chief, which may be seen in the place referred to, exemplifies this variety.

Kafir of the Amakosa.

Kafir of the Bechuana

London & New York, H. Baillière 1855

in all respects, and approximate still further to the features, and colour, and general physical character of the more cultivated races of mankind. The figure which accompanies this page was furnished by Dr. Andrew Smith as a characteristic specimen of the Bechuana races.

The Kafirs, as we are assured by Mr. Bunbury, are in general tall, though not gigantic, and extremely well proportioned. He says their fine forms and easy attitudes reminded him of ancient statues. They are more remarkable for activity than strength, in which, like other savages, they are inferior to Europeans. The colour of most of them appeared to be a deep amber brown, frequently approaching to black, while in some instances it had a tinge of yellow or red. They are so bedaubed with red ochre that it is difficult to ascertain their real colour.

The Kafirs, according to Colonel Smith, who commanded in the late Kafir war, are an uncommonly intelligent, acute, high-spirited, and brave people, although, like the ancient Spartans, they consider theft no crime. Their belief in witchcraft leads to even worse horrors among them than those which were perpetrated formerly in Europe on the same account.* The victims, however, are not poor old women, but rich men, who are worth plundering. They evidently believe in some supernatural power, since their chief Makanna succeeded in persuading his countrymen that he had a divine mission.

The Kafirs sometimes display the peculiar accumulation of fat over the glutei muscles, which is more common among the Bushmen. The widow of Gaika, as we are assured by Mr. Bunbury,† had a hump which rivalled that of the celebrated Hottentot Venus.

Professor Lichtenstein gives the following description of the physical characters of the Kafirs:—

"The universal characteristics of all the tribes of this

* This is a trait which is common also to the Fijis, and some other races in Melanesia.—ED.

† Mr. Bunbury's "Travels in South Africa," vol. i. p. 159.

great nation consist in an external form and figure varying exceedingly from the other nations of Africa. They are much taller, stronger, and their limbs much better proportioned; their colour is brown; their hair black and woolly; their countenances have a character peculiar to themselves, and which does not permit their being included in any of the races of mankind above enumerated; they have the high forehead and prominent nose of the Europeans, the thick lips of the Negroes, and the high cheekbones of the Hottentots; their beards are black, and much fuller than those of the Hottentots. Their language is full-toned, soft, and harmonious, and spoken with cluttering; their root-words are of one or two syllables; their sound simple, without diphthongs; their pronunciation is slow and distinct, resting upon the last syllable. Their dialects differ in the different tribes, but the most distant ones understand each other."

OF THE NATIVE TRIBES OF THE COAST OF MOZAMBIQUE.

The coast of Mozambique is that part of the sea-border of Africa which is washed by the channel that separates the island of Madagascar from the mainland. The name is taken from that of a town and fortress, built by the Portuguese in 1508 to be the seat of government over the neighbouring countries of Africa, which they had partially subdued and colonised. The Mozambique coast extends from the river Inhambane northward as far as Cape Delgado.

The history of this eastern coast reaches much further back than that of the west of Africa. The Phœnicians traded to it, and probably had settlements on it; and the Ophir of Solomon and Hiram is supposed to have been situated on this part of the continent, and to have given to it that name which the Romans perhaps learned from the Carthaginians, and made the perpetual designation of this whole quarter of the world. In the year of our era

950, Ebn Haukal mentioned the coast of Zinjbar, or Zinguebar; and Massúdi shortly afterwards described Sofala as a country rich in gold, and covered with corn and with towns, but without snow, rain, or ships. It was often visited by Arabs and by foreign merchants from India, "who came thither," as Massúdi says, "to buy children and transport them into various countries of the world." The slave-trade was practised, therefore, not only before Christian, but before Mohammedan merchants navigated these seas. The king of Zanghi, or Zanguebar, commanded an army who were mounted on oxen like the present Kafirs; the people traded also in gold, ivory, and steel. Such was the state of things in this part of Africa more than eight centuries ago.*

The Portuguese overpowered the Arabs on the African coast, and expelled them from the borders of the Zambesi, or Cuama, the great stream which falls into the sea of Mozambique, and forms the harbour of Quilimani. This river was regarded as the principal inlet to the riches of the inland country, which was expected to rival the more celebrated regions of South America in its mines of gold and silver. The remains of the Moslemin were miserably destroyed by their European visitors in 1569; and in the following year the Portuguese made an expedition into the interior, for the conquest of the country and working of its mines. But they found enemies of a very different character from the feeble natives of Peru whom the Spaniards had so easily subdued; the Africans resisted them with obstinacy, and finally baffled all attempts to subjugate them.

* There is a short vocabulary of the language of the African slaves in Western India, called Seedees, in Lieut. Burton's "History of Sindh" (London, 8vo. 1851), p. 372. Three-fourths of the words there given belong unmistakeably to Kafir dialects;—the numerals are 1, moyà; 2, perhí; 3, tahtú; 4, mme; 5, tháno; 6, thandatú; 7, mfúngat; 8, mnání; 9, mpyá; 10, kummí. These may be compared with the Suaheli, Nika, and Kamba, p. 418; the only word not Kafir in one dialect or other, is the equivalent for nine.—ED.

The whole region behind the Mozambique coast was, before this period, according to the intelligent Dom João dos Sanctos, inhabited by the great nation of the Mucarongas long subject to the one sovereign of Monomotapa;* but this empire had been divided, like that of the Manikongo, into several independent, though still powerful states. One of these, still called Monomotapa, to the north, was larger than the rest, and extended in length and breadth upwards of 200 leagues. The second was the kingdom of the Quitive, on the river Sofala; Sedanda on the Sabia, and Chiconga or Manien, are still well known. The natives of all these countries were one race, and spoke the Mucaronga tongue. To the northward of these were the people of Abutua, which reached across Africa to Angola, and abounded in fine gold.

The Portuguese concluded their vain attempts to conquer the country by making a treaty with the Quitive, or sovereign, who accorded them a free passage through his territory on the condition of a yearly tribute of 200 pieces of cloth. An expedition, under the command of Barreto, in 1570, was not without fruit in respect to the extension of geographical knowledge. Barreto traversed the mountains of Lupata, denominated the "Spine of the World." Afterwards he founded the settlement of Senna on the Zambesi, and that of Tete, sixty leagues higher up the river, and got possession of the silver mines of Chicova. But the warlike Mongas massacred their garrison at Tete, and forced them to return to Senna. This was in 1600. The Portuguese still have factories on the Zambesi, and claim possession of the Mozambique coast. The port of Quilimani, at the mouth of the Zambesi, is the chief entrepôt of their trade.

The sources of the Zambesi are unknown: the river flows from the highlands of the interior; it traverses, for a great distance, the so-termed silver plains of Chicova,

* Probably meaning the empire of the *Mono* or *Mani*, or sovereign of Motapa.

through which it is said to be navigable, till it reaches the cataracts of Chicoronga, and descends through them into the second level of the eastern border of the great African plateau, which, according to Ritter, is the still elevated region of the Mucarongas, the subjects of the Quitive of Monomotapa. Through the mountains of Lupata it again falls by a series of rapids extending eighteen geographical miles, which the same writer compares to the falls of the Indus at Attock and those of the Ganges at Hurdwar and of the Niger at Bammakou, into the lower level or littoral plain of Eastern Africa, on which are the Portuguese town of Senna and the tracts occupied by the Negro nations of the Mozambique coast. These three regions of successively lower elevation have different temperatures, and, according to the notices that have been collected, present all the phenomena of very different climates, and all those various peculiarities of organic nature which respectively belong to them. In the interior or higher region, according to the Portuguese traveller Pereira, whose statement has been confirmed by later testimony, there is a great lake termed the Lake of Zambri in the country of the Movizas, a civilised people, whose sovereign is said to live in great magnificence, and to be clothed in silk and gold. This lake is termed by the natives N'Yassa, or the *Inland Sea.* "It is situated to the westward of a chain of lofty mountains, beyond which is an extensive highland plain. The lake becomes visible to the traveller who has ascended this bordering chain at a great distance, in the midst of the plain, studded with innumerable islands; it is said to contain fresh water, but no hippopotami or crocodiles, though these creatures abound in the rivers below the mountains. The natives of this country are mountaineers, and they display that superiority, both in their physical and social state, which often distinguishes the inhabitants of elevated countries in Africa from those of the lower and hotter regions. The Moviza, the Mucamango, the Muchiva, or the Monomuezi, nations inhabiting the plains above the sources of the great rivers, are said to be of a bright brown complexion, tall, vigorous, handsome, like the Amazuluh, or the fairest of the Bechuanas, near the Cape of Good Hope. The fairest tribe are said to be the Wambungo:* these people are termed *whites* by the neighbouring black races, and it is supposed that they have given the foundation to the story of white nations inhabiting the interior of Africa."†

The people of the middle region, or the Mucarongas of Dos Sanctos, are plainly allied, as we shall find, to the nations of the Mozambique coast. I shall cite the quaint description which this old writer has given of their physical and moral characters:—

"The Quiteve's people," as he says, "are the strongest of the Mucarongas, and the best archers and most expert at the azagay." "The Quiteve, for so the king is termed, is of curled hair, a gentile, which worships nothing." "I believe for certain that this Caphar nation is the most brutal and barbarous in the world, neither worshipping God nor any idol, nor have image, church, or sacrifice" . . . . "only they believe the soul's immortalitie in another world. They confess that there is a devill, which they call Musaca. They hold monkeys were in past time men and women, and call them the 'old people.'" "Every September the king goes to a high hill to perform obites or exsequies to his predecessors there buried." "In this feast the king and his nobles clothe themselves in their best silks and cottons. After eight days' festivall they spend two or three days in mourning; then the devill enters into one of the company, saying that he is the soul of the deceased king."

"The Cafres of Quiteve are as black as pitch, curled, and wear their hair full of hornes made of the same hair, which stand up like distaffs, wearing slender pins of wood within their locks to uphold them without bending. The

* Query, Mpungwe.—ED.

† "Edinburgh Review," No. 124, p. 352.

vulgar go naked, both men and women, without shame, wearing only an apron made of a monkey's skin.

"In Mucaronga, some parents as black as pitch have white, gold-locked children, like Flemmings. Whilst I was in the country, the Quiteve nourished one white childe in the court as a strange prodigie. The Monomotapa kept two other white Cafres, with like admiration."*

Modern travellers describe the natives of the coast of Mozambique as a race of Negroes. Mr. Salt has given an account of two nations in this region. One of them is the Monjou, who inhabit the inland country, and are probably the Mujaos of Portuguese writers. He says they are Negroes of "the ugliest description, having high cheek-bones, thick lips, small knots of woolly hair, like peppercorns, on their heads, and skins of a deep, shining black." These people may be the Mucarongas.† The natives of the coast are termed by Salt, and by Captain Owen, and many other writers, Makúa and Makúana; these are the proper Negroes of Mozambique, well known in the slave countries of the Portuguese. I have seen an individual of this race, who was brought to England by Dr. Natterer from the Brazils; he was a tall Negro, very black, with woolly hair, and features resembling those of the natives of Guinea. He said that Makúani is the name of the Negroes of Mozambique, and that the neighbouring tribes are termed M'chauva [Muchiva?], M'nijempani, Mlomoi, and Maravi. A short vocabulary of his language, which he gave me, proves it to be a dialect of the Kafir speech. The *m'* or *ma* forming the initial of these names is a Kafir prefix.

The high country in the interior of Africa, in the latitude of Mozambique, is situated under a very different climate from that of the coast; and it was to be expected that the native inhabitants would display a different physical character. As in other parts of the world, so also in

* Purchas's "Pilgrims," vol. ii. p. 1548–1551.

† A short vocabulary of the idiom of the Makua and Monjou, given by Mr. Salt, proves these nations to be allied to the Mucarongas.

Africa, the high mountainous tracts of the interior are the abodes of races of lighter colour than the natives of low countries on the coast. We have made this observation to the northward, in the high regions of Atlas, and in the East, in Abyssinia, Kaffa, and Enarea, and now find the same remark to hold good in the countries inhabited by the Great South African race.

The tribes of Mozambique were the first people called Kafirs by Europeans, who acquired the epithet from the Mohammedan navigators of the Indian Ocean. There are many nations of them, all, so far as evidence extends, speaking dialects cognate with the language of the Kafirs in the south; but they are not generally termed Kafirs by modern writers. The names of these tribes, beginning with Ma, or Mani, and Mone, afford some slight presumption of affinity in their idioms: the vocabularies which have been collected confirm this suspicion, and lead us to agree with those missionaries and travellers who regard all the nations of the eastern part of South Africa as branches of the same stock with the Amakosah and Amazuluh.

The features of the natives display the same varieties as in other parts of the African coast. Captain Owen says, the farther our travellers advanced from the coast, the more they observed the natives to improve in appearance. Of those of Moroora, many seem firmly knit, stout, and elegantly proportioned; some are perfect models of the human form. They go naked, with the exception of a piece of cloth barely sufficient for decency of appearance. Some have their beard shaved, others only in part, but many not at all. In this latter case, the hair—for it is worthy of remark that they have not wool—grows long, is neatly plaited, and turning in slender curls communicates to the countenance a wild and savage aspect; in this resembling the people of Madagascar, whose covering is

* For further information on this subject, I must refer my readers to the second volume of my "Researches into the Physical History of Mankind," treating on the ethnography of the African nations.

Native of Mozambique.

neither wool nor hair, and is dressed in a similar manner. The variation here noted from woolly to merely frizzled hair, or the difference of description, is often disconnected in the accounts of cognate races, or of the same tribe seen by different travellers. The mode of dressing the hair practised by these people is similar to that used by the Kosas, as well as by the nations of the mountainous regions, particularly the Mucaronga.

FIG. 79.

Mozambique.

The accompanying figure displays a specimen of the physical character of Mozambique Kafirs: it has something of the Negro character, though improved. The head of a native of Mozambique, in the opposite plate, which is taken from the atlas of Rugendas, exhibits a physiognomy which might well pass for European, were it not for the black colour and the woolly hair.

OF THE NATIVE TRIBES OF THE COAST OF ZANZIBAR.

To the northward of Cape Delgado and of the Mozambique Channel and the Island of Madagascar, the sea-border of Africa is termed the coast of Zanzibar. This reaches to the Equator; from thence northward to Cape Guardafui and the Straits of Babelmandeb, is the coast of Ajan, or that of the Sumali. The Sumali are the race of people who inhabit this coast: they are a tribe altogether distinct from the Suaheli or Suhaili who possess the coast of Zanzibar. These two nations divide between them all the maritime tract of Eastern Africa, from the great projecting Cape of Guardafui to the Channel of Mozambique.

The inhabitants of all this eastern coast have received some portion of foreign culture from the trade which has been carried on immemorially in the Indian Ocean. Settlements have long existed at the different havens of the coast, which have been the resort of traders from various ports of Arabia and of India. In later times, since the maritime discoveries of the Portuguese, these places have been visited by European merchants. The native inhabitants are no longer savages or pagans; they may be considered as semi-civilised nations, and they profess the Mahommedan religion, which implies some degree of elevation above the condition of idolaters or fetish-worshippers.

The Sumali who have the northern part of this coast reach from the Gulf of Aden to Magadoxo. They are a pastoral people, and in their seaports are addicted to commerce and navigation. The seaport of Barbara belongs to them; there they hold a fair or mart, and exchange the gold, ivory, and slaves brought from the interior of Africa, for the gums, myrrh, and incense of Arabia. To the southward of the Sumali, the Suaheli occupy a similar position. They are more rude than the former people, and differ from them in physical characters. A late voyager has contrasted the fine, regular features of the Sumali, their soft hair, flowing down their shoulders in soft ringlets, and artificially changed to a flaxen colour, with the jet-black complexions and woolly hair of the Suaheli.*

* Bird: "Journal of Royal Geographical Society," vol. iv. p. 194.

An interesting fact in the ethnology of Eastern Africa has been made known by a comparison of the languages of these nations with those of the barbarous people who inhabit the adjacent countries in the inland. By this clue we have discovered that the Sumali and the Suaheli are not foreigners who have come across the sea to colonise the coast of Africa, but are akin to the tribes of the mountains and forests in the interior behind the sea-border which they inhabit. The Sumali speak a dialect of the language of the Galla, and the Suaheli are proved by their idiom to be a branch of the Great South African race, to which the Kongoese and the Kafirs belong.

The extremely unhealthy climate of the eastern coast of Africa has prevented the growth and increase of Portuguese colonies. Although settlements were made on the coast of Melinda and Mozambique some hundred years ago, they have never flourished, and there is now scarcely any population of Portuguese origin on the whole extent of the sea-border. The same cause probably impeded in earlier times the increase of Arabian colonies; and in still more remote ages were, perhaps, the only obstacles which prevented the existence of Phœnician cities on the coast of Ophir which might have rivalled the fame of Utica, and Carthage, and Gades, on the shores of the Mediterranean. To this cause the Sumali and the Suaheli are indebted for their present existence as distinct parts of the human family.

The whole length of the maritime tract from Cape Guardafui, near Aden, to Cape Delgado, opposite the northern extremity of Madagascar, has been claimed of late years by the Imam of Muscat. The pretensions of this new potentate, as it has been observed, are not founded on the right of conquest or acquisition by any means, but on the maxims of the policy of our times, which allows the possession of it to none of the European powers. The English have restored to him the island of Mombas, and have thereby obtained an additional claim to his friendship and alliance. He has conquered some other places on the coast, or they have voluntarily surrendered themselves to him, and are subject to him so long as he leaves them unmolested under their own governments. The commerce which Europeans carry on upon this coast has been hitherto very profitable. Copal, valuable furs, annually about 6000 elephants' teeth, and spices from Zanzibar, are exported, whilst all European wares are admitted; and the trade carried on by the natives is only to Madagascar, Arabia, and India. The Imam is in the meantime the sole great merchant of the country, and employs his twenty great and smaller war-galleys chiefly in commerce. In spite of all his treaties with the English, he permits along the whole of this long tract of coast a very profitable slave-trade to be carried on; a slave may be purchased on the coast for two or three dollars, while the profit obtained from each slave in the trade amounts to forty or fifty dollars. The Mohammedans excuse the capture and sale of slaves by reason that the captives thereby obtain the privilege of Islam; but experience proves that this is only a pretence, and even after the slave's conversion he is just as cruelly treated as before by his *believing* owners.*

The following extracts contain the latest information respecting the Suaheli.† They are part of a communication from the Rev. Mr. Krapf, sent to Von Ewald, and published by that learned writer in the "Zeitschrift der deutschen morgenländischen Gesellschaft:"—

"The inhabitants of all this narrow line of coast, from the fourth degree of south latitude to Mozambique, are termed Suaheli (that is, in Arabic, inhabitants of the sea-coast): they are themselves Mohammedans. Their language, however, proves that they are the aboriginal people of this country, since, though mixed with foreign words, it is funda-

* Krapf. See "Zeitschrift der deutschen morgenl. Gesellsch." Th. i.

† The word Suaheli is derived from the Arabic *Sahal*, signifying "a plain," and it means merely a lowlander. The Suaheli call themselves Wa-zumba.—ED.

mentally allied to other languages spoken further inland. These people formerly undertook, either in conjunction with the Portuguese, or else alone, many warlike expeditions into the interior, in order to carry off slaves and other booty. But in later times the pagan tribes of the interior have pressed more towards the sea-coast, and have destroyed many of their places. Even Melinda has been given up to the Mohammedans through fear of the Gallas. Islam, which elsewhere in Africa makes such rapid progress, seems in this part to set up no pretence of the kind. Nomadic and pagan Gallas at present frequent the sea-coast from the equator to about the fourth degree of south latitude: their number may be computed at eight or ten millions. The ferocity which in this people inspires so much terror in Abyssinia is in these countries still more remarkable. Here, for instance, they are known to be excessively fond of the blood of goats, sheep, and other animals, and they open their veins in order to suck the blood." Krapf observed the extreme leanness of the goats belonging to these Gallas, which was explained to him by reference to this circumstance. "The Gallas in Abyssinia who till the soil have not this custom, and are otherwise distinguished in language, government, and many other particulars, from these nomadic tribes of the sea-coast. For the rest, these maritime Gallas live in a sort of subjection under the more powerful tribes in the interior, for whom they are obliged to defend the sea-coast against the Mohammedans. Their caravans go from thirty to forty miles inland to a country which is traversed by a great river, and resorted to by the Abyssinians. The country described is probably Jingiro and Kaffa.

"To the southward of these Gallas, and behind the Suaheli, dwell the Wanika, Ukuafi, and Matambas, people very different from the Gallas in manners, language, and physical conformation. Among these races the Ukuafi are the most remote from civilisation; they do not bury their dead, but leave them to be devoured by wild beasts. The Wakamba go generally quite naked, but are obliged to put on clothing when they resort occasionally to the sea-coast. The Wanika, who live in the forests, about 200,000 in number, are pagans, though they have no images: they are in the habit of preparing a strong drink from cocoa-nuts, and are much addicted to intoxication and other vices. They are fond of certain games in which the young men engage, and in which one of the company must always become a victim. Still further towards the south are the abodes of the Masambara, and beyond them are the Msegûa tribes, opposite the isle of Zanzibar, through whose country a caravan-road leads far into the interior of Africa.

"Although scarcely any regulations of society exist among these tribes, except that in every village the oldest man of the place becomes a sort of king, the nature of the whole country to the southward of the equator is such as by itself would seem likely to lead its inhabitants to a higher culture. It is not, like the region further northward, spread out in level deserts of sand, but is full of hills and forests, and fertilised by frequent showers."

Physical Characters of the Suaheli.—We have some accounts of the Suaheli in an excellent memoir by Mr. Bird, published in the "Journal of the Royal Geographical Society." In this we are assured that the Suaheli are of a jet-black colour, and that they have woolly hair. It is observed that they have not the thick lips or the protruding mouth which are characteristic of genuine Negroes.

Captain Owen has mentioned the Suaheli repeatedly, but he has not fully described them. He merely remarks that they are Mohammedans, and that they differ in person and character both from Arabs and from native Africans, meaning Negroes.

[The zeal and learning of our missionaries, and particularly of the Rev. Dr. Krapf, have recently added very considerably to our knowledge of Africa south of the equator, and have confirmed most satisfactorily the expressed opinions of the author that nearly the whole of that vast territory, with the exception of the small space still inhabited by the Hottentots, is held by people of one family as closely allied in language to one another as are the Indo-germanic races,—perhaps even more so; the analogy, so far as the languages are yet known, being more like that between Gothic, Lithuanian, Slavonic, Celtic, Greek, Latin, and Sanskrit, to the exclusion of Albanian, Armenian, and any other more remote or doubtful branches. This territory, which we continue to call Kafir, is encroached upon by tribes of the Galla family, all of whom appear to be essentially nomades and warriors, while the Kafirs are certainly cultivators, and therefore stationary; and in compensation, the Kafir area, in one quarter at least, goes over to the north of the Equator. The notices we have of habits and customs, and of mental character generally, coincide with the evidence afforded by language: the testimony of physical characteristics is not so complete, our informants having been rather interested in describing the mental than the bodily qualities of the people they saw; but is only deficient, never antagonistic. In general, the personal characters are mentioned as compared with those of Negroes. Dr. Krapf says expressly that all the people from the sources of the Nile to the Cape of Good Hope are distinguished from the Negroes by their less intense colour, which he calls brownish, by their less projecting lips, and less woolly hair.*

Dr. Krapf's many years' residence in South Africa gave him greater opportunities than have fallen to the lot of any man, to obtain a knowledge of the inhabitants; he spoke with fluency several of the languages, and made occasional incursions far into the interior, always accompanying the discharge of his duties as a missionary by an anxious inquiry into the languages of tribes still farther

* "Church Missionary Intelligencer," vol. ii. p. 56.

advanced, with a view to facilitate the progress of future missions beyond the point to which he was himself able to penetrate. He thus collected fifteen vocabularies, five of which, in Kafir dalects,—the Suaheli, Nika, Kamba, Pokomo, and Hiau*—he published at Tübingen in 1850, with one of the Galla language, all in parallel columns. He also published a Grammar of the Suaheli language. The following information respecting the Kafir tribes is condensed from the prefaces to these valuable works, and from the journals of Dr. Krapf and Mr. Rebmann, printed in the "Church Missionary Intelligencer." The Rev. Mr. Rebmann accompanied Dr. Krapf in some of his journies, and on two occasions in 1848-49 he visited alone the more remote countries of the Jaggas, of whom he brought back interesting information.

The Suahelis, who call themselves, in their own language, Wa-zumba, live on the eastern coast of Africa, south of the line. The language is generally understood, from 1½°N. to the Mozambique country south, by all the Mahometans of South-East Africa. It is the vernacular tongue of Melinda, the first place on the eastern coast visited by the Portuguese, and so poetically described by Camoens. The language is the most cultivated of the Kafir tongues, and is almost indispensable to a traveller in East Africa,

* The Editor has taken the liberty to remove the Kafir prefix, which he thinks not only awkward but positively incorrect. Dr. Krapf calls these languages Kisuaheli, Kipokomo, Kigalla, &c. The fact is, that all the Kafir tongues have certain particles distinguishing singulars from plurals (and sometimes duals), adjectives from substantives, and one kind of substantive from another. Dr. Krapf, in the narrative of his journeys into Sambara in 1852, speaks of the Kisambara language, spoken by the Wasambara, who live in Usambara; and now and then mentions a Masambara, one of a Kisambara family. Different dialects have different particles: in the language which the Editor would wish to call Chuana, a native of the country is a Mochuana, two are Buchuana, the people generally are the Bichuana, and the language is Sichuana: and the latter words have become current in English, to the puzzlement of readers of African intelligence. Wherever the Kafir prefix has not become part and parcel of the English appellation, the Editor omits it.

who by its aid will easily be able, as we are informed by Dr. Krapf, to master any of the dialects of the interior. The New Testament has been translated into this language according to the dialect of Mombas. It is spoken by about 400,000 people.

The Nika tribes [Kinika, Wanika, &c.] occupy the higher country between 3° and 5° south lat., beginning 15 or 20 miles from the sea. They are pagans, but they worship a Supreme Being, whom they call Mulugnu, offering to him prayers and sacrifices. They also offer sacrifices on the graves of their deceased relatives, generally of rice and palm wine. This custom, whether it be worship or a mere mark of respect to the deceased, is common to most Kafir tribes, but milk is the usual offering among those of the interior. The Wanika are well provided with wine, and much addicted to excess; they are a drunken race, according to Dr. Krapf, and the preference of wine to milk as an offering is thus accounted for. They are also more sensually disposed than the rest of the Kafirs, and they use the privilege of divorce, which is accorded to all the tribes, to a much greater extent than the rest. The Government is a loose sort of republic, and the language is intelligible without much difficulty to the Jaggas, Kambas, and Taitas, far in the interior. They number about 60,000 souls. The Gospel of St. Luke has been printed at Bombay in the language of this tribe.

The Kambas [Wakamba, Ukambani, &c.] are 400 miles from the coast, but they are also found elsewhere, being the special traders of South Africa, and therefore more migratory than Kafirs generally, easily establishing themselves in various localities. In the course of their trade they go to the centre of the continent to procure ivory, either by barter, or by hunting the wild elephant, and they return to the coast at Mombas to exchange their merchandise for the articles they want themselves. They are of a cheerful disposition, and live on terms of friendship with all the tribes of the interior, of Kafir race; but have no intercourse with the Masai, Kuafi, and Gallas, who are nomades, and, as a consequence, plunderers. Most of the Kambas have long hair, which they dress in very many small twisted strings, frequently made up with little white beads. They also place strings of beads of various colours round the neck, loins, and ankles; and wealthy persons wear a great number of small brass or iron chains, very neatly made. They grease their bodies with butter and red ochre, like all the African tribes seen by Dr. Krapf. Their houses are circular, without windows, having a low and narrow door through which the inhabitants creep ; their furniture is of course scanty ; their beds are made of a cow's skin laid over a frame of bamboo or other wood, in form not unlike a four-post bedstead. They use a chair, which is neatly made, and carried about when they travel, for they do not sit upon the ground like most of the other tribes. Their dwellings usually contain a good provision of fire-wood, carefully cut, split, and dried, and neatly piled up in a corner. Their food is principally Indian corn, in the form of pudding or gruel, but they take also some meat and milk, and they prepare an intoxicating drink called uki, made from the juice of the sugar-cane. They are talkative and merry, but the men generally enjoy themselves in small parties, drinking and chattering and laughing, while the women are employed in domestic matters or in cultivating the ground. The wealthy marry ten or more wives, whose business is to attend to the care of the husband's property, which may be scattered about in various hamlets, the head wife alone living in the establishment of the husband; so that polygamy appears rather to be the engagement of a household of servants and stewards than a real multiplication of marriages. The Kambas marry at fifteen, and even twelve years of age, though it is not at all uncommon to find persons of twenty or twenty-five years old unmarried. Dr. Krapf thinks that marriage is checked by the large amount required to be paid for a wife by her parents, and by a singular custom among the Kambas, according to which the bridegroom is required to carry off his bride by force, after the preliminaries are completed. This is attempted by the help of all the friends and relatives that the man can muster, and resisted by the friends and relatives of the woman; and the contest now and then terminates in the discomfiture of the unlucky husband, who is reduced to the necessity of waylaying his wife, when she may be alone in the fields or fetching water from the well. When the lady is brought home the price is paid, and all contest is ended. The habit of begging, which is found so annoying by travellers in Africa, is scarcely known to the Kambas of the interior, though it is common enough among such as have had intercourse with the Mahometans of the coast. Dr. Krapf found these Kambas to be "great liars and most boisterous beggars."

The belief in sorcery, in the power to produce rain and thunder, and to put a charm, called utzai, into the house or plantation of an enemy to destroy him, is universal among them, and is found also in many other Kafir tribes. But by no means in them exclusively: the Negroes have some of these practices; the Mongols and Fins of Europe and Asia all believe in the power of affecting the weather; the navigators of the Scandinavian coast buy favourable winds of the Lapland witches, and some very curious accounts of the storm-producers among the Mongols are given by Mons. Quatremère in his notes to the "History of the Mongols" of Rashid-eldin (see the "Collection Orientale," Paris, 1836, vol. i. p. 428, et seq.)

The Kambas are not without mechanical skill; they smelt the iron ore of their country, produce iron of excellent quality, and form swords, knives, and hatchets,—useful, though somewhat rough; and are very expert in the manufacture of fine points for their arrows. They fashion their clay into pots which stand the fire, and they make tobacco pipes which are found perfectly serviceable. The bark of a tree is pounded and converted into fibres, which are twisted by the women into thin strings; and of this they make bags which are far better than those met with on the coast.

The produce of their skill in such fabrics, and of their hunting expeditions in the wilder regions of Kikuyu, Mbè, and Uimbu, to the north-west of their own country, together with the cattle, goats, and sheep reared upon the rich pastures of Ukambani (Kamba country), give them the means of carrying on an extensive trade; and they have profited by this power to make themselves the most wealthy tribe of Eastern Africa. Many individuals in the interior possess several hundred head of cattle, besides sheep and goats; and from their trade with the coast they obtain cloth of various colours, beads, brass wire, red ochre, pepper, salt, and the many other articles which constitute wealth and luxury in Africa. There is no general government among the Kambas, but an irregular sort of patriarchal or clannish system prevails, and the judgments pronounced by the heads of families, or by the most influential men of a district, if not repugnant to what is considered the custom of the country, are invariably obeyed. It would appear that superior wealth, or age, or acknowledged wisdom, which may consist in eloquence or fame of witchcraft, constitutes power in the non-monarchical communities of Kafirland. The wealth of the Kambas, and their intercourse with the Mahometans of the coast, have recently introduced among them the curse of slavery, but it has not appeared in the more detestable form of selling slaves; they only purchase for domestic purposes,—a crime shared by too many white nations. The Kamba nation may amount perhaps to 80,000 persons; a missionary station will probably be established in their country, "as the first link of an equatorial mission-chain," which will probably be the means of making known and Christianising all South Africa, with which they have extensive intercourse. The Gospel of St. Mark is printed in their language.

The Pokomo tribes live on the river called on our maps Quilimancy [Kilima, mountain; mansi, water], three or four degrees south of the equator. The Gallas give the name of Maro to this river, which is also called Dana and Pokomo. The language of the Pokomos has received some Galla admixture, from their constant intercourse with the Gallas, to whom they are subject. They are a commercial and agricultural people, raising rice and corn for the purpose of barter with the Gallas for ivory, which they sell to the Suahelis for manufactured articles. They navigate the Quilimancy in small boats, but avoid the upper river, their intercourse not extending into the interior.

The Wahiau live on the N.E. of the lake Nyassa, which Dr. Krapf believes to be the Maravi of our maps. The Doctor learned the language of a slave brought from the country, which appears, from the accounts he received, to be the great mart of east African slaves. He heard an account of the capture of 7,000 of the Hiau people by the Mawizi, a tribe on the S.W. of the lake, who must be the Moviza of our maps. The most brutal acts of cruelty, according to his informants, accompanied this capture; they may be deemed incredible, but the concurrence of native information left no doubt of the main fact.

Of the above tribes Dr. Krapf has printed vocabularies, as stated above.

The Sambara nation, between the 4° and 6° of south lat., and 100 miles from the coast, were also visited by Dr. Krapf, and described in the fourth volume of the "Church Missionary Intelligencer." The country is mountainous, and the people are named Eldonio (*i. e.* mountaineers) by the Kuafis, a neighbouring nation probably of Galla origin. Dr. Krapf found the Sambaras quiet, intelligent, and desirous of improvement; peace and order prevailed generally, and "a foreigner was not more safe in the metropolis of France or England than in most parts of Usambara," (p. 110). The food, general habits, and customs of the people, resembled those of the Kambas, whose language was not so dissimilar as to be unintelligible, but the country being poorer they were less commercial, and polygamy was less common. The government is monarchical; the consent of the king is required before a foreigner is allowed to enter the country, but when that is obtained he is protected, and, as in Abyssinia, an officer is appointed whose especial duty is to guide him and supply him with food. The monarch, who is absolute, may appoint a viceroy to any portion of his dominions, and the office is generally hereditary, going to the eldest son born subsequently to the appointment of the father: in one place Dr. Krapf found a woman in the viceroyalty, whose husband was a prince consort, who was not permitted to interfere in the government. Like the Israelites, the Sambaras have towns of refuge where a manslayer is safe from the avenger of blood. In the same manner he is safe if he can touch the person of the king. A runaway slave who can succeed in reaching the house of any near relative of the king, can no longer be reclaimed by his master, but the master is empowered to receive back the price of the slave from the slave-dealer who sold him. On this account slave-dealers in their way to the coast always avoid passing through Fuga, the capital town and royal residence, where so many opportunities occur to deprive them of their prey. The dress of the Sambaras is composed either of skins, or of a sort of fine matting made of rice-straw, and the women ornament their persons with ear-rings and large strings of beads, amounting in some cases to five or six pounds' weight.

The Jaggas, called in their own tongue Kirima, were visited by Mr. Rebmann, who passed some months in their country at the beginning of 1848, and again at the close of that year and the commencement of the following. It seems hardly possible that the people described by Mr. Rebmann can be the same with the Jaggas so famous in the early accounts of South Africa for their extraordinary ferocity and barbarism, but the name, and to a certain extent the geographical position, seems to leave little doubt. There may have been amelioration in the lapse of time, but the difference may perhaps be more probably accounted for by the different points of view from which these independent Kafirs were seen by the peaceful missionary arrived amongst them as a benefactor anxious to conciliate, and the warlike if not ferocious Portuguese seeking the subjugation of their country, and too often cruelly treating the people: the manly vigour with which an uncivilised tribe defended their independence would probably have been represented by any civilised people of that date as brutal ferocity. Mr. Rebmann describes the Jaggas as being of a "darkish black;" he found them a clean, industrious, and healthy people, and generally friendly; the women make a sort of embroidery with beads, and help to take care of their flocks of sheep and goats; and the men build houses, plant trees, make fences, and form water-courses for the purpose of irrigation. They carry on a good deal of trade by barter with the neighbouring tribes, named Dafeta, Ugóno, and Kahe, and hold frequent assemblages of these and of many more remote tribes at various spots, called sangarras, or markets, resembling the fairs of Russia and India. They have no towns, like most other Kafir tribes, but each family has its own separate area or farm-yard, surrounded by a fence strong enough to keep out wild animals, within which are generally built three or four cottages: such habitations are spread much about the country, at distances of half a mile or more from each other. The government is an absolute monarchy, like that of the Sambaras; the religion is a kind of adoration of their deceased relatives, to whom they offer sacrifices of milk, and address prayers. The snow-capped mountain of Kilima-njaro is in the Jagga country.

The missionaries at Rabbai, near Mombasa, have from time to time heard of a people called Alá, found in groups scattered through a large section of Eastern Africa, from the interior region beyond the Jaggas to Bondei and the Nika country near the coast. They are called Masaka by the Nikas, Wassi by the Sambaras, and Wandurobbo by the Kuafi. Another tribe, called Ariangulo, living in a state of dependence among the Gallas, is believed to be of the same race. The habits of these people are those of hunters, and consequently nomades. They are skilful archers, but they employ their weapons only against game or wild beasts, carefully avoiding the presence of any tribe excepting their own. Their language is said to be unintelligible to any of the other people of Africa, but no specimens of it have been given, nor have we seen any notice of their physical characteristics, though from their vicinity to the coast, and the circumstance that some of them are said to be held in slavery by individuals of known Kafir tribes, it might not be difficult to obtain more information respecting them. Dr. Krapf believes them to be remains of some aboriginal tribe which once peopled a large part of East Africa. It would be interesting to examine their language, which may perhaps show them to be a remnant of some Hottentot tribe, and would thus afford additional probability to the opinion that the Hottentot area at some former period has embraced the whole of South Africa. The Hottentots, so far as we know, have always receded before the Kafirs, and we cannot suppose any territory now Hottentot to have been ever Kafir. But where shall we get our Kafirs from? Their present wide extension over a large part of the earth's surface, their languages allied to each other at least as closely as those of the Indo-germanic race, and their general physical and moral resemblance, would argue that they have been for ages where they are now found.]

CHAPTER XVII.

OF THE RELATIONSHIP BETWEEN THE DIFFERENT BRANCHES OF THE GREAT SOUTH AFRICAN RACE.

THERE is nothing in the general character of the various nations which I have described that would entitle us to refer them all to one group, or to conclude that they are more nearly related to each other than to other African tribes. There are, indeed, great physical differences between some of them. The fierce and enterprising and energetic Kafirs of the Amakosah and Amazuluh races, tall and handsome, with almost Iranian countenances, and of a brown or copper colour, which has been thought to resemble that of the Red Warriors of North America, are very different people from the indolent Negroes of Mozambique or the black Suaheli. The proof of consanguinity between these nations depends on the evidence afforded by their languages. But as this seems to place a great weight on an argument which requires a particular scrutiny before it can be allowed to afford adequate testimony to such an inference, it will be requisite to show that the phenomena are such as admit no other explanation, and that there is no way of escaping the conclusion. This can, as I think, be done by examining the kind of analogy which has been traced between these languages, and by showing that it cannot have arisen from the intercourse between the several tribes,—that it is such as to preclude all idea of the operation of after-causes, and must needs be primitive or primordial, and growing out of the original development of the several languages. When the fact of the kindred origin of these nations is once demonstrated and allowed to have been established on the evidence of their kindred idioms, there will be found many circumstances that tend to confirm it; but it could never have been arrived at by any other method of proof.

The discovery of this connexion of languages has been very gradual, and the proofs have been brought to light accidentally. The earliest notices of the South African languages were obtained by Portuguese and Italian missionaries in the empire of Kongo. A grammar of the language of Kongo, by Hyacinth Brusciotti à Vetralla, was published at Rome in 1659. This work, though of small extent, is sufficient to explain the principal peculiarities of the language. Some other treatises on the languages of Loango and Angola were afterwards written, and were known to the authors of the "Mithridates;" and since their time, a more copious grammar, with a dictionary or vocabulary of the Kongoan, Bunda, or Angolan idiom, has been compiled by Father Cannecattim.

These three principal languages of the Kongo empire are distinct from each other, but the distinction is little more than that of cognate dialects. Vater compares it to the difference between English and Danish. The old writers say that the difference between the Loangoan and Kongoan and Angolan is nearly equal to that which distinguishes the Castilian from the Portuguese; and by one writer it has been compared to the difference between the Venetian and the Calabrese dialects.

Although the Portuguese had settlements on the eastern as well as the western coast of South Africa, it does not appear that any knowledge was attained by them of relationship between the languages and the races of the people in these two regions, nor was the fact that they were connected known to the authors of the "Mithridates."

The first traveller who made inquiries into the history of the Kafirs and their language, and their relations to other African tribes on the eastern coast, was Professor Lichtenstein. The extensive diffusion of this language on the eastern parts of Africa may be considered as his discovery. He professed to draw his information in part from Mauritz Thoman, a Jesuit, who resided many years on the coast of Mozambique. Lichtenstein says that after much research, and after studying the works of Portuguese writers and visiting the eastern coast of Africa at two different times, and at places remote from each other, he came to the conclusion that all the tribes of people as far northward as Quiloa are allied to the Kafir race.

But the very remarkable fact, that the nations of Western Africa are of kindred language with those of the East, was first pointed out, as I believe, by Mr. Marsden. In an appendix to the narrative of Tuckey's Voyage to the Zaire this discovery was announced. Mr. Marsden says that he had, many years before the date of that voyage, collected a short vocabulary at Bencoolen from the mouth of a Negro servant, a native of Mozambique; and that he had recognised a decided resemblance between the words of that vocabulary and those to be found in specimens of dialects spoken in Kongo and the adjacent countries, given by Oldendorp and Brusciotti, as well as in the vocabulary from Delagoa Bay obtained by White. The opinion which he had formed from these data was confirmed by examining the vocabularies obtained by Captain Tuckey of the dialects of Malemba and Embomma, in Kongo. Specimens of the analogy between all these dialects are to be seen in Mr. Marsden's appendix.

Lastly, our acquaintance with this family of languages has been greatly extended by the late researches of Dr. Krapf among the nations of Africa much further to the northward than Mozambique or the eastern side of Africa. Of these languages nothing was formerly known further than what could be collected from a short vocabulary of the language of the Suaheli collected by Mr. Salt. In the second volume of my "Researches into the Physical History of Mankind" this vocabulary was collated with those of the Kafir and Kongo languages, and a near resemblance in the words, arguing an extension of the same family of languages over the coast of the Suaheli, was pointed out. We have lately obtained from Dr. Krapf much more satisfactory information. After that excellent missionary, whose exertions in Abyssinia had already obtained for him the esteem and admiration of the Christian world, was banished from that country, he sought a new field for his labours further southward, and fixed his residence at a spot on the coast opposite the island of Mombas, in a region as yet unknown. The people of this coast are the Suaheli, called formerly Suahili and Sowhylese by different writers. Dr. Krapf penetrated sixty miles into the interior of the country, and here began his work by studying the languages of the Suaheli and the Wanika. He collected a vocabulary of the former, consisting of more than 10,000 words, prepared a short grammar, and translated into the same dialect the Book of Genesis, and the Gospels, and the Acts of the Apostles.* He communicated to the celebrated philologist Von Ewald the results of his researches; and the last-mentioned writer has published from the version, as a specimen, fourteen verses of the Gospel of St. John, to which he has added a most able and interesting analysis of the grammatical structure of the Suahelian idiom. This paper throws the greatest light on the nature and essential structure of the language, and enables us at once to ascertain its relation to the idioms of the Kafir nations, as well as to those of the nations of Kongo. We had, previously to this time, two short grammars of the Kafir languages by Wesleyan missionaries, one representing the idiom of the Amakosah, and the other the Sichuana of the inland nations.

From a comparison of these sources of information I have collected the following remarks illustrative of the history and relations of the languages spoken by the Great South African family of nations.

It has been observed by Von Ewald, that the most remarkable phenomenon in the structure of the idiom of the Suaheli relates to the peculiar conception of material objects which it displays. It observes no distinction of genders in the ordinary sense of the term, and has neither a masculine nor a feminine form in verbs or nouns. On the other hand, it has a distinct form for the living and the inanimate, according to which, words are modified as they are by the distinction of genders in other languages.

Von Ewald says that he had long ago observed the same phenomenon in the Sanskrit, and traces, though more disguised, of the same construction in the Semitic languages. He is of opinion that the distinction of male and female does not belong to the primitive groundwork, or was not

* The additional pages at the close of the preceding chapter will give some idea of the increased information afforded by Dr. Krapf since the above was written.—Ed.

made in the original development of human speech, "*so much as that of the more strongly and more weakly personal, or the animate and inanimate.*"

This phenomenon is more conspicuous in the South African than in any other known language; and Von Ewald considers the Suaheli as strikingly exemplifying the opinion which he had expressed in the investigation of other languages before the peculiarities of the Suaheli became known to him.

But these African languages carry further a sort of metaphysical distinction between objects, which they separate into different classes, on a principle which it is not easy to define, but which I shall presently exemplify.

It must be remarked, in the first place, that the inflections of words are chiefly effected in these languages by prefixed particles, of which there is a great variety. In the High-Asiatic languages every change of meaning is indicated by a post-fixed particle. The South African take quite the opposite method, in which they remarkably agree, as I have before noticed, with the Coptic.

These prefixes mark the numbers of nouns, and different prefixes are used, not only in reference to animate and inanimate objects, but also to other subdivisions of these objects, founded on some metaphysical distinction. Thus the names of rational and irrational beings require different articles or prefixes, and these are again subdivided, as also are the names of inanimate things.

Thus nouns designating rational beings have *'m* or *um* for the prefix of the singular, which is changed into *va* (in Kosa Kafir, *aba*) in the plural, as *'mtu* (a person), *vatu* (persons), *'msungo* (an European), pl. *vasungo*.

Nouns in the Suaheli, designating irrational creatures, have no plural ending, but adjectives connected with them have *va* as in the former: thus *zimba va-kuba va-vili* means two great lions, the order of words being reversed.

In inanimate things the plural is formed by *ma* or *mi*, as *makasha* (chests) from *kasha*, *miti* (trees) from *mti*.

Vi is found in other instances, as *vi*tu *vi*dogo, little things, the plural of *ki*tu *ki*dogo.

The preceding observations are taken from Von Ewald's remarks on the Suaheli language. I shall now extract the following table from Boyce's Kafir Grammar, in order to show that this language follows the same principle of inflection, and for the purpose of displaying its effects more fully.

Mr. Boyce divides the Kafir nouns into declensions by the different prefixes used. The six forms are thus displayed. The first changes the prefix

1.	Um	into aba;	as, um-ntu (a person), pl. aba-ntu.
	u	o;	u-Faku (Faku), pl. o-Faku.
2.	i	ama;	i-hashe (horse), pl. ama-hashe.
	ili	ama;	ili-zwi (a word), pl. ama-zwi.
3.	in	izin;	in-hlu (a house), pl. izin-hlu.
	im	izim;	im-azi (a cow), pl. izim-azi.
4.	isi	izi;	isi-tya (a basket), pl. izi-tya.
5.	ulu	izin;	ulu-ti (a rod), pl. izin-ti.
	u	o, i, or im;	u-lwimi (a tongue), pl. i-lwimi; u-bambo (a rib), pl. im-bambo.
6.	um	imi;	um-lambo (a river), pl. imi-lambo.

It is remarked that *in*, in the third declension, when prefixed to nouns of living objects having sex, has the plural in *ama*, as,—

In-doda, man; ama-doda, men.
In-kazana, girl; ama-kazana, girls.
In-kwenkwe, boy; ama-kwenkwe, boys.

A great part of the system of inflection is regulated by a complex euphonical method, which it would be impossible to explain in a short compass: it pervades the whole grammatical structure of that language. I must refer my readers to Von Ewald's memoir, and to the grammars of the Kafir Kosa and Sichuana by Messrs. Boyce and Archbell, for a further illustration of this subject.*

* These classes, as well as the further characteristics noticed, are found in more or less completion in almost all the languages of South Africa examined, and in several of those of the people north of the equator, universally called Negroes.—Ed.

Another peculiarity in these languages is calculated to remind us of the structure of the complex languages of America: I allude to the insertion of abbreviated pronouns in the middle of compound verbs. The pronouns become *infixes* instead of suffixes; and of the infix-pronouns there is a great variety, corresponding with the classes of prefixes to nouns. I shall only take one example from Von Ewald, in which the pronoun is inserted between the prefix-particle, denoting the tense of a verb, and the verbal root itself:—

ame-m-finika, he covered *him*; *i. e.*	mtu, the man.
ame-i-finika, he covered *it*;	müesa, the table.
ame-u-finika, he covered *it*;	mti, the tree.
ame-ki-finika, he covered *it*;	kitu, the thing, or dsuo, the book.
ame-li-finika, he covered *it*;	neno, the speech.

Von Ewald observes that the Suaheli language has a very soft and euphonious intermixture of consonants and vowels, and that every word terminates with a vowel. The roots may therefore be dissyllabic, and a change of vowels at the terminations of the roots may serve to distinguish verbs and nouns. Thus *soma* is the verb to read, and *somo* becomes a noun meaning the act of reading. A noun thus distinguished from the verb may serve for an infinitive mood, but is incapable of forming a plural. Forms standing for the *agents* are derived from verbs by prefixing *m*; as *msoma* (or *msomi* or *msomai*), reader; *msêma*, speaker; *muóni*, seer (from *ona*, to see); all of which, like simple participles, may be joined with the accusative, as *msêma maneno*, the speaker of the word, as if "locutor verbum." The formation of more distinctly ideal words is like that of *utakâtifu*, purity, from *takâtu*, to be pure; *uharibifu*, destruction, from *haribu*, to destroy.

The signs of tenses likewise precede the verbal root, as formative particles in this language generally are placed rather before than after the roots. The present is *apenda*, he loves, from *penda*, to love; the past tense, *amependa;* the plusquam-perfect, *alipenda;* the future, *atapenda.* The imperative is in short, *penda ;* in plural, *pendani ;* the optative from the present, *apende.* The negative verb prefixes an *h*, as *hapendi*, he loves not; *hapendŭi*, he is not loved; but *sipenda* is love not (imperative). A participle from the present, *apendai*, is equivalent to *amba* (he) *kuamba* (who) *apenda* (loves).

In all these traits a striking and decided analogy exists between the Suaheli language and the Kosa and Sichuana Kafir, and the dialects of Kongo.

The causative form in verbs is produced by infixing an *s* or *es*, which is sometimes reduced to a mere vowel, as *kuĕsa*, to raise, from *kuea*, to rise; *somesha*, to cause to read, from *soma*, to read; *lettea*, to send, from *letta*, to bring; *pigia*, to cause to beat, from *piga*, to beat.

I may here observe that the causative form is contructed precisely in the same manner in the Kafir dialects, both the Kosa and the Sichuana, and likewise in the language of Kongo, according to Brusciotti à Vetralla.

The passive is formed by inserting an *o* before the terminating vowel, as *pendŏa*, to be loved, from *penda*. Sometimes there is a slight irregularity: as *uáwa*, to be killed, from *úa*, to kill; *haribiwa*, to be destroyed, from *haribu ; suiliwa*, to be hindered, from *suia*.

In the Kafir dialects the passive is formed exactly in the same way. *Tanda*, loving, makes *tandwa* (according to Mr. Boyce's orthography), equivalent to *tandoa*, in the passive. In the Sichuana, *kekang*, buying, is *kekoang* in the passive, being bought, according to Mr. Archbell's grammar.

The reflective form is made by prefixing *dshi* (*ji*), as *dshipenda*, to love one's self; *dshifunsa*, to learn, from *funsa*, to teach.

Mr. Archbell's grammar of the Sichuana contains little more than a collection of paradigms of declensions and conjugations. We have, however, enough to demonstrate a strict grammatical analogy between these languages and the Suaheli.

The same observation may be applied to the dialects of Kongo in comparison with the Suaheli. Brusciotti à Vetralla observes, that what other languages effect by changes in the terminations of words, is done in the Kongo languages by prefixes, or, as he terms them, "*principiatives*." He says that the "principiatives" set before nouns have eight forms, which are connected with variations in the articles. Proper names, and names of men and of animals, when joined with adjectives or the verb substantive, have certain articles. The other classes of nouns have peculiar prefixes. Brusciotti gives the following examples:—

When the "principiative" or prefix begins with *e*, the article *ria* is used, and the following variation takes place:—

Sing. *En-tondo ria n'Ziampunga*, the praise of God.
Plur. *Ma-tondo ma n'Ziampunga*, the praises of God.

In the second form the initial syllable is *mu*, *u*, or *o*, the article *ua*, and the plural is made by taking *mi* from the initial syllable of the noun.

In the third, fourth, fifth, sixth, seventh, and eighth forms, the articles are *quia*, *yo*, *kua*, *ka*, *lua*, *tua*, which make in the plural *y*, *za*, *tua*, *tu*, &c.

Something very similar to this is found in the Angolan language.

The personal pronouns in the Kosa and Sichuana Kafir display a near relation to those of the Kongo and Angolan languages. I shall add the ten numerals and a few common words as specimens of the resemblance of these several idioms.*

* The following table is corrected and arranged from materials obtained since the author's death, furnished by Dr. Krapf. Grammars have since then been published in several South African dialects, and the Rev. J. Appleyard has communicated much valuable information in his sketch of the History and Grammar of the Kafir language, published in 1850. The Galla and Namaaqua words are added for the sake of comparison, and the Kuafi, corrected from Krapf's Vocabulary of that tongue, published in 1854, is separated from the Kafir dialects, because the language appeared to the Editor to be of a totally distinct class; though he is at present unable to say where it should be placed.—ED.

Numerals in the Languages of Southern Africa.

	1	2	3	4	5	6	7	8	9	10
I. Kafir Languages.										
Kosa	Inye	Bini	Tatu	Ne	Hlanu	Tandatu	Xenxe	Mboxo	Itoba	Ishumi
Sichuana	'Ngue	Pedi	Taru	'Ne	Tlanu	Tataru	Shupa	Diheramanwa-namabede	Diheramanwa-namangwahéla	Shumi
Zulu	Nye	Mbíli	Ntatu	Ne	Thlanu	Tatisitupa	Kombile	Kyiyangalobili	'Agatisile	Ikyumi
Delagoa Bay	Chingea	Bizi	Rarou	Moonau	Thanou	...	...	...	...	Koumau
Mozambique	Moosa	Pili	Thara	Saessé	Thana	Thana moasa	Thana pili	Thana saessé	Looko	Mino komili
Suaheli	Mmoja	Mbíli	Tátu	Nne	Táno	Setta	Sábaa	Nane	Kenda	Kumi
Nika	Mmenga	Mbíri	Táhu, háhu	Nne	Tsáno	Tandāhu	Fungáhe	Nane	Kenda	Kumi
Kamba	Umue	Ili	Idátu	Inna	Idăno	Dandātu	Monsa	Niania	Ikenda	Ikumi
Pokomo	Mmóza	Mbii	Háhu	Nne	Záno	...	Fungáhe	...	...	...
Hiau	Yumpépe	Siwíri	Sitátu	Jéje	Sáno	...	Tanona siwíri	...	...	...
Msegúa	Mosi	Pili	Tatu	Kanne	Shano	Endātu	Fungáte	Nane	Kenda	Kumi
II. Empire of Kongo.										
Kongo (Daniell)	Mosa	Meola	Tatoo	Meale	Tourroo	Sambavo	Sambade	N'ana	E'vauh	Coomy
Ambriz (Daniell)	Bosa	Cola	Tatoo	Keale	Tarroo	Sambaavoo	Samboide	Emannah	Avou	Ecoomy
Loango (Oldendorp)	Boose	Soli	Tattu	Ena	Tanu	Sambaan	Samboari	Nane	Voa	Kumi
Kongo (ditto)	Moschi	Meere	Sitattu	Siza	Sitan	...	Samboari	Sinan	Sivoa	Sikumi
Mandongo	Omo	Boelli	Batati	Anna	Attani	Sanu	Nshumi	Mpumo	Kifa	Kumi
Malemba	Basey	Meoly	Tatau	Si-ja	Tanoo	Sanbanu	Sambodi	Enanu	Evana	Kumi
Embomma	Mosey	Cole	Tatoo	Yaea-kea	...	...	...	...	...	...
Sonho	Mochi	Solle	Satu	Msia	Sanu	Samánú	Samboari	Nane	Eoua	Kumi
Bunda, or Angolan	Mochi	Yari	Satu	Uana	Sanu	Samannu	Sambuari	Naqui	Ivoa	Kunhi
Mpongwe	Mori	Bani	Raru	Nai	Otanu	Ozubar	Urwakime	Innanai	Iunogumi	Ikumi
Galla	Tóko	Lama	Zadi	Afur	Zan	Dya	Torba	Zadeta	Zagala	Kudan
Kuafi	Obo	Arre	Uni	Oton	Imiet	Ille	Nabshana	Isiet	Sal	Tomon
Namaaqua	Kwii	Kam	Nun	Haka	Kōre	Nanni	Huuku	Kayssa	Kōizi	Diizii

	Kosa	Sichuana	Delagoa Bay	Mozambique	Suaheli	Nika	Kamba	Pokomo	Hiau	Msegua	Kongo Dialects, Malemba Embomma	Galla	Kuafi	Namaaqua
Man	Uhmto	Motu	Monhee	Mantu	Mtu, *pl.* watu	Mútu	Múndu, *pl.* ándu	Múntu	Múndu, *pl.* wandu	Mtu	Moontau	Nama	Aito	Kip
Woman	Umfaai	Massari	Aduhast	Mahe, mekõnque	Mtúmke	Mutshetu, mutumúje	Mundu, muka	Muke	Mundu, yunam, kongue	Mfiëre	Kentou, quinto	Niti	Endangili	Tarras
Father	Bao	Hara	...	Tete	Baba	Baba	'Adza	Baba	Dáde	Dadi	Tata, bantu	Aba	Baba	Iip
Mother	Mao	Ma	...	Mama, amaoo	Máma	Máyo	Múaido, ignis	Máma	Amáo	Mlela	Mama	Háda	Yeya	Iis
Brother	Um-klhueh	Mogolue	Molupa-liĩka	Molupahaka, aloombo	Ndúgu	Ndúgu	Endui, muina	Ndúgu	Mlóngo	Endugu	...	Oboléza	Enganashe	Kaap
Earth	Umhlaba	Lehatsi	...	...	Nti	Zi	Ndí	Nsí	Jirambo	Zii	...	Lafa, adu, biftu	Anhepo	Hüp
Sun	Ilanga	Tsatsi	Diambo	Ezooah	Dahua	Dzua	Kua	...	...	Zua	Ezooloo, tengua	...	Engolo	Tsoris
Moon	Inyanga	Khueri	...	Molungo, moyse	Mesi	Mesi	Muéi	Mesi	Mesi	Muesi	Tangua, mooezy	Jia, bati	Lubbo	'Khăp
Water	Maasi	Metse	Matee	Maschi	Máji	Mázi	Mánsi	Mázi	Méssi	Madshi	Maza, muza	Bizáni	Engarre	Kammi
Bread	Inhloko	Bogobi	...	Mutuwe	Kitǒa, mukáte	Dshitǒa, mukáhe	Matǔe, mukáe	Mukahe	...	Mtui	Noone, noonee	Budena	Lukünïa	Birip

It would probably be tedious to many of my readers to pursue this subject further at present. What I have collected is quite sufficient to establish a near and truly kindred relation between the languages of South Africa in the east and west, of which it appears difficult to imagine any other explanation than that obvious one afforded by the hypothesis, otherwise probable from local circumstances, of a common original. The South African idioms constitute a particular family of languages, and afford an instance of a peculiar, and in some respects singular development of human speech. They are, however, not without external relations, though it is difficult to say what place will ultimately be assigned to them among the different groups of languages. In what relation they, and the languages of Africa in general, stand to the Semitic or Syro-Arabian family, is, as M. von Ewald has observed, a problem not yet solved. Some words have been recognised in the Suaheli similar to Semitic words, but it is possible that these may have been introduced by Arabian, or even by old Phœnician traders on the eastern coast. In one respect these languages coincide remarkably with the Coptic. I allude to the law by which both prefix all modifying particles and the whole apparatus of small and abbreviative words which answer the end of inflections ; while other languages, either in part or universally, suffix them. In the complex system of verbal conjugation, which may be seen displayed in Boyce's Grammar, they certainly make some approach towards the involving method of the North American languages, of which Mr. Howse's Grammar of the Cree, or Algonquin Knistenaux, exhibits the construction. Compared with the simple jargons of the tribes on the coast of Guinea, the languages of Kafirland, with the kindred dialects, certainly indicate a higher development of intellect among the native races of Africa.*

* It is scarcely necessary to say that increased philological information necessitates a considerable modification of these conclusions. The Kafir complexity is chiefly euphonic, and has no resemblance to the American

One objection will be offered to the supposition that all the nations who speak the various dialects of this mother

---

grammatical system; at the same time it is far surpassed by the languages of the Australians, whose intellectual development is of so low a character: we should almost be inclined to regard the simplicity of a language as a mark of superiority of intellect. It may be observed here that the grammars of the South African languages since published by Dr. Krapf, and the researches of Dr. William Bleek, have enabled us to see with greater evidence the diffusion of the same system of languages throughout South Africa. As our grammatical knowledge extends, we find traces of the same structure far north of the Kafir area: the learned Bishop of Sierra Leone (Introduction to Yoruba Grammar, p. 7 and 31) finds it in the Timmani, Bullom, and Sherbro', and he particularises the eleven Kafir-like modifications of the Timmani verb. A few Timmani fragments, printed in 1847, by the Rev. C. F. Schlenker, of the Church Missionary Society, have enabled the Editor to see the identity of the Timmani and Kafir pronouns, of the initial changes (compare the Timmani genitive particles wah, rah, yah, mah, with the Sechuana waga, loga, yaga, baga, &c.), and of some other striking peculiarities of structure. Some of the Fulah modifications, though much less in degree, are indications of a like affinity. There are Kafir-like resemblances of structure even in the Galla language, though they seem to be rather accidental than constituting an affinity: we allude to the formation of a causative verb by the addition of a sibilant. The Kafir *soma*, for example, makes *somesha*, and *kuea*, *kuësa*; so the Galla *debia* makes *debiza*, and *loa* makes *loza*. The passive, too, is made in Kafir by *w*, as *tanda*, *tandwa*, and the Galla passive by the cognate *m*; as *ega*, *egama*. The structure of the Hottentot languages proceeds upon a wholly different principle, and the following note, drawn up from such an insight into the Namaaqua dialect as the Editor could get from reading the Rev. Mr. Schmelen's version of the Gospels, will, he believes, prove its total and radical distinction from the Kafir languages. The language is also an interesting study of itself, on account of its remarkably simple and yet comprehensive and expressive structure, and from its possessing some features, such as the grammatical gender and accusative case, usually considered as peculiar to the most highly organised languages. Its few affinities, strange to say, appear to be rather with Coptic and Semitic, than with anything else. The vocabulary is very limited, and many words, as in Chinese, appear to have the same sound. In Chinese, a distinction is made by a varied intonation, and the Editor is inclined to think, though in opposition to the valuable opinion of Dr. Bleek, which is not to be neglected, that the remarkable inarticulate clicks used by the Hottentots may have been adopted for a similar purpose.

In the Namaaqua, nouns have two genders,—real grammatical genders,

tongue are of one origin, and that is, the great extent of their physical diversity. The tribes of the coast of Ajan

---

as in the Semitic, Roman, and Celtic languages, distinguished by their terminations: *p* is masculine (sometimes *mi*) and *s* feminine. Thus *iip* is "father," and *iis* "mother;" *kaap* is "brother," *kaas* "sister;" *khāp* "moon," *tsōris* "sun." They form their plurals respectively by *koe* and *ti*, as *kaakoe* "brothers," and *kaati* "sisters." There is also an indefinite form terminating in *i* for the singular, and *n* for the plural; as *kooi*, "a man," *kooin*, "men;" *kamaui*, "a robber," *kamaun*, "robbers;" *kamaup*, and *kamaukoe*, would be "the robber," "the robbers." There are two dual forms, one appropriated to a pair, like the Semitic dual, the other to two individuals, as in Greek.

Some words appear to take either gender, as *moep*, or *moes*, "the eye;" and frequently the difference of gender shows a modification of meaning, the feminine denoting a smaller object, or a part of it: as *hawoop*, "shoe," *hawoos*, "sandal;" *hoemmi*, "mountain," *hoems*, "hill;" *nanoep*, "the sky," *nanoes*, "a cloud;" *hayp*, "tree," *hays*, "stick," &c. &c.

There is a copious declension, formed, as in the Finnish language, by terminations, which may be called post-positions; the genitive has its distinct form, ending in *di*; and the accusative, terminating in *a* like the Arabic, is regularly used.

The adjective goes before the substantive, and by the addition of *ze* it becomes an adverb: as, *kay*, "good," *kayze*, "well," *amma*, "true," *ammaze*, "truly."

The pronouns are very copious, and have distinct forms for almost every conceivable modification of meaning; the second persons, as well as the third, distinguish the genders, as do the Semitic pronouns, and the third persons have the indefinite form, like the nouns; as *ayip*, "he," *ays*, "she," *ayi*, "he" or "she," indefinite. The dual is complete, and the first persons dual and plural distinguish the inclusive and exclusive values, as in Polynesian, and some American, Dekhanic, and Tartar languages. All are completely declined, and all have abbreviated forms for the complements of verbs or of nouns, or for combination; and this is done with a regularity and simplicity which admit of no mistake. An example or two will show this:—The pronouns of the singular number are *tita*, "I," *zaats*, "thou, m." *zaas*, "thou, f." *ayip*, "he," *ays*, "she;" the abbreviated objective forms end in *i*, and the nominatives in a consonant, except the first, which is *ta*. We have then, with the verb *maa* "to give," *maati*, "give me," *maatits*, "thou givest me," *maatip*, "he gives me," *maabiita*, "I give him," *maassip*, "he gives her" (or thee, f.), *maatziita*, "I give thee," &c. These forms, be it observed, are used only in indirect sentences; in the direct way the nominative is put first, without abbreviation, as *tita maabii*, "I give it," *zaats maati*, "thou givest me," &c. &c.

are, as we have seen, of a jet black, while the Bechuana are of a light brown, the Amakosah being somewhat darker. In Kongo there are various complexions; the features also differ. The nomades of the high plains beyond the tropics have often features which approach the Arabian type, and an Arabian origin has been assigned to them, whilst the natives of the Mozambique coast have nearly the Negro characters. But there is enough that is peculiar in the hair and colour of all these tribes, to preclude the notion of an Arabian parentage. On the other hand, the deviation in physical characters is not greater than that which is to be found in the Dekhan among tribes of the native Tamulian family, where we may compare the tall, handsome, and comparatively fair Tudas of the Nilgherry Mountains with the puny tribes of black people who are to be found in the low plains of Malabar and Coromandel.

In like manner the physical characters of these nations, though differing considerably in different parts,—all, however, presenting the same difference within the limits of one and the same tribe,—may all be reduced to one description, or admit of the same general remarks. On the sea-coast, and among the more savage races, as the Makua of

---

The verbs make all modifications by the addition of certain syllables; the past tense prefixes *ke*, the perfect *ko*, the future *nii*, the conditional *ka*; the infinitive postfixes *za*, the passive *hii*, the reflected verb *ssen*; as *ays nii maa*, "she will give," *tita ka maa*, "I would give," *maaza*, "to give," *maahiiza*, "to be given," *maassen*, "to give one's self," &c. &c.

The Namaaqua tongue is provided with a fair supply of conjunctions, a part of speech which is generally very deficient in uncultivated languages; with the exception of the simple copulatives, they come at the close of the sentence to which they belong; an example is *'ays 'ayp ko ha ammaka*, "because her hour is come;" literally, "her time has come because."

It is very singular that the consonants of the form-syllables, *p*, *b*, *n*, *s*, &c., very rarely occur in nouns or verbs, as if they had been borrowed from a language of a wholly distant phonology.

Enough has been said to prove the peculiar character of the Hottentot languages, and their utter disconnection with Kafir; any further detail upon a subject so little calculated to interest readers generally, would be superfluous.—Ed.

Mozambique, they have much of the true Negro physiognomy. Yet even here a milder and more intellectual expression is observable than among the natives of Guinea. Their hair is woolly, and their colour black, but their skulls, as may be seen by a variety of crania from the Mozambique coast in various collections, are more vaulted and capacious in the anterior part, and have much less of the prognathous character. The sketch of a Mozambique Negro, inserted in a previous page, will exemplify the above remark. But a great many of the people of Kongo, Benguela, and Loango, as well as of the natives of the eastern countries on the opposite side of the continent, recede greatly from the Negro physiognomy. Professor Christian Smith, who accompanied the late expedition to the river Zaire, coincides with the old Portuguese navigators in this statement.

In proof and illustration of these remarks, I have selected several portraits from the excellent work of Rugendas, which display the character above described in the natives of South Africa. One of them is the portrait of a native of the Mozambique country. It has the tattooed stars which appear to be the characteristic ornament of that people, and which are seen upon the preceding portrait engraved on wood. The features and expression are almost European. Very similar observations will apply to other figures copied from the same work, one of which is marked a native of Loango; the other a woman of Benguela.

I shall here advert once more to the figures of a Kongo cranium, of which several delineations have been given.

In Plates III. and IV., facing page 111, I have given two representations of the skull of a native of Kongo. One displays the form of the basis, and the other the front view. The front view, as may be seen at a glance, bears a strong resemblance to two other skulls represented in the same plate. Both of these belong to races who have

Native of Benguela

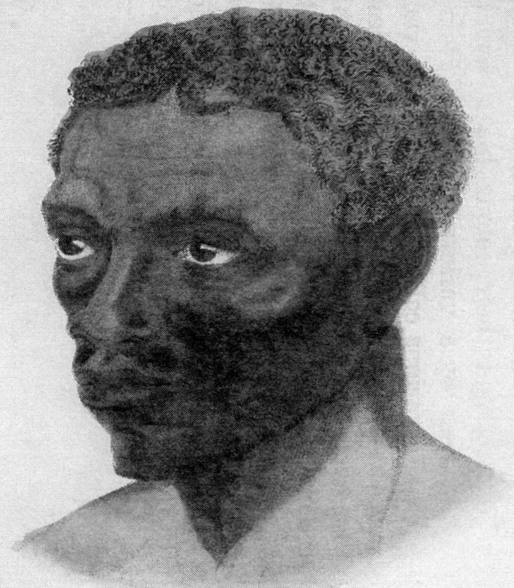

Native of Angola

crania of the pyramidal form, and broad flat faces, though not in the greatest degree. One of them is the skull of a Chinese; the other that of a native American, a Chitimacha of Louisiana. In all these the zygomatic arches project laterally in nearly equal degrees; the orbits are wide, and rather far apart; the nasal bones rather flat; and the transverse diameter of the face below the eyes nearly plane, or with very little convexity; the foreheads rather conical. All these are characters of the pyramidal skull, though they appear not so strongly marked as in the Esquimaux and other Polar races. Plate IV. exhibits the bases of the same three skulls, and these are very much alike: the Kongo head is not more prognathous than the others, but it is somewhat more elongated. For the rest, the Kongo skull is heavier than the others, displaying in this respect an African character; while the large round sweep of the zygomatic arches, and the breadth of the diameter of the anterior third part of the cranium, exhibit approximations to that form of the head which is so common among the nomades of Northern Asia.

From what has been said, it will be evident to the reader that it is vain to attempt to reduce the nations of Africa, even if we confine our view to the so-termed woolly-haired tribes, under any particular stock or number of original races. We may call them all Negroes, if we define that expression to mean people with woolly hair; but they agree in no other character; and even this seems arbitrarily assumed as a mark of separation, since there are tribes who have hair that nearly approaches to this character, as the Galla and some of the Nubian races before described, and are yet excluded by a general consent from the class to which the Negro belongs. As for the form of these skulls, we find all the three principal types of the human cranium among these woolly nations, the Soudanians having elevated foreheads and capacious heads, without the prognathous countenance; the Ibos, narrow and elongated skulls; and the Hottentots, broad-faced and pyramidal ones.

Since these pages were written, I have received from New York a grammar, recently published, of the language of the Mpongwe, the people on the Gaboon river, near Cape Lopez and Cape St. Catherine, whose country extends 300 miles in the interior. This language, the structure of which is said by the American missionaries who composed the grammar to be beautiful and philosophical, is a cognate of the Suaheli. We have thus reason to believe that the South African race reaches nearly up to the Equator, both on the eastern and western side of the continent.

[Taking into consideration all the facts in relation to the languages of Africa which have come to the knowledge of the Editor, he would provisionally map out the whole continent in the following manner, premising that it is merely a rough attempt, awaiting further information:—The northern division, extending from the Atlantic on the west to the Red Sea on the east, and from the Mediterranean on the north to an irregular line on the south, which will include the Great Desert, and reach an undefined Negro and Kafir frontier near the Equator as it proceeds eastward, is all Semitic, or at least what has been called Sub-semitic; including the Berber, Tuaric, and Abyssinian languages, and it is believed, the Galla in its different branches. These will have to be subdivided into smaller families, as is done with the great Indo-Germanic class; but we have not yet sufficient data for doing this with any degree of minuteness. The Hottentots, as before stated, occupy the extreme south, and all the rest is occupied by Negroes and Kafirs. From the notes occurring here and there in the preceding pages, it will be seen that we are inclined to class these in one great group. About the Kafirs there can be no hesitation, and not much as to the fact that Kafir languages and Kafir physical and moral characters graduate in many instances into such as are universally termed Negro, as we proceed from south to north-west. But there are Negro tongues which seem to elude classification or graduation; and taking some that have been carefully investigated, as the elaborately varied Wolof, the simple Mandingo, the intonated Ghâ or Accra, the Ashanti and the Mongol-like Bornu, we seem to have the phenomenon of wholly different families of languages in a space much smaller than could be anticipated. Further researches may, and probably will, disclose principles uniting the whole in one great class; and we anticipate valuable results from the expected publication of the vocabularies of 200 Negro languages recently brought from Africa by the Rev. Mr. Koelle, in which he has very judiciously inserted a considerable number of phrases that may enable us to see more of their structure than we can do from the vocabularies usually furnished. The negroes hitherto have been considered as constituting one race rather from physiological than philological evidence.]

CHAPTER XVIII.

OF THE PELAGIAN RACES. 1. MALAYO-POLYNESIAN RACE. 2. PELAGIAN NEGROES. 3. ALFORAS.

After surveying the population of Africa, we are naturally led to direct our attention to the extensive regions of the globe lying to the eastward of that continent, which, though formerly supposed to be occupied by one great southern land, is in reality a vast expanse of ocean, interspersed with groups of islands of various extent and elevation. Disjoined and widely separated, these insular tracts are found to contain races of inhabitants more nearly connected with each other, and at the same time much more widely scattered, than any of the families of men who occupy the continuous lands of Asia and Africa. The habitable tracts of this region lie principally, but not entirely, within the tropics. In longitude, it may be considered as reaching in its greatest extent, namely, from Madagascar to Easter Island, through nearly half the equatorial region of the globe. The whole of this region is made, by Malte-Brun, to constitute a fifth great division of the globe, under the name of Oceanica. Some of the islands in it are of great elevation, which are principally volcanic; and although in others the presence of fiery mountains has not been ascertained, we know already, as Malte-Brun has observed, a greater number of volcanoes in Oceanica than in any other portion of the world; in all the most elevated lands volcanic rocks are found, and craters either now burning, or effete, or still emitting smoke. The low islands are of a different description: they have for their foundation reefs of coral rocks, generally disposed in a circular form, and enclosing a lagoon. There is no region of the world which affords a greater variety of local conditions, and none which opens a better field of observation to those who are desirous of tracing the influence of physical agencies on the organisation of living bodies, and particularly on that of the human kind.

The human inhabitants of Oceanica divide themselves into three groups. One of these may be termed a race or family of nations, since a real kindred or community of origin has been proved, by affinity of language, to exist among them. The two others probably constitute as many races, since we seem able to trace them from one cluster of islands to another; but certainty is yet wanting on this point. I shall distinguish them by the following names. The first is the race termed by different writers Malayan, Polynesian, and Oceanic. The identity, or the near affinity, of the Malays and Polynesians has been doubted, and even denied, by writers of great authority;* but it has lately been fully established through the researches of Baron William von Humboldt.† I shall term these people the

---

* Crawford's "History of the Indian Archipelago."

† See the great work of W. von Humboldt, entitled "Ueber die Kawi Sprache auf der Insel Java, nebst einer Einleitung über die Verschiedenheit des menschlichen Sprachbaues und ihren Einfluss auf die geistige Entwickelung des Menschengeschlechts."

Malayo-Polynesian, or, in short, the Malayan race. The second group consists of tribes of people of darker complexion, with hair crisp, and more or less resembling African Negroes: they are spread over many islands, within a narrower range than the Malayan race. I shall term them the Pelagian Negroes. They have often been called Papuas; but we have seen that this last designation belongs properly to a mixed race, descended partly from the people last described, and in part from another tribe with straight hair. The mixed people are termed hybrid Papuas by MM. Quoy and Gaimard, and other French writers. A third distinct group consists of tribes who differ in physical characters from the two former. They are the Alfoers, Alforas, Haraforas, of different voyagers. They are savages of dark colour, lank hair, and prognathous heads. To this group the natives of Australia belong. I shall term them collectively Alforas. By the name of Pelagian races I mean to designate collectively the whole assemblage of nations inhabiting Oceanica.*

The Malayan stock may be subdivided, in a manner that will much facilitate the description, into three branches. The first branch is the Indo-Malayan, comprehending the Malays proper of Malacca, and the islanders of the Indian Archipelago, as the inhabitants of Sumatra, Java, Celebes, the Moluccas, and the Philippines. These last nations resemble the proper Malays, both in language and in physical characters, much more nearly than do the Polynesian tribes. To the Indo-Malayan branch may, perhaps, be associated the natives of the Caroline Islands and the Ladrones, who appear to be nearly related to their neighbours, the natives of the Philippines. 2. To the second, or Polynesian branch, belong the Tonga Islanders, the New Zealanders, the Tahitians, and the Hawaii: these are the four principal groups of the Polynesian family, arranged according

* I use this name Pelagian, because the term Oceanic, as well as Polynesian, has been by different writers appropriated to one particular branch of this stock.

to the indications of their languages. 3. The third branch are the Madecasses, or people of Madagascar.

Blumenbach placed all the Pelagian nations in one class of human races, and, in his system, they constitute one of the five varieties into which all mankind are by him distributed. At the time when Blumenbach made his classification, the distinct line which separates the Pelagian Negro and the Australian races from the Malays was hardly recognised. He otherwise would not have placed all these nations in one group, or have assigned to them one common description. Neither would he have stationed the Malays at all, as he has done, in a place intermediate between the Caucasian and the Æthiopic varieties, or have assigned them a peculiar form of their own. The Australians, and some other tribes in these regions, have, it is true, some characters in which they resemble African Negro races; and they might be arranged in the same, or in a proximate department of the human species. But the Malays, properly so termed, have no traits in common with the Negroes, nor do they make any approach to the Æthiopian type. Neither do the Polynesian tribes bear any real resemblance to the Negro in the shape of their heads. If, therefore, Blumenbach's arrangement be preserved, the Malays, and all the nations akin to them, must be excluded from this fourth variety of mankind, and it must comprehend only the two remaining groups, namely the Pelagian Negroes and the Alforas. In adverting to the question, what place in the ethnological system belongs to the Malayo-Polynesian race, we are led to the statement of a fact which manypersons will not be disposed to admit,—that the entire group of these nations, though, strictly speaking, one race, do not display the same physical type. Many late voyagers, indeed, have been struck by the great difference, in this respect, which exists between the natives of the Indian Archipelago, of the Malayan stock, and the remote Polynesian races; and on this ground they have pronounced them to be of distinct origin.

Great as the physical difference is between these nations, it will be found by those who give due weight to the evidence offered by late researches into their history, that there is full and complete proof of the unity of descent in the whole class, and that there is no probable way of explaining the diversities that exist between them, unless we attribute these diversities to the spontaneous variations which display themselves in tribes of people who have inhabited from immemorial ages different climates, and have existed, in many respects, under different physical conditions.*

---

* The division into three groups made by the Author is in the main correct, though the extensive and valuable information received since his death in relation to the Pelagian races, and some linguistic researches prosecuted at home, enable us to draw the line more definitely; and, further, to show in some degree the relation which the first two of the groups named bear to each other. Dr. Prichard himself recognised the incorrectness of the name Alforas, which Mr. Earl's investigations proved to be merely a Portuguese term signifying outcasts, or separated tribes, and its improper application to any division of the natives of the smaller islands (see note in p. 21). But as the natives of the great insular continent of Australia, whom he included under the Alforas, are wholly different in physical features, moral character, and structure of languages, from all the other Pelagian races, they may remain the sole owners of the name. The Editor has no objection to any name whatever as a mark of distinction, and will not pretend to suggest any partial changes: for a nomenclature wholly new, the time is not yet arrived, though it may come by and by. The Malayo-polynesians and the Pelagian Negroes of the Author, as is shown by the structure of their languages, and by the mental character of the people, however variously developed, are of one great family, in the same sense as are the Germanic races and the Persians: all the languages yet investigated have like grammatical characters, pronouns resembling, verbal structure the same; and although the languages beyond the Polynesian line have very distinct vocabularies, yet they graduate from tribe to tribe, and island to island, in such a way as to render it impracticable to cut off from the family even the most remote branches. We have the phenomenon indicated by Dr. R. G. Latham as being the normal condition: one pervading language (the Polynesian here) extending over a very large area with little dialectic variation, and an adjacent population split up into tribes speaking a great number of idioms, all allied to the great body, but differing from each other far more decidedly than the most distant dialects of the language spoken by the first-mentioned people. There is in the case before us one

CHAPTER XIX.

MALAYO-POLYNESIAN RACE.

I. *Indo-Malayan Branch.*

THE Malays, properly so termed, are well known to all voyagers in the Indian Archipelago as a people of short and slender stature and small limbs, with flat faces, and features resembling the Chinese; they are, in complexion, considerably darker than that race, yet much fairer than

---

great line to be drawn, coinciding to a certain extent with that indicated by Dr. Prichard:—the people whom he calls Polynesians speak languages not only similar to each other in structure, but in vocabulary also, to such a degree of resemblance that tribes separated by a quarter of the globe's circumference might with little trouble understand each other; at all events an educated European who can read, for example, the New Zealand language, will have little difficulty in comprehending the meaning of a book in the language of the Sandwich Islands. On the other side, the idioms of the Pelagian Negroes, whom we may call Papuans, vary so greatly in their vocabularies that even in small islands two or more languages mutually unintelligible are frequently in use: in a Church Missionary voyage around the Papua Islands [Pelagian Negroes], with several natives on board speaking English, who had been competently educated in the College of Auckland, and were good interpreters in 26 of the islands, it was estimated that they visited districts containing 200,000 inhabitants, speaking 40 distinct languages, averaging 5000 persons only to each tongue. We have before us translations of small portions of Scripture in several of the tongues spoken in New Caledonia and the more eastern islands, and an examination of their structure fully confirms what is above stated. The languages examined are but very few among the many spoken by these races, and the specimens received being only Scripture extracts, often rather paraphrastically translated, and but scanty in amount, may not have enabled the Editor to see deeply into the structure of these idioms—and he admits that he is generalising rather largely on a small basis—but, so far as they go, they seem to prove that the languages are allied to those of the other Pelagians in the same way as the Teutonic to the Slavonic tongues; the grammar having much resemblance, the pronouns being often almost identical, but the bulk of the words different. We find the transition well marked in the Fiji, an idiom which is allied to both these divisions of language, in words as well as grammar. Geographically, this might be expected. The New Zealanders may probably be also considered as partaking somewhat of the second class, or Pelagian

the Hindús. They inhabit the southern part of the Peninsula of Malacca, where they have many towns, or cities. They likewise possess a considerable part of the Island of Sumatra, the people of Menangkabao being Malays, and speaking the Malayan language, properly so termed. On the coast of most of the islands of the Indian Archipelago they have formed settlements, and carry on traffic in most parts of the Indo-Chinese seas; they are the Phœnicians of the Eastern seas. All the dispersed people thus far described are Malays in the strictest sense of the term; they are people of one dialect, and nearly of the same manners and cultivation. There are numerous

---

Negroes; certainly very much less so than the Fijis; but their decided though recently abolished cannibalism, the distinction into two great families—the Maoris, and the darker Mangamangas—and, we may add, some few features of the language, all point to a Papuan intermixture. The language of the Tonga Islands has even more Fiji analogies, though decidedly Polynesian on the whole; the physical character also indicates intermixture. Some scanty vocabularies would seem to show that the so-called Micronesian groups will be included under this, or another distinct division of the same great family, but there is not sufficient material at hand for coming to a decision. The preponderance of evidence in regard to the Negritos of the Philippines is that they speak the languages of the more civilised natives of the first or Indo-Malayan group, though so corrupted as to be scarcely intelligible to them. Of many of the islands, and of the large island of New Guinea, we have only short vocabularies, often little more than numerals, but these, on analysis, shew decidedly a Malayan or Polynesian basis. We expect the fuller detail of the characters and divisions of these tongues from Mr. Logan, the penetrating and indefatigable editor of the Singapore Journal, who has studied this subject more extensively and scientifically than any other man, and has already published very valuable papers in relation to it. We may add that, under very opposite moral conditions, the mental qualifications of the whole family are alike; all live in fixed habitations, all cultivate the ground, all observe something like a government and political arrangements, all have manufactures more or less rude, and all, when not alarmed by fears or experience of treachery, have shown an aptitude, and even considerable anxiety, to receive European improvements and education. Twenty-five candidates for scholarship were carried to New Zealand on the return of the missionary voyage above alluded to, and many more were rejected for want of accommodation. It is unnecessary to show how totally opposite all this is to the state of things in Australia.—ED.]

tribes besides them who speak cognate dialects of the same speech, and differ in their degrees of civilisation. The Orang Benua are a race of savages who live in the mountainous tracts in the interior of the Peninsula; they are conjectured to be the original stock of the whole race. The inhabitants of other parts of Sumatra, exclusive of the people of Menangkabao, are likewise of this class, as well as the original people of the Sunda Isles.

The people of Sumatra are thus described by Mr. Marsden: the description refers principally to the Malays of that island:—

"Their eyes are uniformly dark and clear, and in some, especially the southern women, bear a strong resemblance to those of the Chinese, in the peculiarity of formation so generally observed of that people. Their hair is strong, and of a shining black: it is constantly moistened with cocoa-nut oil. The women wear their hair long, sometimes reaching the ground. The men destroy their beards with chunam, or quick-lime; and their chins are so smooth that an uninformed person would imagine them naturally destitute of hair. Their complexion is properly yellow, wanting the red tinge that constitutes a tawny or copper colour. They are generally lighter than the Mestees, or half-breeds of the rest of India: those of the superior class, who are not exposed to the rays of the sun, and particularly the women of rank, approaching to a degree of fairness."

The people of Java are described by Sir S. Raffles as short, well made, slender, their extremities small. "Their forehead," he says, "is high; the eyebrows well marked, dark, and distinct from the eyes, which are somewhat Chinese, or rather Tartar, in the formation of the inner angle; the colour of the eye is dark; the nose somewhat small and flat; the cheek-bones are usually prominent; the beards very scanty; the hair of the head lank and black, but sometimes waving in curls, and partially tinged with a deep reddish-brown colour; the countenance is

A Malay.

Woman of the Marian Islands.

mild, placid, and thoughtful." The natives of Celebes are said by Labillardière to be short, of a yellowish complexion, and to have features somewhat resembling the Chinese. A nearly similar description is given of the natives of other islands in the Indian Archipelago.

Blumenbach has figured and described the cranium of a Bugis of Celebes in his fifth decade of skulls. Viewed in front, this skull resembles, as he says, the Mongolian in its great breadth, jugal bones, the flatness of the nasal bones, and the distance of the orbits: the jaw was prominent, and like the African. This last character, however, is not general in the Malayan race.

M. Lesson was so struck with the difference in physical characters between the islanders of the Indian and the Pacific Oceans, that he positively denies the Malayan origin of the Polynesian tribes. To the natives of the Caroline or New Philippine Islands, who are well known to belong to the same stock,* he gives the appellation of Pelagian Mongoles, and constitutes them a particular family. He says that they have decidedly the obliquely-placed eyes which characterise that race; their countenance broad, or extended transversely, and the nose flattened; the natural complexion of a citron-yellow, but becoming brown on exposure. The Oceanic race, by which name he designates the Polynesian tribes, is, on the other hand, in his opinion, the most beautiful and the most regular in features of all the nations who inhabit the isles of the Great Southern Ocean.

The Plates here selected to illustrate this variety of our species are portraits of a Malay, and of a native of the Marian Islands, exemplifying the character above described. It will be seen that the countenance of both approaches considerably to the Chinese physiognomy, and is strikingly different from that of the Polynesian tribes who will next be mentioned.

* Le Gobien says, "La langue des Carolines a beaucoup de rapports avec la Tagala."

2. *Of the Polynesian Branch of the Malayo-Polynesian Race.*

The fact which I have in the preceding pages ventured to assert—namely, that the Polynesian nations, though belonging to a different physical type, are nevertheless genuine descendants, or really cognate tribes, of the Malayan family—is, for obvious reasons, one of considerable moment in its bearing on the natural history of mankind. I cannot attempt, in the present work, to exhibit in detail the proofs, founded chiefly on a minute and elaborate comparison of languages, which lead to this conclusion. They form one of the principal inferences to be collected from the great posthumous work of William von Humboldt, which occupies three quarto volumes of the Transactions of the Royal Academy of Sciences at Berlin. To this work I must for the present refer my readers who are desirous of investigating the subject.*

The Polynesian races display considerable variety among themselves, both as to physical and moral characteristics.

The Tahitians are considered by Lesson as the type of the whole Polynesian race. He says that all the Tahitians, almost without exception, are very handsome men: their limbs are of graceful proportions, but at the same time robust; the muscular parts are everywhere covered with a thick cellular tissue, which softens the contour of their projecting lines. Their physiognomy has generally a mild, and gentle, and frank expression. The head of the Tahitian would be European, were it not for the spreading out of the nostrils (*l'épatement des narines*), and the too great thickness of the lips.

Blumenbach has figured the skull of a Tahitian, and one of a native of the Marquesas, who are very nearly related to the Tahitians. He remarks that the former is

---

* In the last volume of my "Researches into the Physical History of Mankind," the reader will find a brief statement of this evidence.

somewhat narrow in form, but remarkably prominent at the summit; the upper jaw somewhat prominent; a ridge extending from the middle of the forehead over the vertex. The forms of these skulls in Blumenbach's plates are among the finest in his Decades. Mr. Lawrence has remarked, in reference to them, that the Tahitian skull does not differ in any essential points from the European formation. The front and lower part of the forehead may be a little contracted and slanting. The face is altogether large, and the upper jaw fully developed: its alveolar portion, too, projects slightly in front. He says, "The head of a native of Nukahiwah, one of the group called the Marquesas Islands, presents a very beautiful and symmetrical organisation, corresponding to the descriptions of the great stature, fine proportions, and strength of these islanders.

FIG. 80.

A Native of Tahiti.

Except that the face is larger, its lower part especially more considerable and prominent than in the best models

of the Caucasian variety, and that the jaws and teeth altogether have a marked projection, this head is not very essentially distinguished from that form. The forehead is, indeed, more slanting than in the intellectual European heads." Mr. Lawrence concludes that the Marquesas, the Society, Friendly, and Sandwich Islanders, might almost be arranged under the Caucasian variety.

The natives of the Society Islands, including Tahiti, are, according to Cook, of the largest size of Europeans. The men are "tall, strong, well-limbed, and finely shaped. The women of the superior rank are also in general above our middle stature, but those of the inferior class below it; and some of them are very small. Their natural complexion is that kind of clear olive, or *brunette*, which many people in Europe prefer to the finest white and red. This refers to the females of the better class, who are sheltered from the wind and sun; they have no tint in their cheeks which we distinguish by the name of colour. Their hair in general is black, but in some it is brown, in some red, in others flaxen; but in the children of both sexes it is generally flaxen." "Nothing," says Anderson, "could make a stronger impression at first sight on our arrival here than the remarkable contrast between the robust make and dark colour of the people of Tongataboo, and a sort of delicacy and whiteness which distinguish the inhabitants of Otaheite. The women struck us as superior in every respect."

The people of the Marquesas are very nearly related to the natives of the Society Islands, and they may be almost considered the same nation. They have similar features, and an equal variety of complexion. Captain Cook thus describes them:—"The inhabitants of these islands collectively are, without exception, the finest race of people in this sea. For fine shape and regular features they, perhaps, surpass all other nations. The men are tattooed from head to foot; this makes them look dark; but the women, who are but little punctured, and youths and young children, who are not tattooed, are as fair as some Europeans. The men are in general tall,—that is, about five feet ten inches, or six feet. Their hair, *like ours*, is *of many colours*, except red, of which I saw none." The Spanish writers expressly mentioned red hair at the Island of La Madalena, which Cook did not visit: perhaps they may have given that term to auburn or flaxen hair. They observe different modes in trimming the beard, which is generally long. Their clothing is the same as at Tahiti and made of the same materials, but not so plentiful, nor is it so good.

The Hawaii, or Sandwich Islanders, are another branch

FIG. 81.

A Native of the Sandwich Islands.

of the Polynesian stock in the arrangement of nations by Humboldt; they stand next to the Tahitians. Their language is nearly allied to the Tahitian. Their physical characters have been described by M. Choris :—

"Les enfans, en venant au monde, sont complètement noirs ; la jeune fille la plus jolie, et la plus délicate, qui s'expose le moins à l'action de l'air et du soleil, est noire ; celles qui sont obligées de travailler constamment à l'ardeur du soleil, sont presque de couleur orangée."

The hair of these people is sometimes crisp or frizzled, approaching to the woolly appearance ; in other instances, soft and flexible. M. Choris says, "Les grands se distinguent aisément du peuple ; ils sont de haute taille, et gras ; leur teint est brun foncé ; ils ont les cheveux moins longs que les gens du commun, souvent crépus, et courts ; les lèvres généralement assez grosses ; tandis que le peuple est petit et maigre, a le teint plus jaune, les cheveux plus lisses."

The adjoining coloured plate, from the Atlas of M. Choris, exhibits characteristic portraits of two natives of the Sandwich Islands.

The New Zealanders.

The skulls of the New Zealanders differ somewhat from those of the nations already mentioned ; but the deviation is inconsiderable. There are many in different collections in England, and several may be seen in the Museum of the Royal College of Surgeons ; the annexed figure represents one of them.

FIG. 82.

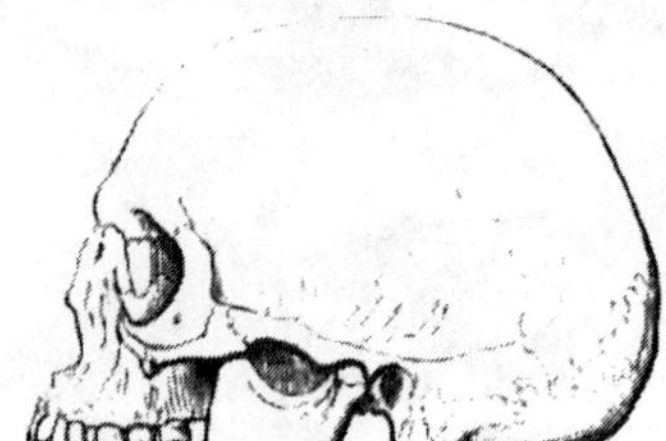

Skull of a New Zealander.

The Ombai Islanders are a tribe of this race.

It seems that there is great variety in the complexion of the New Zealanders. We have seen that many of them were, according to early voyagers, of a colour which is de-

scribed as "a pretty deep black;" and a late writer, Crozet, divides them into white, brown, and black people. The latter are of smaller stature than the former; but there is no clear indication of their belonging, as some have conjectured, to a different stock. It has been supposed that New

FIG. 83.

A Native of Ombai Island.

Zealand was inhabited by a tribe resembling the Australians before the Polynesian race arrived, and that the darkest people are descended from these aborigines.* But no evi-

* See the note in p. 432–3. If Papuans [Pelagian Negroes] be substituted for Australians, the opinion expressed in the text will coincide with the suspicion indicated in that note.—ED.

dence of any such fact has been found: the language of the people gives no testimony of intermixed descent; it is a simple Polynesian dialect. Similar physical varieties are traced among all the other races scattered through the Great Southern Ocean; and if we admit this conjectural explanation of the phenomena of variety in regard to one of these insular tribes, we must adopt a similar hypothesis in regard to almost every other group of islands in the Pacific; and even this will afford no way of accounting for the appearance of a type so nearly European in several of them. The mixture of Malays with Australians, or with any people resembling the aboriginal inhabitants of the Indian Islands or Austral countries, would never give origin to a form so nearly approaching the European as that displayed by the handsome and xanthous inhabitants of the Marquesas.

[In a paper by Dr. Thompson, printed in the Journal of the Statistical Society, it is stated that the average height of males near Auckland is 5 feet 6¾ inches; one man, a chief, was measured, whose height was 6 feet 5½ inches. Their bodies generally are 1½ inch longer than those of Europeans, and their legs, from the knee joint to the feet, as much shorter. Their feet are broader than ours, and nearly an inch shorter.—Ed.]

The Tonga Islanders.

The Tonga Islands, formerly called the Friendly Islands, of which Tongataboo is one of the largest, are inhabited by a tribe of people nearly resembling the New Zealanders. Their language, according to Mr. Anderson, bears the greatest affinity imaginable to the idiom of that people.

In their physical character, they are described as seldom above the common stature, of strong and stout form, great muscular strength rather than beauty, and not subject to the obesity which is observed among the

Tahitians. "Their features," says Mr. Anderson, "are very various, insomuch that it is scarcely possible to fix on any general likeness by which to characterise them, unless it be a fulness at the point of the nose, which is very common. But, on the other hand, we met with hundreds of truly European faces, and many genuine Roman noses amongst them. Few of them have any uncommon thickness about the lips. The women have less of the appearance of feminine delicacy than those of most other nations.

Fig. 84.

Matabula of the Tonga Islands.

The general colour is a cast deeper than the copper-brown; but several of the men and women have a true olive complexion, and some of the last are even a great deal fairer: this, as we are told, is the case principally among the better classes, who are less exposed to the sun. Among the bulk of the people, the skin is more commonly of a dull hue, with some degree of roughness. There are some albinos among them.

"Their hair is in general straight, thick, and strong, though a few have it bushy and frizzled. The natural colour, I believe, almost without exception, is black; but some stain it brown, purple, or of an orange cast. In this custom, they resemble the islanders to the northward of the New Hebrides."

The Tonga Islanders are divided into several distinct hereditary castes, to whom different offices are appropriated by fixed institutions. One of these castes are the Matabulas, who are a sort of middle class, below the *Egais*, or nobles, but above the common people. The preceding sketch gives the portrait of a Matabula, from M. d'Urville's collection. It displays the character which the hair assumes in many of the tribes of the Southern Ocean.

The Samoan Archipelago and its Inhabitants.

The Samoan islands are situated near the confines of the three great Oceanic provinces into which the vast regions of the Pacific have been divided by late geographers. On the western, or the Asiatic side of that ocean, and between the Samoan Archipelago and the insular empire of Nippon, is situated Micronesia, so named by the late much-lamented Admiral Dumont d'Urville, who has been followed by many writers of recent times. Micronesia is a region of small islands: it comprehends many insular groups, widely dispersed, of which the particular islets are mostly of small extent. Their inhabitants are said to differ in some respects from the Polynesian tribes in general—that is, from the various nations, the Tongans, Tahitians, Hawaiians, and Maorians [New Zealanders], who people the principal groups of distant Oceanica. The Micronesians have been thought to approach more nearly to the Tagalan and Bisayan races of the adjacent Philippines; and by a celebrated naturalist, who has traversed the Pacific in one of the naval expeditions sent by the late French government to pursue nautical discovery in the Austral seas, these people have been termed Pelagian Mongoles. They are regarded by M. Lesson as foreigners in Oceanica, and by him supposed to have descended from the high table-land of Central Asia, as an offset of that race who, according to their own mythological tradition, issued by aid of fire and blast from the iron-bound valley of Irguenekonn. The opinion of M. Lesson has been, if I am not mistaken, sufficiently refuted by Admiral Lütké, who has displayed in full the proofs of relationship between the dialects of the Micronesian islanders and the Polynesian idioms. It seems, on the whole, evident that the Micronesian islanders differ somewhat in physical characters and habits from the rest of the Polynesians, but the differences are not such as are usually typical of separate races—I mean of races which have been immemorially separate, and without indications of original consanguinity. The idioms of these islanders differ only as dialects from the languages of the great Malayo-Polynesian family. To which group of these nations the Samoan islanders are to be referred, whether to the Micronesian, the Tongan, or the Maorian, has not been proved. It seems not improbable that they will be found to be in some respects intermediate between these subdivisions of the Oceanic race.

Another region of the Great Ocean, which has been separated by geographers from Polynesia, and made a distinct province of the Pacific, approaches and almost touches on the limits of the Samoan Archipelago. This province may be termed "Kelænonesia," or the "region of islands inhabited by blacks." It lies to the southward of Micronesia, and to the westward of the central spaces of Oceanica. Kelænonesia presents a striking contrast to the beautifully variegated groups of the Polynesian islands, covered with rich vegetation, and spread out in clusters of gems under the sunny sky of the great Ocean.* The more extensive

* Dumont d'Urville, "Voyage Pittoresque autour du Globe." Paris, 1835.

lands of Kelænonesia contain denser masses of lofty mountains and unexplored wildernesses covered with primeval forests. Unlike the lively, cheerful Polynesians, the natives of these gloomy retreats, ferocious and sullen, of repulsive and menacing aspect, have ever shunned the approach of strangers. The moral and physical characters of these savage people distinguish them equally from the agile, graceful, and comparatively fair Polynesians. Some of the tribes of Kelænonesia recede further than others from the almost Asiatic beauty of the Marquesans and Tahitians, and even exceed, as it is said, in ugliness the most ill-favoured brood of the African forests, whom they rival in the sooty blackness of their complexions. We shall form a correct idea of this region if we represent Australia as its nucleus or great continental centre. The outskirts of Kelænonesia, or Oceanic Negroland, stretch themselves into far-distant spaces to the eastward, northward, and westward of Australia, and form a crescent of islands and groups of islands which presents its convex front towards the more open seas of eastern Oceanica.*

Situated near the junction of these departments of the Great Ocean, the Samoan Archipelago appears likely to become the centre of a widely-spreading influence, and the Christian mission which, since the misfortunes of Tahiti, has there established the seat of its active operations, is already beginning to produce a strong impression on the surrounding insular nations. The influence of this mission may be expected before long to open a way into the darkest parts of Pelagian Negroland, on the history and languages of which a new light is very soon to be diffused. Some brief notices of the Archipelago, which has hitherto been very obscurely known to Europeans, cannot fail, I think, to be interesting to the students of ethnology.

The chain of the Samoan islands occupies an extent of almost 100 leagues from east to west, nearly under the fourteenth degree of southern latitude. The most westerly

---

* See the note in pp. 431, 432, and 433.—Ed.

islands are the largest in this chain. They are smaller in extent towards the east, and Rose island, the last in this direction, is a mere rock.

The principal isles of the Samoan chain are named as follows :—

Opoun [Manua], Leone [Ofu?], and Fanfoue [Orosenga], separated by narrow channels from each other, are elevated lands covered with wood; at a distance they appear to be one island.

Maouna [Tutuila], is a mountainous and woody island; it is about seventeen miles long, and six or seven in width, and has two islets at the eastern and western extremities.

Farther westward is Oïolava [Upolu], a delightful and still more fertile island, forty miles long, and ten miles at its greatest breadth. Several islets adjoin the eastward and westward extremities of Oïolava; to the westward is the fertile and populous islet of Platte [Manono].

Pola [Savaii], the most westerly of the group, is a magnificent island; its beauty and fertility have been extolled by La Pérouse and Kotzebue. The western part of this island forms an immense cone, which is compared by Kotzebue in form to Mouna-Roa, the lofty volcano of Hawaii, and in height to the Peak of Teneriffe. This island is one hundred leagues in circuit.*

It was supposed by the historian of "Discoveries in the Southern Ocean,"† that the Samoan islands were first seen by Admiral Roggewein in 1722, and that they are the group named by him Isles of Baumann, after the captain of the ship Tienhoven. Roggewein, however, placed these islands under the twelfth degree of south latitude. His

---

* The Editor has added the native names of these islands: it is curious that one of them should have the same name with that one of the Sandwich Islands which it resembles, Savaii and Hawaii being different in pronunciation only. Hawaii is as near an approximation to Savaii as the organs of a Sandwich Islander could accomplish.—Ed.

† "History of Discoveries in the Great Southern Ocean," by Captain Burney, R.N., 3 vols. 4to.

description of them agrees with that of the Samoan chain; he says that they were islands of pleasant appearance, and were covered with fruit-bearing trees and leguminous plants. They were intersected by mountains and smiling valleys, some of them being ten, fifteen, and twenty leagues in circuit. Every family on these islands governed itself, and the tribes were classed as at Easter island. The natives came out to sea to meet the Dutch, and offered them fish, cocoa-nuts, bananas, and other fruits, for which they only received some worthless trinkets. Roggewein supposed the population to be very large; he judged from the crowd of people he saw upon the sea-shore. He says the men were white, and only differ from Europeans in having their complexion darkened by the heat of the sun; their bodies were painted of divers colours; their arms were bows and arrows; their countenances had a gentle and kind expression, and they were lively and cheerful. He says they were the most honest and civilised people in the Southern Ocean. They took the Dutchmen for gods, and grieved at their departure.

It is probable that the isles visited by Roggewein were the Samoan group, but the discovery is commonly attributed to Bougainville, the first navigator who accurately described them. Bougainville was acquainted with all the principal islands. He gave an account of the inhabitants, which differs widely from that of Roggewein; he says the people are not so mild in disposition as the natives of Tahiti. "Their countenances are more savage, and their disposition more false and cunning. Their most remarkable characteristic is their skill in navigation. Their canoes are better constructed than those of any other oceanic tribe, and seem to fly over the water with great rapidity." Bougainville called the group, from this circumstance, the Islands of Navigators, a name which they have retained on maps from that era.

La Pérouse spent some time on the island of Maouna, where he had many adventures, and lost one of his best officers. He described the inhabitants as a tall, athletic race; he says the ordinary stature of the men was five feet ten inches, and the proportion of their limbs colossal; the females were tall, slender, graceful, and sometimes beautiful. His account of their moral character is by no means very favourable. Kotzebue was the next writer of celebrity who gave an account from his own observation of the Samoan islanders; but I believe their name was first made known by M. Mariner, who spent some years in captivity in the Tonga islands. In his time the natives of these islands had frequent intercourse with the people of the Samoan Archipelago. Among these Mariner obtained much information respecting the Samoans, but he modified their name according to the peculiarity of the Tongan dialect.*

The most full and detailed account yet published of the Samoan islanders is that which has been given by Mr. Wilkes, the commander of the exploratory voyage sent out by the United States of America. We have, however, still more recent information in the papers published by the Christian mission to the Samoan Archipelago, the members of which not only exert themselves with zeal and remarkable success in their sacred calling, but seize every opportunity that permits itself of collecting materials for the history of the native tribes with whom they have intercourse, and their languages. It is from them that we are likely to obtain a satisfactory account, not only of the Polynesian tribes in this part of the ocean, but likewise of the yet unexplored nations of Kelænonesia.†

* Mariner termed this group the Hamoan Islands, and by that name they have been lately designated in European maps. The Tongan language, like almost all the Polynesian dialects, the Fiji and the Samoan excepted, wants the sibilant consonant. Like the Greek and the Persian languages, and the ancient British, all of which repudiate sibilants to a considerable degree, these dialects supply their place with aspirants and gutturals. Thus, Samoa becomes in the Tongan Hamoa.

† The following is a curious and almost prophetical passage in one

The missionaries began their operations in the Samoan Archipelago in 1830, and at the end of the six following years six English missionaries were settled on those islands. Their labours now extend over ten islands, two of which are nearly as large as Tahiti, and contain a population of between fifty and sixty thousand souls. Beyond the limits of the Samoan group they have likewise exerted themselves in establishing missions to several islands in the chain of the New Hebrides, New Caledonia, and the Loyalty group.* At the time when the Samoan islands were visited by Mr. Wilkes and the American expedition, 14,850 are said to have been converted to Christianity.

The mythology of the Samoan islanders is very similar to that of the Tongans and other Oceanic tribes of the Polynesian race. It contains the same legend of Tangaloa, the god who fished up the islands from the depths of the sea.

Physical Characters.—The Samoan islanders are described by the missionaries as a people of yellowish brown complexion and black hair, who in their features and stature bear a resemblance to the Polynesian tribes, and likewise to the Malayan race, distinctively so termed.

Among the Polynesian islanders the men of Samoa are said to rank in personal appearance as second only to the

---

of the works of the late Admiral Dumont d'Urville on the Pacific Ocean. It occurs in his account of the Samoan, or, as he termed it, Hamoan Archipelago:—

"Après avoir complété leur travaux évangéliques dans la Polynésie Orientale, les missionaires s'ouvriront probablement ces terres de l'Ouest, plus sauvages sans doute, mais plus riches et plus essentielles à convertir. Là, peut-être, le Christianisme aura quelques martyrs, mais la tâche accomplie n'en sera que plus utile et plus glorieuse: à eux d'ailleurs est resérvé l'honneur d'éclaircir de graves questions géographiques, qui demandent pour être tranchées qu'on ait tout ensemble et la foi de l'apôtre et la conscience du savant!"—*Voyage Pittoresque.*

* See the first number of the "Samoan Reporter," published by the missionaries for the purpose of spreading information respecting the history of these and the neighbouring islands. [See subsequent notes by the Editor relative to the still further extension of these missions.]

Woman of the Samoan Islands.

Man of the Samoan Islands.

London & New York, H. Baillière, 1855

Tongans; the women are rather ill-formed and stout. When very young, some of them are pretty, and their colour is light, being little darker than that of a brunette or South American Spaniard. The girls are lively, have a good expression of countenance, and, what is rare in Polynesia, some degree of bashfulness.

"The average height of the men is five feet ten inches, and some of the chiefs, whose limbs are well rounded, would be called fine-looking men in any part of the world. Their features are not in general prominent, but are well marked and distinct, and are all referable to a common type." This type is thus minutely described:—

"The nose is short and wide at the base, the mouth large, and well filled with large and white teeth, with full and well-turned lips; the eyes black, and often large and bright; the forehead narrow and high, and the cheekbones prominent. It was observed that some of them had the eye turned up at the outer corner, like the Chinese. Of beard they have but little, but their hair is strong, straight, and very black. Little difference was perceived in the shape of the head between the two sexes. The general form of the skull is broad and short, and it is highest near the crown."*

Two natives of the Samoan Archipelago were lately brought to England by the Rev. Mr. Stair, one of the missionaries who had been resident in those islands. I have availed myself of the kindness of that gentleman, and have taken the opportunity afforded me of obtaining correct portraits of these persons, which will furnish the best idea of the physical characters of the race.

The groups now enumerated and described appear to comprise the most numerous of the nations into which the Polynesian race is subdivided. But there are other offsets of this stock, less known, but perhaps not less peculiar.

* "Narrative of the United States Exploring Expedition," vol. ii. p. 131.

The inhabitants of Easter Island may be considered as one of these. In many respects, they differ considerably from the other tribes, from whom they are separated by a vast space in the Great Southern Ocean. Another curious and interesting people are the inhabitants of the small Island of Tikopia. They are described in the Notes of MM. Quoy and Gaimard, appended to Captain Dumont d'Urville's voyage round the world. The plate adjoined contains the figure of a Tikopian, accurately copied from M. d'Urville's picturesque Atlas.

[All the tribes who come under the denomination of Polynesians appear to have adopted with readiness the Christian religion, and the elements of civilisation. The Sandwich islanders, who were the first population of any extent that received the faith and habits of the people of Europe, are now wholly professors at least of Christianity, and they have regularly-conducted ecclesiastical establishments, colleges, and ordinary schools. But in their schools, where the mental powers of the race are best appreciated, they show the same rapidity of acquisition in the lower branches of knowledge, with a deficiency of the higher faculties, which is observed in other of our colonies, and even in the less favoured races of Eastern Europe. According to Lieut. Walpole, in 1849, "The masters [of the schools at Woahu], say that in all the early parts of their education they are exceedingly quick, but not in the higher branches; that they have excellent memories, and learn by rote with wonderful rapidity, but will not exercise their thinking faculties." The capital of the Sandwich Islands, Honolulu, can boast of its theatres, hotels, and ball-rooms, as well as churches, and the richer natives have the houses and dress of Europeans; but the people generally are stated to live and clothe themselves much as they did before the white man came to reside among them; even those who conform in public to the foreign customs are said to recur to their old habits, when at home and unseen. The most

Natives of Tikopia.

unfortunate circumstance noted is the steady decrease in their numbers, which unmistakeably forces itself on our attention. In 1849, while the births were 1422, the deaths amounted to 4320, more than three times as many. Such a proportion, if continued, will soon leave the Hawaians among the "things that were." A similar observation is made in the Friendly [Tonga] Islands. The Rev. Walter Lawry says they do not live long. "The females are women at thirteen, and grow old women before thirty. Their food is very simple, and mostly vegetable; but in size they far outstrip Europeans,—so also, as they think, in personal attractions and beauty. But, alas! they quickly pass away, and are gone."* Some authorities, however, declare the Tonga islands to have an increasing population. The same decrease in numbers is also observed in our thriving colony of New Zealand; but this may be accounted for by the horrible practice of female infanticide, which was very prevalent during the last generation; giving rise to a visible scarcity of young women among the native tribes at this day. This cause of decrease has now wholly ceased, and we may expect that here at least the Polynesian may not perish before the European. In the language of Governor Grey, who is speaking of the English intercourse with the natives, "both races already form one harmonious community, connected by commercial and agricultural pursuits, professing the same faith, resorting to the same courts of justice, joining in the same public sports, standing mutually and indifferently to each other in the relation of landlord and tenant, and thus insensibly forming one people."

May not the New Zealanders owe their exemption from the fatality which appears to attend the appearance of Europeans among the Polynesians, to the slight intermixture of the more energetic Papuan, which has been suspected, as alluded to above?

They now vie with Englishmen in many of their pursuits:

* Second Missionary Voyage, 1851.

they are expert riders and breeders of horses, they understand perfectly how to make a bargain, they erect buildings, cultivate land, and form good roads, far beyond the limits of the English settlements. The more opulent among them become ship-owners, landlords, and millers, the latter being especially a favourite occupation; the poorer people make roads, till the ground, tend cattle, build houses and ships, fish for whales, and navigate ships generally; according to good authority, the most regular, clean, and orderly of all the coasting vessels plying between Auckland and the Bay of Islands, is owned and manned wholly by natives, and is preferred by the public as a conveyance for passengers, before all the others. They resort readily to the English law-courts, becoming even annoyingly litigious; and their favourite conversation is said to be "religious and political discussion, and the general news of the day." Of their skill in military tactics, and great courage in fight, we have had some unpleasant experience, and they have decidedly abandoned all their ancient barbarous warlike customs, conducting their combats with us in the most chivalrous spirit, and carefully avoiding injury to all but actual combatants. From men capable of such an advance we may hope much, and we cannot fear that the English mixture will produce any deterioration among them. The only drawback we know is, that they do not acquire English enough for steady intercourse,—the English rather learn their language; a result fatal to the mental progress of the native, and injurious to that of the Englishman. It is perhaps accounted for by the great facility of the New Zealand language; we would not willingly attribute it to the same want of national stamina which has made the Spaniard and Portuguese in South America forsake their own tongues and European usages, to acquire the difficult idioms and listless habits of the Guaranis, and kindred tribes.]

3. *Of the Madecassians, or Natives of Madagascar.**

It has long been known that the language spoken in the Island of Madagascar bears some resemblance to the Malay. Some writers, adopting a conjecture which seems at first sight most probable, have assumed that this resemblance is the merely casual effect of commercial intercourse between the trading Malays and people on the sea-coast of that island. This is not the fact, as it has been fully proved by Baron William von Humboldt.

Through the whole Island of Madagascar only one language is spoken. There are particular dialects in different parts; but the diversities between them are but slight, and such as do not constitute what can be termed cognate or sister languages. This was the testimony of Flacourt, who wrote a history of Madagascar in 1658, and likewise completed a dictionary of the language; and it is confirmed by all later accounts that are worthy of regard.† The people differ, as we shall see, considerably in their physical characters. Some tribes resemble the woolly-haired blacks on the opposite coast of Africa, and others are more like the Malays; but they have all one language.

The learned authors of the "Mithridates" compared this language, as far as they had materials enabling them to investigate its nature, with the Malayan; and they came to a conclusion that the connexion between them was not original, and that each idiom had a distinct basis. But this opinion has been entirely refuted by Humboldt, who has set the question for ever at rest, and has demonstrated the Madecassian to be a genuine and real offspring of the great Malayo-Polynesian language. The mass of the population in this island must be considered as of Malayan descent. From what part of the Great Ocean they ori-

* The people of this island are often called Malecasses, or Malgasches, the *d* and *l* being interchangeable. Madecasses, or Madecassians, is the form of the name adopted by Baron W. von Humboldt.

† Humboldt's Kawi Sprache, vol. iii. p. 326.

ginated cannot be ascertained; their idiom contains numerous words common to it and the remote Polynesian dialects, and wanting in the Proper Malay; on the whole, it bears, perhaps, the nearest affinity to the Tagala, the prevailing language of the Philippine Islands.

Though so many English persons have visited the Island of Madagascar of late years, we have great reason to complain that none of them have thought it worth while to give us correct information respecting the races of people who inhabitit, and the diversities of their idiom and physical characters.* It is chiefly from French voyagers that we have obtained what information we possess on these subjects. Flacourt, the Abbé Rochon, and other old writers, have taken much pains to collect materials for the history of the Madecasses. A later account of the different races is to be found in the narrative of M. J. B. Fressange, which was published by Malte-Brun in his "Annales des Voyages."† I extract chiefly from it the following particulars.

"The Madecassians," says Fressange, "are one of the finest savage races known: they are of great stature (*d'une stature très grande*), and of agreeable figure, well-shaped in all their proportions, and of an olive colour." This general description he afterwards modifies: "Their character is serious and reflective: they are incontinent and revengeful, lively, susceptible at once of the most brilliant qualities and the greatest vices. Hospitality is reckoned honourable through the whole island." The people of the interior differ much from the preceding description; they are of short stature, with Malay features, lank and long hair; they are knavish and deceitful, and bear little or no resemblance to the natives of the coast.

The Madecasses believe in a Supreme Being, infinitely

* I must except an interesting paper in the fifth volume of the "Journal of the Royal Geographical Society," by Captain Lewis, R.N.

† A more detailed enumeration of the different tribes may be seen in the voyages of M. de Froberville to Madagascar and the Comoro Isles, published in Paris in 1811.

good, and likewise in an evil genius. They believe in the immortality of the soul.

Madagascar is divided into different provinces, whose inhabitants differ in character, person, and manners. In the northern part are the Antavarts, People of the North, or People of Thunder, because thunder comes generally from the north. Next to them are the Bestimessaras, Good People, or Great People. 3. Betanemènes are people inhabiting a red country. 4. The Antaximes are People of the South. This is the succession of tribes along the coast: in the interior are the Ambarivoules, or people living at the feet of mountains covered with bamboos. The third tract, reckoning from the coast, is occupied by the Bézonzons, the Amayes, or Antamayes, the Ancovesovas, or Ambolambs, the Andrantsaïs, the Antsinaxes, and the Saclaves. The provinces of Queen Borbétoe and of the Bay St. Augustin are little known, and the western coast is seldom visited.

The Bestimessaras are the finest race in the island: they are a pastoral and agricultural people, of mild character; their chief place, the village of Andévourante, sends out 10,000 armed men. The Antaximes are a rude and predatory tribe; on this part of the coast the people are black, and have woolly hair. The Antamayes, whom Rochon mistook for Arabs, resemble the Malays in features and complexion, and blacken their teeth with betel; they inhabit a high steppe between two ranges of mountains, eighty leagues in length; their plains are covered with flocks, and their villages are situated on hills. The Ancovas, Ovah, or Ambolambs, are divided into two nations, the North and South Ovahs; the despots of both tribes carry on war between themselves for the traffic in slaves; the people resemble the Antamayes, but are of fairer colour.

The Andrantsaïs are a pastoral people, of rude and cowardly character. In the villages of these people there are sometimes born dwarfs; and this is the race which has been reputed to be a nation of dwarfs, and described under the name of Kimòs. They ignore any such epithet. M. Fressange saw one dwarf from their country, but says that they are only occasionally seen, and that no race of dwarfs exists in Madagascar.

It seems that circumcision is practised through the whole island; but it is not the Mohammedan custom.

Of all the Madecassian tribes, the Ovahs are the most remarkable; they were described under the name of Virzimbers by Robert Drury, in the account of his captivity in Madagascar, about eighty years ago. Of late they have become the dominant tribe; Radama was a chieftain of the Ovahs, who subdued under his power nearly the whole island. The province of Ovah is the smallest in Madagascar, and it is situated at the distance of 160 miles from the nearest coast.

Although the Ovahs are said to resemble the Malayan race, it does not appear that they have all the peculiarities of the genuine Malays. Several men of distinction from the Island of Madagascar were in London some years ago on a mission from the Queen of the Ovahs, the widow of Radama; their portraits were taken by a good artist, and it is remarkable that they all bear the most striking resemblance to each other. If we may consider them as specimens of the Ovah race, it must be allowed that this tribe has acquired a peculiar physiognomy, having nothing of the Chinese type, to which the Proper Malays approximate; neither has it the almost European character of the Polynesian Islanders. Their hair is curly and bushy, but it is not woolly; neither is there, in general, any thing indicative of an approach to the Negro character. The coloured plate opposite is copied from one of these portraits.

Natives of Madagascar

CHAPTER XX.

THE PELAGIAN NEGROES.

BLACK, woolly-haired people, resembling in their features and colour the Negroes of Guinea, are widely spread in the Indian Archipelago. They inhabit the interior of many islands, and, according to Mr. Crawford, there are traces of them in others where they are no longer found. Dampier, and other early navigators, found them spread along the northern coast of New Guinea, New Britain, and New Ireland; for, besides the hybrid Papuas, already described, it seems, from the account of voyagers, that there are in these countries tribes much more resembling the Africans, with short woolly hair. At what period they spread themselves over these regions cannot be determined; neither do we know the source from which they originated. It is remarkable, however, that the mountainous country in the interior of the Malayan Peninsula is inhabited by woolly-haired tribes, who are well known under the name of Samangs,* and are supposed to be the aborigines of the land, which they divide with the Orang Benúa, inhabitants of the plains. The latter are said to resemble the Malays. A similar people are known in the Andaman Islands, in the Bay of Bengal; and these are the most eastern points to which they are to be traced.†

* A short notice of the Samangs, by Mr. John Anderson, Secretary to the Government of Penang, appeared some years ago in a Penang newspaper, and was reprinted in the second volume of Mr. Logan's "Journal of the Eastern Archipelago," p. 425. A partly civilised Samang, residing at Jan, was seen by Mr. Anderson: he was quiet and inoffensive. "His height was 4 feet 9 inches; his hair woolly and tufted; his colour a glossy jet black; his lips were thick, his nose flat, and belly very protuberant, resembling exactly two natives of the Andaman islands, who were brought to Prince of Wales Island [Penang] in the year 1819." See *infrà*, p. 462.—ED.

† The Editor's views with regard to the subjects of this chapter are briefly stated in pp. 429–431. He has preferred to call them Papuans, in

Pelagian Negroes have long been well known as inhabitants of the interior of the Penang Islands, in the Archipelago of the Philippines, where they occupy rocky and mountainous tracts in the inland parts. One of the small islands is named from them "Isla de los Negros:" in other islands they are termed "Negritos del Monte." They are called Aïgta and Inagta, which, according to Don Francisco Garcia de Torres, means "Blacks." Igolote is another appellation given to them. We have numerous descriptions of these people in the writings of Catholic missionaries who have resided in the Philippine Islands.

It appears, from these reports, that there are two races of Blacks in the interior of the Philippine Islands. The

---

accordance with general usage, the restriction of the term to the supposed hybrid races having been tacitly abandoned by common consent. His views are founded on a consideration of the grammatical structure of a very few of the languages of this race, and those spoken by a small section only of the islanders of the New Hebrides and New Caledonia. There appears to be no other source of linguistic information yet accessible; for mere lists of words, and these but scanty, are of little use. He would also attach value to the statement of Torres and de la Fuente, cited by the Author, that the languages of the Negritos of the Philippines are the Bobolan, Bisayan, &c., only "corrupted" and mixed with foreign words, which can hardly be the result of intercourse; the separation of the tribes is too decided. The testimony of missionaries who spoke these languages far outweighs the negative evidence of Mallat and de la Gironière, who did not understand them; a Frenchman with a fair knowlege of our language, on hearing the English spoken by many of the Sierra Leone Negroes, would find it wholly unintelligible. In regard to the Andamanners, Tasmanians, people of New Guinea, and others, we can only adduce some general resemblance of habits, manners, and physical features, as rendering the connection probable. The most recent and copious details respecting the Papuans of the Indian Archipelago are given by Mr. Earl, in the first volume of the Ethnographical Library, 1853. Capt. Erskine's "Islands of the Western Pacific" contains the best and fullest notices we have of the Eastern division of this race. The Editor would willingly limit the term Papuan to the subjects of the two last-mentioned volumes, and would continue the appellation of Negritos to the races inhabiting the northern islands: this was certainly the practice of the author himself in his latest writings.—Ed.

following account was taken from the narrative of the Abbate Bernardo de la Fuente :—

"The Negroes of the Philippine Islands are of two races. One of them is supposed, in those countries, to be descended from the Malabars, or Sepoys; because, although their skin is perfectly black, their hair is long, fine, and glossy, like that of other Indians, and their countenances are not deformed in the nose and lips, as those of the Negroes of Guinea. These people, whether in a state of slavery or freedom, are tolerably civilised in their manners. There is another race of Negroes, termed Aïgta, who wander about dispersed among the mountains : these have somewhat of the deformity of features, and they have crisped hair, like that of the natives of Guinea. Of these Negroes, some are found in the Isle of Luzon ; and they are very numerous in the Isla de los Negros, of which they suppose themselves to be the original inhabitants. The said race of Negroes seems to bear upon themselves the malediction of Heaven; for they live in the woods and mountains like beasts, in separate families, and wander about supporting themselves by the fruits which the earth spontaneously offers to them : it has not come to my knowledge that a family of these Negroes ever took up their abode in a village. If the Mohammedan inhabitants make slaves of them, they will rather submit to be beaten to death than undergo any bodily fatigue; and it is impossible, either by force or persuasion, to bring them to labour. Not far from my mission at Buyunan, in the island De los Negros, there was a horde of Negro families who had traffic with some barbarous Indian people, and were by these given to understand that I counselled them to receive baptism, in order that the government might force them to pay the tribute : in consequence of this, I could never reclaim one of them ; and I believe that very few Negroes have been converted, for I only found the name of one in a register containing the baptisms of two hundred years. I ever maintained with these Negroes a gentle and friendly intercourse, hoping that the grace of the Lord might fructify in their hearts; and I began to discover that they trusted me and obeyed me in many particulars." He adds, "That their language was the Boholan, and that they were supposed to descend from African Negroes:" a conjecture of as little weight as that which derives the other race of straight-haired black people from the Malabars. The same writer was informed, that in the interior of the island were Negroes with perfectly red eyes, who were cannibals; but he never saw any one of them.

A very interesting account has lately been given by Captain Gabriel Lafond (of Lavey) of a tribe of these Negroes inhabiting the island of Lasso, where they are found in places of difficult access. One of their mountain villages was visited by M. Lafond, who represents the inhabitants as living in the rudest manner. This writer agrees with Le Gentil in describing them as nearly naked savages, with flat noses, and hair like wool or cotton. They precisely resemble the Negroes of the Isle of Luzon; they were lean, of light and active form; their stature was remarkably small, being little above four feet, and nearer to four than to four and a half. In this extreme smallness of stature the Inagta or Igolote resemble some of the Samangs of the Malayan mountains, who are described by Crawford as a very diminutive race. M. Lafond admits that in other places their stature is greater.

The plate opposite gives probably a correct portrait of a female of this race. It was taken from the collection of the French artist, M. Choris, who accompanied the Russian voyage of circumnavigation under Kotzebue.

It is very remarkable that M. Lafond, as well as all the missionaries who have been acquainted with these Negro tribes of the Philippines, agree in the statement, that they speak dialects of the Tagala and Bisaya languages. These are the principal idioms of the Philippine islands, and are known to be dialects of the Malayan language. The Abbate Torres says, "La lingua dell' Isola detta de' Negri

Girl of the Isle of Luzon

è la Bisaya stessa, col miscuglio di moltissime parole forestieri;"* and by De la Fuente, who says, " La loro lingua è Bohalana, poichè in essa mi parlavano, sebbene adulterata."†

[Much information in regard to the Negritos of the Philippines is contained in Mallat's splendid work on those Islands; and P. de la Gironière's "Souvenirs de Jala-jala,"‡ the result of twenty years' residence, affords some very amusing reading, which is no doubt authentic on the whole, though somewhat coloured and heightened for the sake of effect. Mons. Mallat describes the Igorrotes, Tinguianes, or Itanegs, Yfugaos, Gaddanes, Ibilaos, Itetapanes, Guinaanes, and the Aetas or Itas. The last-named people, which are also called Aigtas or Ajetas, he names especially Negritos, but apparently for no sufficient reason. He says they speak different dialects, varying from tribe to tribe; but gives no specimens which could lead us to infer the relation of those languages to those of the Islands generally.§ He is of opinion that these several tribes, and the other unchristianized people in the islands, are all mixed races between the aboriginal Negritos and the Malays, Chinese, and Japanese, who have accidentally reached the islands, a circumstance of not unfrequent occurrence.

" The Negritos (p. 93) are small, well-made, and nimble; the nose is not broad, [peu épaté], the hair is frizzled. They are less black, and much less ugly than the negroes of the African coasts, because, instead of living, like those negroes, in the open air, exposed to the saline exhalations of the sea, and burning heat of the sun, they take shelter, during the violent heat of the day, under the shade of

* The language of the Isla de los Negros is the Bisayau, mixed with very many foreign words.

† Their language is Boholan, for they spoke to me in that language, though corrupted.

‡ J. Mallat: Les Philippines, &c. Paris, 1846, two volumes. P. de la Gironière, Vingt années aux Philippines, Paris, 1853.

§ Vol. ii. p. 170.

forests which are so high and so thick that the sun's rays cannot pierce through.

"The Negritos dwell on the tops of the highest mountains; their sole dress is a little wrapper of bark around the body; they feed upon roots, wild fruits, and such game as they kill with arrows, which they shoot with incredible skill. . . . . They are spread over the desert places throughout the whole of the islands, and they are far from being the most ferocious of the pagan tribes." The Plate opposite, from Mr. Mállat's work, represents a male and female of this race.

M. de la Gironière (p. 273), compares them for their form and colour to the New Zealanders. Afterwards (in p. 297), he says the Ajetas or Negritos are of an ebon black like the African negroes; that their features are not unlike, though the lips are less prominent; their hair is woolly, and forms an odd-looking sort of crown about the head; which we should suppose to be like the coiffure of Dampier's "mop-headed Papuas;" their eyes are yellowish, but quick and brilliant like those of an eagle. When young, they are well made, but their shelterless habits, and very precarious life of alternate gluttony and starvation, soon produces a large abdomen, and slender extremities. "The old women, especially, are hideous; their decrepit limbs, protuberant abdomen, and very extraordinary hair, give them the look of furies, or of old witches," p. 299. On the whole, he thought them more like monkeys than human creatures,—their gestures were absolutely the same, and their voices like the squeak of those animals. He could not understand their language, but an old woman among them who spoke Tagala was his interpreter. Mons. de la Gironière was called upon to give names to all the young children of the tribe with which he associated for a day or two, because, as the old woman informed him, "We have but a very few words to talk with among ourselves, and all our children are named from the place where they are born, which causes great confusion; we therefore bring

P. Van Oore ad nat. pinx.

Maddey lith 3 Wellington St. Strand

NATIVE OF DOURGA STRAIT. NEW GUINEA.

London, H. Baillière Publisher & at 290 Broadway New York

OUTANATA, NEW GUINEA.

London, H. Bailliere Publisher & at 290 Broadway New York.

them to you to give them names." This does not look very probable; the old lady's language was perhaps not very intelligible. They use poisoned arrows, and eat their game almost raw.

Marriage among the Ajetas is a voluntary contract, made without any ceremony, but is maintained inviolate, and only one wife is allowed. They have a great respect for old age, and each tribe, amounting to about 60 or 80 persons, is always governed by one of the oldest of the body (p. 303). They have also great veneration for the dead; they place the bow and arrows of the deceased over the grave, and for many years they continue to pay visits to the place of burial to deposit tobacco and betel, for the use of the spirit of the departed. Mons. de la Gironière gives a good deal more information respecting this race, which, considering the short stay he made amongst them, is rather suspicious; he could hardly have obtained his information from the other people of the islands, who appear to shun all intercourse with the Negritos.

Mons. Mallat gives further descriptions of the various wild tribes inhabiting the Philippines; from which we make a few extracts:—

"The Igorrotes (p. 99) are tall; their colour is that of a roasted quince, called by some coppery; they have large and black eyes, turned upwards at the outer angle; their cheeks are large and salient; hair smooth, but very hard, and of a lustrous black."

Mons. de la Gironière's account agrees with that of Mons. Mallat; but he makes the colour a deep bronze, the nose flattish, and the head disproportionately large.

The Itetapanes and Gaddanes (Mallat, vol. ii. pp. 102 and 110), are like the Negritos, but have round eyes, and large and flat noses. The Guinaanes and Yfugaos are savage and cruel, and decidedly cannibals; they throw the lasso with much skill, and, like some of the Borneo tribes, kill their enemies for the sake of the head, with which they ornament their huts; and they themselves wear an additional ear-ring for every head they cut off. Colonel Galbey, in 1831, found one man with twenty-two such trophies. These races are not devoid of industry, and they cultivate the land with some skill.

The Tinguianes, according to Mallat, (p. 104-7), are not unlike the civilised Tagalas in colour, size, features, and temper; but, unlike them, they are indolent, and mostly pagans. He believes them to be of Chinese descent.

M. de la Gironière visited a Tinguiané village, (p. 113), and was surprised to find a fine race of men, of a slightly bronzed complexion, smooth hair, aquiline nose, and regular profile; and women really handsome and graceful. "I might have thought myself," he says, "among the inhabitants of the South of France, had it not been for the costume and language." The dress of the men was a mere girdle; the women had also a little apron, very narrow. The men covered their heads with a sort of turban made of fig-tree bark, but the women ornamented their hair with beads of coral, pearls, and grains of gold: their hands were painted blue, and on their arms they had a tight sleeve or bracelet, which is put on in youth, and never taken off, so that the wrist is tightly compressed, and the hand horribly swollen, which is considered a great beauty. They are clean in their persons, and they bathe frequently; their habitations by day are little bamboo and straw huts, but they pass their nights in a very small kind of straw nest, which they build as high as they can in lofty trees, sixty or eighty feet from the ground: a necessary precaution against their ferocious enemies, the Guinaanes. Their religion appears to be a sort of fetishism. They have only one wife, from whom divorce is rare, but they may have as many concubines as they can afford to keep, having a separate hut for each. At the death of any of the tribe, the body is laid out on a bench: all his friends meet to feast on what he has left behind him, and to pronounce orations in his praise; after which, the body is surrounded by fire, and slowly dried, an operation which usually lasts fifteen days;

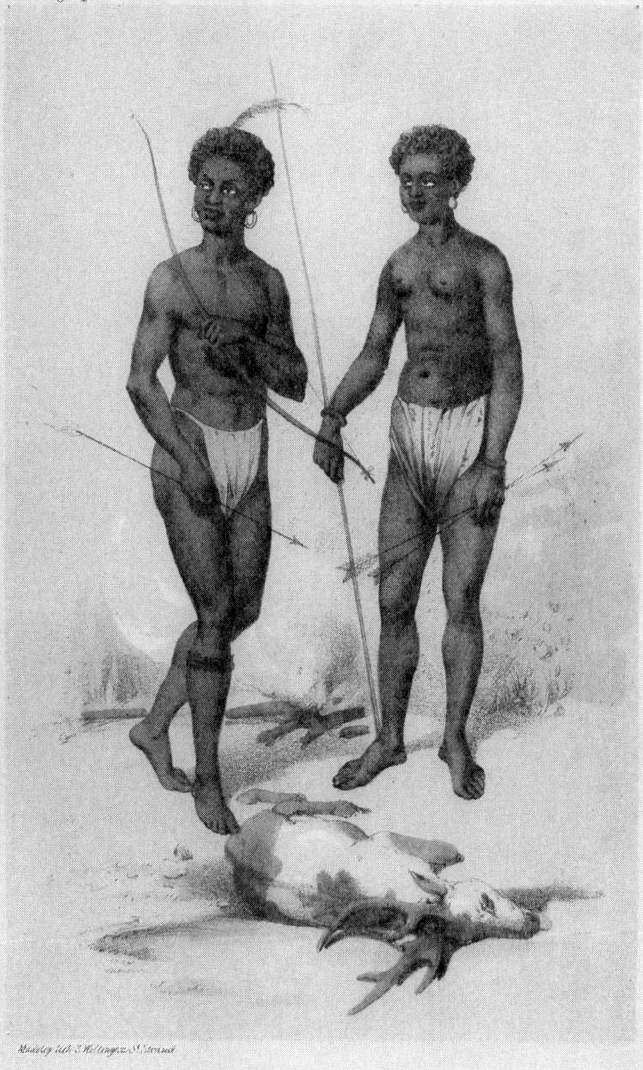

Maudsley lith. 3 Wellington St. Strand

AHETAS.

(or Negritos of Luzon.)

it is then deposited in a hole under his hut. M. de la Gironière (p. 148), considers the Tinguianes to be descendants of the Japanese.

The several uncivilized tribes in the islands appear to resemble either the Ajetas or Tinguianes, with slight differences.]

From the southern extremity of New Britain and New Ireland, tribes of Pelagian negroes are spread along the chains of Louisiade and Solomon Isles to Santa Cruz, and thence still farther to several of the New Hebrides and to New Caledonia. The ethnography of these last countries is, however, but imperfectly known; and several voyagers assert that, although the hair of the New Caledonians is crisp and much curled, it is not like that of the African. The island of Mallicollo appears to contain a particular race of small slender negroes, whose countenances are said by Cook to be remarkably prognathous. Lastly, the Tasmanians, or natives of Van Diemen's Land, now almost entirely exterminated, are decidedly of the Pelagian Negro stock. The compressed, elongated form, with prognathous jaws, may be recognised in the outline of a Tasmanian skull which is here annexed.*

FIG. 85.

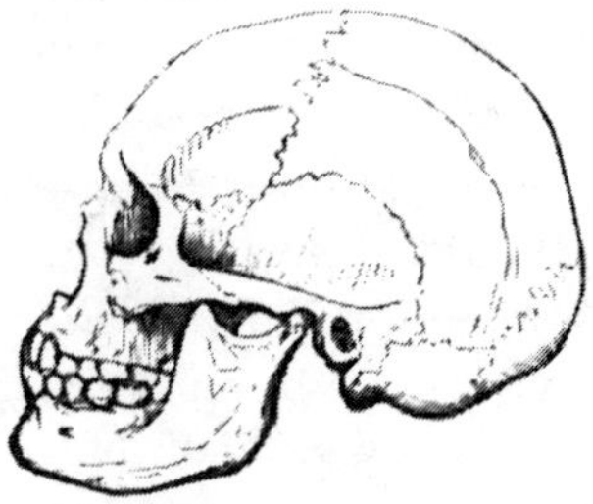

Skull of a Tasmanian.

* The people of Van Diemen's land appear to be on the point of becoming extinct, without leaving on record enough of the language to aid the philologer in his estimate of the class it belongs to: the Editor has made an attempt, by the kind assistance of Captain Erskine, to obtain something of it, but as yet unsuccessfully. From this gentleman he has learned the curious fact that the few Tasmanians left, amounting to two or three dozen, have nine distinct dialects among them, so different, that they have found it expedient to adopt English as the medium of communication. In his "Journal of a Cruize among the Islands of the Western Pacific," Captain Erskine, in p. 378, has a note upon the curious distinction between the populations of the adjoining islands of New Holland and Van Diemen's Land in physical characteristics generally, and particularly in the flowing

[Much has been added within these few years to our knowledge of those groups of the Western Pacific Islands, which include New Caledonia, the Loyalty Islands, and the New Hebrides, containing a population estimated roughly at 80,000. Many missionary voyages have been made among these groups under the auspices of the Bishop of New Zealand, two of which, at least, were conducted by that excellent prelate in person: youths have been brought away from several of the islands, placed in the college of Auckland for education, and have subsequently been carried back again to serve as the heralds of Christianity, and as aids to future missionaries. According to the last intelligence we have received, published this year (1854), in the Samoan Reporter, recording some details of the tenth missionary voyage, there were 25 schools, with 1400 scholars, one-third of whom could read well, and many write, in the single little island of Anaiteum, while cannibalism, war, the strangling of widows, and infanticide, had almost wholly ceased.

A very interesting narrative of a visit to the Papuan Islands, (meaning those above mentioned) in 1849,* in the course of which Captain Erskine, the conductor and narrator of the Expedition, met the little vessel of the Bishop of New Zealand, and had the benefit of his previous acquaintance with the natives, forms the chief source of what is here stated; and a Report of the missionary voyage of 1850, which included the Solomon's

---

silky hair of the former, and almost woolly hair of the latter, which justifies the separation made by Dr. Prichard between these and his Alforians. The remarkable resemblance between the baskets manufactured by the natives of Van Diemen's Land, and those of the Papuans of the Loyalty Islands, is an evidence of consanguinity which the Editor estimates highly; he has examined the articles which Capt. Erskine brought to England, and is satisfied that so perfect an identity of texture, different too from any thing made by native tribes elsewhere, could not have been produced by other causes than such as may be referred to affinity of race.—ED.

* Journal of a Cruise among the Islands of the Western Pacific, &c., by John Elphinstone Erskine, Capt. R. N. 8vo. London, 1853.

Native of Balad in New Caledonia

Native of Aneiteum

and Queen Charlotte's islands, as well as those above named, drawn up by the Rev. John Inglis, and printed in New Zealand in 1851, affords valuable additions to Captain Erskine's observations. Both these gentlemen agree in depicting the natives of all the islands as generally intelligent, active, good-tempered, and industrious; inclined to be perfectly friendly with the English, learning our language readily, adopting our habits willingly, and polite and even polished in their general behaviour; while at the same time, by a revolting contrast, they eat their fellow creatures, strangle widows, and even such of the children of a deceased parent as are unable to support themselves, put their aged relations to death, and exhibit a remorseless cruelty in war. Their languages vary remarkably,—there are several mutually unintelligible dialects in New Caledonia alone, and each of the smaller islands has at least one of its own; it was estimated by the Bishop of New Zealand, that, on the average, a language is spoken by 5000 individuals only. The Rev. John Inglis (p. 22), would call the whole of these islands Polyglottia, or the Polyglot Islands; he contrasts the Papuan and Polynesian languages, and considers them wholly distinct, and even opposed in words and structure: but if he had taken into consideration all the languages of the Malayan family, and compared them with that of Anaiteum, in which he was conversant, we think he would have modified his opinion: he does, in fact, subsequently (p. 25) admit the probability of finding affinities by further investigation, and a fuller knowledge.

Capt. Erskine describes the New Caledonians as a fine and intelligent race of men, black, woolly-haired, and resembling the Fijis in general appearance. The figure in the opposite plate, the portrait of a man of the district of Balad, is from his portfolio. The women were much under subjection to the men, but they were not restrained in their intercourse with the whites, in the course of which they conducted themselves with strict propriety.

On the banks of the river up which the party proceeded, they found "neat trimly-kept houses, standing often in very beautiful situations on its banks, with well-constructed landing-places, and a few trees placed in regular order on what appeared to be mown lawns. . . . . . . The face of the hills above the river is covered with rectangular fields, surrounded by channels for irrigation, which, as far as can be seen from below, is conducted on a careful and scientific system, levels being carried from the streams, which, at this season of the year, afterwards flow into the river at intervals of a quarter of a mile" (p. 355). In the course of the day, he saw some poles with heads upon them, which he was informed were those of women put to death for breaking the tabu,—a decided Polynesian characteristic. The natives had scarcely any covering but a mere girdle, though they appeared to suffer from cold and wet, and were very probably restricted to this deficiency of dress by want of means, for the chief and his brother wore frocks; and one of the people was detected in the attempt to steal a seaman's shirt. Some of them wore a sort of cylindrical hat, not unlike the paper cap used by carpenters at their work, and many frizzled their hair out behind into a globular queue. Mr. Inglis says (page 9) they use a large mat, of a size sufficient to cover them completely when it is cold or rainy: this was not seen by Captain Erskine, but in an island 240 miles long there must be variety of usages. He further states that "they manufacture coarse earthen pots for the cooking of food, similar but inferior to the earthenware made by the natives of the Fiji islands; thus furnishing one proof of the relationship or common origin between the natives of the two groups" (p. 11.)

The New Hebrides are peopled by a race having a general resemblance to the New Caledonians, though differing considerably among themselves in particular characters, so that each island is said to have a population which may be recognised as peculiarly its own. The portraits of two

Lavandulu an Erromango Boy

Man of Erromango

A Native of Aneitum

Erumanga natives on the opposite plate, and the figure of a native of Anaiteum, facing page 469, all from the portfolio of Captain Erskine, are characteristic of these islanders. The people of Anaiteum* are shorter and less athletic than the average; the little dress they have is like that of the New Caledonians, but they wear the hair tied up in small locks, and like strings, which are brought together in a bunch behind, looking like a bundle of whipcord,—a mode found besides only in Tana, and in a small part of Erumanga. The opposite plate† gives a good idea of this kind of head-dress. They sing beautifully, according to Mr. Inglis, "greatly surpassing any thing I have heard among the New Zealanders (p. 15)." In Tana, the people are short but athletic, with shining, black, downy skin; their features are not disagreeable, but they smear themselves with black and red earths that give them a very ugly appearance. Like the people of Anaiteum, they are very fond of music; two mouth-organs were brought from Tana by Capt. Erskine, one of 14, the other of 18 pipes, both in the key of G. These instruments were out of tune when examined by the Editor, but both appeared as though intended to have the common chord in the minor key, with an additional sixth. The Tanese are good agriculturists. The inhabitants of Vate are tall and handsome, they have good foreheads and straight noses, approaching the aquiline form; some of them are tattooed; the women are tall and thin, they wear the hair close cropped, have a broader waist-belt than the men, and a square mat by way of an apron. They wear also a sort of tail of matting, suspended from the waist-belt, with a loose fringe at the end, 18 inches in length, and reaching to the calf of the leg. The Vate people are better workmen than those of Tana; their spears are beautiful, their bracelets are made

---

* This island is called Aneiteum, Anáttom, Anatám, &c. The name in the native language is Aiteum; the *an* being a preposition meaning "at." We have followed the orthography which is nearest to the real name.—ED.

† From the portfolio of Captain Erskine.

of small rings ground out of shells, exactly resembling chain-armour, and so neatly strung together in alternate black and white rows or figures, that the inside resembled a coarse woven cloth. Their houses are "of tolerable dimensions, of an oblong form, with slightly curved roofs, closed at the sides, but entirely open at one end." The village of Sema, to which Capt. Erskine and the Bishop were "conducted by a good path, bordered in parts by enclosed provision grounds, apparently very productive," was composed of several such houses in no regular order, and of one great common house, 100 feet long by 28 wide, which was exhibited with evident pride" (p. 331). Their language approached so near to the Samoan, that the general meaning could be followed by one who spoke that tongue. According to Mr. Hardie, who visited the Island shortly after the departure of Captain Erskine, "the people are most inveterate cannibals. Enemies slain in war are eaten by them. They will go to other villages and exhume bodies that have been buried two, three, or more days, bring them home, cook and eat them. It is their custom, when they wish to make peace, to kill one or more of their own people, and send the body to those with whom they have been fighting, to eat. On the death of chiefs, it is a frequent custom to kill one, two, three, or more men, to make a feast for the mourners. When parents are unwilling to have the fatigue of rearing their children, or when they find them a hindrance to their work, they often bury them alive" (p. 334).

This is quoted by Capt. Erskine from the Samoan Reporter for November 1849. A better character was given by the Rev. Mr. Turner, who was there in 1845, though he confirms much of what is stated by Mr. Hardie; but at the same time he says, "Upon the whole, they are among the most inviting heathens we have met with in these seas."

In the Loyalty Islands, between New Caledonia and the New Hebrides, Capt. Erskine found similar characters, though he thought there was a Polynesian admixture discernible in features and language. In Uea, also called Eningeha and Mondavi, the colour of the skin was less dark than in Vate; but there was much diversity in this respect. The hair in some cases was long and flowing, in others crisp, in about equal proportions. In this little island there are three tribes, speaking different dialects. According to information received from an intelligent man named Edwards, who had resided some months on the islands, the men were honest and upright, the women chaste and faithful. In Lifu, the colour of the skin was lighter than in Uea, and the same diversity in the hair was found as in that island (p. 367). A Lifu boy, since dead, was brought to England some years ago, and examined by Dr. R. G. Latham, who noticed a reddish tinge, clearly perceptible under a cross light, in his otherwise black and frizzy hair."* Dr. Latham was inclined to attribute this to alkaline washes; but as an interval of five years had elapsed since such application was made, it would seem that new hair must have grown, unaffected by any wash. According to the Samoan Reporter for September 1845, the people were inveterate cannibals, but the efforts of the missionaries had induced many persons to abandon the habit. "Bula, a chief . . . . has had as many as sixteen cooked bodies laid before him at a meal. Now, he not only abstains from it himself, but he declares that death will be the penalty to any of his family who ever again tastes human flesh." According to the same authority, they believe in a Creator, and in a future state of existence, a sort of Hades, which they call Locha; they preserve relics of the dead, and pay homage to them. They are industrious, and they build good and large houses, of circular shape. There are two tribes on this island, speaking different languages. In Mare or Nengone, the remaining island of the Loyalty group, the physical character resembled that at Lifu, but the people generally had

* Varieties of Man, by Dr. Robert Gordon Latham, p. 262.

remarkably fine eyes, and high, well-formed foreheads. No clothes were worn by the men, nor even by many of the women, who were tattooed. The people on the western coast of this island were nominally Christians; on the eastern coast still Pagans; but all were equally peaceable and well-behaved. The social state of the island may be inferred from the existence of a village of 300 or 400 inhabitants, to which the Bishop and Capt. Erskine were invited, and which possessed a large circular house, exactly resembling those of New Caledonia, the common meeting-place of all the population, in addition to the smaller private habitations. The people make spears, curiously carved clubs, and very beautiful baskets of peculiar manufacture. According to the last received intelligence from Mare (Samoan Reporter for Jan. 1854), the people of Mare are steadily improving; hundreds can read well, and the people have erected large six-roomed houses, in the hopes of inducing missionaries to settle among them.

In all these islands, the characteristic Polynesian custom of the taboo prevails; but the use of Kava does not appear to reach west of the New Hebrides. All practise dancing on a large scale, apparently more as a ceremony than an amusement. Mr. Inglis met on one occasion a dancing party of four or five hundred in Tana, assembled in an open irregular space, to celebrate the removal of the taboo from the bread-fruit trees; and he says that for two months in the year the New Hebrideans meet daily at mid-afternoon, and continue dancing till day-light next morning. After visiting all the groups above mentioned, he comes to the conclusion that the inhabitants are all of one race, much the same in their physical, moral, and social features, but quite distinct from the inhabitants of Eastern Polynesia.

In Sept. 1850, in the course of a second voyage among the Eastern Papuans, Capt. Erskine visited some of the Solomon islands: he has allowed the Editor to peruse his MS. journal, which he may perhaps hereafter publish. Capt. Erskine found the people of these islands strikingly like

Native of Solomon Island

those of the New Hebrides; they were perhaps lighter coloured generally than the latter, but not more so than many individuals among these, and on the whole he says they looked like *black Chinamen;* they were well made, though small, and they had curly, not woolly, hair. They resembled most nearly the people of Niue. He found them friendly, good-tempered, and perfectly honest in all their dealings with the people of his ship, showing a complete contrast to what former travellers had related of their barbarity and ferocity; in fact, they were excessively timid on board ship, and although they exhibited a little more confidence on shore, they were still never offensively forward. In most of the islands the men had no clothing, and the women very little; but they had shell armlets well made, with the shells disposed so as to form a showy pattern. The plate facing this page* represents a man of the Solomon Islands with a pair of such armlets. Some of them wore a curious ornament on the nose like the horn of a rhinoceros, and others had an appendage behind, which would easily account for the stories of men with tails. Capt. Erskine saw the peculiar nose-ornament of mother-of-pearl, mentioned by Surville, whose account was in general accurate. Some few persons were tattooed. They manufactured handsome bowls, skilfully inlaid with pearl-shells, and their canoes were beautifully carved and ornamented. He visited several large villages, the houses of which were very good, and in some instances divided into separate apartments, well arranged, though dirty. In one village, he found a circular well, ten feet in diameter, surrounded by a loose coral wall. Here he found some of the inhabitants dancing. They were ready to barter cocoa-nuts for anything useful, but they more especially liked empty bottles; and in the course of this trade, a man who was wounded rather severely by a bottle which a careless sailor threw from the ship, good-temperedly admitted that it was an accident. In some cases, bits of printed

* From the portfolio of Captain Erskine.

paper were preferred to useful articles. Capt. Erskine learned that the native name of the island called on our maps St. Cristoval, is Toro; Guadalcanar, the natives call Gela or Kela; Surville's Isle des Contrariétés is Utáqua.]

Notices of the Black Races in the Groups of Islands near the Samoan Archipelago, and of their Languages.

The Samoan Archipelago, as I have observed, is situated in that part of the Southern Ocean which approaches the confines of Kelænonesia. By this name I distinguish that great region containing the abodes of the Papuas and other black races. The great chains of Solomon's Isles and the New Hebrides, forming a vast semicircular sweep, projecting towards the east, and fronting the central Pacific, seem to constitute the natural boundary of this region. But a wide space intervenes between these islands and the Samoans. In the midst are the insulated abodes of two distinct races of people, who approximate, in many characteristics, to the Papuan tribes, from whom, however, they are distinguished in other particulars; they are even contrasted with those nations in some respects. Their languages likewise differ from those of the Papuas, and appear to be very peculiar dialects of the Polynesian speech.

These races are the inhabitants of Rotuma and of the Fiji or Viti Archipelago. The former are intermediate between the Solomon's Isles and the Samoan group; the latter are between that group and the New Hebrides. They were visited by Captain d'Urville, who has given some new information respecting them and their inhabitants. They are called Viti by the inhabitants; and it seems that Fiji is the corruption of the name in the Tonga language. The natives call themselves Kaï Viti, and their neighbours of the Friendly Isles, Kaï Tonga, or the people of Tonga, from the root *Kaï*, which means to eat or to live. M. d'Urville has given the portrait of a Viti Islander named Tomboua Nakoro, "who

Tomboua Nakoro, a Fiji

was," as he says, "a man of gentle manners, of an agreeable physiognomy, and mild character;" and appeared to M. d'Urville much superior to all the savages whom he had seen. His general aspect and countenance, his complexion, which could only be called swarthy (*basané*), his whole conformation, recalled to M. d'Urville's mind the type of the Arab. "Son intelligence ne cédait pas à celle de ces hommes naguère si célèbres dans les arts et les sciences." "His conduct on board ever displayed an union of gravity, propriety, reserve, and equanimity. He never abandoned himself, like his countrymen, to immoderate transports of joy or grief, of anger or delight, under any circumstances."* The physical characters of this man were equally remarkable. His hair, ample and frizzled, even resembled that of the Papuas. What gave him a most strange appearance was, that the anterior part of it was a fine black, while the back part was of a deep red, the effect, as M. d'Urville supposed, of an art practised by these islanders.* (See plate opposite.)

M. d'Urville coincides with the general opinion respecting the origin of the Viti Islanders. He thinks that the black race, having advanced thus far eastward, have resisted in these islands the progress of the Polynesians in an opposite direction. But I think there is no room to doubt but that the Malayan race spread from west to east; and it is very probable, as M. Lesson conjectured, that the Polynesian race had peopled the distant groups in the Great Pacific before the progress of the Pelagian negroes in a similar direction took place. We have not yet sufficient information respecting the Viti Islanders to afford any conclusive evidence on this subject; and W. v. Humboldt has shown that there are strong grounds for doubting the general opinion respecting them.

* A very good and comprehensive monograph relative to the Fiji Islands and their inhabitants will be found in Captain Erskine's "Cruise among the Islands of the Western Pacific," which also contains the curious narrative of the English sailor Jackson, who resided two years among the natives, where he became almost like one of themselves.—Ed.

FIG. 86.

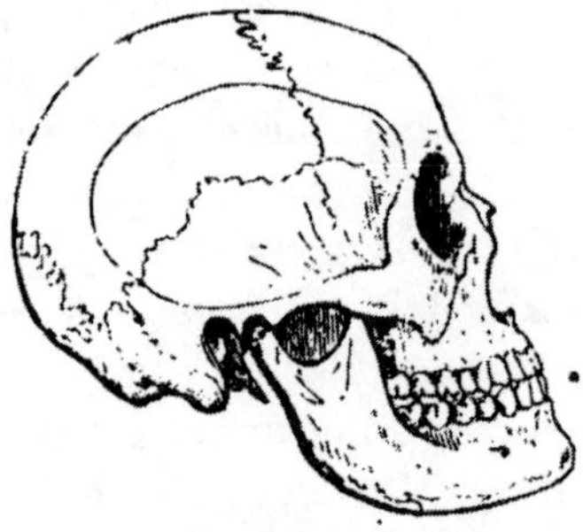

Skull of a Viti Islander.

The sketch accompanying these outlines represents the cranium of a Viti Islander, which is in the College of Surgeons. It is taken from the work of Mr. Martin, who observes that it resembles the Tasmanian skull in the ample size of the coronal ridge, from which the head slopes down on each side, in the convexity of the parietal bones, and the narrowness and lateral compression of the forehead.

The missionaries settled in the Samoan islands have repeatedly visited, not only these intermediate islands, but likewise many of the New Hebrides and of the more distant isles adjacent on New Caledonia. Being well aware of the importance of gaining a knowledge of the languages of these races, they seem to have availed themselves of the opportunities which these visits have afforded them, and it is much to be regretted that the fruits of these researches have not all been published.* The last numbers, however, of the periodical work which issues from the Missionary Press, entitled the "Samoan Reporter," contain some specimens of several languages of those nations; and from these I have thought it worth while to select a few, and compare them with words of the same signification in the Polynesian dialects. The words of these last I have taken from Dumont d'Urville's Vocabulary of the Madecassian, Malayan, Mawian or Maorian, Tongan, Tahitian, and Hawaiian. The words taken from the "Samoan Reporter" are from the following languages:—

* The Rev. Mr. Heath, a most enterprising and meritorious missionary, now in the Samoan islands, put into my hands, some years since, a grammar of the language of Tana, which he had composed while resident in that island. It was his intention to publish it immediately; but this was not done, and the author soon afterwards returned to the Samoan Islands.

1. The Samoan, which, as it will be seen, resembles generally the other Polynesian languages. The most striking peculiarity is the possession of a sibilant consonant, which is wanting to all other known dialects of the Polynesian, except the Fijian.

2. The language of the Rotumans, to whom I have before alluded. The people of Rotuma are very peculiar in their physical characters, which are but little known. They are tall, finely-made people, of almost black colour, with straight flowing hair. Their skulls are massive and heavy, almost approaching the weight and density of the crania of African negroes, with the jaws considerably projecting.*

3. Words in the language of the Fiji islands.

The grammatical structure of this language has been investigated by Mr. Norris, who has availed himself for this purpose of a translation of some parts of the New Testament made by missionaries.† The result to which he has arrived is that the Fijian is really a Polynesian dialect, though offering peculiarities not found in any other, and having a vocabulary so peculiarly modified that it requires some examination to perceive the resemblances, while the other Polynesian idioms display the proofs of their affinity at a glance. The Fijians are a very interesting people, of almost black complexion, with frizzled but not woolly hair, very rude and savage in their habits, but possessed of greater physical and mental energy than any of the fair Polynesians. In natural capabilities they seem to be superior to any other tribe of the Pacific, though perhaps descended from a mixture of the Tongan race with some

* I have only seen specimens of the skulls of the natives of Rotuma in the collection of Dr. Busk, surgeon to the Seamen's Hospital in the Dreadnought. From that gentleman's information, and from the inspection of the skulls, I have derived the account above given of the physical character of the Rotumans.

† His analysis may be seen in the last volume of my "Researches into the Physical History of Mankind," pp. 249—254.

Papua tribe. This hypothesis, however, was rejected by Baron William von Humboldt, who observed that the Fijian language displays affinity to the western forms of the Malayo-Polynesian idiom, viz. the Madecassian and Malayan, while receding from the peculiarities of the Eastern or Oceanic idioms. The Fijians have a mythology and traditions of their own, differing from those of the Tongans, Samoans, and Tahitians.*

4. Words in several languages of other Black Races.

These are arranged in the "Samoan Reporter" under the two designations of—1. Group of the New Hebrides, comprehending Naiea and Fotuna, Anaiteum, Tana, and Vate Land. 2. Group of New Caledonia; including Lifu, Nengone, and New Caledonia properly so termed.

I have selected the words in the following pages.†

---

* The note on the Fiji language communicated by the Editor some years ago to the Author, and inserted in his "Physical History of Mankind," was founded on the first printed pages in that language. A grammar and dictionary have been since published, as well as a version of the New Testament; showing some difference in dialect, or else increased knowledge of the language. But the alteration does not in any way affect the conclusions there arrived at. Mr. Hale, an opponent of those conclusions, admits that a fifth part of the vocabulary and nearly all the grammar are Polynesian; which is admitting every thing. See United States Exploring Expedition vol. vi. p. 174.—Ed.

† The following pages show that considerable modifications have now to be made in the statements of these paragraphs; but they are nearly all in the way of development rather than correction. The list of languages is augmented, and freed from the many typographical errors of the former edition; it is also ordered geographically, which is in this case tantamount to a philological arrangement. Most of the islands in the list are known, though some, perhaps, by other names. Vate is called in some maps Sandwich Island; Lifu is Chabrol, and Nengone is found under the name of Mare or Britannia Island. Anaiteum should more properly be Aitẹum, the initial syllable being a preposition, which is omitted when not wanted: as in the plural form "Ilpu Aiteum," designating the people of the island. The variety found in the five districts of New Caledonia show how much the languages differ within a very limited locality.—Ed.

Languages.		Heaven or Sky.	Earth or Land.	Sun.	Moon.	Star.	Water.	Rain.	Mountain.
	Malay	Lángit	Tanah, Benua	Matahari	Búlan	Bintang	Ayer	Ujan	Gunong
	Madecass	Lanitra	Tany	Masoandro	Volana	Kintana	Rano	Orana	Tendrombohitra
Polynesia	Hawaii	Lani.	Honua	La	Mahina	Hoku	Wai	Ua	Mauna
Polynesia	Tahiti	Rai	Fenua	Mahana	Marama	Fetia	Pape	Ua	Moua
Polynesia	New Zealand	Rangi	Whenua	Ra	Marama	Whetu	Wai	Ua	Maunga
Polynesia	Tonga	Langi	Fonua	Laa	Mahina	Fetuu	Uai	Uha	Mounga
Polynesia	Samoa	Langi	Fanua	La	Masina	Fetu	Vai	Ua	Maunga
	Fiji	Langi	Vanua	Singa	Vula	Kalokalo	Wai	Utha	Maumi
	Rotuma	Langi, Oroit	Hanua	Asa	Hula	Hethu	Vai	Usa	Solo
Micronesia	Tobi	—	—	Yáro	Mukum	Uish	Táru	Ut	—
Micronesia	Tarawa	Kárawa	Benua, Tan	Aai, Tāai	Makainga	Tuitui	Ran	Karu	—
Micronesia	Mille	Lŭng	Rărrŭn	Al	Allŭng	Edju	Renuin	Ut	—
New Hebrides	Niua and Fotuna	Rang	Fanua	Ra	Marama	Fatu	Vai	Ua	Ora
New Hebrides	Anaiteum	Nohotang	Nobohtan	Nangesenga	Nmahouc	Nmuiteu	Nwai	Nuopfa	Neduon
New Hebrides	Tana	Neai	Lunha	Meri	Maukua	Kumhao	Nui	Nesan	Takuar
New Hebrides	Fate	Insau	Launa	Alo	Atalang	Masi	Vai	Usa	Tof
New Hebrides	Erumanga	Pakhop	Maap	Nitminen	Tais	Masi	Nu	Mampi	Hua
Loyalty	Lifu	Thenganra	Lapa, Meak	Thu	Teû	Uatasith, Thint	Tim	Mani	Hunsuet
Loyalty	Nengone	Aue	Nonte	Tu	Siakole	Watiakole	Ui	Ele	Petiti
New Caledonia	Duauru	Okua	Nu	Ni	Mue	Ve	Ui	Igi	Ngwi
New Caledonia	Murare	Kua	Ngweh	Ngi	Boe	Vio	Qui	Uigi	Undu-ngweh
New Caledonia	Nikete	Koe	Hoa	Ingarat	Nuea	Raamea	Que	Nonduhe	Bakwe
New Caledonia	Yengin	Lepodang	Paatah	Ningat	Pue	Tanik	Ue	Kut	Ungduat
New Caledonia	Balad	Koema	Dilis	Aat	Malok	Pidu	Ue	Ora	Yut

Group	Languages.	Sea.	Stone.	Lightning.	Thunder.	Wind.	Light.	Darkness.
	Malay	Tassek	Batu	Kilat	Tágar	Anghin	Taráng	Kalám
	Madecass	Ranomasina	Vato	Helatra	Kotrokorana	Rivotra	Magava	Maizina
	Hawaii	Kai	Pohaku	Uila	Hekili	Makani	Malamalama	Pouli
	Tahiti	Tai, Moana	Ofai	Uira	Patiri	Matai	Maramarama	Pouri
Polynesia	New Zealand	Moana	Kowatu	Uira	Whatitiri	Matangi	Maramatanga	Pouri
	Tonga	Tahi	Maka	Uhila	Mana	Matangi	Mama	Bouli
	Samoa	Moana	Maa	Uila	Faititili	Matangi	Malamalama	Pouliuli
	Fiji	Waitui	Vatu	Liva	Kurukuru	Thangi	Rarama	Butobuto
	Rotuma	Seas	Hathu	Onga	Thui	Langi	Tafa	Mahsum
	Tobi	Tāt	Vās	Vijik	Ngepà	Yang	—	—
Micronesia	Tarawa	Taari	—	Itet	Bĭ	—	Mārrăm	—
	Mille	Lâjet	Rŭkkah	Darrŏm	Dâru	Gŭtto	Mainsina	Marok
	Niua and Fotuna	Tai	Fatu	Vashiri	Ngulungulu	Matangi	Ao	Ouri
	Anaiteum	Njop	Nhat	Nauainàbit	Inmunuka	Mtinjop	Nadiat	Manepven
New Hebrides	Tana	Tasi	Kapuir	Maruapen	Karuarua	Matangi	Maraven	Pitau
	Fate	Ntasi	Nemuka	Napila	Tefa	Nlang	Nikapu	Kapmat
	Erumanga	ûntak	Navat	Ame-taropis	Tarapis	Matang	Nen	Nelawakabat
Loyalty	Lifu	Nagetha	Eta	Samek	Hendring	En	Laihe	Thint
	Nengone	Jere	Et	Uasisinet	Nine	Iengo	Lane	Riti
	Duauru	Injo	Nu	Iuea	Treo	Kuie	Ijaija	Une
	Murare	Tyo	Lu	Ivea	Tio	Kuia	Ngi	Bidi
New Caledonia	Nikete	Napue, que	Sanki	Tonoho	Nito	Dewhang	Kamia	Ngare
	Yengin	Hal-ue	Paik	Niuk	Niuk	Dan	Mala	Wudan
	Balad	Koot	Boai	Ndan	Ndyu	Uru	Aat	Honbaat

It will be perceived from the examination of the vocabulary, that many of the languages spoken by the black races contain numerous words which resemble the Polynesian. Whether these words have been adopted by the Papua tribes in their accidental intercourse with Polynesians, or belong to both races from primeval times, is a problem yet to be solved. The former opinion seems at first the more probable, but it is doubted much by those who have most carefully studied the languages of these nations.

CHAPTER XXI.

OF THE ALFORIAN RACE.

THE Alforians are a people of peculiar physical characters, who are supposed to inhabit the interior of New Guinea, and many of the larger islands to the southward of the Indian Ocean. They are termed Haraforas, Alfoërs, and Alfourous: the real name is uncertain.

The Alforians of New Guinea are named Endamênes by M. Lesson, who has given the following account of them. He says, "That they live in the most miserable manner: continually at war with their neighbours, they are solely occupied in endeavouring to preserve themselves from attacks, and escape the snares laid for them. The custom prevalent among the Papuas of the coast, of putting their prisoners to death, and erecting their spoil as trophies, accounts for the difficulty we find of observing them even in New Guinea; and two or three men reduced to slavery, whom we saw at Doréry, are the only individuals we have met with. The Papuas described them to us as of a ferocious character, cruel and gloomy, possessed of no arts, and passing their whole lives in seeking subsistence in the forests. But we cannot regard this hideous picture, which each people draw of its neighbouring tribe, as authentic. The Endamênes, whom we saw, had a repulsive physiognomy,—flat noses, cheek-bones projecting, large eyes, prominent teeth, long and slender legs, very black and thick hair, rough and shining, without being woolly. Their beards were very coarse and thick. An excessive stupidity was stamped upon their countenances, probably the effect of slavery. These savages, whose skin is of a very deep, dirty brown or black colour, go naked. They make incisions upon their arms and breasts, and wear in their noses pieces of wood nearly six inches long. Their character is taciturn, and their physiognomy fierce; their motion is uncertain and slow. The inhabitants of the coast gave us some details of the Endamênes, but such as seemed to us dictated by hatred; and as their accounts differed, whether because the sense of what they told us was badly understood, or they related to us statements which they did not themselves credit, with the intention of inspiring us with fear, we think it useless to make a race of men known by false or inexact descriptions, whose history is still enveloped in obscurity."*

Captain Forrest was, at least, one of the first English voyagers who described the Alforas; but we derive more information respecting them from Dr. Leyden, who contributed very much to the ethnology of the Indian Archipelago. According to Leyden, the Tirún, or Tedong, are a people of Alforian origin. He says, "These tribes live chiefly on the north-east coast of Borneo, and are reckoned

* The two or three slaves seen by M. Lesson at Doréry were in all probability specimens of the normal man of New Guinea, but degraded by misery and slavery; the outcast tribe, as found in India and Ceylon; the Fingo or Bushman of New Guinea, as described in the preceding chapter. There can be no doubt that M. Lesson's suspicions of the truth of his informant were fully justified. We have also the direct testimony of M. Macgillivray, the naturalist to the expedition which explored New Guinea under Captain Stanley, in 1850. After speaking of the Harfours as described by former voyagers, he says, "I mention these Harfours for the purpose of stating that no people answering to the description of them given above were seen by us in New Guinea, or the Louisiade Archipelago." See Narrative of the Voyage of H. M. S. Rattlesnake, &c., vol. ii. p. 77.—Ed.

a savage and piratical race, addicted to eating the flesh of their enemies. With their language I am totally unacquainted; but it is reckoned peculiar. It is very probable, however, that they are only a tribe of *Idán*, whom again I imagine to be only a race of *Haraforas*, or *Alfoërs*, as they are termed by the Dutch, who seem to be the most original race of all the Eastern islands, excepting, perhaps, the Papuas. The Idán are sometimes termed Marút; they are certainly the original inhabitants of Borneo, and resemble the Haraforas equally in stature, agility, colour, and manners. The Haraforas are indigenous in almost all the Eastern isles, and are sometimes found on the same island with the Papuas, or Oriental Negroes. They are often lighter in colour than the Muhammedan races, and generally excel them in strength and activity. They are universally rude and unlettered; and where they have not been reduced to the state of slaves of the soil, their habits have a general resemblance. In their manners the most singular feature is, the necessity imposed on every person of, some time in his life, embruing his hands in human blood; and in general, among all their tribes, as well as the Idán, no person is permitted to marry till he can shew the skull of a man whom he has slaughtered. They eat the flesh of their enemies, like the Battas, and drink out of their skulls; and the ornaments of their houses are human skulls and teeth, which are consequently in great request among them, as formerly in Sumatra, the ancient inhabitants of which are said to have had originally no other money than the skulls of their enemies. The Haraforas are found in all the Moluccas, in Celebes, the Philippines, and Magindano, where they are termed Subano or Manubo; and the ferocious race mentioned by Marsden, who live inland from Samanka, in Sumatra, and are accustomed to atone their own faults by offering the heads of strangers to the chiefs of their villages, are probably of the same description."*

* "Asiatic Researches," vol. x. p. 217. These Idán are Dayaks.—Ed.

From later accounts given of the Dayaks, by Mr. Earle and others, I think it very doubtful whether they belong to the Alforian race. They appear more similar to the Malays; but until we have specimens of their language, it will be impossible to form any opinion on sure grounds.*

[*The Australians.* The aborigines of New Holland are proved by their languages to have no affinity with Pelagian tribes of any class, and if the term Alforian is retained, it will be convenient to restrict it to this race, who may be termed a people apart. In the great insular continent to which they appertain, and beyond whose shores they do not pass, having an area equal to that of Europe, and reaching from the middle of the temperate to far within the torrid zones, differences of feature and habits may be expected, but there is an unmistakeable physiognomy characteristic of them all. In languages the variety is much greater, so that even neighbouring tribes are wholly unintelligible to each other; but their grammatical structure, so far as is known, and we have grammars more or less complete of half a dozen tribes at least, divided by the whole extent of the country, is remarkably like in all.† We have

---

* The just suspicion of the Author is now fully confirmed. A version of the New Testament in the Dayak language, and an analytical Grammar by Gabelentz, clearly show the close affinity of these people to the proper Malays; the Malay language is much nearer to the Dayak than to the Tagala, or Madecass, or Polynesian, where the affinity is generally admitted.—ED.

† In the fifth volume of his "Researches into the Physical History of Mankind," Dr. Prichard inserted (p. 277 *et seq.*) a few notes which the Editor of the present work communicated to him on some striking analogies which he believed he had discovered between the Australian languages and those of the south of India. The Editor has no reason to withdraw from any statements there made, but a variety of occupation has not allowed him to make any attempt to add to the few facts mentioned. He would, however, strengthen the philological evidence by a remark or two on other analogies between the Australians and the Peninsular Indians. The peculiar usage by which hereditary succession is drawn from the female parent instead of the male, is noticed in page 268 of the volume of the Physical History

numerous descriptions of the people from all parts of the island, beginning with Dampier in the 17th century, and all agree in general characters. Two of the most recent we select; one taken on the North-west by Captain Stokes, of

---

noticed above, as existing in Australia, and among the Nairs of Malabar; and that singular weapon, the boomerang, as striking a characteristic of Australia as the black swan or kangaroo, has its analogy or prototype in the Colley stick of the Dekhan, a couple of which have been for several years in the Museum of the Royal Asiatic Society, where they may be compared with a genuine boomerang. In regard to other analogies, some notes, written by George Windsor Earl, Esq., two years ago, in compliance with a request of the Editor, may be found of interest. Mr. Earl's lengthened residence at different periods on the extreme points of Australia made him acquainted with the natives of the remotest tribes, but he expressly alludes in these notes to the tribes about Port Essington in the North, where he lived until the breaking up of that Establishment. The analogies pointed out by Mr. Earl are not given as conclusive, but they were spontaneously made by him, and not drawn out by leading questions: the notes are merely the written expression of what had frequently been stated verbally.

"*Complexion.*—Upon this point the Australians and Coromandels are identical, being also many shades darker than the Malayo-Polynesians who occupy the intermediate islands. Among the Coromandels, individuals are often met with who are so much fairer than the others, as to be remarkable; but this is also the case on the north and north-western coasts of Australia, where nearly every traveller has observed individuals so much fairer than others, as to lead to the supposition that they were of foreign origin (see Captain King, Major Campbell in the Royal Geographical Society's Journal, Messrs. Grey and Lushington, &c.)

Features.—A great variety of features exists both among the Australians and Coromandels, from an almost European regularity down to the very coarsest development that I have met with in any race of mankind. This coarse development is more common with the Australians than with the Coromandels, among whom I have chiefly observed it in individuals of the boatman caste, who are often so like Australians that they would pass without remark if met with among the native tribes of the North Coast. The resemblance, however, does not hold among the better-featured, for although more European-like faces will be met with among the Australians than the Coromandels, yet the former never have that steady thoughtful cast of countenance which is so prevalent with the latter.

Stature and Proportions.—In point of stature, the Australians and Coromandels correspond very closely, the average height being greater than that of the Malayo-Polynesians; indeed, very little inferior to the European

H. M. S. Beagle, and the other drawn from the tribes at no great distance from the East coast, by Dr. Thompson, who also examined natives from various parts of the country, and communicated the result of his observations at a meeting of the Ethnological Society of London, in January 1853. Dr. Thompson says the natives are of middle height, with spare body, the hands and feet of good proportion, arms and legs long, particularly the latter. Head inclined to round rather than to oval, forehead somewhat broad but low, cheek-bones rather high, eyes sunken, eyebrows arched,

---

standard. The Coromandels are better proportioned, and their limbs are more rounded and muscular.

Physical Capacity.—The Australians can stand most fatigue in travelling or hunting, but they are utterly incapable of continued labour, such as the Coromandels habitually undergo. Both races are remarkable for their powers of endurance under rough treatment; indeed, they are the only people of the East who have shown themselves capable of contending successfully with Europeans in wrestling-matches and prize-fights.

Mental Capacity.—Upon this point a fair comparison cannot be drawn until the Australians have been domesticated. They are by no means deficient in quickness and intelligence, and readily acquire little handicrafts. For example, an Australian who has once seen a gun-lock cleaned and put together, can generally do it himself without assistance. The only steady employment that the Australians have yet been put to is that of policemen, for which they have shown themselves well adapted. This is also a favourite occupation with the Coromandels, the police force of the Straits Settlements being chiefly composed of them.

General Habits.—The Australians and the lower classes of Coromandels agree exactly upon one point,—a love of indolence, which is indulged in until aroused into active exertion by an appeal to the feelings, or by the necessity of seeking subsistence, their better halves being generally the monitors on these occasions. In their mode of conducting their quarrels, there is also a resemblance which cannot fail to strike those who are acquainted with both people. The mutterings, spittings, frantic abuse, and apparent struggles to get loose from their friends to annihilate their opponents, are acted with the same gestures, only the Australians are rather more violent in their contortions, as they have no clothes to tear.

I have never yet met with any natives of the Coromandel coast who are scarified with raised cicatrices like the Australians. If this was ever practised among the former, there ought to be some relics of it among the hill tribes. I have seen many with the septum of the nose bored, but a ring has always been worn, instead of the bone or feather of the Australians."

whiskers very small in quantity,—occasionally, however, there is a good deal of beard on the chin, which is rounded and not very prognathous; the lips are prominent and thick, especially the upper one, the mouth is expressive of determination; the skin is dark brown, approaching to black, and usually very smooth; the hair is inclined to be long, soft, and silky,—it is usually quite glossy, but always curly. The women, whilst young, are well proportioned; the hands and feet of many of them are very small. Their manners and speech are quick, lively, and animated; they are easily excitable, and very revengeful. All the tribes have distinct marks on the breast, back, shoulders, and arms, produced by longitudinal or transverse gashes. The Kingbar tribe always have these markings transversely. All the tribes about Moreton Bay speak one language, and have the same characteristics. Dr. Thompson further stated that the slight differences observable between the various tribes scattered over the whole of that extensive region might be easily accounted for by varieties in the climate, or in the supply of food, and he concluded his notice by expressing his opinion that many of the aborigines were, occasionally at least, cannibals.

The observations of Capt. Stokes extended about 200 miles, from Port George IV. to Roebuck Bay. He says, "They agreed in having a common character of form, feature, hair, and physiognomy. The average height of the males may be taken to be from five feet five inches to five feet nine inches . . . . they are almost black . . . . Their limbs are spare and light, but the muscle is finely developed in the superior joint of the arm, which is probably owing to their constant use of it in throwing the spear. Some tribes are entirely naked, while others wear girdles of skin and leaves, hardly sufficient, however, to serve any purpose of decency, much less of comfort. Their hair is always dark, sometimes straight and sometimes curled, and not unfrequently tied up behind; but we saw no instance of a negro or woolly head among them. They wear the beard upon the chin, but not upon the upper lip, and allow it to grow to such a length as enables them to champ and chew it when excited by rage,—an action which they accompany with spitting it out against the object of their indignation or contempt. They have very overhanging brows and retreating foreheads, large noses, full lips, and wide mouths; in some cases they want the two fore teeth in the upper jaw, and while in any one tribe in which the custom prevails it seems to be unanimous, it does not appear to be by any means universally diffused along the whole north-western coast.

"No instance of the use of a canoe or proa was seen or heard of along the whole N.W. coast.*

For more extended details respecting the New Hollanders we may refer to the 5th volume of Dr. Prichard's Physical History of Mankind. With reference to the complicated and artfully contrived laws for marriage, and the constitution of society, mentioned in p. 267 of that volume, we subjoin an extract from a lecture delivered by the Rev. William Ridley at Sidney, in November 1853, which explains those curious regulations more fully than we have seen elsewhere. This lecture, which is of exceeding interest in many respects, relates to the Kamilaroi tribe, a numerous body residing N. W. of Sidney. The language is spoken, according to Mr. Ridley, "along a hundred miles of the Bundarra, on Mooni Creek, and at least eighty miles of the Barwan; all down the Peel and Namoi, over Liverpool Plains, and even on this side of the great dividing range about Murrurundi. It is also spoken on the Bolloon, where the blacks are still very numerous."† Mr. Ridley

* Discoveries in Australia, vol. i. p. 88.

† Threlkeld's grammar of an Australian language, printed at Sidney in 1834, is said by Hale,—who reprinted it in the great work so frequently mentioned,—to be the Kamilaroi; but Mr Ridley, whose evidence is decisive, calls Threlkeld's the Lake Macquarie language, and notices the very great similarity of structure, and differing vocabulary. Mr. Hale also gives a grammar of the Wiradurei language spoken in Wellington Valley, two hundred miles west of Lake Macquarie, of which the same degree of resem-

gives a grammatical sketch and some specimens of the language, in which he proposes to print Scripture extracts, and to teach the natives to read them. He proceeds: "From the small but unquestionable success which I have had in my first few weeks' attempt at speaking Kamilaroi, I expect in a few months, or a year at most, to have a considerable amount of correct Bible translations. There are [a] few Kimilaroi blacks who can read English, and it is a common remark (of which Mr. Watson's school furnishes many illustrations), that when blacks are put early to school, they learn very quickly."

The following is Mr. Ridley's account of the castes and rules of descent of the Natives who are the subject of his lecture:—

"The castes are distinguished by peculiar names. There are four names of men—*ippai*, *murrí*, *kubbi*, and *kumbo;* and four of women—*ippata*, *mata*, *kapota*, *buta*. Every black has one of these names by birth. There is one variation:—In some tribes *baia* is used instead of *murrí*, and it is much more convenient, for *mŭrrĭ* is a general word for black man; and *murrí* is apt to be confounded with it.

"In one family all the sons are called *ippai*, the daughters *ippata;* so that if you find a black man's name is *ippai*, you may be sure all his brothers are *ippai*, and his sisters *ippata*. In another family all the sons are *murrí* or *baia*, all the daughters *mata*. If you ask a *mata* the names of her brothers, you will find they are all *murrí* or *baia*, and all her sisters *mata*. In another family all the sons are *kubbi*, and the daughters *kapota*. In another family all the sons are *kumbo*, the daughters *buta*. By the foregoing names all the blacks are divided into four classes.

"The following rules of intermarriage are most strictly observed:—

blance may be predicated. Hale says that the name of Kamilaroi is unknown to the people themselves, but it is applied to them by the Wiradurei. He derived his grammar or its materials from Mr. Watson; no doubt the gentleman mentioned by Mr. Ridley.

I. *Ippai* may marry an *ippata* (of another family), or any *kapota*.
II. *Murri* may marry only *buta*.
III. *Kubbi* may marry only *ippata*.
IV. *Kumbo* may marry only *mata*.

"Any attempt to infringe these rules would be unanimously resisted, even to bloodshed; but it seems they never dream of attempting to transgress them.

"Polygamy is allowed, and is common; but how many soever a black man's wives may be, they all have (and that from their birth) the right name.

"The following rules of descent prevail:—

I. The children of *ippai* by *ippata* are all *kumbo* and *buta*.
II. The children of *ippai* by *kapota* are all *murri* or *baia* and *mata*.
III. The children of *murri* or *baia* are all *ippai* and *ippata*.
IV. The children of *kubbi* are all *kumbo* and *buta*.
V. The children of *kumbo* are all *kubbi* and *kapota*.

"By tracing out the effect of these rules, you may perceive that descendants of every family come, in the course of a few generations, into the privileged class of *ippai;* while the sons of these aristocrats inherit not their father's rank, but belong to the *kumbo* or *murri* caste.

"They have commonly distinctive names added to their family titles: these distinctive names are often taken from animals; and when they associate with the whites they adopt another name, by which they are known among them. Many blacks are much averse to letting white people know their peculiar names, although they at once tell their family name. Simon of Kollemungul has the family name *Ippai*, and the cognomen *Nurrai,* which means a brown snake. Simon would not tell me his name *Nurrai,* but another black, perhaps owing Simon a grudge, whispered it to me as a grand secret. Another black, known among the whites

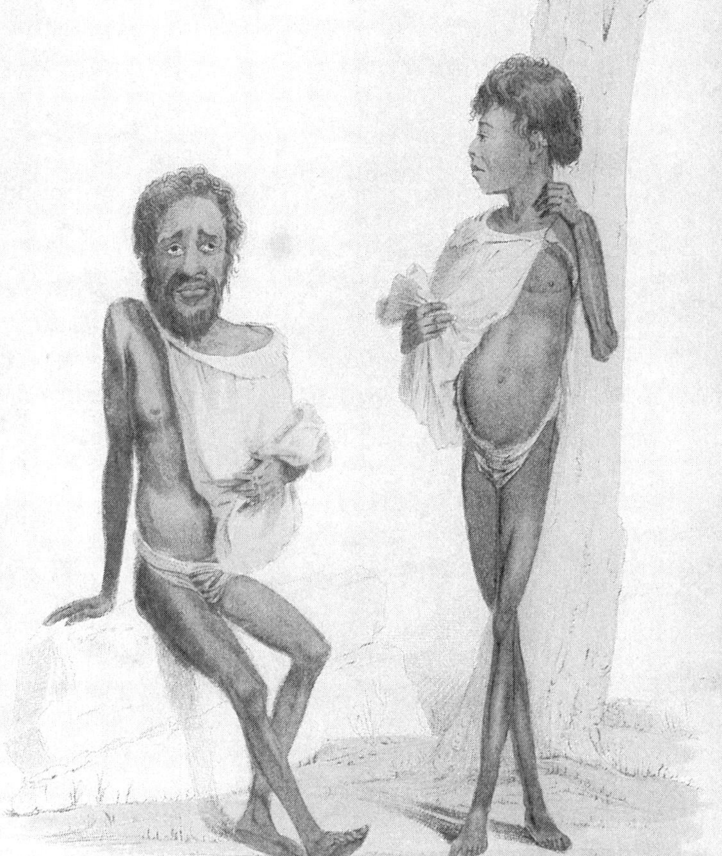

Natives of King George's Sound.

as Jacky of Goonal, has the names *Kubbi Mute* (*mute* meaning opossum); his father was of course *Kumbo*, also called Dinoün (emu).]

The subjoined portrait gives a good specimen of the Australian physiognomy.

FIG. 87.

Australian.

The skull of an Australian is figured in the annexed sketch. It bears a great resemblance to the Tasmanian already described, especially in the ridge-like form of the coronal arch, and the general contour of the head. This resemblance is a fact worthy of remark in the natives of two adjoining countries, differing as they do in other particulars; the one a lank, and the other a woolly-haired race.

FIG. 88.

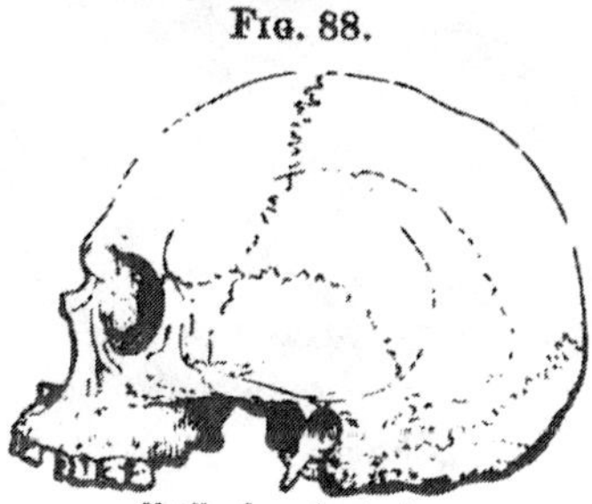

Skull of an Australian.

The lean and half-starved form of the Australians, and the disproportionate size of their limbs and head, are strongly exemplified by the plate representing two Australian figures, which is taken from the magnificent Atlas of M. d'Urville.

CHAPTER XXII.

OF THE NATIVE RACES OF AMERICA—COLLECTIVE SURVEY.

The aboriginal people of America are generally considered as a department of the human family very distinct from the inhabitants of the Old World. The insulated situation of the continent, and the fact that it was so long unknown, and the tribes which it contains so long cut off from intercourse with other nations, are among the circumstances which have contributed to produce this impression. The American nations, taken in the aggregate, are neither among themselves so uniform and unvaried in their physical and moral qualities, nor is the line of distinction between them and the rest of mankind so strongly marked and so obvious, as most persons imagine. Yet it must be admitted that certain characters are discoverable which are common, or nearly so, to the whole of this department of nations; that there are strong indications, if not proofs, of a community of origin, or of very ancient relationship, among them; and that in surveying collectively the people of the New World, we contemplate human nature under a peculiar aspect. On comparing the American tribes together, we find reasons to believe that they must have subsisted as a separate department of nations from the earliest ages of the world. Hence, in attempting to trace relations between them and the rest of mankind, we cannot expect to discover proofs of their derivation from any particular tribe or nation in the Old Continent. The era of their existence as a distinct and insulated race must probably be dated as far back as that time which separated into nations the inhabitants of the Old World, and gave to each branch of the human family its primitive language and individuality.

The traits which serve to characterise the native Americans collectively, are, as I have said, not so obvious as by some they are supposed to be. These nations are called "Red Men;" but there are tribes equally red, and perhaps more properly deserving that epithet, in Africa and Polynesia. And the Americans are not all of the hue denominated "red," that is, of a copper colour: some tribes, as we shall see, are as white as many European nations; others brown or yellow; others are black, or at least they are, by travellers, described as very much resembling in colour the Negroes of Africa. Anatomists have distinguished what they have termed the American form of the human skull; they were led into this mistake by regarding the strongly marked characteristics of some particular tribes as universal. The American nations are spread over a vast space, and live in different climates, and the shape of their heads is different in different parts. Nor will any epithet derived from their habits of life apply to all the tribes of this department: the native Americans are not all hunters: there are many fishing tribes among them; some are nomadic; others cultivate the earth, and live in settled habitations; and of these, a part were agriculturists before the arrival of the Europeans; others have learned of their conquerors to till the soil, and have changed the ancient habits of their race, which, as we may hence infer, were not the necessary result of organisation or congenital and instinctive propensity. If we wish to form a correct idea of the characteristic qualities which really form the bond of association between the American races, and constitute their peculiar distinction, we must inquire somewhat more deeply into the subject.

The most decided and most clearly marked evidence of relationship between these nations is to be found in the characteristic structure of their languages. This is a subject on which light has been thrown of late years, principally through the labours of American philologers. Hervas,* indeed, collected some materials for this purpose; but Dr. Smith Barton of Philadelphia was the first who made any notable attempt to classify the idioms of North

* "Catalogo delle Lingue Conosciute," &c., by Don Lorenzo Hervas, 4to. Cesena, 1784.

America. Humboldt and Vater pursued the work on a more extended scale, and with much more ample resources; but it is to M. Du Ponceau that we owe the most important elucidations.* The history of American philology is a subject far too extensive to be entered upon in the present work, and I shall only adduce the general result, which, as the celebrated traveller Humboldt observes, is a fact of great importance to the history of mankind. "In America," Humboldt says, "from the country of the Esquimaux to the banks of the Orinoco, and again, from these torrid banks to the frozen climate of the Straits of Magellan, mother tongues entirely different with regard to their roots have, if we may use the expression, the same physiognomy. Striking analogies of grammatical construction have been recognised, not only in the more perfect languages, as that of the Incas, the Aymara, the Guarani, the Mexican, and the Cora, but also in languages extremely rude. Idioms, the roots of which do not resemble each other more than the roots of the Sclavonian and Biscayan, have resemblances of internal mechanism similar to those which are found in the Sanskrit, the Persian, the Greek, and the German languages."

These observations were made many years since by M. de Humboldt. They have been confirmed by more extensive research, and the conclusion is thus stated by Mr. Gallatin:—

"Amidst that great diversity of American languages, considered only in reference to their vocabularies, the similarity of their structure and grammatical forms has been observed and pointed out by the American philologists. The result appears to confirm the opinions already entertained on that subject by Mr. Du Ponceau, Mr. Pickering, and others, and to prove that all the languages, not

* American ethnography has also derived important aids from the learned works of Messrs. Pickering and Gallatin. We may expect to find new elucidations of the subject when the posthumous work of the greatest European philologer, W. von Humboldt, long promised by M. Buschmann, shall make its appearance.

only of our own Indians, but of the native inhabitants of America, from the Arctic Ocean to Cape Horn, have, as far as they have been investigated, a distinct character common to all, and apparently differing from any of those of the other Continent with which we are most familiar."*

It must be observed that the idioms of the Esquimaux are included among the American languages; and this is the mature opinion of Mr. Du Ponceau, and other writers who have carefully examined the subject. We must, therefore, reckon the Esquimaux in the class of nations among whom the ancient culture of language peculiar to the New World was originally spread. They belong to the American stock, though differing from many other tribes in some of their most striking characters; but they are not the only nations of the New World who thus differ.

There are, in the second place, many remarkable traits in the moral and social state of the American nations which indicate some near relation between them, and serve to distinguish them from the races of the Old World. These phenomena have been differently accounted for by writers who have contemplated the subject in different points of view; but whatever supposition may be adopted as to their nature and origin, their tendency is to exalt the antiquity of the American race, and to carry back to a remote period the era of its separation from the rest of mankind. A learned and ingenious writer, who has attentively studied the character of the American aborigines, and who has availed himself for that purpose of more ample resources for acquiring accurate knowledge than have fallen to the lot of many persons, has been led to adopt the opinion, that the nations of the New World are not in a state of primitive barbarism or living in the original simplicity of uncultivated nature, but that they are, on the contrary, the last remains of a people once high in the scale of civilisation and mental improvement, now almost worn out and perishing, and sunk into the lowest stage of

* "Archæologia Americana," vol. ii.

decline and degradation. Among many of the American tribes Dr. Martius has observed the remains of ancient institutions of a kind which seems to imply the existence of much refinement and of an artificial state of society. Of this description are,—a complicated form of government, regulated despotisms or monarchies, privileged orders, hierarchical and sacerdotal ordinances, systematic laws the results of reflection and a settled purpose connected with marriage and inheritance and family relationships, and other customs which are strongly contrasted with the simple and unreflective habits of rude and uncivilised nations.*

The languages of these nations abound, as he says, with words expressive of metaphysical views and abstract conceptions. Their opinions respecting a future state, and the nature and attributes of invisible agents, are strikingly different from those of nations who have never emerged from primitive barbarism. Another fact which tends, as M. Martius observes, to confirm the opinion that the natives of the New World have fallen from a state of greater refinement, is their use, from immemorial ages, of certain domesticated animals and cultivated plants, and the notions which they entertain of the first acquisition of these possessions. Of such animals and plants the people of the Old World have their peculiar stock, and the American nations have their own, entirely different. In the Old World we know not whence our horses, our dogs, cattle, and the various kinds of cerealian gramina, were obtained; and the American nations are equally at a loss, when we inquire for the original stock of the dumb dog of the Mexicans, the llama, the root of the mandioca, the American corn, and of the quinoa. In the ancient world there were traditions of some mythical benefactors of mankind, Ceres, Triptolemus, Bacchus, Pallas, and Poseidon, who had contributed their gifts, corn and wine, the sacred olive,

* "Martius, über die Vergangenheit und die Zukunft der amerikanischen Menschheit."

and the horse, and we infer that all these had been known from periods of remote antiquity. In America, likewise, tradition refers the knowledge of cultivated plants and domestic animals, and the art of tilling the earth, to some fabulous person who descended from the gods, or suddenly made his appearance among their ancestors, such as the Manco-Capac of the Peruvians, and the Xolotl and Xiuhtlato of the Toltecas and Chichimecas.

The remains of ancient sculpture and architecture spread over Mexico, and Yucatan, and Chiapa, as well as over the high plain of Quito and other parts of South America, and the extensive works of art, consisting of fortifications and other relics discovered in the Tenessee country as well as in the inland parts of New Mexico on the Rio Gila, afford some further support to the hypothesis of M. Martius.

The possession of arts and acquirements, the most simple improvements of human life, and such as belong to the very infancy of human society, distinctively appropriate, and the origin of which is recorded by mythical legends peculiar to each division of mankind, seems to carry back the era of their separation to the first ages the world.

Whether we adopt the opinion of M. Martius, that the American nations, in general, have fallen from a higher degree of mental culture into their present barbarism, or attempt otherwise to account for the phenomena which have led to that supposition, it must be admitted that many traits are discoverable in the moral and intellectual history of the native American tribes which serve to distinguish them and give them a sort of national character common, at least, to the great majority of the race. The structure of their languages, to which we have adverted, indicates, perhaps, more reflective habits, and a more accurate observation of relations, than the rude idioms of many other races. The national customs and institutions, and many other traits which appeared so remarkable to M. Martius, if they are not fully sufficient to establish his hypothesis, prove, at least, habits of thought and reflection, and a cultivation of mind, very different from the state of savages in general. We may also observe among the nations of America some moral characteristics which serve to distinguish them: with a certain vigour and energy of character they are said to combine a tendency to cruelty and revenge; the social affections appear to have, in general, less influence over them than over most other races of men. The Bedouins of the Arabian desert are cruel and vindictive; but their evil passions have a more transitory influence over them than the stern malice of the Americans. The contrast between the nomades of Asia and of America is in many respects striking; it has been drawn by one of the most eloquent of modern writers, who has himself had opportunities of observing both races in their native wildernesses. I shall terminate these remarks by citing M. Chateaubriand's* description, and it will perhaps interest my reader to observe, that in one particular very different conclusions have been drawn from a contemplation of similar facts by the German philosopher and the French poet:—

"Ce qui distingue surtout les Arabes des peuples du Nouveau-Monde, c'est qu'à travers la rudesse des premiers on sent pourtant quelque chose de délicat dans leurs mœurs; on sent qu'ils sont nés dans cet Orient, d'où sont sortis tous les arts, toutes les sciences, toutes les religions. Caché aux extrémités de l'Occident, dans un canton détourné de l'univers, le Canadien habite des vallées ombragées par des forêts éternelles et arrosées par des fleuves immenses: l'Arabe, pour ainsi dire, jeté sur le grand chemin du monde entre l'Afrique et l'Asie, erre dans les brillantes régions de l'aurore, sur un sol sans arbres et sans eau. Il faut, parmi les tribus des descendants d'Ismaël, des maîtres, des serviteurs, des animaux domestiques, une liberté soumise à des lois. Chez les hordes Américaines l'homme est encore tout seul avec sa fière et cruelle independance: au lieu de la couverture de laine il a la peau d'ours; au lieu

* Chateaubriand, "Itinéraire à Jérusalem."

de la lance, la flèche ; au lieu du poignard, la massue : il ne connoît point et il dédaigneroit la datte, la pastèque, le lait du chameau : il veut à ses festins de la chair et du sang. Il n'a point tissu le poil de chèvre pour se mettre à l'abri sous des tentes : l'orme tombé de vétusté fournit l'écorce à sa hutte. Il n'a point dompté le cheval pour poursuivre la gazelle ; il prend lui-même l'original à la course. Il ne tient point par son origine à de grandes nations civilisées ; on ne rencontre point le nom de ses ancêtres dans les fastes des empires : les contemporains de ses aïeux sont de vieux chênes encore debout. Monuments de la nature et non de l'histoire, les tombeaux de ses pères s'élèvent inconnus dans des forêts ignorées. En un mot, tout annonce chez l'Américain le sauvage qui n'est point encore parvenu à l'état de civilisation, tout indique chez l'Arabe l'homme civilisé retombé dans l'ètat sauvage."

However different the conclusions at which these writers have ultimately arrived, they appear to have participated with all other reflecting persons who have contemplated the same phenomena in one impression as to the leading traits in the character of the American aborigines. Attentive observers have been struck, as I have said, with manifestations of greater energy and mental vigour, of more intense and deeper feeling, of a more reflective mind, of greater fortitude, and more consistent perseverance in enterprises and all pursuits, when they have compared the natives of the New World with the sensual and volatile, and almost animalised savages who are still to be found in some quarters of the Old Continent. They have been equally impressed by the sullen and unsocial character, by the proud apathetic endurance, by the feeble influence of social affections, by the intensity of hatred and revenge, and the deep malice-concealing dissimulation so remarkable in the dwellers amid the dark solitudes of the American forests, where some have imagined that the descendants of the First Murderer have sought to hide themselves from the eyes of men and benevolent beings :

Φοιτᾷ γὰρ ὑπ' ἀγρίαν ὕλαν
ἀνα τ' ἄντρα καὶ πέτρας, ὡς ταῦρος
μέλεος μέλεῳ ποδὶ χηρεύων.

Few additions have been made of late, in a connected and systematic form, to our previous acquaintance with the native races of America. The magnificent publication of Dr. Morton, which far exceeds in its comprehensiveness and in the number and beauty of its engravings any European work that has yet appeared on national varieties of the skull, comprises nearly the sum of our information on the distinctive characters of the head and skeleton in the several tribes of the New World; and the Synopsis of Indian tribes by the learned and Honourable Albert Gallatin is still the chief work of authority on the ethnology of the Northern Americans, and the only work in which these races are classified according to the extent of knowledge as yet acquired by the distinctions and affinities of their languages. The only part of the North American continent which lay beyond the professed scope of M. Gallatin's survey, was the region between the Rocky Mountains and the Northern Pacific. This chasm in North American ethnology has been in some measure supplied by an excellent memoir of Professor Scouler on the tribes inhabiting the country to the northward of Nootka Sound, which appeared some time since in the "Journal of the Royal Geographical Society."*

* A vast accession of materials has within a few years resulted from Government enterprise in the United States. This can be little more than referred to, the mass of matter being far too great for present limits in the most meagre outline, and with the severest compression. The bulky volumes on the Indian Tribes of the United States, by Dr. Henry R. Schoolcraft, published in imperial quarto, at Philadelphia, by authority of Congress, already amount to four, beautifully printed and splendidly illustrated; and the information they afford is immense on every subject connected with the aboriginal tribes in the States, now including all the territories acquired from Mexico. The Journals of Major Emory and of Lieut. J. W. Abert, printed by order of Congress, have also furnished a considerable accession of valuable matter; and the philological volume of the American Exploring Expedition may be consulted on the North-Western Tribes, concerning

Dr. Morton has observed a number of important facts which must be noticed with reference to the physical history of particular races of Americans. But the types of organisation which prevail among these races are too comprehensive, and the deviations, as far as they are yet known, too evanescent or too feebly marked to afford a basis for discriminating the native inhabitants of the New World into ethnical groups. I shall, however, cite from Dr. Morton's work the general results of his comparison of American skulls.

He says: "After examining a great number of skulls I find that the nations east of the Alleghany Mountains, together with the cognate tribes, have a head more elongated than any other Americans. This remark applies especially to the great Lenapé stock, the Iroquois, and the Cherokees. To the west of the Mississippi we again meet with the elongated head in the Mandans, Ricaras, Assiniboins, and some other tribes. Yet, even in these instances, the characteristic truncation of the occiput is more or less obvious, while many nations east of the Rocky Mountains have the rounded head so characteristic of the race: as the Osages, Ottoes, Missouris, Dacotas, and numerous others. The same conformation is common in Florida: but some of these nations are evidently of the Tolteca family, as both their characters and traditions testify. The heads of the Caribs, as well of the Antilles as of Terra Firma, are also naturally rounded: and we trace this character, as far as we have had opportunity for examination, through the

---

whom the author laments his deficiency of means of knowledge. A good deal of information on the tribes of the Southern border is furnished by J. R. Bartlett, who conducted the United States and Mexican Boundary Commission from 1850 to 1853, and who in the course of his official labours collected materials for a work on American ethnology, including carefully checked vocabularies of the native tribes, which he is preparing for publication. The information which he has already communicated in his "Personal Narrative" is valuable, and will be noticed in its place. Some of the volumes published by the Smithsonian Institution also contain information of interest.—ED.

nations east of the Andes, the Patagonians, and the tribes of Chili. In fact, the flatness of the occipital portion of the cranium will probably be found to characterise a greater or less number of individuals in every existing tribe from Tierra del Fuego to the Canadas. If the skulls be viewed from behind, we observe the occipital outline to be moderately curved outwards, wide at the occipital protuberance, and full from these points to the opening of the ear. From the parietal protuberances to the vertex there is a slightly curved slope, producing a conical or rather a wedge-shaped outline.

"Humboldt has remarked that there is no race on the globe in which the frontal bone is so much pressed backwards, and in which the forehead is so small. It must be observed, however, that the lowness of the forehead is in some measure compensated by its breadth, which is generally considerable. The flat forehead was esteemed beautiful among a great number of tribes; and this fancy has been the principal incentive to the moulding of the head by art.

"Although the orbital cavities are large, the eyes themselves are smaller than in Europeans; and Frézier asserts that the Puelche women whom he saw in Chili were absolutely hideous from the smallness of their eyes. The latter are also deeply set, or sunk, in the head—an appearance which is much increased by the low and prominent frontal ridges.

"Among the North American Indians, there is scarcely any decided obliquity in the position of the eyes, which is so universal among the Malays and Mongoles; but Spix and Martius have observed it in some Brazilian tribes, and Humboldt in those of the Orinoco: and among the Pouris, the Prince de Wied describes a man who bore in this and other respects a marked resemblance to a Kalmuk.

"What has been said of the bony orbits obtains with surprising uniformity: thus the superior margin is but slightly curved, while the inferior may be compared to an inverted arch. The lateral margins form curves rather mediate between the other two. This fact is the more interesting on account of the contrast it presents to the oblong orbit and parallel margins observable in the Malay. The latter conformation, however, is sometimes seen in the American, but chiefly in those skulls which have been altered by pressure on the frontal bone.

"The nose constitutes one of the strongest and most uniform features of the Indian countenance: it mostly presents the decidedly arched form, without being aquiline, and still more rarely flat.

"The nasal cavities correspond to the size of the nose itself; and the remarkable acuteness of smell possessed by the American Indian has been attributed to the great expansion of the olfactory membrane. But the perfection of this sense, like that of hearing among the same people, is perhaps chiefly to be attributed to its constant and assiduous cultivation. The cheek-bones are large and prominent, and incline rapidly towards the lower jaw, giving the face an angular conformation; the upper jaw is often elongated, and much inclined outwards, but the teeth are for the most part vertical; the lower jaw is broad and ponderous, and connected in front. The teeth are also very large, and seldom decay; few present marks of disease, though the teeth are often worn by the mastication of hard substances."

Interesting and important as these observations are, they yet do not afford us the means of separating the races of America, and in arranging them according to affinity between different tribes. We shall find, as in the Old Continent so in the New, that tribes of different physical characters come into the same families of nations. Dr. Morton's remarks above cited afford an instance; since the Mandans, Minetaris, and Osages, placed in one class with reference to their skulls, are known to be tribes of the great family of the Sioux, to whom also belong the Dacotas, and other tribes characterised by a different conformation of the head.

The affinity of languages affords the only secure ground for ethnological arrangements; and this method has been followed by the great philologers of the American race, Du Ponceau, Pickering, and Gallatin. We must pursue it as far as it leads us, and when it fails, we must be content with such probabilities or approximations to historical truth as geographical circumstances and all other obtainable lights may be found to furnish. On these foundations, I shall now endeavour to enumerate in particular classes the principal families or groups of nations into which the aborigines of America divide themselves.

CHAPTER XXIII.

INHABITANTS OF CENTRAL AMERICA. 1. RACE OF TOLTECAS, CHICHIMECAS, AZTECAS.

In many parts of the world are to be found tracts of great elevation, where the climate and soil, and all the productions of the earth, are remarkably different from those of the adjacent lowlands; but nowhere else do we observe contrasts so striking in all the forms of living and inanimate nature as when we compare the lofty plain of Anahuac with the low intertropical countries of America. The chain of the Cordillera, which, in Peru, is cleft into parallel ridges, supporting between them broad valleys, becomes, in the latitude of Mexico, a concentrated mass of mountains, which itself constitutes the table-land, and over the surface of which peaks 16,000 and 17,700 feet in height are scattered. The whole high region of Mexico is divided into four great uplands of different character and different natural productions. The first, comprehending the high valley, so termed, of Toluca, is raised 8530 feet above the sea; the valley of Tenochtitlan, where the royal city of Montezuma stood, 7460; that of Actopan, 6553; and the fourth, which is termed the valley of Istla, 3343. The rocks and mountains of Anahuac have the forms of ancient towers, and buttresses, and cones, or pyramids: great lakes, as those of Texcuco, Christobal, and Chalco, variegate its surface, of which they occupy nearly one-fourth part. In these treeless plains, various forms of the cactus, the prickly manguey, or agave, and other plants of singular shape, overspread the soil, where the dumb dog and the bald wolf of Mexico or the xoloitzcuintli, and various lacertine reptiles, wander. In such a country, where the seasons have neither a proper summer nor winter, and the climate is neither that of the temperate nor of the torrid zone, the Spanish invaders found a people equally singular, equally removed from the rudeness and simplicity of savage life, and from the softer and more gentle manners which civilisation has elsewhere produced, combining great knowledge and skill in many useful and ornamental arts with the reckless cruelty of the fiercest barbarian. The Aztecas were diligent cultivators; they had not only the practice of working mines, and producing for use all the metals which their soil concealed, but could set gems in silver and gold, and perform fine works of art, which, as Clavigero says, astonished the workmen of Europe. The natives of Mexico erected stupendous edifices, which rivalled those of Egypt, and although they could not yet attain to the greatest of human inventions, perhaps only once achieved by men under the most favourable auspices, that of symbols representing the sounds of words, they had long aspired after it, and had contrived a method of recording events, and handing down to memory the passages of their ancient history. The Mexicans had even made great advancement in science, and had a solar year, with intercalations on the principle of the Roman calendar.* They

* This is not quite accurate; the Mexican estimate of the length of the year was really nearer the truth than that of the Roman [Julian] Calendar; but there were eighteen months of twenty days each, together with five odd days in every year, and the intercalations were made at remote periods. The most curious fact relating to Mexican astronomy, is its obvious analogy

appear to have been influenced by a deep sentiment of religion, though singularly perverted; had orders of priests performing the rites of a stately ceremonial, and splendid pomps and processions in honour of the gods, whom they worshipped through these mediators and with sacrifices of of the most appalling cruelty, connected, as it appears, with the universally prevailing sentiment of mankind which calls for atonement and expiation. The accounts left by the "conquistadores" hardly suffice to furnish an adequate idea of their social state; but, so far as we can form an opinion, it does not appear that the civilised Aztecas had derived from their cultivation of arts any moral improvement or mitigation of that sullen malignity which seems common to the native tribes of the New World. Their gods had no attribute of clemency or mercy; they were demons, unrelenting avengers of guilt, the creatures of an evil conscience.

It is well known that the Mexicans professed to have records of considerable antiquity; these consisted of historical paintings, of which the traditional explanation was repeated orally by native Mexicans to some of their conquerors, and to Spanish and Italian ecclesiastics. They had also calendars carrying back the notion of time, and marking the different passages of their history.* The authenticity of these documents, and of the interpretation assigned to them, requires a more critical research than has yet been made. To the Abbé Clavigero, however, and Professor Vater, and M. de Humbolt, they have

---

to that of Eastern Asia; the peculiar mode of grouping the years in cycles being similar to that which is in use to this day among the Chinese, Japanese, Mongols, Manchús, Tibetans, &c.; and if the symbols and characters of the Mexican astrology were ever in actual use as regulating the civil calendar, which its connection with the practice prevailing at the epoch of the Spanish conquest renders probable, the systems are identical, and must have been at some remote period the common property of Eastern Asia and Western America.—ED.

* See the magnificent collection of the historical paintings of the Mexicans by Lord Kingsborough, folio, London, 1830.

appeared worthy of credit; and though the style of representation in the earliests parts is evidently mythical, they will continue to hold their place among the archives of nations; and as they are the only records of the past ages of the New World, to be objects of study to all those who attempt to investigate its history. The principal events recorded in these documents are the successive arrivals of three migratory nations in Anahuac from distant rigions in the north-west.* These nations were the Toltecas, the Chichimecas, and the Nahuatlacas. The latter were a band of seven tribes, one of which were the Aztecas, or proper Mexicans. The country whence the Toltecas issued was named Huehuetlapallan. Thence their progress began in the year 554 of our era; and this is the very oldest epoch in the history of the New World. They arrived at Tollantzinco, in the land of of Anahuac, in 648, and at Tula in 670. In the reign of the Toltec king Ixtlicuechahuac, in 708, the astrologer, Huematzin, composed the Divine Book, or Teo-amoxtli, which contained in hieroglyphics their history, their laws, their calendars, and their mythology. The Toltecas are said to have constructed the pyramid of Cholula, on the model of the pyramid of Teotihuacan. These are supposed to be the oldest of all the pyramids of the New World; Siguenza believed them to be the work of the Olmecas, more ancient inhabitants, of a different race from the Toltecas. It was under the Toltec dynasty, or even more early, that the Mexican Buddha, Quetzalcohuatl, appeared, a white man, bearded,

* The curious account of a voyage made to Foo-sang, a country which must have been the N. W. coast of America, in the 5th century, A.D., translated from the Chinese annals by Mons. De Guignes in the 28th volume of the Mémoires de l'Académie des Inscriptions (p. 503), proves, if genuine, a degree of civilization in that region, at least equal to that of the Mexicans at the period of the Spanish conquest. The narrative attributes the civilization of Foo-sang to the effects of the Buddhist religion, preached there by five bonzes from Samarkand, A.D. 458. The Mexican tradition and the Chinese narrative certainly afford each other some degree of support, however slight it may be deemed.—ED.

and accompanied by strangers in black garments. High-priest of Tula, he founded religious ceremonies, while his brother, Huemac, exercised secular authority, and a double dynasty arose like the temporal and ecclesiastical Dairis, or Emperors of Japan. Pestilence destroyed the Toltecs in 1051; they migrated southwards, but some remained in Tula. The Chichimecas, a barbarous people, issued from their unknown country, Amaquemecan, and arrived in Mexico in 1070. Lastly, the Nahuatlacas, or Seven Tribes, began their migration in 1170; they consisted of the Sochimilcas, the Chalcas, Tepanecas, Acolhuas, Tlahuicas, Tlascaltecas, or Teo-chichimecas, and Aztecas, or Mexicans, all of whom, as well as the Chichimecas, spoke the same language as the Toltecas. They issued from a country far to the northward called Aztlan, in 1064, or in 1160, according to another account. The Aztecs separated themselves from the other tribes; in 1325 they built the city of Tenochtitlan, the ancient Mexico, on the banks of the lake Texcuco.*

Such is the outline of the history of the ancient Mexican race, as it seems to be portrayed in the historical painting of which the Spanish conquerors obtained possession, and, as they supposed, the correct interpretation. We may, at least, infer from hence that tribes of the Mexican race, for the Toltecas and Aztecas, and the other tribes above mentioned were one race, since they all spoke the same language, had ascended the central plain of Anahuac from the countries lying somewhere towards the north, and that their arrivals had been successive, and had continued for some centuries before the discovery of America. By the writers before cited the substance of these accounts appears to have been fully credited.

---

* Among the most interesting, and probably the most authentic remains of the literature of this singular race, are the hymns composed by Nezahualcojotl, king of Texcuco, in honour of the Supreme Being, and his elegy on the instability of human greatness, as proved by the fate of the tyrant

The portraits of the ancient Aztecas, as Humboldt has observed, and some of their divinities, are remarkable for the depression of their forehead, giving a small facial angle; and this is a form which seems to have entered into the *beau idéal* of the race, and which many other American nations imitate by artificial compression of the head. The characteristics of the present Mexicans are thus described by Clavigero:—

"The moral and physical qualities of the Mexicans, their tempers and dispositions, were the same as those of the Acolhuacans, the Tepanecans, the Tlascalans, and other nations, with no other difference than what arose from their different mode of education.

"The Mexicans are of a good stature, generally rather exceeding than falling short of the middle size, and well-proportioned in all their limbs. They have good complexions, narrow foreheads, black eyes, clean, firm, regular white teeth; thick, black, coarse, glossy hair, thin beards, and generally no hair upon their legs, thighs, and arms; their skin is of an olive colour.

"There is scarcely a nation upon earth in which there are fewer persons deformed; and it would be more difficult to find a single hump-backed, lame, or squint-eyed man among a thousand Mexicans than among a hundred of any other nation. Among the young women of Mexico, there are many very beautiful and fair; whose beauty is rendered more attractive by the sweetness and natural modesty of their behaviour.

"Their senses are very acute, especially that of sight, which they enjoy unimpaired to the greatest age. Their minds are at bottom, in every respect, like those of the other children of Adam, and endowed with the same powers; nor did the Europeans ever do less credit to their own reason than when they doubted of the rationality of

---

Tezozomoc; translated into Spanish by the great nephew of this king, who was baptized by the name of Ferdinand Alva Ixtilxochitl.

the Americans. Many persons allow the Mexicans to possess a great talent of imitation, but deny them the praise of invention,—a vulgar error, which is contradicted by the ancient history of that people."

2. *Original Inhabitants of Mexico, and other parts of Central America.*

We have seen that the Aztecas, or Mexicans, as well as their kinsmen and predecessors, the Toltecas, were foreigners in Anahuac, who entered that country from the north, and that the first body of this race entered Mexico about 640, as it is supposed, after the Christian era. Previously to that time, the same region had been inhabited by various races, some of whom had arts and civilisation, while others are said to have been barbarians. The former were spread far through Central America, as the splendid buildings of Palenque, and other places which have been lately described by Mr. Stephens, fully testify. Among the most ancient tribes, according to Clavigero and Humboldt, were the Olmecas, who are supposed by Boturini, one of the great collectors of Mexican antiquities, to have peopled the West India Islands and South America. They are known to have extended their migration to Leon de Nicaragua. The Olmecas divided the land of Mexico with the Xicalancas, the Coras, the Tepanecas, Tarascas, Mixtecas, Tzapotecas, and the Othomi.

The Othomi and Totonacs were two barbarous races who inhabited the country about Lake Texcuco, before the arrival of the Chichimecas, who were of the Mexican race. The Othomi are a very remarkable people, from the circumstance that, while all the other known languages of America are polysyllabic, and abounding with complicated constructions, the Othomi, as it has been proved by a late writer, a native of Mexico, Don E. Naxera, whose discovery has been particularly noticed by a great philologist, Du Ponceau, was a monosyllabic dialect. It would seem to belong to the same family of languages with the Chinese and Indo-Chinese idioms.*

Farther to the northward, and beyond the northern boundary of the Mexican empire, dwelt the Huaxtecas. It was discovered by Professor Vater that the Huaxteca idiom is nearly allied to the languages of Yucatan and Guatemala; and this confirms the history of the Aztec conquest of Anahuac. Huaxtecapan is separated from those southern districts by the whole of Acolhuacan, and by a great part of the Mexican empire. The people must have been cut off from each other by the immigration of the Mexicans. Between the Maya, which is the idiom of Yucatan, the Poconchi of Guatemala, and the northern Huaxteca, Vater has proved the existence of an extensive analogy; and there is reason to believe that the Maya was the common language of Cuba, Jamaica, and Hispaniola. In the neighbouring Chiapa at least ten languages are enumerated; the people of this country had hieroglyphical paintings, and a computation of time analogous to that of the Mexicans. They also, according to their tradition, came from the north under a patriarch, Votan, and had historical paintings. Between Chiapa and Mexico were the Zapotecas and Mixtecas, who had peculiar languages and systems of mythology.

The Tarascas, who inhabit the fertile and extensive country of Mechoacan, to the north-west of Mexico, were always independent of that kingdom. They had a sonorous and harmonious language, distinct from all others. Their country was very populous, and in arts and cultivation they were equal to the Mexicans, who could never subdue them; but their king submitted voluntarily to the Spaniards.

Before we leave the nations of Anahuac, it may be worth

* Dr. Latham shows reasons for doubting the alleged isolation, glossarially, and even grammatically, of the Othomi among American languages; 'admitting at the same time that, of all the tongues of the New World, its structure, from being either anaptotic or imperfectly agglutinate, is the most remarkable." See his "Varieties of Man," p. 408.—Ed.

while to remark, that although they differed so much in language, they generally considered themselves as descended from the same race, and that they had even mythological stories which accounted for the diversities of their languages. Acosta has preserved one of these tales, in which the Tarascas are asserted to have spoken originally the languages of the Aztecas, and to have emigrated with that people from Atzlan. According to this tale, the Aztecas, arriving after a long peregrination at Mechoacan, were desirous of settling in so pleasant a country, which was, however, too small for the whole nation. Their god, Huitzilopochtli, consented that a part might remain, and, while they were bathing in the lake of Pazcuaro, advised the others to steal their clothes, and pursue their journey. The former party were so incensed on being thus robbed, that they resolved to separate themselves for ever from their thievish brethren, and accordingly adopted a new language, the Tarasca.

Gomara relates that an allegory was current among the Mexicans, of a more extensive meaning. An old man, named Iztac-Mixcoatl, and his wife Itancueitl, had six children, each of whom came to speak a different language, called Xolhua, Tenoch, Olmecatl, Xicallancatl, Mixtecatl, and Otomotl, the names appropriated to six of the principal nations of Anahuac.

3. *Traces of the Aztec Migration.*

In the countries lying to the eastward of the Gulf of California, between the sea-coast and the highest ridges of the Cordillera, and reaching northward as far as the great rivers Gila and Colorado, many traces are found of the temporary abodes of the Aztecas during their migratory march, which probably took place through this region. Ruins have been found in various places in the countries above mentioned, lying to the south of the Gila, which, connected with local traditions remaining among the inhabitants, are supposed to mark the different stations of the Aztecas in their journey towards Anahuac: these vestiges are said to coincide with and confirm the accounts transmitted by the Mexican historians. Near Nayarit are seen earthen mounds and trenches, which tradition assigns to the Cora. These people are said to have raised them as a defence against the Aztecas, when in their way from Hue'colhuacan to Chicomoztoc, where the Seven Tribes separated. Stations of the Aztecas are supposed to have been recognised by some extensive remains; the most celebrated of these is near the river Gila, where there are ruins of edifices built like those of Mexico, and manifestly the work of a people advanced in arts; they are termed the Casas Grandes. Nations speaking various languages inhabit the provinces of Sinaloa, and Sonora, and in the missions of New Biscay, which lie between Mexico and the river Gila. According to Ribas, all the languages of Sinaloa contain numerous words resembling the Mexican: of such, he says that he could furnish a long catalogue, which appears to prove that some ancient connexion subsisted between the people of these countries and the Mexicans; their languages are said, however, to differ from the Mexican in grammatical structure.

The mountains of Tarahumara and of Pimeria Alta, extending from New Biscay into Sonora, give name to the missions of those countries. The natives of Tarahumara have a peculiar language. The Eudeve and Opata, in Pimeria, are said by Clavigero to resemble the Tarahumara so closely, that they must all have sprung from the same root. But the language of the Cora, a nation inhabiting the missions of Nayarit, and that of Tarahumara above mentioned, have long been known to bear a decided relation to the Mexican. The Cora agrees with the Mexican, according to the result of Vater's researches, not only in its vocabulary, but very remarkably in its grammatical structure. This resemblance is of such a description as to prove that the Cora nation are descended, at least in great part, from the same stock as the ancient Aztecas.

The farthest vestige of what may be considered as Mexican civilization toward the north is in the neighbourhood of the Yaquesila, which flows into the Rio Colorado. The Moqui, and other tribes who inhabit this region, are said by the missionaries who visited those countries in their journey from the missions of Pimeria, to reside in towns, or villages, containing two or three thousand inhabitants. They are clothed, and their houses have several stories and terrasses, and are constructed in the same manner as the Casas Grandes, and the houses of ancient Mexico.*

CHAPTER XXIV.

OF THE ESQUIMAUX, OR KARALIT.

THERE are two races among the aborigines of North America, and only two, who may be traced nearly across the whole continent, from the Pacific to the Atlantic Ocean. These are the two northern races of the Esquimaux and Athapascas. There are several dialects among them, but the proximity of these to each other is astonishing, if the extent of space over which they are spread is considered.

The Esquimaux, though they hunt during their short summer, are obliged to draw their principal sustenance from the sea, and consequently they are rarely found more than 100 miles from the sea-coast. The name of Esquimaux is derived, according to M. Charlevoix, from an Algonquin or Abenaqui word, and means "Eaters of raw fish." They call themselves by different names in different places, but their most prevalent designation is Karalit. The Esquimaux inhabit the shores of all the seas, bays, inlets, and islands of America, north of the 60° of north latitude; from the eastern coast of Greenland, in longitude 20°, to the Straits of Behring, in longitude 167° west. On the Atlantic, they reach eastward along the coast of Labrador

* See an account of these people in Chapter XXIX.

to the Straits of Belle-isle, and within the Gulf of the River St. Lawrence. Towards the west, they may be traced along the shores of the Pacific to the extremity of the Peninsula of Alaska, and thence to the neighbourhood of Mount St. Elias, where they border on the Kolushi. The Konæges and Tschugazzi are the southernmost tribes of Esquimaux that are known in this direction,* as reaching the western side of North America, along the shores of the Pacific. The whole length of the coast of the Esquimaux is computed by Mr. Gallatin to be not less than 5400 miles, without reckoning the inlets of the sea.

I have already described the form of the skull peculiar to the Esquimaux. The description given by Crantz of the Greenlanders may well apply to the whole race. He says that they are for the most part under five feet in stature. He adds, "That they have well-shaped and proportioned limbs; their face is commonly broad and flat, with high cheek-bones, but round and plump cheeks; their eyes are little and black, but devoid of sparkling fire; their nose is not flat, but small, and projecting but little; their mouth is little and round, and the under lip somewhat thicker than the other." "They have universally coal-black, straight, strong, and long hair on their heads, but no beard, because they root it out. Their hands and feet are little and soft, but their head and the rest of their limbs are large. They have high breasts and broad shoulders: their whole body is fat."

M. Charlevoix, in his history of New France, has given a very good description of the Esquimaux, and there are some remarkable particulars in his account. He says, "Il est certain que de tous les peuples connus de l'Amérique, il n'en est point qui remplisse mieux que celui-ci la première idée que l'on a eue en Europe des sauvages. Il est presque le seul où les hommes ayent de la barbe, et ils l'ont si épaisse jusqu'aux yeux, qu'on a peine à découvrir

* "Synopsis of the Indian Tribes of North America," by the Honourable Albert Gallatin. "Archæologia Americana," Vol. ii. p. 10.

quelques traits de leur visage. Ils ont d'ailleurs je ne sçai quoi d'affreux dans l'air, de petits yeux effarés, des dents larges et fort sales, des cheveux ordinairement noirs, quelquefois blonds, forts en désordre, et tout l'extérieur fort brut. Leurs mœurs et leur caractère ne démentent point cette mauvaise physionomie. Ils sont féroces, farouches, défiants, inquiets, toujours portés à faire du mal aux étrangers.

"Leurs cheveux blonds, leurs barbes, la blancheur de leur peau, le peu de ressemblance et de commerce qu'ils ont avec leurs plus proches voisins, ne laissent aucun lieu de douter qu'ils n'ayent une origine différente de celle des autres Amériquains." [The plate opposite is the portrait of a young Esquimaux, now a student at S. Augustin's College in Canterbury. It is copied from an excellent photograph which was taken for this work.]

CHAPTER XXV.

ATHAPASCAS, OR CHEPEWYANS.

THE name of Athapascas has been given by Mr. Gallatin to a widely-spread nation in North America, termed Chepewyans by Mackenzie, who had a very imperfect idea of their extension. This designation is derived from the original name of the Lake of the Hills and the adjoining country, which is in the centre of the territory possessed by the tribes of this race.

The country of the Athapascas reaches from the western shore of Hudson's Bay, across the whole American Continent, to the confines of the Kolushian tribes, immediately on the coast of the Pacific. Its southern boundary is the river Missinippi, or the Churchill river, which falls into Hudson's Bay. This boundary line ascends from the mouth of that river to its source, and is thence continued in a direction nearly due west; the country of the Atha-

Kalliherua.

(An Esquimaux.)

pasca race reaches from this line northward to that of the Esquimaux. The Athapascas may thus be considered as occupying the whole interior of North America to the northward of the latitude of the Missinippi, behind the coast of the Kolushians, or to the eastward of them, and to the southward of the Esquimaux, whose enemies and neighbours they are through the whole frontier of that race to the westward of Hudson's Bay. The Northern Indians, the Beaver Indians, the Mountain Indians, the Tacallas, or Carriers, the Sussees, are all tribes of Athapascas, in the midst of whose territory is the whole chain of the Rocky Mountains to the northward of the 52° north latitude.

Mackenzie has described the Chepewyans, or Athapascas. He is unwilling to include them under the name of native Americans. He says, "Their progress is easterly, and, according to their own traditions, they came from Siberia; agreeing in dress and manners with the Eastern Asiatics. They have a tradition among them that they came originally from another country inhabited by very wicked people, and had traversed a great lake, which was narrow, shallow, and full of islands, where they suffered great misery, it being always winter, with ice and deep snow. At the Copper Mine River, where they made the first land, the ground was covered with copper, over which a body of earth has since been collected to the depth of a man's height. They believe, also, that in ancient times their ancestors lived till their feet were worn out with walking, and their throats with eating. They describe a deluge, when the waters spread over the whole earth, except the highest mountains, on the tops of which they preserved themselves."*

* On the authority of Professor W. W. Turner, who read a paper on the subject before the American Ethnological Society, "a close analogy exists between the languages of the Apaches [in Texas] and the Athapascans." See J. R. Bartlett's Explorations and Incidents in Texas, &c., New York, 1854, Vol. i. p. 326. The statement is given by a trustworthy writer, though

CHAPTER XXVI.

THE GREAT ALGONQUIN-LENÁPE AND IROQUOIS RACES.

The greater part of Canada, and of the country now belonging to the United States, which lies to the eastward of the Mississippi, was inhabited at the era of its discovery by tribes belonging to two principal races. The Algonquins and the Lenni-Lenápe, or Delaware Indians, were two of the most powerful and celebrated tribes in one of these races; to the other belonged the people who were termed by French writers Iroquois. These names, as above set down, may be made to comprehend the two races respectively, though neither was a general appellation. Both races were subdivided into a great number of tribes, who formed individually distinct nations, though they respectively recognised their kindred to each other. The Algonquin-Lenápe were the most extensively spread people in all Northern America. The territory of the Iroquois was nearly surrounded by lands belonging to that race; for that reason, and because the two nations have ever been nearly connected in history, I shall describe them, as Mr. Gallatin has done, in one section.

The limits of the Algonquin-Lenápian territory towards the north is the river Missinippi, which separates them from the Athepascas, or Chepewyans. The whole course of that river, from its source in the Rocky Mountains to its mouth in the Hudson's Bay, divides the Athapascas on its left bank from the Algonquin nations on the right. The latter, however, are also found on the east side of Hudson's Bay, and a continuation of nearly the same line forms their northern limit through the land of Labrador, where, there being no Athapascas, they border immediately on the Esquimaux. On the east, they were extended along

---

not of his own knowledge: the fact appears very unlikely, except in so far as there is a close analogy between the structures of nearly all American languages.—Ed.

the coast of the Atlantic, from the mouth of the River St. Lawrence to the vicinity of Cape Hatteras; this is the eastern boundary of the country occupied by the Algonquins and Iroquois. The southern limit is as follows:—An irregular line drawn from Cape Hatteras to the confluence of the Ohio and the Mississippi separates the Iroquois and the Algonquin nations on one side from the territories of the southern people on the other, who will be mentioned in the following chapter. On the western side, the Algonquin race is generally limited by the river Mississippi, from the point before mentioned up to its source. Farther northward, the tribes of this race are separated from the Sioux by the Red River, which falls into Lake Winnipeg. Thence northward to the Missinippi the line is unknown.

The Iroquois, a people distinct from the Algonquins but similar to them, and waging almost perpetual warfare with them, consisted formerly of two separate bodies. The northern Iroquois were entirely surrounded by Algonquin-Lenápian tribes; they occupied countries difficult to define, extending from the neighbourhood of Lake Huron to the Ohio. The southern Iroquois were the Tuscasoras in Virginia and North Carolina.

History of the Algonquin-Lenápe.

From the Atlantic to the Mississippi the names of rivers and mountains are, as Dr. Barton observes, chiefly Algonquin words; examples are those of Massachusetts, Connecticut, Monongahela, Alleghany, Muskingum, Savannah, and Mississippi. One great branch of the race were the Delaware Indians, or Lenni-Lenápe. Their traditionary history, as collected by Heckewelder, is as follows. The Lenni-Lenápe, or Original People, as their ancestors have handed down, dwelt long ago in a very distant country, in the western part of the American Continent. For some reason, now forgotten, they determined on migrating to the eastward, and accordingly set out together in a body. After a long journey, and many nights' encampment—by which they mean the halt of a year in one place—they at length arrived on the Namæsi-Sipu, River of Fish, or Mississippi, where they fell in with the Mengwe, or Iroquois, who had likewise emigrated from a distant country, and had struck upon the river somewhat higher up. Their object was the same as that of the Lenápe; they were proceeding to the eastward, until they should find a country that pleased them. With this nation, destined to be their future enemies and destroyers, the Lenápe formed a confederacy, and both united their forces against a common foe. This was a powerful nation, whom their spies had discovered in the country eastward of the Mississippi, termed Talligewi, or more properly Alligewi, who had built many large towns on the rivers flowing through their land. These people were a remarkably tall and stout race, higher in stature than the tallest of the Lenápe; they were finally overcome by the latter, and being expelled from their territory, fled down the Mississippi, whence they never returned. The Alleghany river, or Ohio, is still called after them by the Delawares, Alligewi-Sipu, or River of the Alligewi; and the chain of mountains also preserves their name. The conquering nations divided the country eastward of the Namæsi-Sipu among themselves. The Lenápe took possession of, and gradually migrated into, the country to the south, and settled on the four great rivers,—Delaware, Hudson, Susquehannah, and Potomac; and the Mengwe, or Iroquois, occupied the lands farther northward, in the vicinity of the great lakes, and on their tributary streams. This migration, according to the tradition of the Lenápe, was the cause of the division of their race into several bodies. Some remained beyond the Mississippi, and another body near that river on the eastern side; but the larger number settled on the Atlantic. This vast body of the Lenápe on the Atlantic became divided into three tribes, termed the Unamis, Unalachtigo, or Turtle and Turkey, who settled near the sea, from the Hudson River to beyond the Potomac, and the Minsi, or Wolf tribe, farther westward: these people were commonly called Monseys.

From these three tribes, comprising the nation termed Delawares by the Anglo-Americans, have gradually descended many other divisions of the same race, who continued to acknowledge the Lenápe as their parent stock, or as their *grandfather*.

Northern Tribes of the Algonquin-Lenápe Race.

The northern tribes belonging to this family of nations are the Knisteneaux, or Crees, who border towards the north on the Athapascas, and reach from Hudson's Bay to the Rocky Mountains, the Algonquins and Chippeways, or Ojibways, the Ottawas, and the Potowatomis and the Mississagues. The north-eastern division, in Mr. Gallatin's enumeration, are the Algonquins of Labrador, the Micmacs, the Etchemens, and the Abenaquis. These nations have been described by Charlevoix, La Hontan, and other French writers on the history of Canada.

Individuals belonging to several northern tribes have been brought, within a few years, to London, and have furnished specimens of the physiognomy of the native American race. The most remarkable are the Ioways, from the Rocky Mountains, and the Ojibways.

The Ojibways, also called Chippeways, are reckoned by M. Gallatin a tribe of the northern branch of the great Algonquin-Lenápe family, to which are likewise referred the Knistenaux, or Killistenos, or Crees, the Algonquins proper, or Nippisings of Charlevoix, the Ottawas, the Potowatomies, and the Mississagues. All these nations speak dialects which are nearly allied, and are more or less easily intelligible to each other, while the idioms belonging to other branches of the same great family, as those of the Lenápe, or Delaware Indians, the Mohicans, the Nanticoks, and the Illinois, are much more remote. The Knistenaux and Algonquins are the most northern of the northern branch: they inhabit Canada and the country on the river St. Lawrence. The Chippeways, or Ojibways, are intimately connected with the Ottawas; these were considered by the French Catholic Missionaries as the same people. The original position of these people is said to have been on the Ottawa River, where they dwelt chiefly on an island, and exacted tribute from all canoes passing into the country of the Hurons. After the almost total destruction of the Hurons by the Five nations, in 1649, the people of the Algonquin-Lenápe race, who had lived on that river, abandoned their ancient abodes; and a part of them passed to the south-western extremity of Lake Superior. The Chippeways are now situated around Lake Superior, extending north-west towards Lake Winnipeg, and west to Red River.

A very interesting account was given long ago of the Chippeways by Carver, who resided some time among them; and they have been described lately by Professor Keating and by Mr. Catlin. The following account has been given by this last writer of the tribe and of the party of Ojibways who have lately been exhibited in London.

"The tribe amounts in number at this time to about 25,000 persons. They occupy the eastern and north-eastern and northern shores of Lake Huron, also the whole northern and southern shores of Lake Superior, the head-waters of the Mississippi, and even extend over an immense tract of country to the north and west of the Lake of the Woods, reaching nearly to Lake Winnipeg and Hudson's Bay. In a political point of view the Ojibways are more important to Great Britain than any other American tribe residing within the territory claimed by that kingdom. The Ojibways are composed of about thirty bands, each having at its head a chief, and they are all subservient to one supreme head. The party now in England consist of nine individuals, six of whom are men and three females: they came from the eastern shore of Lake Huron. Of the men, one is a war-chief, fifty-one years of age, who is said to have

THE WAR DANCE, BY THE OJIBBEWAY INDIANS.

distinguished himself, like the old chief, in the year 1812, by the side of the great warrior Ticumak. There are also three young men denominated warriors, and an interpreter, a half-bred Indian, who is named Not-een-a-akm, or the Strong Wind. This young man, who is dressed in a semi-civilised costume, speaks French and English as well as the Ojibway language. He is twenty-two years of age. He is the son of a French Canadian named Candotte, who rendered the British Government some essential service during the last war in the capacity of Government interpreter. His mother is an Ojibway woman.

"The principal man of the party is Ah-quee-we-zaints, 'the Boy,' an old chief, now seventy-five years of age. His stature is six feet one and a half inches, and his countenance intellectual and benevolent.

"Of the three females, two are wives of young men belonging to the party, and the third, a little girl ten years of age, and daughter of one of the band. They are all dressed in skins, and their dresses are ornamented with a profusion of beads of various colours, and with rows of elks' teeth."*

[Of all these tribes the Crees have made the greatest advances towards civilization; the accounts received from time to time by the Church Missionary Society in London, and made known in their publications, are evidence of this, and a notice of a geological work† inserted in the Literary Gazette of July 1853, gives a striking instance of the pro-

* A perfectly civilized and well-educated Chippeway, named Kah-ge-ga-gah-bowh, who was in London a few years ago, (1851), excited a good deal of attention by his agreeable manners, and the interesting nature of his discussions on the condition and prospects of his countrymen. He gave some public lectures on these subjects, in which he expressed himself with an ease and propriety quite unexpected in a man who had for the greatest part of his life lived wholly in the forests with his countrymen, and who did not know any language but his own, until he was above 12 years of age. Kah-ge-ga-gah-bowh was born in 1818, on the river Trent, near Rice Lake, in Upper Canada.—ED.

† David Dale Owen's Geological Survey of Wisconsin, Iowa, and Minnesota. Philadelphia, 1853.

gress made by one body of the nation. The Reviewer quotes the author as speaking of a settlement of five hundred Crees at a place called Prince Rupert's Landing, near the Fort Garry Colony, and not far from where the Red River joins Lake Winnipeg. The author says, "These Indians support themselves mainly by the produce of their farms, which they cultivate with their own hands. They dwell in comfortably squared log buildings, erected, thatched, and whitewashed by themselves. They are acquainted with the use of the simpler farming utensils, and the mechanical operations necessary to keep their farms and houses in order. Each family cultivates from five to ten acres of land, which is kept well fenced. They mow their own hay, and feed their cattle on it in the winter. A few occasionally hunt during a month or more in the summer, when their crops do not require much attention; but this is more for recreation than for support. Some of the men occasionally contract with the Hudson's Bay Company to transport their goods to and from York Factory on Hudson's Bay." The author informs us that this extraordinary change in Indian habits and character has been wrought by the example of a judicious missionary named Smithhurst, who thoroughly understands their language. The care with which this excellent man cultivated his own farm and garden first drew their attention, and the example given by a teacher whom they reverenced, showed them palpably the superior certainty of support derivable from agriculture, over anything they could obtain from their old source of livelihood, the chase; and this has induced them gradually to fall into habits leading to results which they could feelingly appreciate. In spite of the ridicule of their neighbours the Chippeways, who contemptuously style them grubs and earth-worms, they have persevered, and "have gathered around their permanent homes the implements and appurtenances, and even some of the comforts and luxuries, belonging to the establishment of the thrifty farmer."]

The eastern division comprises all the tribes of New England. The Delaware, or Lenni-Lenápe, were acknowledged, according to La Hontan, by a long list of nations, as their primitive ancestors, or, in the Indian phrase, as their grandfather. The Minsi, and the Mohicans, or Mohegans, the Nachitoches of Maryland, the Susquehannahs, the Pohatans of Virginia, and the Pamlicos of North Carolina, belong to this division of the Algonquin race. The languages of these nations have been grammatically examined, and grammars and dictionaries of some of them have been made by various writers of the United States, among whom are the celebrated Jonathan Edwards, Eliot, Heckewelder, Zeisberger, Pickering, and the great philologer of the New World, the venerable Du Ponceau.*

---

* The history of these nations presents many curious and interesting passages; particularly the accounts of the wars of Uncas, chief of the Mohicans, and the wars of King Philip, Sachem of the Wampanoags. They are detailed with great clearness in the classical work of Mr. Gallatin.—DR. PRICHARD.

A copious grammar of the Cree language, combined with an analysis of the Chippeway dialect, from the pen of Joseph Howse, Esq., who was twenty years a resident in Prince Rupert's Land, was printed in London in the year 1844. This is a valuable contribution to American philology; but it is a fact of greater interest in the history of the aboriginal American, that the Crees have recently learned to read and write for themselves, not with the Roman alphabet, like the Cherokees, but by the aid of a syllabarium devised for their use a few years ago by the Rev. James Evans, a Wesleyan missionary, who became almost an Indian himself, and who was "skilful in all departments of Indian exertion; so that he may be said to have become a naturalized denizen of the woods and lakes" (Ch. Miss. Intell. vol. iv. p. 68). Mr. Evans's syllabary is composed of simple forms representing different consonants, which receive different vowel sounds by a change in position; so that, for instance, ¬ stands for ma, ┌ me, ┘ mo, └ mu; modifications are made by dots and small lines. Portions of the New Testament have been printed in this character at Rossville, near Norway-house on Lake Winnipeg, and St. John's Gospel has been received in England. It is said that the Crees learn to read rapidly in this character, though it is fair to state that some of our missionaries who speak the language object to it, though they admit that it is "valuable for the old Indians;" no doubt because it is more easily acquired: an important admission in its favour. According to a notice in the "Albany Evening Journal," Mr. Evans died in November 1846.—ED.

It was with the Lenni-Lenápe, or Delawares, that William Penn made his celebrated treaty. In his time the Delawares had been subjugated and "made women" by the Iroquois, so that Penn and his followers were obliged to purchase the right of possession from the Delawares, and that of sovereignty from the Five nations.

The western branch of the Algonquin race are the Menomonies, called by the French "Folles Avoines," or "Wild Oats," the Miami, or Illinois tribes, the Sauks, Foxes, and Kickapoos, and, lastly, the Shawnees. A long list of inferior names might be enumerated: I have confined myself to the prominent tribes.

The Iroquois Tribes.

The Iroquois, entirely distinct from the Algonquin race, have been singularly associated with that family of nations in the various passages of their history. The northern Iroquois consist of two divisions,—the eastern, who are the famous Confederacy of the Five nations, and the western, or Four nations, of which the Wyandots, termed by the French Hurons, are the principal tribe. When the Five nations were engaged in deadly feud with the Algonquin tribes, the Wyandots were the head and principal support of the Algonquin confederacy, and even the Delawares, who claim to be the elder branch of the Lenápe race, recognise the superiority of the Wyandots, whom they still call their *Uncles*: the right of ancient sovereignty is conceded to them. Their real name is probably Yendots; they concentrated themselves near Lake Huron, and have cultivated agriculture more than any other native race. The Iroquois nations in general were a people of superior character to the Algonquin tribes, and had gained a decided ascendancy over them before the discovery of America. Most of these tribes are now nearly extinct,—the result in part of their intestine warfare, and in part of the small-pox and other diseases, and the vices introduced among them by Europeans. The French Catholic missionaries were indefatigable in their attempts to convert them to Christianity, and eight or ten Jesuits suffered death among the Hurons in the pursuit of this work of piety.

Physical Characters of the Algonquin and Iroquois.

It does not appear that there are any very strongly marked differences in physical character between the nations belonging to these two races.

The descriptions given by Mackenzie of the Knisteneaux, and Professor Keating's account of the Potowatomis near Lake Michigan, may serve for a general portrait of the Algonquin-Lenápe. They are as follows :—

"The Knisteneaux are of moderate stature, well proportioned, and of great activity; their complexion is of a copper colour, and their hair black, which is common to all the natives of America." To this observation some exceptions are afterwards mentioned by the writer himself. "It is cut in various forms, according to the fancy of the several tribes; and by some is left in the long, lank flow of nature. They very generally extract their beards, and both sexes manifest a disposition to pluck the hair from every part of the body and limbs. Their eyes are black, keen, and penetrating; their countenance open and agreeable; and it is a principal object of their vanity to give every possible decoration to their persons. A material article in their toilets is vermilion, which they contrast with their native ochre, white and brown earths, to which charcoal is frequently added. Of all the nations I have seen on this continent, the Knisteneaux women are the most comely; their figure is generally well proportioned, and the regularity of their features would be acknowledged by the most civilised people of Europe; their complexion has less of that dark tinge which is common to those savages who have less cleanly habits.

"The Potowatomi are for the most part well-proportioned, about five feet eight inches in height, possessed of much muscular strength in the arm, but rather weak in the back, with a strong neck, and endowed with considerable agility; their voice is feeble and low, but when excited, very shrill; their teeth are sound and clean, but not remarkable for regularity. In persons of feeble habit or of a scrofulous tendency, the teeth are found to decay much faster than in others. Dentition is said to be a painful process among Indian children,—a circumstance which we had not expected. Their complexion is very much darkened by exposure to the sun and wind, while those parts which are kept covered are observed to retain their native brightness. Children are red when new-born; after a few years they assume a yellow colour." Some other observations are added, tending to prove that all the organs of sense are very perfect in these tribes, as well as the physical powers in general. Kalm has described the Hurons, and some other tribes of the Iroquois nation. From his account, it appears that they do not differ remarkably in person from the Algonquin race. He says, "The Hurons are tall, robust people, well-shaped, and of a copper colour; they have short black hair, which is shaved on the forehead from one ear to the other. The Anies, another Iroquois tribe, speaking the Huron language, are equally tall. The Hurons seem to have a longer, and the Anies a rounder face; the Anies have something cruel in their looks; both the Hurons and the Anies are taller than the Mickmacks; the latter speak a different language." They have already been mentioned as an Abenaqui tribe, and therefore of the Algonquin race. Kalm says, "I have not seen any Indians whose hair was so long and straight as theirs. Almost all the Indians have black, straight hair: however, I have met a few whose hair was pretty much curled; but the Indians of Canada have been somewhat intermixed with the French."

The Mohawks are a tribe of the race of Iroquois. A portrait of the Mohawk chief, Thayendaneega, may give some idea of their type of countenance.

I have selected from Mr. Catlin's admirable collection

Nah-pope

(The Soup)

A Sauk Warrior

Muck-a-tah-mish-o-kah-kaik.

The Black Hawk.

A Sauk Chief.

of original paintings two portraits of warriors of the tribe of Sauks and Foxes, more properly termed, according to Mr.

FIG. 89.

Thayendaneega, a Mohawk Chief.

Gallatin, the Musquakiúk, or "Red Clays."* They belong to a western branch of the Algonquins, and may serve as specimens of the Lenápian races. One of them is the celebrated chieftain Black Hawk, the other Nah-pope, a warrior of the same tribe. (See *Coloured Plates.*)†

---

* "Archæologia Americana," Vol. ii. p. 61.

† "The Iroquois and Algonkins exhibit in the most typical form the characteristics of the North American Indians, as exhibited in the earliest descriptions, and are the two families upon which the current notions respecting the physiognomy, habits, and moral and intellectual powers of the so-called Red Race are chiefly founded" ("Varieties of Man," by Dr. R. G. Latham, p. 333).—ED.

CHAPTER XXVII.

OF THE ALLEGHANIAN RACES, OR NATIONS LIVING TO THE SOUTHWARD OF THE LENAPE AND IROQUOIS.

In the southern parts of the territory of the United States, there were formerly a multitude of distinct races; that is, of races speaking distinct and wholly unconnected languages. Most of these have become extinct: those who survive are some remnants of the Catawhas, the Cherokees, the Choctaws, and the Chickasas, and the tribes partly or wholly included in what is termed the Creek confederacy: these are the Muskhogees, of the race of the Seminoles, the Uchees, and the Natchez, and some others. As all these nations live on the Southern parts of the Alleghany Mountains, or in the neighbourhood of rivers which take their rise in that chain, I shall adopt, in describing them, the collective term above expressed, not because it is a very good one, but because it is the best I can find.

The Cherokees.

The history of the Cherokees has been admirably sketched by Mr. Gallatin, to whom I must refer the reader for more extended information. Their name, rightly pronounced, is Chilakees, or more properly Tsalakies. Their territory was to the north and south of the south-westerly continuation of the Appalachian Mountains. In the time of Adair, who lived in their country, the number of their warriors was estimated at 2300: they are now 15,000, including about 1200 Negroes in their possession; so that, as Mr. Gallatin observes, they appear to have increased.

It is probable that the Cherokees are originally a branch of the race of Iroquois. Dr. Barton and Mr. Gallatin agree in the opinion that there is an essential, though remote affinity, between the languages of these races. Their idiom is now a written language; a native

Cherokee, Sequoyah, termed by the Anglo-Americans Guess, has invented for writing it a syllabic system of letters, which, according to Mr. Gallatin, is better adapted for expressing the words belonging to it than our alphabetic characters. The Cherokees have now written laws, and seem likely to improve in civilisation, and to preserve their name to future ages, and to prove to the world, what some prejudiced persons have denied, that the native races of America are capable of receiving and appropriating the blessings of Christianity. We are informed by Mr. Catlin, who visited the settlement of the Cherokees, and Owahs or Muskhogees, on the river Arkansas, in Lousiana, that they have fine farms and immense fields of wheat, and live in good houses. He adds, "The Creeks, as well as the Cherokees and Choctaws, have good schools and churches established amongst them, conducted by excellent and pious men, from whose example they are drawing great and lasting benefits."*

2. The Catawhas, akin to the Woccons, the Cheraws, and Congarees, are feeble remains of a distinct nation who occupied the country on the Cheraw and other districts to the eastward of the Cherokee territory. Their language has some affinities to the Muskhogee.

3. The Muskhogees form seven-eighths of what is termed

* Several small books printed by the Cherokees in their own language and peculiar syllabary have passed through the Editor's hands; among them, portions of Scripture, amounting to nearly the whole of the New Testament, and some religious tracts; all neatly and carefully executed. An almanack printed also in this language contains a detailed notice of the native executive government, a list of their district courts, and an account of their religious associations and educational establishments. The number of free schools for primary education was stated at twenty-two, and the institution of two high schools, one for each sex, was then (1851) in contemplation, for applicants who could sustain a good examination in the ordinary subjects of instruction, and affording board and education free for four years at least. "Thus," concludes this account, "the Cherokee Nation is better provided for, in respect to schools, than many portions of the United States, and we are happy to say that a large proportion of the people are disposed to avail themselves of their privilege."—Ed.

the Creek confederacy. The Seminoles, or properly, Isty-Semole, that is "Wild Men," speak the same language, but are not included in the confederacy. Several other small tribes of distinct races are included in this league, among whom are reckoned the remains of the once celebrated Natchez, who came from the Mississippi, and the Uchees, ancient inhabitants of the country on the Coosa river.

4. The Chickasas and Choctaws, properly Chahtas, which means "Flat Heads," different nations, but of one race, formerly inhabited most of the country on the Mississippi, as far upwards, or nearly so, as the Ohio. Mr. Gallatin is of opinion that the language of this race is remotely allied to the Muskhogee.

The numbers of these southern nations, according to the estimate of the American War Department, are as follows:—

The Cherokees		15,000
The Choktaws	18,500	24,000
The Chikasas	5,500	
The Muskhogees, Seminoles, and Hilchitees		26,000
The Uchees, Alibamons, Coosadas, and Natchez		2,000
		67,000

The Alleghanian races preserve among them many remarkable customs, once common, more or less, to many American nations, which indicate a cultivation of mind, and even a refinement in political institutions, wonderful when compared with their general habits. These were the people among whom Adair fancied that he recognised the institutions of Judaism. The Cherokees had a city of refuge or peace, Echotah,* where even murderers found a

* The name of the Cherokee town in Georgia, where a newspaper in the language was printed in the year 1828, was New Echotah. A copy of that paper, seen by the Editor, contained a deprecatory but desponding article on the dreaded compulsory banishment of the nation beyond the Mississippi; which was soon after carried into effect by the American government with a deplorable loss of life, and a serious check to the commencing civilization of the Cherokees.—ED.

temporary asylum. A perpetual fire was there kept up, and it was the residence of the "*beloved men*," in whose presence no act of violence could be committed; these were different persons from the war-chieftains of tribes. Charlevoix and Du Pratz saw the temple, and the sacred and perpetual fire of the Natchez. They worshipped the sun and fire. According to Charlevoix, most Indian nations are divided into three tribes, or clans, each of which is named after some animal, as the Wolf, the Turtle, and the Bear, of the Hurons. No man was allowed to marry in his own clan, or a woman who had the same "Totem," or clan-name, as his own; and according to Loskiel, the division into clans originated in the intention to prevent the possibility of marriages among blood-relations. These institutions were not peculiar to the southern tribes, as they prevailed extensively among the Lenápe, and among the Sioux, a great family of nations to the westward of the Mississippi.

Physical Characters.

The following account of the Cherokee and Muskhogee, or, as he terms them, Muscogulges, is from Mr. Bartram's travels in America. "The males of the Cherokees, Muscogulges, Seminoles, Chicasaws, Choctaws, and confederate tribes of the Creeks," says Bartram, "are tall, erect, and moderately robust; their limbs well-shaped, so as generally to form a perfect human figure; their features regular, and countenance open, dignified, and placid; yet the forehead and brow, so formed, will strike you instantly with heroism and bravery; the eye, though rather small, yet active and full of fire, the iris always black, and the nose commonly inclining to the aquiline. Their countenance and actions exhibit an air of magnanimity, superiority, and independence. Their complexion is of a reddish brown, or copper colour, their hair long, lank, coarse, and black as a raven, and reflecting the like lustre at different exposures to the light. The women of the Cherokees are tall, slender, erect, and of delicate frame; their features formed with perfect symmetry; the countenance cheerful and friendly; and they move with a becoming grace and dignity.

"The Muscogulge women, though remarkably short of stature, are well formed; the visage round; features regular and beautiful; the brow high and arched; the eye large, black, and languishing, expressive of modesty, diffidence, and bashfulness; they are, perhaps, the smallest race of women yet known, seldom above five feet high, and I believe that the greater number never arrive to that stature; their hands and feet not larger than those of Europeans of nine and ten years of age; yet the men are of gigantic stature, a full size larger than Europeans; many of them above, and few under, six feet, or five feet eight or ten inches. Their complexion is much darker than any of the tribes to the north of them that I have seen. This description will, I believe, comprehend the Muscogulges, their confederates, the Choctaws and the Chicasaws, excepting, however, some bands of the Seminoles, Uchees, and Savannaws, who are rather taller and slenderer, and their complexion brighter.

"The Cherokees are yet taller and more robust than the Muscogulges, and by far the largest race of men I have seen; their complexion brighter and somewhat of an olive cast, especially the adults; and some of their young women are nearly as fair and blooming as European women."

Mr. Catlin has given a very interesting account of the settlement of the Cherokees and Muskhogees in Louisiana, whither they have been removed by treaty with the United States government. He says, "They occupy a country in the states of Mississippi and Alabama; but by a similar arrangement, and for a similar purpose, with the government, have exchanged their possessions there for a country adjoining to the Cherokees, on the south side of the Arkansas, to which they have already removed, and on which, like the Cherokees, they are laying out fine farms,

Tuch-ee,
a Cherokee War Chief.

London, H. Baillière, 1843.

and building good houses, in which they live, in many instances surrounded by immense fields of corn and wheat. There is scarcely a finer country on earth than that now owned by the Creeks; and, in North America, certainly no Indian tribe is more advanced in the arts and agriculture than they are. It is no uncommon thing to see a Creek with twenty or thirty slaves at work on his plantation."*

The annexed coloured Plate of Tuch-ee, a Cherokee warrior, from an original painting by Mr. Catlin, affords a specimen of the race, and is interesting as the portrait of a very remarkable person. He was the leader of a colony of his kindred into the remote interior of America. An account of him will be seen in page 121 of the second volume of Mr. Catlin's work.

---

* The country appropriated to the Indians beyond the Mississippi is said to be fertile and healthy. About 100,000 persons now dwell within it, principally Cherokees, Choctaws, Chickasas, and Muskhogees, all pretty nearly equal in point of civilisation; there are also remnants of fourteen other tribes within the territory, the chief of whom are the Senecas, Shawnees, Delawares, and Kikapoos. They are apparently advancing, and if not checked by a nation boasting higher principles, they will continue to do so. But the danger which menaces them on the part of the United States government is candidly stated by Schoolcraft, a not unpatriotic American, who views with much apprehension the course of emigration to the Gold Regions precisely through the Indian territory. He says, "Whether this new tide of emigration be successful or unsuccessful, will those who compose it spare to trample on the red man? will they suddenly become kind to him to whom they have been unkind? will they cease to desire the lands which their children want? will they consent to see the nation separated by an Indian State? will they award honours—nay justice, to that State? Twenty years will answer that question" ("American Indians," p. 389). It is to be feared that the words of the Forty-third Annual Report of the American Board of Missions (1852), speaking of the last removal of the Cherokees, may give the only answer:—"The ancient and cherished fatherland of this interesting people was wanted for another race. They made their appeal to natural right, to solemn treaties and international law; but it was all in vain. An iron purpose demanded their removal, and go they must" (quoted from the "Church Missionary Intelligencer" for March, 1854).—Ed.

Tribes between the Mobile River and the Mississippi, and thence to the Red River.

A number of small tribes formerly inhabited the country between the Mobile and the Mississippi.

The Chitimachas were a distinct tribe, who, according to their own traditions, had come from the west; they are now reduced to 300 souls, and live incorporated with the Creeks, but preserve their language. In the third and following plates of this volume, facing page 111, there is an engraving of a skull of a Chitimacha chief, brought from a tumulus near the Mississippi by Dr. Daubeny, to whose kindness I am indebted for it. It bears, as may be seen, a striking resemblance to a Chinese cranium, represented in the same plate. The Chinese face is somewhat flatter, but the difference is trifling.

The most complete account of the small tribes still existing to the westward of the Mississippi, and thence to the Red River, has been drawn out, as Mr. Gallatin says, by Dr. Sibley, of Natchitoches; they consist of tribes who have crossed the Mississippi within memory, and of others considered as native. The first class embraces the Appalaches, the Alabamas, and many others; the second, the Caddoes and other tribes less celebrated. It is remarked of the Caddoes, that they formerly lived 300 miles up the Red River, on a prairie near an eminence, on which they say, that after all the world had been drowned in a flood, the Good Spirit placed one family of Caddoes, from which all the Indians have originated.

CHAPTER XXVIII.

OF THE NATIVE AMERICAN RACES TO THE WESTWARD OF THE MISSISSIPPI.

1. *Of the Sioux and Pawnees.*

THE Sioux, and the tribes belonging to the same stock, are one of the most widely extended families of nations among the aboriginal races of North America. The history of this people is interesting in many points of view, and particularly on account of the physical varieties displayed in some of their tribes. The whole family of the Sioux is divided by Mr. Gallatin into four departments, or separate stems. These are—1. The Winibagoes; 2. The Sioux proper, or Dahcotas, and the Assiniboins; 3. The Minetari and tribes allied to them; 4. The Osages, and other kindred tribes in Southern Louisiana.

1. The Winibagoes, known by that name among the English, who derived it from the Algonquins, are the Puants of the French: among themselves they are called *Hochungorah*, or the Trout Nation. Their abode is on the the Fox river of Lake Michigan, and thence northward to the Winconsin. They are about 4600 souls.

2. The Sioux proper, or Naudowesies, who call themselves Dahcota, and sometimes the "Seven Fires,"* are divided into seven tribes. They occupy extensive tracts on the Upper Mississippi, and on St. Peter's river; and some extending as far to the westward as the Missouri. The four most eastern tribes of the Dahcotas are called "Gens du Lac," and "People of the Leaves." The first of these cultivate the land in a country eastward of the Mississippi, extending from the Prairie du Chien to the Spirit Lake, a tract extending through three degrees of north latitude,

* This appellation is "ocheti shakowing," the seven council fires: these are named in the introduction to the Dahcota Dictionary, mentioned in the note on page 541:—1. Mdewakang, village of the Holy Lake, 2000 in number; 2. Wahpekute, leaf shooters, 500 to 600; 3. Wahpetongwang, village in the leaves, 1000 to 1200; 4. Sibitongwang, village in the marsh, 2500; these four eastern bands are called by the Missouri Dahcotas, Isangti, as a general name: 5. Ihanktongwangna, 4000, subdivided into four branches; 6. Ihanktongwang, 2400, both terms meaning End village; 7. Titongwang, Prairie village, 12,500, subdivided into eleven branches. The usual names for five of those bands are given in the text. The detached Sioux of Red River, known as the Assiniboins or Stone Indians, are said to have sprung from the Wazikute, one of the subdivisions of the Ihanktongwangna, or Yanktoana: the Dahcotas call them Hohe.—ED.

viz. from 43° to 46°. The western tribes are the Yanktons, Yanktoanas, and the Tetons. It is believed that the whole Sioux nation amounts to about 20,000 souls. The Assiniboins, or Stone Indians, are a detached body of the Sioux who live on the Red River of Lake Winnipeg. The Shyennes have also been taken for Sioux; but it is reported that they have a peculiar language.*

The Sioux are a people of singular and interesting character, and they preserve the original habits of the North American aborigines much more than the eastern races. Carver, who travelled in their country 100 years ago, drew a lively picture of their manners. The missionary Heckewelder supposed their language to be distantly allied to the Iroquois; but in this he is not supported by later writers. "The Dahcotas," says Professor Keating, who travelled in their country some years since, "are a large and powerful nation of Indians, and distinct in their manners, language, habits, and opinions from the Chippeways, Sauks, Foxes, and Nahiawah, or Kilisteno, as well as from all other nations of the Algonquin stock. They are likewise unlike the Pawnees and the Minitaris, or Gros Ventres." Major Pike says, "Their guttural pronunciation, high cheek-bones, thin visages, and distinct manners, together with their own traditions, supported by the testimony of neighbouring nations, put it, in my mind, beyond the shadow of a doubt that they have emigrated from the north-west point of America, to which they had come across the narrow straits which in that quarter divide the two continents, and are absolutely descendants of a Tartar tribe." Pike, however, must have been mistaken in one respect; for we are assured by Professor Keating that the Dahcotas have no tradition of ever having emigrated from any other place: they believe that they were

* The Shyenne vocabulary, communicated by Lieut. J. W. Abert, shows that they are Algonquins; which was also stated by Dr. Latham at the meeting of the British Association held at Oxford in 1847, from a comparison of the numerals. See his "Varieties of Man," p. 331.—Ed.

created by the Supreme Being upon the lands which they at present occupy.*

3. The third branch of this family of nations are the Minetari; their language is of the same stock, though remotely connected with the Dahcota.

Among the Minetari nation are included three tribes,— the Mandans, a small tribe, the stationary Minetari, and the tribe called Crow Indians. The proof that these three are of one kindred, and that allied to the race of Sioux, is to be found in the affinity of their languages, of which full evidence has been adduced by Mr. Gallatin. The moral and physical history of these several tribes presents some most curious traits. The Mandans, being of lighter complexion than their neighbours, are supposed by many to have given rise to the story of Welsh Indians in North America. They have among them a singular tradition as to their origin: they say that they came from under ground by means of a great vine, which, breaking under the weight of some of them, has left behind a part of their nation, whom they expect to join after death. Of the Mandans and Minetaris, we have some striking and remarkable details in the graphic description of Mr. Catlin.

4. The fourth division of the Sioux race comprehends several nations spread through the southern parts of the great Missourian valley, and inhabiting the banks of rivers which flow into its channel. They are the Osages, or Wausashe, on the river Osage, the Kansas, the Ioways, the Missouris, the Ottoes, the Omahaws, or Mahaws, and the Puncas. The affinity of these nations to the Sioux

* There is a good and extensive grammar and dictionary of the Dahcota language edited by the Rev. S. R. Riggs, and printed at Washington in 1852. It constitutes the 4th volume of the Smithsonian "Contributions to Knowledge." It contains a catalogue of printed books in this language, mostly portions of Scripture, catechisms, hymns, and religious tracts. The Book of Genesis, and almost all the New Testament, is included among these publications. The learned Conon von der Gabelentz also published a small Dahcota Grammar at Leipzig in 1852.—ED.

has long been known.* The Osages consider themselves as indigenous; but the tradition of the last five tribes is that they came from the north together with the Sioux Winibagoes, who remained near Lake Michigan, while they proceeded further south.

The Pawnees, of whom there are two nations, the Pawnees proper and the Ricaras, or Black Pawnees, settled at the ground on the river Platte, to the westward of the Ottoes. They have a distinct language from all others in America; unless, as Mr. Gallatin observes, it should be found that the Panis of the Red River have a kindred dialect.

Of the Physical and Moral Character of the Sioux and other Nations on the Missouri.

We are informed by Mr. Gallatin that the only agricultural tribes to the westward of the Mississippi are the Sauks and Foxes of the Algonquin race, to the northward of the Red River the Pawnees, and among the nations of the Sioux family, only those which belong to the southern group, besides the Mandans and the Stationary Minetaris. "The six western tribes of the Dahcotas, the Assiniboins, the Crows, and all the other tribes not yet enumerated, whether east or west of the Rocky Mountains, cultivate nothing whatever, and those east of the Rocky Mountains subsist principally on the meat of the buffalo. But whether erratic or agricultural, there is a marked difference between the habits and character of all the Indians who dwell amidst the dense forest which extends from the Atlantic to the Mississippi, and those of the inhabitants of the western prairie. These are every where less ferocious than those on the eastern side of the Mississippi. Like all savages, they put to death the prisoners taken in battle; but the horrid practice of inflicting on them the most excruciating torture for days together, does not appear to have prevailed any where beyond the Missis-

* Pike's "Exploratory Travels," p. 172.

sippi. These observations seem, however, to apply more forcibly to the southern cultivating tribes of the Sioux family and to the Pawnees. Dr. Say, during his residence among the Omahaws, collected some important facts, which are equally applicable to their neighbours on the south of the Missouri, of either of those two families.

"They reside in their villages at most five months of the year, principally for the purpose of planting, cultivating, and gathering maize, and few other vegetables. Two winter months are employed by the men in hunting beaver and other fur animals. During the rest of the year the whole population remove to the buffalo-grounds, subsist on its meat, and preserve a portion of it.

"They address prayers to *Wahconda*, the Creator and Preserver of the world, to whom they ascribe infinite power and omnipresence. But, although they believe in a future life, it cannot be said that this vague belief has any important influence over their conduct. Like all the other Indians, they put more faith in their dreams, omens, and jugglers, in the power of imaginary deities of their own creation, and of those consecrated relics to which the Canadians have given the singular appellation of *medicine*."

The Missouri Indians of the male sex exceed in height the ordinary average of the Europeans; but the women are in proportion shorter and thicker. The average facial angle is 78°, that of the Cherokees being 75°; the transverse line of direction of the eyes is rectilinear; the nose aquiline; the lips thicker than those of the Europeans; the cheekbones prominent, but not angular. The recently born infants are of a reddish brown colour, which after a while becomes whiter, and then gradually assumes that tint, which is not perfectly uniform amongst all the Indians, and which, for want of a better approximation, we call copper-colour. They designate that of the Europeans by words which mean *white* or *pale*. Theirs is not the effect of exposure, as all parts of the body present the same appearance. The women marry very young, bear children from the age of thirteen to forty, and have generally from four to six.

The Mandans are a branch of the same stock as the Dahcotas; but there is much difference between these nations with respect to their physical characters. The following is Mr. Catlin's account of the last-mentioned tribe of the Sioux family of nations, whom he takes for the descendants of Prince Madoc's Welsh Army. The account of their physical characters is very remarkable. They differ considerably from those of the Sioux and other tribes of the same race, and display some of the most singular variations of colour that are to be found among the American nations. Mr. Catlin says, "In the Mandan village a stranger is struck at once by the different shades of complexion and various colours of hair which he sees around about him, and is at once almost disposed to exclaim, 'that these are not Indians.'

"There are a great many of these people whose complexions appear as light as half-breeds; and amongst the women particularly there are many whose skins are almost white, with the most pleasing symmetry and proportion of features; with hazel, with grey, and with blue eyes; with mildness and sweetness of expression, and excessive modesty of demeanour,, which render them exceedingly pleasing and beautiful.

"Why this diversity of complexion I cannot tell, nor can they themselves account for it; their traditions, so far as I have learned them, afford us no information of their having had any knowledge of white men before the visit of Lewis and Clarke, made to their village thirty-three years ago. Since that time there have been but very few visits from white men to this place, and surely not enough to have changed the complexions and customs of a nation. And I recollect perfectly well that Governor Clarke told me, before I started from this place, that I would find the Mandans a strange people and half white.

"The diversity in the colour of hair is also equally as

Mah-to-toh-pa
(the four Bears)
2nd Chief of the Mandans

great as that in the complexion; for in the numerous group of these people (and more particularly amongst the females, who never take pains to change its natural colour, as the men often do), there may be seen every shade and colour of hair that can be seen in our own country, with the exception of red or auburn, which is not to be found.

"And there is yet one more strange and unaccountable peculiarity, which can probably be seen nowhere else on earth; nor on any national grounds accounted for, other than it is a freak or order of nature, for which she has not seen fit to assign a reason. There are very many, of both sexes, and of every age, from infancy to manhood and old age, with hair of a bright silvery grey; and in some instances almost perfectly white.

"This singular and eccentric appearance is much oftener seen among the women than it is with the men; for many of the latter who have it seem ashamed of it, and artfully conceal it by filling their hair with glue and black and red earth. The women, on the other hand, seem proud of it, and display it often in an almost incredible profusion, which spreads over their shoulders and falls as low as the knee. I have ascertained, on a careful inquiry, that about one in ten or twelve of the whole tribe are what the French call "*cheveux gris*," or "grey hairs;" and that this strange and unaccountable phenomenon is not the result of disease or habit, but that it is unquestionably an hereditary character which runs in families, and indicates no inequality in disposition or intellect. And by passing this hair through my hands, as I often have, I have found it uniformly to be as coarse and harsh as a horse's mane; differing materially from the hair of other colours which, amongst the Mandans, is generally as fine and soft as silk."

As the physical character of the Mandans is so curious and remarkable, I have selected three portraits from Mr. Catlin's collection which represent individuals of this race painted by himself in the Mandan village. Plate 49 is the portrait of Mahtotohpa, or "The Four Bears," who is the second chief of his nation, and the most popular man of the Mandans. Mr. Catlin designates him as a high-minded and gallant warrior, and a polished gentleman.* The two female portraits which follow are Plates 50 and 51 of Mr. Catlin; and the account of the individuals of the Mandan tribe whom they represent is to be found in p. 92. The colour of the hair described as grey is remarkable in one of them; but the complexion is much darker than it really is in very many of the race.

The description of the Minetaris and Crows, two other tribes belonging to the same branch of the Sioux race, is very remarkable, as an instance of variations in the same stock. The Crows are remarkable for the length of their hair, which, in men, sometimes reaches to the ground; they are generally handsome, and well clad. Every man in the nation oils his hair with a profusion of bear's grease. Mr. Catlin says, "The form of the head peculiar to this tribe may well be recorded as a national characteristic, and worthy of further attention, which I shall give it on a future occasion. This striking peculiarity is quite conspicuous in the two portraits of which I have just spoken, exhibiting fairly, as they are both in profile, the *semi-lunar* outline of the face before-mentioned, and which strongly characterises them as distinct from any relationship or resemblance to the Black-feet, Shiennies, Knisteneaux, Mandans, or other tribes now existing in these regions. The peculiar character of which I am speaking, like all other national characteristics, is of course met by many exceptions in the tribe, though the greater part of the men are thus strongly marked with a bold and prominent anti-angular nose, with a clear and rounded arch, and a low and receding forehead, the frontal bone oftentimes appearing to have been compressed by some effort of art, in a certain degree approching to the horrid distortion thus produced among the Flat-Heads

* He is described in vol. i. p. 114, of Mr. Catlin's work.

Mi-neek-ee-sunk-te-ka

The Mink

A Mandan Girl

Sha-kó-ka

Mint

A Mandan Girl

Meach-o-shin-gaw

The Little White Bear. A Konza Warrior

Wah-no-nee-sah.

The Surrender.

An Otoe Chief.

beyond the Rocky Mountains. I learned, however, from repeated inquiries, that no such custom is practised among them; but their heads, such as they are, are the results of a national growth, and therefore may well be offered as the basis of a national *character*."

Mr. Catlin has likewise described the Osages, Konzas, Mahas, and Ottoes, whom he recognised as constituting one nation. The annexed portrait of a Konza warrior, Meach-o-shin-gaw, or "The Little White Bear," Plate 52, was engraved from Mr. Catlin's original painting. The broad and square conformation of countenance is exemplified by the portrait of Wah-ro-nee-sah, or "The Surrounder," an Ottoe warrior, likewise painted by Mr. Catlin. Plate 53.

2. *Tribes on the Sides of the Rocky Mountains: Black-feet.*

In the country lying to the westward of the Minetaris, and between that people and the Rocky Mountains, traversed by the southern branch of the Saskatchawan river, which descends from that chain towards Lake Winnipeg, and by the upper channel of the Missouri and Yellow-Stone rivers, are the buffalo-plains, inhabited by two Indian nations of distinct language, the Black-feet, and the Rapid or Fall Indians. The Black-feet are a very powerful and numerous people; they are estimated at 30,000 souls.*

Mr. Catlin says that the Black-feet are one of the most

* Mr. Gallatin has had the kindness to communicate to me vocabularies of the languages of the Black-feet Indians, of the Crows or Upsarokas, and of the Gros Ventres, or Rapid or Fall Indians, who call themselves Ahnenin. These vocabularies are in manuscript; they were collected since the publication of Mr. Gallatin's work by Mr. Mackenzie, a very intelligent man, who resides at the juncture of the Yellow-Stone and the Missouri rivers, as principal agent of the St. Louis American Fur Company, and who trades principally with these three nations. They appear to belong to three distinct families; but the Crows speak a dialect decidedly cognate to that of the Sedentary Minetaris and Mandans, confirming the opinion of Mr. Gallatin, that this tribe belongs to the great Sioux family.

numerous tribes. They occupy the whole country above the sources of the Missouri, from the mouth of the Yellow-Stone river to the Rocky Mountains. They are fierce and warlike, and carry war amongst their enemies in every part of the Rocky Mountains. The Black-feet proper are divided into four bands, or families, as follows:—The Pa-e-guns of 500 lodges; the Black-foot Band, of 450 lodges; the Blood Band, of 450 lodges; and the Small Rover, of 250 lodges. These four bands, constituting about 2500 lodges, averaging more than ten to the lodge, amount to about 30,000 souls.*

The Shoshonees, or Snake Indians, in the high tracts on both sides of the Cordillera of North America, are in perpetual warfare with the Black-feet, who prevent them from hunting in the buffalo-grounds. They are described by Lewis and Clarke as remarkable for lean and squat bodies and high cheek-bones. [Some of the Shoshonees have horses and fire-arms, and derive their subsistence from the chase and from fish. Others, to the north, have no horses, are armed with bows only, and live on acorns and roots; these the hunters call Diggers, and consider the most miserable of the Indians.]†

Farther southward, on the Arkansas and the Platte, are the Paducas, consisting of several nations, viz. the Ietans, termed by the Spaniards Cumanches,‡ and the Kiawas and

* Gallatin, "Archæologia Americana," p. 133. According to Hale, the numbers and power of these tribes are very much diminished. He says, p. 220, "A few years since, the number and warlike spirit of the Black-foot tribes made them the terror of all the western Indians on both sides of the mountains. They were reckoned at not less than thirty thousand souls, and it was not uncommon to hear of thirty or forty war-parties out at once against the Flathead [Salish], the Upsarokas [or Crows], the Shoshonees, and the Northern Crees. But in the year 1836 the small-pox carried off two-thirds of their whole number, and at present they count not more than fifteen hundred tents, or about ten thousand people. Their enemies are now recovering their spirits, and retaliating upon the weakened tribes the ravages which they formerly committed."—Ed.

† Hale, page 219.

‡ The Cumanches are called in their own language Na-uni; signifying

Utahs, who, according to Pike, speak the language of the Paducas. These three tribes form one nation of considerable extent. The name of Paducas belongs to the whole race; it is the term given them by their neighbours the Pawnees.

Their chief positions are indicated by Pike. The Kiawas wander about the sources of the river Platte; they possess immense herds of horses, and are at war with the Pawnees and Ietans, as well as with the Sioux. The Utahs wander on the sources of the Rio del Norte. The Ietans are a powerful nation, entirely erratic, without any attempt at cultivation, subsisting solely by the chase. Their wanderings are confined to the frontiers of New Mexico on the west, the nations of the lower Red River on the south, the Pawnees and Osages on the east, and the Utahs, Kiawas, and various unknown nations, towards the north. Pike says, "the Utahs and Kyaways reside in the mountains of North America, and the Ietans on the borders of the Upper Red River, Arkansas, and Rio del Norte."*

The Apaches are a nation of Indians who extend from the Black Mountains of New Mexico to the borders of Cogquilla, keeping the frontiers of three provinces in a continual state of alarm. They formerly extended from the entrance of the Rio Grande to the Gulf of California. The Nanahaws are situated to the north-west of Santa Fé; they are supposed to be 2000 warriors strong. "This nation," adds Pike, "as well as all the others to the west of them, bordering on California, speak the languages of the Apaches and Lee Panis, who are in a line with them to the Atlantic."

From the name of this last nation, Lee Panis, Vater conjectures them to be related to the Pawnees; but this does not appear to have been Pike's opinion.

"live people." Schoolcraft says their language is cognate with that of the Shoshoni group. See Indian Tribes, vol. ii. p. 126 and 134.

* "Exploratory Travels," pp. 214 and 194.

The natives of the high regions on the sides of the Rocky Mountains, like the people of elevated countries in the Old Continent, have a lighter complexion than those of the low plains. Mr. James declares that the Kiawa and Kaskaia Indians have often, during early youth, hair of a much lighter colour than that of the nations on the Missouri. He says, "A young man, of perhaps fifteen years of age, who visited us to-day, had hair decidedly of a flaxen hue, with a tint of dusky yellow."*

It appears that a deviation of a similar kind from the more common complexion of the American nations, exists in the race of the Apaches, who have been mentioned in the last chapter as occupying the mountainous regions of Northern and New Mexico. To this kindred belong the Lee Panis, who, according to Pike, roved from the Rio Grande to some distance into the province of Texas. "Their former residence," he says, "was in the Rio Grande, on the sea shore." The mountainous region approaches near to the coast. "The Lee Panis," adds the same traveller, "are divided into three bands; they have *fair hair*, and are generally handsome; they are armed with bows, arrows, and lances."

In the northern districts of the great chain of Rocky Mountains which were visited by Sir Alexander Mackenzie, there are several nations of unknown language and origin. The Atnah† nation is one of them. Their dialect appears, from the short vocabulary given by that traveller, to be one of those languages which, in the frequent recurrence of peculiar consonants, bears a certain resemblance to the Mexican. Some of the tribes which were found on the heights, and on the western borders of the great mountain-chain, recede considerably in their physical character from the general traits of the North American aborigines. A

---

* Keating, vol. iii. p. 47.

† This tribe must not be confounded with the Shushwaps, to whom the name of Atnah is given by their northern neighbours, the Tahkali. The Shushwaps belong to the next chapter.—ED.

people, whom Mackenzie terms Rocky Mountains Indians, are said to have a complexion of a swarthy yellow. The natives of Friendly Village to the westward have round faces, with round cheek-bones, and a complexion between the olive and copper colour. They have small *grey eyes* with a *tinge of red* and *hair* of a *dark brown colour* inclining to black. They are a distinct people. Another tribe nearer to the mountains is described in similar terms. "The colour of their hair is *grey*, with a tinge of red; they have all high cheek-bones, more remarkably the women." There are considerable deviations from the supposed uniformity in the physical characters of the American aborigines. The varieties of colour tending towards a lighter tint in the hair, eyes, and skin, in the elevated region, are phenomena similar to those which appear in other divisions of mankind. The hair is brown in these nations.

CHAPTER XXIX.

OF THE NATIVE AMERICAN RACES ON THE COAST OF THE PACIFIC OCEAN. 1. BLACK TRIBES OF CALIFORNIA. 2. TRIBES ON THE COLUMBIA RIVER. 3. WHITE RACE OF THE NORTHERN COAST.

THE American coast which borders on the Pacific, traced from Mexico northwards to the land of the Esquimaux, is divided into two nearly equal parts by the channel of the Columbia river. That river is the only great stream that is known to take its rise in the Rocky Mountains, or Cordillera of North America, and discharges its waters into the Pacific. It flows through the whole western lowland, the region intercepted between the Rocky Mountains and the sea. The breadth of that lower region varies: in the 35° and 40° north latitude, it is supposed to be about 900 miles wide; the inland part of it, lying nearer to the foot of the Rocky Mountains, is separated from the narrow stripe which runs along the coast by a long chain of inferior mountains. These inferior hills appear to take their rise to the northward from the cluster of hills named Mount St. Elias, which may be seen marked on all late maps near the Pacific in latitude 60°. Thence they take their course about 100 miles from the sea, and pass southwards in a line almost parallel to the coast: from these hills all the rivers take their rise which fall into the Pacific between the above limits, with the exception of the Columbia, a greater stream, which comes, as I have said, from the Rocky Mountains. The maritime country, to the westward of the lower chain, is inhabited by people who differ from the tribes in the interior.

In the present chapter I shall briefly survey the natives of the coast from Mount St. Elias southwards, including the Californian nations. They may be divided into three sections: 1. Tribes inhabiting the peninsula, or projecting land, of California, and a part of the coast farther northward termed New California. 2. Tribes on the coast of Nootka Sound, and the adjacent islands, and the shores of the Columbia River, who have lately been designated as the Nootka-Columbian race. 3. Races of the northern coast who reach from Vancouver's Island northward as far as Mount St. Elias, and the countries of the Esquimaux.

1. *Californian Nations, including the Tribes of New California.*

We are assured by a late writer that there are frequently in the Spanish mission of California not less than ten different races of native people, each speaking a peculiar language.* But the most correct accounts we have of this

* Kotzebue's "Voyage to California." Remarks by the naturalist of the Expedition, vol. ii. page 51.—DR. PRICHARD.

It would appear from the observations of Hale (p. 223), that this coast exceeds the Caucasus in the number of its languages. "It is a remarkable fact," he says, "that while the interior of the country west of the Rocky Mountains is occupied by a few extensive families, the whole coast, from the neighbourhood of Behring's Straits to Cape St. Lucas, is lined with a

country, drawn from the information of missionaries who have resided among the natives, reduce their languages to four, and ultimately to three, which are the mother tongues of all the remainder.* These are the Cochimi, Pericu, and Loretto languages; the former is the same as the Laymon, for the Laymones are the northern Cochimies; the Loretto has two dialects, that of the Guaycuru and the Uchiti; the three nations and languages are nearly equal in extent in California. A long list of barbarous names, the designations of peculiar tribes, may be found in the histories of this country, which it would be useless to extract.

The climate of California is hot and dry to an excessive degree: the earth is barren, abounding in rocky and sandy districts, and deficient in water. The circumstances of the climate are, in short, in every respect, opposite to those of the north-western tracts, which abound in hills, covered with snow and with verdant forests. It was long ago well known that the Californians are of much deeper hue than the natives of America in general. La Pérouse compares them to the Negroes in the West Indies.† He says, "The colour of these Indians, which is the same as that of Negroes, a variety of circumstances, and, indeed, every thing that we observed, presented the appearance of a plantation in the island of St. Domingo." In another passage the same writer expresses himself more positively and minutely. He says, "The complexion of the Californians very nearly resembles that of those Negroes whose hair is not woolly: the hair of this nation is long

---

multitude of small tribes, speaking distinct idioms. A few of these...... are allied to the families of the interior, but the greater number are entirely unconnected with these and with one another. In Oregon.... the variety of idioms has been found to be much greater than was anticipated; probably no other part of the world offers an example of so many tribes with distinct languages, crowded together within a space so limited."—Ed.

* "A National and Civil History of California," by Father Miguel Venegas. Translated. London, 1759. Vol. I. — Also Mithridates, part iv. p. 183.

† "Voyage de La Pérouse autour de Monde."

and very strong, and they cut it four or five inches from the root." (Plate 54.)

M. Rollin, a naturalist and an able writer, who accompanied La Pérouse, says, "that the Californians have little resemblance to the natives of Chili; they are taller, and their muscles are more strongly marked; but they are not so courageous or intelligent. They have low foreheads, black and thick eye-brows, black and hollow eyes, a short nose depressed at the root, and projecting cheek-bones; they have rather large mouths, thick lips, strong and fine teeth, and a chin and ears of the common form. They are very indolent, incurious, and almost stupid. In walking they turn in their toes, and their step is tottering and infirm." The Californians have their chins more covered with hair than the Chilians.

It seems, from this description, that colour is not the only circumstance in which the Californians make an approximation to the characters of person prevalent in some other tropical countries; as among the Negroes of Guinea, New Guinea, and the New Hebrides. The shape of their heads and features may be compared with those of the nations last mentioned. [A similar account is given in the narrative of the American Exploring Expedition. "The natives of this class are chiefly distinguished by their dark colour. Those of Northern or Upper California are a shade browner than the Oregon Indians, while some tribes in the peninsula are said to be nearly black. In other respects they have the physiognomy of their race,—broad faces, a low forehead, and long, coarse hair. They are the lowest in intellect of all the North American tribes, approaching to the stupidity (?) of the Australians. They are dull, indolent, phlegmatic, timid, and of a gentle submissive temper."—Vol. vi. p. 199].

To the northward of California the coast is termed New California. In the countries here claimed of old by the Spaniards, the indigenous inhabitants are little known. M. Choris has given some representations and portraits of

Natives of California

PLATE IV.

Hunters of Bay San Francisco

the natives of Port San Francisco within this region. They appear to be a fine race of people, and to resemble in their complexion, which is very dark, the proper Californians. The portraits of Californians engraved for this work, as well as the figures of natives of Port San Francisco, are taken from Choris's "Voyage Pittoresque." (Plate 55.)

[The personal narrative of Mr. J. R. Bartlett,* who conducted the United States and Mexican Boundary Commission a few years ago, contains incidental notices of several of these Californian tribes, which have hitherto been described chiefly from the accounts, evidently exaggerated, brought by chance travellers on their way to the Gold-diggings. The industrious habits of these tribes, their agriculture, their domestic manufactures, their fixed habitations congregated in villages of considerable size, together with their courage, pleasing manners, and intelligence, all concur to make them the most interesting of the aboriginal populations of America. Their social condition appears to be not much unlike that of the Mexicans at the epoch of the Spanish conquest; certainly not so high in its actual degree, but of a similar kind. The remains of large well-built stone edifices, called locally Casas Grandes, well-defined traces of canals for irrigation, and immense remains of very fine old pottery, show that the people have suffered a declension from a higher position in civilization, such as probably will always accompany a state of separation from the masses of humanity who constitute the civilised world; and, in the case under consideration, the inroads of surrounding tribes of more warlike character and far inferior cultivation must have tended to the same melancholy result; and this is a cause of deterioration still visibly

* Personal Narrative of Explorations and Incidents in Texas, New Mexico, California, Sonora, and Chihuahua, connected with the United States and Mexican Boundary Commission during the years 1850, 51, 52, and 53. By John Russell Bartlett, United States Commissioner during that period. 2 vols. 8vo. New York, 1854.

in operation, and unhappily not likely to be diminished by the now constant access of an European and American population, confessedly hostile to the aborigines everywhere. The locality of these semi-civilised tribes may be roughly stated as extending from 27° to 37° of North latitude, in a line running SE. to NW., including the province of Sonora on the eastern shore of the Gulf of California, the valleys of the Colorado and Gila rivers which fall into the Gulf in a united stream, and the country between the Colorado and the Pacific. The Pimos and the Coco-Maricopas,* who live together on the Gila, with whom Mr. Bartlett was in constant intercourse for nearly a fortnight,—two tribes so like each other that he was for some time unable to distinguish between them,—may be described here as typical of the whole family.† The languages of these united tribes, to which we shall add brief notices of the most important of the others, are different, that of the Pimos being soft and melodious, while the Coco-Maricopa is harsh and guttural: the only other distinction is, that the Pimos bury their dead, while the Coco-Maricopas burn theirs. The tribes live together without any division between their villages. Mr. Bartlett believes that the civilisation of the Coco-Maricopas is derived from that of the Pimos, following in this the observations of Major Emory (p. 132), who compared their condition with what it was when seen by his guide, Carson, in 1826.

The Pimos and Coco-Maricopas are of clear-brown complexion, different from the red-skins east of the Rocky Mountains, and from the olive colour of the South Californians. The women have good figures, full chests, and finely formed limbs; owing, in a great measure, to their erect carriage under the burdens they are in the habit of

* The "Notes of a Military Reconnaissance from Fort Leavenworth in Missouri, to Van Diego in California," &c., by Major W. H. Emory, printed at Washington in 1848, contains some good incidental notices of the Pimos and Coco-Maricopas.

† Collected from Chapters 30, 31, and 32 of his Personal Narrative.

conveying on their heads: many of them are models of beauty. The men have small and slender limbs, and are physically quite inferior to the tribes between the Mississippi and the Rocky Mountains; "readily accounted for by their different modes of life." The dress of both sexes is chiefly a sort of blanket or cloth, which the women wrap round their loins, letting it fall to the knees, while with the men it is the mere body-cloth common to many of the aboriginal tribes. The women sometimes fasten their cloth with a belt, which is manufactured by themselves in handsome patterns, consisting of a variety of figures in brilliant red, blue, and buff wools on a white ground, like the ancient pottery found so extensively over their country, though more commonly they keep it in place by merely tucking in one end. The women wear nothing on the head, nor

FIG. 90.

Pimo Man and Woman.

do they tie up their hair, but let it hang loosely over the back and shoulders as a protection from the sun, merely cutting it over the eyebrows in front. The men have a head-band like the belt just mentioned, which they twine gracefully round the head in several folds, allowing the braided ends to hang down to their shoulders. They have also a woollen cord of different colours, nearly an inch in diameter, which they use as a hair-ornament. Their hair when loose hangs down to their knees, but they usually club it in a large mass on their backs.

Their houses are built of stakes and rushes; they are of a circular form, from fifteen to twenty-five feet in diameter, and from five to seven feet high, so that in some of them a man cannot stand upright: they are in fact used chiefly to sit and sleep in: the doorway is about three feet high; many of them are plastered all over with mud. They have outside a kind of shed, or bower, a mere roof open on all sides, where they pass most of their time. The villages consist of from twenty to fifty houses, surrounded by gardens or cultivated fields, which are intersected by small canals of irrigation, leading water from the Gila: these fields are fenced in with crooked stakes, wattled with prickly brushwood.

FIG. 91.

FIG. 92.

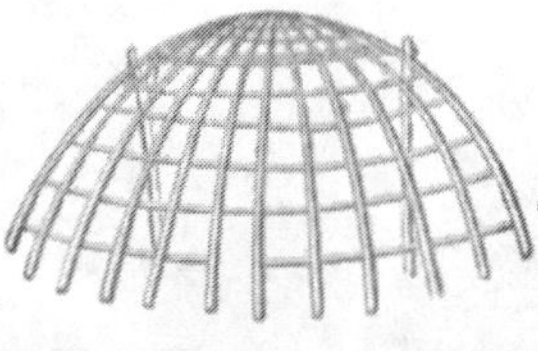

FIG. 93.

They possess considerable numbers of horses and cattle, which are left to graze near the village during the day, and at night are brought into the corrals, or yards, for safety. Some of them have recently obtained a few carts and waggons from passing emigrants, which they use with oxen for agricultural purposes: they occasionally plough with oxen, but more commonly they turn up the ground with hoes. Their agriculture is more systematically pursued than by other tribes; their lands are better irrigated, their crops are larger, and the flour they make from their wheat and maize is quite as good as the Mexicans make, except in their grist-mills, their own means of grinding being limited, by the account of Major Emory (p. 133), to a large stone slightly concave, surmounted by another slightly convex, intended to fit into it; the corn placed between the two is crushed by the pressure of the hand. Similar implements are found among the ancient ruins before mentioned, called the Casas Grandes. The cotton raised by them is excellent; specimens carried home by Mr. Bartlett were pronounced by the merchants to be equal to the best Sea-Island cotton.

The machinery for spinning and weaving their cotton is of a very primitive order. The spinner uses a spindle of thin wood, two feet in length, passing through a block of thicker dimensions, like a child's teetotum, but of larger size, which is twirled round with one end resting in a wooden cup held between the toes of the workman. The supply of cotton is rolled upon the left arm, from which it is drawn out by the left hand, and conducted to the spindle which is twirled round by the right hand. The loom for weaving is still ruder: the threads of the warp are rolled upon two sticks, and stretched on the ground by means of upright stakes; and the alternate threads are lifted by a piece of cane to afford passage to the shuttle, which is nothing more than a pointed stick with the thread wound round it. The action of the reed of our looms is produced by a smooth sharp-edged ruler of hard wood, which is inserted after the passage of each thread, to beat it up close. This is but slow work, but the implement is not much ruder than that with which much of the fine Indian muslin was made by the natives of India at no very distant period. The weaving is generally done by the old men, who sit in the manner of our tailors.

The pottery is all red or dark brown, the latter colour made by a mixture of black and red. The articles manufactured are identical with those made and used by the Mexicans; consisting of vases of different sizes, the largest holding two pailfulls, the smallest half a pint; jars with small mouths, resembling bottles; basins of all shapes and dimensions from a milk-pan to a saucer, and oblong vessels of small size, used as dippers. All these vessels are painted or ornamented with black lines forming geometrical figures, showing much taste, of a character resembling those on the head-bands.

The basket-work is remarkably well made of willow twigs, so closely woven as to hold water; it is ornamented with geometrical figures in the same colours and patterns as the pottery. The baskets are of various sizes and shapes: they are most frequently made of a form like basins, and are carried on the head filled with corn or other articles.

FIG. 94.

The moral character of these races is decidedly good; no tribes of the whole continent excel them in virtue and honesty. Bartlett assures us that, although from the first day of his arrival among them they thronged the American camp day and night, he is not aware that they ever took an article that did not belong to them; and the same testimony is borne by Major Emory (pp. 84, 85). They were perfectly docile and inoffensive in their intercourse with the whites, fond of peace, and disliking war; though they do not hesitate to march against the ferocious Apaches when necessary, fighting with bows and arrows, at the use of which they are remarkably expert, boys of ten or twelve years old hitting a little piece of coin three times out ot five at a distance of fifteen yards. It is a not uncommon contradiction in their character that they delight in torturing their prisoners taken in war, equally with the Apaches.

Their ideas of a Supreme Being and future state are vague; their souls after death are supposed to return to the banks of the Colorado where their ancestors lived, and there to be changed into the forms of various animals; their enemies, the Yumas, will also be found there, and, like the Northmen, they believe that the same wars will be continued between them after death as during life. They marry only one wife, and always with the consent of the lady, whose good graces are romantically sought by means of music, the suitor playing his flute in some retired spot near her hut daily for some hours, until she makes known her assent, or he is wearied out by want of success. The wife is well treated, although she has the greater share of hard work, being employed in the domestic labours of grinding corn and fetching water, besides making baskets and taking care of the children, while the husbands do little more than plant and gather the crops and attend to their cattle, which leaves much idle time on their hands. These labours, especially the carrying of water in vessels on their heads, tend to develope the forms of the women, and add greatly to their general beauty, while the men are slender and less muscular.

The number of the Pimos and Coco-Maricopas is supposed by Emory to be decidedly above 3000; but Bartlett, with better means of information, would hardly place them above 2000.

The Yumas, who are also called Cuchans, live on the Colorado near where the Gila joins it, 200 miles westward of the Pimos; they speak a language intelligible to the Coco-Maricopas, though often engaged in deadly warfare with them. They differ from the people above described by being very much attached to warlike pursuits, though they cultivate maize extensively, and raise some patches of melons and squashes. The journal of Lieut. Whipple, an officer of the Expedition who had much intercourse with the Yumas, describes them as large, muscular, and well-formed, with pleasing and intellectual countenances: he says, "they are exquisite horsemen, and carry their bow and lance with inimitable grace."*

The Opates are the first large tribe to the south, in lat. 30° and long. 110¼ W. They live in villages, are quiet and well-disposed, but also noted for their bravery, being the only tribe who can successfully resist the savage Apaches. Their chief is in the pay of the government, and always ready to fall upon the common enemy; they have been often called out, and on each occasion are said to have performed extraordinary acts of valour, one man successfully contending with eight or ten Apaches. The chief was "full six feet high and well-proportioned, with a light complexion for an Indian; large piercing eyes, prominent and high cheek-bones, and a most determined expression of countenance." "His wife, who always accompanied him, was quite small, with a delicate complexion for an Indian, though strongly marked with the characteristics of her race." The artist of the expedition took their portraits, and Mr. Bartlett obtained a full vocabulary of their language.†

The Yaquis, a little further south, were among the first converts of the Jesuits. They are invariably honest, faithful and industrious, and "fill the same place, and perform the same duties, as the lower class of Irish do in the United States."‡ They wear no dress but a bit of cloth round the loins, while the Opates are now never without "a clean white shirt and pantaloons."

---

* See Lieutenant Whipple's Journal, in Vol. ii. p. 110 of Schoolcraft's "Indian Tribes."

† Bartlett, Vol. i. p. 446.

‡ Ibid. p. 442.

Of the tribes north of the Pimos little has been seen. The Mohavis in lat. 34° "are said to be a fine athletic people, exceedingly warlike, and superior to the other tribes on the river."*

To the N.E. on the Little Colorado, about lat. 35°, are the Zunis, not mentioned by Mr. Bartlett. Major Emory, who calls them Soonees, says, "They cultivate the soil, and live in peace with their more numerous and savage neighbours." He adds that most of them are said to be Albinos; a very curious statement, which it would be worth while to inquire into (p. 99). In another place he says, "They resemble the Pimos, except that they live in houses scooped from the solid rock: many of them are Albinos, which may be in consequence of their cavernous dwellings" (p. 133).

The most civilised of all this aboriginal family would seem to be the Moquis; but we have unfortunately no account of these from an authoritative source. Mr. Bartlett says that they are "one of the semi-civilised tribes with which we have had some intercourse. This people cultivate the soil, raise numbers of sheep, live in large villages, and manufacture a superior blanket both of cotton and wool."† The most detailed notice we have, rests on the authority of the San Francisco Herald, which quotes the account of a Captain Walker, who professes to have passed several days in one of these villages. He places them north-east of the Zunis, midway between the Little Colorado and San Juan rivers. His statement informs us that they live on the top of a table mountain, the sides of which are almost perpendicular, only to be reached by a steep flight of steps cut in the solid rock. Here they have built three large villages, where they sleep; by day they cultivate the arable land at the foot of their mountain, raising all kinds of grain, melons, peaches, and vegetables; and tending their large flocks of sheep and goats. They are kind and

* Bartlett, Vol. ii. p. 178.

† Ibid. p. 178.

hospitable to strangers, but they are timid, and offer no resistance to their warlike neighbours the Navajos, who make periodical incursions on them, sweeping off all their stock. Their houses are built of stone, many of them two and even three stories high, all snug and comfortable. Captain Walker saw three Albinos among them. The rest of his account is very similar to what Mr. Bartlett relates of the Pimos and Coco-Maricopas.*

These statements are illustrated by the accounts of Lieut. J. W. Abert, who, in 1846, visited the so-called Christianised tribes dwelling on the Rio del Norte, the western Rio Puerco, which falls into the Norte about 34° 20′ N. lat., and the San José, which falls into the Rio Puerco. On the upper branches of the San José, about 3° east of the position assigned to the Moquis, he visited the "Indian Cities" seen by Vasquez Coronado in 1541,† named Cibolleta, Moquino, Pojuate, Rito, Covero, Acoma, and Laguna, all Indian towns of 350 to 1000 inhabitants, placed upon lofty terraces with steep sides; the

---

* The statements of Captain Walker are confirmed by Dr. Ten Broeck, a surgeon in the United States Army, who visited the Moquis in 1852; extracts from his Journal are printed in the 4th volume of Schoolcraft's Indian Tribes, which had not reached this country when the above was written. Dr. Ten Broeck speaks in high terms of the moral qualities of these Moquis, who are characterised by him as "a simple, happy, and most hospitable people." He mentions a curious fact, that the people of one of the towns called Harno, "within 150 yards of the middle town," speak a different language among themselves from those of the other towns, all of whom have the same language; "the other Moquis say the inhabitants of this town have a great advantage over them, as they perfectly understand the common language, and none but the people of Harno understand their dialect." (p. 88).

† Coronado visited the interior of this country, with 150 European cows and a large flock of sheep. Schoolcraft is of opinion that the immense flocks now possessed by these tribes derive their origin from these. See the Indian Tribes, Vol. ii. p. 309. See also Gallatin's interesting paper on the "Ancient Semi-civilisation of New Mexico," in the Introduction to the second volume of the "Transactions of the American Ethnological Society," New York, 1848.—ED.

houses comfortable, of two or three stories in height, built of stone plastered with mud, and accessible generally by ladders only, which may be drawn up at will. Lieut. Abert does not usually distinguish his Indians by their tribal names, but calls them simply Pueblo (or village) Indians,—a term used by the Spaniards to designate those of the Aboriginal tribes who have submitted to Spanish rule; but the name of Moquino is suggestive of the Moquis in this case. He has furnished engravings of some of the towns: of Acoma, the largest, three views are given, showing the town itself, and its singular and difficult approaches. Some extracts of his notice of this town and its inhabitants, depicted by him with more minuteness than the others, will afford a good notion of all (see his Report, p. 470, 471). After describing some huge rocky masses with horizontal tops and perpendicular sides, which rise 300 or 400 feet above the plain he was traversing, he says, "High on a lofty rock of sandstone, such as I have described, sits the city of Acoma. On the northern side of the rock the rude boreal blasts have heaped up the sand, so as to form a practicable ascent for some distance; the rest of the way is through solid rock. At one place, a singular opening, or narrow way, is formed between a huge square tower and the perpendicular face of the cliff. Then the road winds round like a spiral stairway, and the Indians have, in some way, fixed logs of wood in the rock, radiating from a vertical axis, like steps; these afford foot-hold to man and beast in clambering up. We were constantly meeting and passing Indians, who had their burros (asses) laden with peaches. At last we reached the top of the rock, which was nearly level, and contains about sixty acres. Here we saw a large church and several continuous blocks of buildings, containing sixty or seventy houses in each block; the wall at the side that faces outwards was unbroken, and had no windows until near the top. The houses were three stories high; in front, each story retreated as it ascended, so as to leave a platform along the whole front of the story; these platforms are guarded by parapet walls about three feet high. In order to gain admittance, you ascend to the second story by means of ladders; the next story is gained by the same means, but to reach the azotea or roof, the partition walls on the platform that separates the quarters of different families have been formed into steps. This makes quite a narrow staircase, as the walls are not more than one foot in width. Lieutenant Peck and myself ascended to the azoteas, and saw there great quantities of peaches, that had been cut in half and spread out to dry in the sun.

"We entered some of the houses, and the people received us with great gladness. . . . . . . Each family occupies those rooms that are situated vertically over each other; the lower story is used as a store-room, in which they put their corn, pumpkins, melons, and other eatables. The fronts of their houses are covered with festoons of bright red peppers, and strings of pumpkins and musk-melons, that have been cut into ropes, and twisted into bunches to dry for winter use.

"These people appeared to be well provided with all the necessaries and luxuries that New Mexico can afford. They are quiet, and seem to be happy and generous. . . . . Whenever we approached, they would cry out to us, 'coma! coma!'—'eat! eat!' and point to the peaches. They generally wear the Navajoe blanket, marked with broad stripes, alternately black and white. Their pantaloons are very wide and bag-like, but are confined at the knees by long woollen stockings, and sometimes buckskin leggins and moccasins. The women stuff their leggins with wool, which makes their ankles look like the legs of an elephant."

The Lieutenant further says that these people scarcely know a word of Spanish, but that they have "a smattering of the Roman Catholic religion." In the plain below, they had "large flocks of sheep, herds of cattle, and droves of horses," and in many places they had dug holes to supply themselves and their cattle with water; and in these holes the water never failed.

It is impossible to read this account without being struck with the resemblance of the "Casas Grandes" to the architecture above described, which extends to the towns on the banks of the Rio del Norte, and even still further East. The analogy also to the Aztec towns, as found in the mountainous districts of Mexico by the Spanish invaders, is obvious, and Lieut. Abert cites the account given by Antonio de Solis of the town of Capistlan [Quiabislan], which he describes as "a town strong by nature, seated on the top of a great rock, difficult of access, the way so steep that the Spaniards could not use their hands for fear of their feet slipping."*

The Navajos are probably to be included among this family, as industrious manufacturers and cultivators; they differ from the other tribes by having no permanent villages, but roaming over the country between the San Juan and the Gila. According to the report of Governor Bent, printed in the first volume of Schoolcraft's "Indian Tribes," p. 243-4, they "raise sufficient grain and fruits of various kinds for their own consumption. They are the owners of large flocks and herds of cattle, sheep, horses, mules, and asses. It is estimated that the tribe possesses 30,000 head of horned cattle, 500,000 head of sheep, and 10,000 head of horses, mules, and asses; it is not a rare instance for one individual to possess 5,000 to 10,000 sheep, and 400 to 500 head of other stock. Their horses and sheep are said to be greatly superior to those reared by the New Mexicans. A large portion of their stock has been acquired by marauding expeditions against the settlements of this territory. They manufacture excellent coarse blankets, and coarse woollen goods for wearing apparel.

"Their numbers are variously estimated at from 1,000 to 2,000 families, or from 7,000 to 14,000 souls. The Nabajos,

* Report of Lieut. J. W. Abert, of his Examination of New Mexico in the years 1846-47. In papers printed by order of Congress in 1848.

so far as I am informed, are the only Indians on the continent, having intercourse with white men, that are increasing in numbers. They have in their possession many prisoners—men, women, and children,—taken from the settlements of this territory, whom they hold and treat as slaves."

Several branches of this interesting aboriginal family have been noticed by Spanish writers, deriving their information from the Jesuits and other Catholic missionaries; but the accounts have not excited much attention, and have in fact been suspected of exaggeration, if not invention.*

Until vocabularies of their languages shall be obtained and carefully examined, it is useless to speculate much on their past history. Missionaries acquainted with the Aztec language have testified to the essential difference between that tongue and the dialects of these tribes,† and would thus seem to separate them entirely from the Mexicans; but the difficulty of estimating the affinities of language is too great to inspire full confidence without much more evidence than we possess; while the similarity of architecture, which is almost as positive a test of affinity of race as language itself, such as we see it exhibited in the Casas Grandes, in the early accounts of the Aztecs handed down by the Spaniards, and in the existing dwellings of the tribes under consideration, induce a strong inclination to believe in an ancient connection between them; possibly, as suggested by Gallatin, a simple importation of superior culture among these races by colonists from Mexico, but more probably, we think, a real affinity of blood. Gallatin compares these races with the Mexicans, points out the inferiority of their arts and sciences, but enumerates many particulars of their social, moral, and even intellectual superiority over the more renowned race; and after adverting to the almost universally afflicting results of his

* Schoolcraft's Indian Tribes, Vol. iii. p. 296, *et seq.*

† Gallatin's Semi-civilisation of New Mexico, before mentioned, p. lxxxv.

inquiries into the state of the aboriginal man of the new world, he concludes with the following words:—"If I have dwelt longer on the history of these people than consisted with the limits of this essay, it is because it has been almost the only refreshing episode in the course of my researches."

2. *Tribes of the North-west Coast and the Columbia River.*

The latest and the most accurate accounts that we have obtained of the native tribes of the north-western coast of America, from the neighbourhood of New California to Mount St. Elias and the country of the Esquimaux Tchugazzi, is from the ethnographical memoir contributed by Professor Scouler to the eleventh volume of the "Journal of the Royal Geographical Society." The author, who has visited the country, has collected extensive vocabularies of the native languages, which furnish him with the principal guide for the distribution of the people into groups; and he has made some important observations on the apparent connection of their natural peculiarities with the physical circumstances under which the several tribes exist. "The people of the north-western coast in general," as he remarks, "exhibit characters and manners which strongly distinguish them from the hunting races who wander over the plains of the Missouri. Westerly winds generally prevail on the shores of the North Pacific, and render the climate extremely moist and mild: hence the winters are mild in comparison with those in other corresponding regions of America." At the mouth of the Columbia river, nearly in the latitude of Quebec, snow seldom lies upon the ground more than a few hours, and the natives go about, even in winter, with very slight clothing. The coasts abound in islands, and are broken up into numerous inlets; the natives obtain their food chiefly by fishing, and are become more settled than the hunting nations. Even the inland tribes of North-west America are less exclusively hunters than those who live near the

Missouri; and many of them, living on rivers and fresh-water lakes, obtain great part of their sustenance from the abundant supply of salmon. "It is at least in part," says Dr. Scouler, "owing to these peculiarities in their physical condition that the habits of the Indians of the opposite sides of the mountains present so remarkable a contrast." The coast tribes have made considerable progress in the rude arts. From their settled life, they are more accustomed to continuous labour, and even show considerable aptitude for passing into the agricultural state.

We shall find that the physical characters, and especially the complexion of these tribes, differ at least as much as their moral qualities from those of the inland nations of America.

The same writer has given some valuable information respecting the tribes of several groups in this region; but his remarks chiefly refer to the insular or maritime races. These are divided by him into two families,—the northern and the southern. I shall compare his account of each with the observations of some former writers.

1. The northern family consists of tribes extending along the shores of the Pacific, from the arctic circle and the settlements of the Esquimaux to the northern extremity of Quadra and Vancouver's Island. This tract includes the tribes in the Russian territory, many of whom have been enumerated by Vater, and more recently by Wrangel, under a variety of names,—Kolushi, Ugalyachmutzi, Kinaitzi. According to the researches of Dr. Scouler, these tribes are all connected more or less by affinity in their dialects, and probably have originally one language. Nearly the same conclusion might be collected from the evidence brought forward by Vater, which he derived from the manuscript grammars and vocabularies of Von Resanoff, made in the Russian settlements. To this race Dr. Scouler refers the Haidah tribes of Queen Charlotte's Island, who cultivate potatoes, which they export in fleets of forty or fifty canoes to the different villages of the Chemesyan

nation, where potato fairs are held. It seems that there is a competition among the different Haidah tribes who shall carry the earliest potatoes to the main-land. All the tribes of this family resemble each other in physical features and intellectual character: they are bold, industrious, and ingenious, when compared with the southern family. One custom is common to the northern tribes, which has already been observed by all the voyagers who have visited this coast: it is that practised by females, of perforating the lower lip, and wearing in it a wooden ornament. On the other hand, the habit of flattening the skulls of infants is peculiar to the southern, or Columbian tribes, and is not known among the northern.

2. The southern tribes are termed, by Dr. Scouler, Nootka-Columbians. They include the various hordes who inhabit Nootka Sound and the lower tracts of the Columbia River, and extend thence southward along the coast. They differ from the northern tribes: they are fatter and more muscular; their cheek-bones are prominent; and their complexion, though light, has more of a copper hue. The limbs of both sexes are ill formed. The practice of flattening the head is universal among the Nootka-Columbians, and prevails along the coast from Salmon River, in latitude 53° 30′ north, to Umqua River, in latitude 46° north. Dr. Scouler has described the process used in this operation, which is performed on the heads of new-born infants. The skulls of these people are quite as flat as the remarkable crania brought by Mr. Pentland from Titicaca. It seems to have no effect on the intellect; but Dr. Scouler informs me that the people by whom it is practised are particularly subject to apoplexy.

To the Nootka-Columbian family belong the tribes known by the names of Chenooks, Flat-head Indians,* Clat-

* The proper name of this tribe is Selish, and in spite of the appellation by which we know them, they do not flatten their heads, as observed by the Author in the following page. Hale, p. 205, says that they scarcely differ from the Shushwaps, their immediate northern neighbours; he con-

sop s, Clamooths, Multnomahs, and many others, as well as the tribe called Wacash, who inhabit the island in Nootka Sound bearing the same designation. The most northern tribe of the Nootka-Columbian family are the Haeeltzuk, who are said to be very dirty in their habits, and of effeminate appearance. The following traits, given by Dr. Scouler from the report of M. Tolmac, may serve as a specimen of the moral history of this race :—

"The Haeeltzuk live at peace among themselves, and are the most northern tribe who flatten the cranium. Their chiefs have but little influence except as conjurers. When the salmon season is past, provisions for the winter having been laid in, the feasting and conjuring begin. The conjurer is called Tzeet-tzaiak. The chief retires to the forest, where he secludes himself, pretending to fast, but is secretly supplied with food by a confidant. While there, he is called Taamish, and is supposed to hold communication with the Nawlok. Unexpectedly he makes his appearance in the village, dressed in a robe of black-hair skin, his head bound with a chaplet and a collar of wrought alder bark, which is of a bright red colour. The women, children, and many of the men, fly at his approach; but some one desirous of distinction boldly awaits and presents his bare arm, and from its outward surface the Taamish bites, and swallows one or more large mouthfuls; and whoever meets him is obliged to submit to this ordeal. The biter acquires renown by being able to seize a huge morsel between his incisors, and to remove it with dexterity without the aid of a knife, and the person bitten, by enduring with fortitude. The Indians are as proud of these scars as a soldier can be of wounds acquired in the defence of his country. I have often inquired the reason of this practice, but could only learn that it is *weinah*, or valuable. With respect to the Nawlok, Wacash, the chief Taamish

siders them as "intermediate between the Chenooks and the Sahaptin [Nez-percés]; their features not so regular nor their skins so clear as those of the latter, while they fall far short of the grossness of the former."—ED.

Kee-ahk-gee-ah

a Shawnee Boy

and most successful biter among the Haeeltzuk, informed me, rather reluctantly, as he did not see them, but only heard their cries, that they lived in the mountains, and were not human beings. During the Tzeet-tzaiak, it was improper to meet or travel for any purpose. The Haeeltzuk are commonly reputed to practise cannibalism; but it is only the Taamish who tastes human flesh, and that in the manner I have mentioned."

The portrait of a Chenook youth (Pl. 56), whose head had never undergone the process of flattening, is taken from a painting by Mr. Catlin. Probably the complexion is darker than that of the race in general: it is much darker and redder than the people of Nootka Sound are said to be. Yet they must be the same race, since the people of the Columbia understood those of Nootka with little difficulty.* Of this fact I have heen assured by Dr. Scouler. From Captain Cook and Mr. Anderson we have the following account of the people of Nootka:—

"The persons of the natives are in general under the common stature, but not slender in proportion, being commonly pretty full or plump, though not muscular: neither are they corpulent, but many of the older people are rather spare or lean. The visage of most of them is rather round and full, and sometimes also broad, with high prominent cheek-bones; and above these, the face is often much depressed, or seems fallen in quite across between the temples; the nose also flattening at its base, with pretty wide nostrils and rounded point. The forehead is rather low: the eyes small, black, and rather languishing than sparkling; the mouth round, with large round thickish lips; the teeth tolerably equal and well set, but not remarkably white. They have either no beards at all, which was most commonly the case, or a small thin one on the

* The portrait of a full-grown warrior, belonging to the tribe called Flat-heads, who, however, do not uniformly observe the custom which once gave them a name, is likewise taken from Mr. Catlin's original paintings.

point of the chin, which does not arise from any want of hair upon that part, but from plucking it out; for some of them, particularly the old men, have not only considerable beards on their chin, but whiskers or mustachios. Their eyebrows are always scanty and always narrow; but the hair of the head is in great abundance, very coarse and strong, and, without a single exception, black, straight, and lank, or hanging down over the shoulders; the neck is short; the arms and body rather clumsy; the limbs in all very small in proportion to other parts, with large feet, badly shaped and projecting ankles. Their colour was difficult to determine, their skins being incrusted with dirt or paint: in particular cases when these were rubbed off, the whiteness of the skin appeared almost equal to that of Europeans, though rather of the pale effete cast which distinguishes those of our northern nations. Their children, whose skins had never been stained, also equalled ours in whiteness. A very remarkable sameness seems to characterise the whole nation; a dull phlegmatic want of expression being common to all of them. The women strongly resemble the men, and have no pretension to beauty" (Plate 57).

One trait which distinguishes these people from the native Americans in general is their fondness for music. They display, as Captain Cook informs us, much skill in the composition of their songs. He says, "Their music is not of that confined sort found among many rude nations; for the variations are very numerous and expressive, and the cadence and melody powerfully soothing."

[Mr. Hale pronounces the natives of the region west of the Rocky Mountains to be "on the whole inferior to those east of that chain. In stature, strength, and activity, they are much below them. Their social organisation is more imperfect; the two classes of chiefs, those who preside in time of peace, and those who direct the operation of war,—the ceremony of initiation for the young men, the distinction of clans or totems,—and the various important

Hco-a-hco-a-hcotes-min

a Flat-head Warrior

festivals which exist among the eastern tribes, are unknown to those of Oregon. Their conceptions on religious subjects are of a lower caste: it is doubtful if they have any idea of a Supreme Being."

Mr. Hale proceeds to give certain doubtful analogies and points of similarity between these races and the Australians, and goes on to give an account of their singular mode of life, which is not either strictly nomadic or sedentary. He says, "They have no fixed habitations, and yet they are not, properly speaking, a wandering people. Nearly every month in the year they change their place of residence,—but the same month of every year finds them regularly in the same place." He accounts for this very properly by the fact that the food of these people being chiefly esculent roots, fruits and berries, and fish, their dwelling-place is necessarily determined by the locality in which these necessaries are to be found. At certain seasons fish are in plenty, and the river banks then become their habitations. The various edible roots on which they subsist grow in very different regions, and come to maturity at different times, and this demands further changes of abode. Added to this, many of their chief men go periodically towards the Rocky Mountains to obtain for their tribes, either by hunting or barter, the buffalo skins which are required for clothing; though this does not usually demand a general move of the whole body.*]

3. *White Race of the Northern Coast.*

The northern family are a race more interesting than the Nootka-Columbians in many respects, but more particularly because they furnish an instance of a white American nation, whose complexion, if we compare these people with the black Californians, would seem to bear a relation to climate similar to that which we trace in the Eastern Continent of the world, when we compare the white Europeans with the black Africans. Dr. Scouler in-

* Exploring Expedition, Vol. vi. page 200.

forms us that these people are as white as the natives of Southern Europe, and some of our voyagers have described them as even of lighter hue. Captain Dixon says, "That the natives of Port Mulgrave are so covered with paint that it is difficult to determine what is their complexion." He adds, "We prevailed on one woman to wash her face and hands, and the alteration in her appearance surprised us: her countenance had all the cheerful glow of an English milk-maid, and the healthy red which flushed her cheek was even beautifully contrasted with the whiteness of her neck: her forehead was so remarkably clear that the translucent veins were seen meandering even in their minutest branches." From Von Langsdorff and M. Rollin, the latter of whom accompanied the unfortunate La Pérouse as medical officer and naturalist, we have a similar account. M. Rollin says, "That their hair is often of a chestnut colour."

The following passage of La Pérouse gives the important information, that these races are not Esquimaux, but allied to the hunting tribes of North America.

La Pérouse says, "My voyages have enabled me to compare various nations, and I am certain that the Indians of Port des Français are not Esquimaux; they have evidently a common origin with the inhabitants of the interior of Canada and the northern parts of America." He adds, "Customs entirely peculiar to themselves, and a very singular countenance, distinguish the Esquimaux from all other Americans." They are a people who delight more in fishing than the chase, and, preferring oil to blood, nay, perhaps to everything else, commonly eat their fish raw. The framing of their canoes is always covered with the skin of the sea-wolf very tightly stretched. Nimble and active in all their movements, they differ little from sea-calves, and wanton in the water with as much agility as if they were amphibious; their face is almost square; their eyes and breast large; their figure short. Of all these characteristics not one agrees with the natives of Port des

Français, who are much larger, meagre, far from robust, and very unskilful in the construction of their boats, which are formed of an excavated tree raised on each side with a single plank.

"In size and figure these Indians differ little from us: their features are greatly varied, and afford no peculiar characteristic, except in the stern expression of their eyes. The colour of their skin is very brown, being constantly exposed to the sun: but their children are born as white as any among us. They have less beard than Europeans, but enough to remove all doubt upon the subject; and the supposition, that the Americans are without beards, is an error that has been too readily adopted. I have seen," he adds, "the aborigines of New England, Canada, Nova Scotia, Hudson's Bay, and have found many individuals among these nations with a beard; whence I conclude that those who are destitute of it have got rid of it by artificial means."

The people of Norfolk Sound are described by Dixon; and from the general outlines of his account, as well as from a vocabulary containing the numerals of their language, it seems that they belong to the same nation as the people of Port des Français. They speak, according to Dixon, a different language from that of Prince William's Sound, the natives of which are, as we have observed, Esquimaux. They have also the same habit of cutting through the under lip in females, and making a second aperture to the mouth, which prevails at Port des Français. This and the other customs of the inhabitants of Norfolk Sound connect them also with the natives of Port Mulgrave: they resemble the latter people in their make, shape, and features, and in language. The natives of Port Mulgrave are thus described by Captain Dixon: "They are in general about the middle size, their limbs straight and well shaped."

I must not terminate this Chapter without adding some remarks on the singular languages of those nations. It is observed by Dr. Scouler that the idioms of the Nootka-

Columbians, though a distinct branch, yet indicate traces of remote connection with the dialects of the northern tribes; and it is probable that both these groups of languages originated from one common stock. What is more interesting are the signs of remote affinity which both display to the Azteca-Mexican,—a fact which recalls the tradition that the Nahuatlacas originated from a region far to the north.* It was observed long ago, by Anderson, that the language of Nootka bears a strong resemblance to the Mexican in the terminations of words, and the frequent recurrence of the same consonants. The same phenomena have fallen under the notice of the Baron von Humboldt, who remarks, that "on a careful comparison of the vocabularies collected at Nootka Sound and at Monterey, he was astonished at the resemblance of the sounds and the terminations of words to those of the Mexican: as, for example, in the language of Nootka, *apquixitl* is *to embrace; temextixitl, to kiss; hitltzitl, to sigh; tzitzimitl, earth; inicoatzimitl,* the name of a month. Yet these languages are, on the whole, to be considered as essentially distinct, as it appears from the comparison of their numerals." To these remarks of Von Humboldt, I shall add the following original observations of Dr. Vater. Having taken notice of one circumstance distinguishing the Nootka language from the Mexican, viz. that *tl* in the latter occurs only as a termination of nouns, whereas, in the Nootka language, it is found in words of all sorts, as, perhaps, chiefly in verbs, he adds, "Yet *agcoatl*, a young woman, in the Nootka dialect may bear a nearer resemblance to *çou-atl*, a wife or woman, generally, in the Mexican. At any rate, that frequent recurrence of the same sounds, which in other languages are comparatively rare, as particularly of the *tl*, is

* Words terminating in ATL abound in the Nootkian language as in the Aztec. *Agcoatl*, a young woman in the Nootkian, resembles *çou-atl*, a wife or woman in the Aztec, as Vater has observed. The Nootkian name for the sun, *Opulsztkl*, is compared by the writer of "Cook's Voyage" with *Vitzliputzli*, the name of the Mexican divinity.

a circumstance of some weight." This phenomenon, however, is not peculiar to the Nootka language, but common to it and to the dialect of the Kolushi, and is even more extensively prevalent. "By means of the specimens of different languages, brought to our knowledge by the Russians in the colonies planted of late on the American coast, it appears that this remarkable termination of words is not only common to the language of the Koluschi, but even in the idiom of the Ugaliachmutzi it is so strikingly frequent, that among the words, amounting to about twelve hundred, collected by Herr von Resanoff, nearly the twelfth part of the whole, but these words of all descriptions, and not merely substantives, have *tl*, or sometimes *tli*, or *tle*, for their termination."

[The three tables following are extracted from Schoolcraft's valuable work,—the first on the Indian Population of the United States, which is necessarily and obviously approximate only; another on the Cranial Admeasurements of the Aborigines; and the third, the Synopsis of Indian Tribes.]

ULTIMATE CONSOLIDATED TABLES OF THE INDIAN POPULATION OF THE UNITED STATES.—(From Vol. i. p. 523.)

Names of Tribes.	Number in Tribe.	Total Population.	Names of Tribes.	Number in Tribe.	Total Population.
TABLE I. — Tribes whose Vital and Industrial Statistics have been taken by Bands and Families, under the direction of the Acts of Congress.			Brought forward..		34,704
			Mexico under the Treaty of Guadalupe Hidalgo.		
			A. Indian Population of Texas	24,100	
A. Iroquois Group.....	5,922		B. Indian Population of New Mexico ...	92,130	
B. Algonquin Group*	17,197		C. Indian Population of California	32,233	
C. Dacota Group* ...	6,570		D. Indian Population of Oregon	22,731	
D. Appalachian Group*	5,015	34,704	E. Indian Population of Utah	11,500	
TABLE II.—Tribes of the New States and Territories South and West, including the Acquisitions from			F. Indian Population of Florida	848	183,042
Carried forward		34,704	Carried forward		217,746

* The census, in these groups, has been carried no farther, but is in progress.

Names of Tribes.	Number in Tribe.	Total Population.
Brought forward....		217,746
TABLE III.—General Schedule of the Tribes located East of the Rocky Mountains and the Line of the Mississippi, in high northern latitudes; all of whom, together with those named in Table No. 2, remain to be enumerated, under the operation of the Indian Census in progress.		
Alabamas. (See Muskogees).*		
Assinaboins, south of lat. 49°	1,000	
Apaches. (See Texas, New Mexico, and Utah.)		
Arapahoes..............	3,500	
Absarokes, or Crows...	4,000	
Aurickarees	1,500	
Blackfeet	13,000	
Blood Indians (few reach the Missouri).	500	
Brothertons	600	
Cherokees	26,000	
Creeks	25,000	
Chickasaws (not enumerated)	5,000	
Choctaws	16,000	
Comanches (See Texas.)		
Cheyennes......	2,500	
Caddoes................	2,000	
Chippewas. (See Algonquin Group.)		
Chippewas, west, and Red River, north...	1,500	
Crees. (None in the United States.)		
Chawas. (See Cheyennes.)		
Cayugas. (See Iroquois Group.)		
Cayugas and Iroquois, west	30	
Dionondadies. (See Wyandotts.)		
Dacotas. (See Sioux.)		
Delawares	1,500	
Eutaws. (See Utahs.)		
Foxes and Sacs........	2,400	
Folles Avoines. (See Menomonies.)		
Florida Indians. (See Table 2.)		
Flatheads (See Oregon.)		
Carried forward......	106,030	217,746

Names of Tribes.	Number in Tribe.	Total Population.
Brought forward.....	106,030	217,746
Gros Ventres	3,000	
Green Bay Indians. (See Menomonies and Oneidas.)		
Iowas. (See Dacota Group.)		
Kiowas	2,000	
Kickapoos	600	
Kanzas	1,600	
Kaskaskias	200	
Menomonies...........	2,500	
Mandans	300	
Minitarees.............	2,500	
Miamies	500	
Missouris	500	
Mohawks. (See Iroquois Group.)		
Munsees	200	
Ottowas. (See Algonquin Group.)		
Ottowas, west...........	300	
Otoes	500	
Omahas	2,000	
Oneidas. (See Iroquois Group.)		
Onondagas. (See Iroquois Group.)		
Ogellahs	1,500	
Pawnees	17,000	
Poncas	700	
Pottawatomies	3,200	
Peorias	150	
Piegans. (See Satsika, Blood, & Blackfeet.)		
Piankeshaws...........	200	
Quappas	400	
Ricarees. (See Aurickarees)		
Shawnees	1,600	
Sioux of the Mississippi (not enumerated in No. 1)................	9,000	
Sioux of the Missouri (not enumerated in No. 1)................	,500	
Satsika. (See Blackfeet, &c.)		
Stockbridges	400	
Senecas. (See Iroquois Group.)		
St. Regis Tribe. (See Iroquois Group)		
Seminoles	1,500	
Senecas and Shawnees. (See Iroquois Group)		
Swan Creek and Black River Chippewas (not enumerated in Algonquin Group)......	200	
Carried forward.....	159,180	217,746

* The Muskogees are not given in the Table: their omission may account for the apparent excess in the total amount.—ED.

Names of Tribes.	Number in Tribe.	Total Population.
Brought forward.....	159,180	217,746
Snakes. (See Table 2)		
Shoshonees. (See Tab. 2)		
Tetans	3,000	
Tonewandas. (See Iroquois Group.)		
Utahs. (See Table 2)		
Wyandots. (See Iroquois Group.)		
Winnebagoes. (See Dacota Group.)		
Weas	250	
Yanktons. (See Sioux of the Missouri.)		167,330
TABLE IV. — Fragmentary Tribes still existing within the Boundaries of the old States.		
MAINE—		
Souriquois of St. Johns..............	300	
Passamaquoddies ...	379	
Penobscots...........	277	
MASSACHUSETTS—		
Marshpee............		
Chippaquadie.........		
Christiantown		
Gay Head		
Assonets of Troy or Fall River		
Herring Pond	847	
Hasanamico		
Punkapog		
Natic		
Dudley		
Grafton		
Yarmouth		
[All mixed with the race but 8 or 10.]		
Carried forward......	1803	385,076
Brought forward.....	1803	385,076
RHODE ISLAND—		
Narragansetts	420	
CONNECTICUT—		
Mohegans at Mohegan	300	
Mohegans at Stonington	50	
Mohegans at Groton	50	
NEW YORK—		
Iroquois. (See Iroquois Group)		
Algonquins (not enumerated in Algonquin Group)	40	
VIRGINIA—		
Nottoways, mixed with the African race	40	
SOUTH CAROLINA—		
Catawbas	200	
NORTH CAROLINA—		
Catawbas	250	
Cherokees. (See Table 1.)		
Total in old States ..	3,153	3,153
Grand Total	....	388,229

There may, in addition to these numbers, be from 25,000 to 35,000 Indians, within the area of the unexplored territories of the United States.

[In the official "Report of the Seventh Census of the United States," recently printed, from which extracts are given in the "Companion to the British Almanack for 1855," we find that the Commissioner of Indian Affairs estimated "the total number of Indians of both sexes and all ages," in the United States, on the 10th November, 1853, at 400,764; who were distributed in the following manner:—

California	100,000
New Mexico	45,000
Texas	29,000
Utah Territory	11,500
Oregon and Washington Territories	23,000
Valley of the Missouri	43,430
Indians of the Plains, or Arkansas Valley	20,000

The remainder, for the most part, in Indian Territory West.

The numbers differ a good deal from those given by Schoolcraft, and it is not easy to understand how the Commissioner reconciles the minute exactness of his grand total with the vague estimates which make it up; but we give it as we find it.—ED.]

CRANIAL ADMEASUREMENTS OF AMERICAN INDIANS.—(From Vol. ii. p. 335.)

	No. of crania measured.	Average facial angle.	Average internal capacity.
OREGONIANS.			
UNALTERED BY ART.			
Chenook	4	79	80
From Columbia river	10	76	80
	14		
Average	...	77½	80
Two lowest in series	...	70	67
		74	72
Two highest in series	...	80	91
		80	95
CRANIA ALTERED BY ART.			
From Oregon and California	15	71½	80
Two lowest in series	...	66	71
		67	72
Two highest in series	...	77	86
		77½	91
SHOSHONEES	4	76½	81
Lowest measurements	...	74	72
Highest „	...	80	91
ALGONQUIN.			
Chippewa	2	78½	91
Cotonay	2	77	95
Illinois	1	82	broken
Lenape	8	77½	74½
Massasauga	1	76	79½
Minsi	1	78	broken
Menomonee	8	75½	84
Miami	3	76	89
Natick	4	76	85
Naumkeag	2	80	79½
Narragansett	9	75	88
Ottigamie	4	81	92
Ottawa	4	72	80½
Pottawatomie	2	78	92
Quinipiac	1	70	78
Sauk	2	82	91
Shawnee	1	78	72
	50		
Average	...	77	83¼
Two lowest in series	...	70	71
		72	72
Two highest in series	...	84	95
		86	102
APPALACHIAN.			
Cherokee	2	75½	87
Choctaw	1	74	79
Euchee	1	75	84
Tlascalan [Astec]	1	75	84
Muskogee	3	74	90
Miccosaukie	1	74	74
Seminole	9	76½	88½
	18		
Average	...	75	88¼
Two lowest in series	...	72	74
		74	79
Two highest in series	...	81	97
		82	97
DACOTA.			
Assineboin	1	79	101
Dacota	1	77	90
Otomie	4	74½	78
Minetari	4	77	86½
Mandan	4	74	80¼
Osage	2	78	87
Oteo	3	74½	86
Pawnee	2	76½	73½
Rickaree	3	80	78
Winnebago	2	79	89
	26		
Average	...	77	85
Two lowest in series	...	70	76
		71	76
Two highest in series	...	80	94
		83	101
IROQUOIS.			
Cayuga	1	78	95
Huron	2	74½	81
Iroquois	2	74	96
Mingo	2	77	80
Mohawk	3	73	84
Oneida	1	74	85
	10		
Average	...	75	88¼
Two lowest in series	...	70	77
		73	80
Two highest in series	...	77	95
		78	102½
SUMMARY.			
Oregonian	14	77½	80
Crania altered by art	15	71½	80
Shoshonees	4	76½	81
Algonquin	50	77	83¼
Appalachian	18	77	83¾
Dacota	26	77	85
Iroquois	10	75	88½
	137		
Average of the whole	...	76⅜	83½

The average of 76⅜ degrees facial angle is taken, excluding the flat heads. The three lowest types being measured separately for illustration, when two at least of them should be united for the common average, makes the average lower than it really is; and as Dr. Morton's average was taken without including so many of these lower types, he not having measured the crania, the common average may be safely fixed at 83½ to 84 cubic inches.

SYNOPSIS OF INDIAN TRIBES.—(From Vol. iii. p. 401.)

A. NORTHERN, EXTENDING FROM THE ATLANTIC TO THE PACIFIC OCEAN.

Families.	Languages.	Languages.
	EAST OF ROCKY MOUNTAINS.	WEST OF ROCKY MOUNTAINS.
I. Eskimaux	1. Greenland. Labrador.*	3. Kotzebue's Sound } Behring's 4. Tshuktchi .... } Straits.
II. Athapascas ...	2. Hudson's Bay. Churchill's river, Hudson's Bay.* Copper Mine river,* &c. 6. Cheppewyans. 7. Sussees.	5. Kadiac Island, N.W. coast America. 8. Tahcali or Carriers (Harmon and Hale). 9. Kenai, Cook's Inlet. 10. Tlascani, near mouth of Columbia (Hale). 11. Umquas, sth. of Columbia (Hale) Loucheux,* mouth Mackenzie River, doubtful.

B. EAST OF THE MISSISSIPPI.

Families.		Languages.
III. Algonkins	Northern...........	12. Sheshatapoosh } Northern side Gulf of 13. Scoffies......... } St. Lawrence. 14. Montagnars, Saguenay to Montreal. 15. Eastern Chippeways (Long). 13. Ojibways. 17. Ottowas. 18. Potawatomies. 19. Knistinaux.†
	Eastern	20. Micmacs, Nova Scotia, New Brunswick. 21. Etchemins, New Brunswick, Maine. 22. Abenakis (Penobscots).
	Central Atlantic ..	23. Massachusetts. 24. Narragansets. 25. Mohicans. 26. Long Island.
	Southern Atlantic	27. Minsi. 28. Delawares. 29. Nanticokes. 30. Powhattans. 31. Pamlicoes.
	Western...........	32. Illinois......... } 33. Miamis ...... } Piankishaws* } 34. Saukies, Foxes, Kickapoos.‡ 35. Shawnees. 36. Menomonies.

* This asterisk denotes the languages of which I have no vocabulary.

† The Western Knistinaux have by conquest extended far beyond the meridian of the Mississippi.

‡ The Saukies and Foxes, though Algonkins, have for a long time been settled west of the Mississippi; and the Winnebagoes, though Sioux, are east of that river. The Dahcotas are partly found also there.

B. EAST OF THE MISSISSIPPI—*continued.*

Families.		Languages.
IV. Iroquois............	Western............	37. Wyandotts, or Hurons.
	Five Nations ...	38. Senecas.
		39. Cayugas.
		40. Onondagoes.
		41. Oneidas.
		42. Mohawks.
	Southern	43. Tuscaroras.
		44. Nottoways.
V. Catawbas............		45. Catawba (Woocons extinct).
VI. Cherokee		46. Cherokee.
VII. Chocta, Muskhog		47. Chocta...... } nearly identical.
		48. Chicasa ... }
		49. Muskhoghee.. } The Creek Confederacy; but the Seminoles, though Muskhogs, had separated.
		50. Hitchittee ...
		Seminoles* ...
		Coosadas* ...
		Alibamous*...
VIII. Utchees		51. Utchee ....
IX. Natches............		52. Natches ......

C. BETWEEN THE MISSISSIPPI AND THE ROCKY MOUNTAINS.

Families.		Languages.
X. Sioux	North..............	53. Winnebagoes,* east of Mississippi.
		54. Dahootas.
		55. Yanktons.
		Tetons.*
		56. Assiniboins.
	South...............	57. Quappas, Arkansas.
		58. Osages, Kansas.
		59. Ottoes, Missouris, Ioways.
		60. Omahas, Puncas.
	West	61. Minetarees (stationary).
		Mandans.*
		62. Upsarokas, or Crows.
		Shyennes (doubtful) [Algonkins—ED.]
XI. Gros Ventres ...		63. Ahnenin.
Algonkins (III.)		64. Black Feet, Paegans Blood Indians.
XII. Pawnees		65. Pawnees.
		Ricaras.*
XIII. Kiaways.........		* } Wander on upper waters of Arkansas.
XIV. Kaskaias.........		*
XV. Cumanches		*
XVI. Pania, Towiacks		*Red River (Tawakeroes), Towekas, Wachos?
XVII. Caddoes		66. Caddo, Red River, (Nandakoes, Tachies, Nabedaches.)
XVIII. Adaize.........		67. Adaize........................ } South of Red River.
XIX. Chetimachas....		68. Chetimachas ....
XX. Attacapas.........		69. Attacapas ....
XXI. Natchitoches ...		Natchitoches, Apelousas*

* This asterisk denotes the languages of which I have no vocabulary.

D. WEST OF THE ROCKY MOUNTAINS.

Families.		Languages.
		OREGON (Hale).
XXII. Jelish	Northern	70. Atnahs, north of 49° N. lat.
		71. Flatheads, part do.
		72. Skitsaih.
		73. Piscous.
	Middle	74. Skwalz (Nasqually).
	Western............	75. Tsihailish (Sea-shore).
		76. Cowelitz.
	Southern	77. Nairtahaus, or Upper Killamuks.
XXIII. Sahaptin......	Upper	78. Nez percés.
	Lower	79. Wallawallas.
XXIV. Wailatpu......		80. Cayuse.
		81. Molele.
XXV. Chinook	Lower	82. Chinooks, Clatsops.
	Upper	83. Watlala.
XXVI. Kalapuya......		84. Willamets.
XXVII. Jakon.........		85. Lower Killamuks.
XXVIII. Luturim....		86. Clamets.
XXIX. Shasti		87. Shasties.
XXX. Pulairih.........		88. Palaiks.
XXXI. Shoshonees ...	Eastern	89. Snakes.
	Middle	Bonnarks.*
	Western...........	90. Wihinasht.
		NORTH OF FUCA'S STRAITS, along Pacific.
XXXII. Kituanaha...		91. Coutaria or Flatbows, north of 49° N. lat.
XXXIII. Ugaliach-mutzi......		*Lat. 60, between Pr. William's Sound and Mount St. Elias (perhaps Athapascas).
XXXIV. Koulischen..		92. Sitka, between 52 and 59 lat.
XXXV. Naass		93. Huitala, between 52 and 55 main.
XXXVI. Skidegatz ...		94. Queen Charlotte Island.
XXXVII. Wakash ...		95. Newittee ...... } Vancouver's Island.
		96. Nootka Sound } Vancouver's Island.
		UPPER CALIFORNIA, 32 to 42° N. lat.
		97. Talatui† } River San Sacramento.
		98. Pujari } River San Sacramento.
		99. Sekumre } River San Sacramento.
		100. Tsamak } River San Sacramento.
		101. San Raphael, near San Francisco.
		102. La Solidad, near Monterey.
		103. San Miguel.
		104. Kii, near San Gabrial.
		105. Netela, near S. Juan Capitouro.

* This asterisk denotes the languages of which I have no vocabulary.

† These nine imperfect Californian vocabularies, collected by Messrs. Hale and Dana, are not yet digested, but will probably be reduced to six families.

CHAPTER XXX.

OF THE SOUTH AMERICAN RACES.—GENERAL REMARKS—CLASSIFICATION.

The different races of people in South America have been supposed to be much more numerous than late observations give us reason to believe them. As their languages have become somewhat better known, the number of distinct families has, as in many instances, been materially reduced; aud we can now refer, without hesitation, to comparatively few groups a great variety of dialects which were long regarded as so many distinct forms of human speech. Still, however, the history of the South American languages is in its infancy. It affords, in many particular examples, the means of tracing affinity between nations widely separated; but we cannot find as yet in South American lexicology satisfactory resources for a classification of the native races of this region into different groups. The only attempt hitherto made with any degree of success to distribute these nations into particular departments is by following a geographical outline, or one furnished by physical phenomena. On this principle, as it has been observed by a well-informed and philosophical writer, who has made the history of the South American nations his particular study, we may divide the whole population of this great peninsula into a few groups severally distinguished from each other by marked varieties in their physical organisation, and at the same time establish the important and interesting fact, that these varieties bear a decided relation to the geographical conditions of the several regions in which they are displayed. We must begin by observing, that there is no division of the world, of which the different parts are more clearly severed and distinguished by reference to their physical circumstances, than the great region of South America.

The whole surface of the continent is estimated by M. d'Orbigny to be equal to more than half of Europe. It reaches from the torrid zone to the frozen regions of Tierra del Fuego. Its geographical structure raises it from the level of the sea to that of perpetual snows; its surface presents the utmost variety in its forms and aspect. Towards the west a vast chain of mountains, rising to the clouds, follows the shores of the Great Ocean, covered with ice and snow. At its northern extremity, this chain under the torrid zone presents the most diversified climates; sterile, dry, and burning, in its abrupt descent towards the west; temperate or cold on its immense table-lands; covered with a luxuriant vegetation on its gently inclined eastern declivity. To the eastward, low hills, hot and wooded, present towards the borders of the Atlantic a remarkable uniformity of aspect, of geological composition, and of outward forms. In the midst of these regions so different, are immense plains; at first cold, arid, and rocky, in the southern parts; then temperate, verdant, and with a boundless horizon towards the Pampas; lastly, of burning heat, and covered with forests under the torrid zone. Such are the features of external nature in the regions we are about to contemplate; we shall observe what influences they exercise on the physical and moral characters of the men who people these different tracts.

M. d'Orbigny divided all the South American tribes into three families of nations, that term denoting what we should express by physical types: these greater departments are subdivided into thirty-nine distinct nations. The following table is necessary for explanation of the author's meaning:—

Groups	Branches.	Names of Nations.
1. ANDIAN GROUP.	*1st Branch,* Peruvian.	Quichua or Inca Aymara Chango Atacama
	2d Branch, Antisian.	Yuracarès Mocéténès Tacana Maropa Apolista
	3d Branch, Araucanian.	Auca or Araucano Fuégian
2. MEDITERRANEAN GROUP.	*1st Branch,* Patagonian or Pampéan.	Patagon or Téhuelche Puelche Charrua. Mbocobi or Toba Mataguayo Abipones Lengua
	2d Branch, Chiquitian.	Samucu Chiquito Saravéca Otuké Curuminaca Covaréca Curavès Tapüs Curucanéca Païconéca Corabéca
	3d Branch, Moxean.	Moxos Chapacura Itonoma Canichana Movima Cayuvara Pacaguava Iténès
3. BRASILIO-GUARANI GROUP.		Caribí Guarani Tupi Botocudo

The following remarks will explain the distribution intended by the preceding Table :—

1. The Alpine nations of South America or tribes of the Andian family.

On the chain of the Andes, on its slopes, and on the shore of the Great Ocean, a powerful monarchy, that of the Incas or Quichuas, held in subjection all the mountain tribes from Chili to Quito, without even reaching down into the eastern plains: yet leaving at its southern extremity in freedom the warlike Araucanos and the fishing tribes in the Tierra del Fuego.

All these nations are brought together in one great department: they are the native races of the South American Cordillera from the southern to the northern extremity. The countries which they inhabit are alike in physical structure, and the races of men bear a decided analogy, though with varieties, in the organisation of their bodies.

2. In the central parts of South America, between the region above described and the following, are the countries belonging to the second group; but this region is also made to include the Southern Pampas; viz. all the level plains which lie to the southward of the Rio de la Plata. The following are the subdivisions of the tribes belonging to the department of nations corresponding to this section of the continent. 1. People of the Pampas, including Patagonians and other nations of the plain and open countries on the Paraguay: these may be termed the Equestrian nations of South America. 2. Forest nations dwelling in the small woody valleys of the Chiquitos under the eastern border of the Andian chain. 3. People of the inundated tracts within the province of Los Moxos, where the rivers of South America stagnate and almost form inland lakes. A collective name for the tribes belonging to these three last divisions is yet wanting; I shall term them the Mediterranean nations of South America.

3. Almost from the foot of the Peruvian Andes east,

regions of comparatively level country extend towards the Atlantic. The immense plains through which the Orinoco and the Maragnon, or river of Amazons, and their great tributary streams, take their course towards the sea, constitute a third region, contrasted in its geographical features with the first. This is the abode of the third group of South American nations; among whom are the most extensively spread races of the New World, the Caraibs, the Tupi, and the Guarani; they are distinguished by the name of Brasilio-Guarani nations.

Some revolutions have taken place in the situation and relative position of these nations since the arrival of the Spaniards, of which we must take notice.

Already, before that era, the Caribbees, or Caraibs, of the northern coast had effected extensive conquests in the interior; but the monarchy of the Incas, in Peru, was the most powerful dynasty in South America. The Incas and the Aymaras, reduced under the yoke of Spain and Christianised, have never changed their abode; the proud Araucanos have withdrawn themselves from the Spanish colonies of Chili, and have passed southward into the Pampas to maintain their independence; the Pesherais have remained on their frozen rocks; the Patagonians in their arid plains; the Puelches have left the banks of the River Plate to dwell in the Pampas of the south; the Charruas have been exterminated from the Banda Oriental and Entre-Rios; the Mbocobis and the Lenguas dwell in their old asylum. The nations belonging to the Chiquitos and the Moxos have submitted to Christianity, and remain upon their ancient soil. The Antisian nations have not changed their abode: a part have embraced Christianity; a part remain savages where the Spaniards found them. Slight changes have taken place in the abodes of the South Americans, and, except in the vicinity of towns, where different tribes are blended into a mixed population, and unless where the love of liberty has caused them to withdraw, South America presents nearly the same distribution of races as at the era of its conquest. The numbers of individuals have principally changed.

Three principal nations among the South American tribes have been celebrated from the extent of their migrations; the others have been nearly fixed. The migratory nations are the Quichua, the Guarani, and the Araucanos; we observe the first departing under Manco-Capac, from the Lake and Plain of Titicaca, proceeding northwards towards Cuzco; thence dispersing themselves, in the spirit of conquest, farther northward to Quito, southward to Chili, following either the uplands of the Andes, or the margin of the sea: the Guarani, coasting along the ocean-border towards the north, their savage and warlike bands advancing to the Antilles under the name of Caribbees, and under the same name ascending the Orinoco and the Amazon, and their tributary streams. Elsewhere the Guarani of Paraguay followed the Paraná, and descended southwards to Buenos Ayres, while, at a known epoch, we observe them in great numbers abandon Paraguay, and, turning north-west, traverse the plains of Chaco, and settle themselves under the eastern feet of the Peruvian Andes, where they remain under the name of Chiriguanos. The Araucans have only made partial migrations from the Andes towards the eastern plains. The Guaranis have generally moved from north to south; the other migrations of the American races have issued in various deviations from a central point.

A survey of the numbers of people belonging to each race yet subsisting in South America affords a gratifying consideration, and one that tends to relieve the distressing picture which the history of North America presents. The following table shows the numbers, as far as they can be ascertained, belonging to each race who have been at least received within the pale of Christianity, and those who yet remain in the wilderness of original Paganism. This consideration, if we can separate it from the events of the Spanish conquest, for which it is to be hoped that soldiers, and not the ministers of religion, are responsible, must be allowed, by a comparison with the history of North America, to reflect honour on the Roman Catholic Church, and to cast a deep shade on the history of Protestantism :—

	Christians.	Savages.
Peruvian branch	1,315,452	
Antisian branch	11,857	2,700
Araucanian branch		34,000
Patagonian branch	100	32,400
Chiquitian branch	17,735	1,500
Moxian branch	23,720	3,497
Brasilio-Guarani family	222,036	20,100
Total	1,590.900	94,197

It seems, from this table, that more than a million and a half of the pure aboriginal races live in South America in the profession of Christianity. The American race, through the exertions of missionaries, is destined to survive to future ages; and though it will eventually become mixed with the European, we may look for improvement rather than a dwindling deterioration, since it appears that the mixed descendants are physically a more vigorous offspring than either of the parent stocks.

Physical Characters of the South American Races.

Nothing can be more erroneous than the assertion made by Ulloa, and often repeated, that the South Americans are all of one complexion, and that this complexion is red, or of the colour of copper. Humboldt says, "La dénomination d'hommes rouge-cuivrés n'aurait jamais pris naissance dans l'Amérique équinoxiale pour désigner les indigènes;" and M. d'Orbigny extends the same observation to the southern parts. The complexions of the South American nations, according to this writer, whose observations have been most extensive and accurate, are of two different hues, each of which is found in various degrees of paleness and of intensity: one is an olive-brown, the other yellow. The natives of Peru, of the Pampas, of

Araucania, of the Chiquitos, and the Moxos, are of the olive-brown; the Brasilio-Guarani tribes are of a yellowish cast. It does not appear, from the examination of facts which this writer has instituted, that the shade of colour varies decidedly according to difference of latitude or climate; but it seems to be modified in a remarkable manner by the dryness or moisture of the atmosphere. Where the air is dry, the people are of deeper hue; where moist and foggy, their colour is more dilute. In the shape of the head among South American tribes, no constant observation can be laid down; the form of the cranium varies in every tribe. The Peruvians have most generally heads of an oblong form, somewhat compressed laterally, the forehead a little prominent, short, and falling somewhat backward; the Antisians and Araucans display nearly the same shape. In the people of the Pampas the head is generally rounded, nearly ellipsoid, contracted in length, and but little compressed laterally, with a forehead moderately prominent, and not falling back; in the Chiquitos, the same character is exaggerated, and the head is nearly circular, while in the Moxos it is more oblong; this last form is very nearly that of the Guarani. An artificial deformity of the head is well known in the South American nations; it had its greatest degree in the ancestors of the Aymara, who now resemble the other Peruvians. The Aymara are supposed to be the descendants of the people to whose ancestors belonged the wonderfully deformed skulls of Titicaca.

Most erroneous was also the assertion of Don Antonio de Ulloa, the great enemy of the South American aborigines, that their physiognomy is everywhere the same. "Visto un Indio de qualquiera region, se puede decir que se han visto todos." *i. e.* He who has seen an Indian of any part of the country, may say he has seen them all. This was the erroneous declaration of a prejudiced man. M. d'Orbigny, on the contrary, avers that a Peruvian differs more from a Patagonian, and a Patagonian from a Guarani, than does a Greek from an Ethiopian or a Mongole. Nor is the expression of countenance in these nations always gloomy and severe; it differs in the same nation under the influence of varying moral conditions. The Guarani of Paraguay, of Corrientes and Bolivia, have a countenance expressive of sorrow, dejection, and indifference; they appear neither to think nor feel. The free Guarani, the Guarayos, on the contrary, have an expression of life and animation,—"leur aspect dénote des hommes spirituels."

CHAPTER XXXI.

OF THE ALPINE NATIONS OF SOUTH AMERICA, OR THE ANDIAN FAMILY.

THE Andian family comprehends the principal nations of the whole South American Cordillera, including Peru and Chili, and some of the countries on both sides of that long chain. These nations, though differing in language and manners, have certain traits in common, which justify the assembling of them in one department. Their physical character is defined as follows: "Colour olive-brown, more or less intense; stature small; forehead of little elevation, and retiring; eyes horizontal, never turned upwards at the outer angle." Three branches are comprehended in this stock: the Peruvian, or the nations who inhabited the greater part of the old kingdom of Peru, or the present republics of Peru, Bolivia, and a part of that of Argentine; secondly, the Antisian, or tribes in the country called Antis by the Inca Garcilaso de la Vega, the historian of his native land and race; their countries are situated on the easternmost of the three ridges of the Cordillera; that is, to the eastward of Cuzco: it was by mistake that the Spaniards gave the name, which they corrupted into Andes, to all the three branches of the Cordillera. The third branch of this stock are the Araucanos, the celebrated warlike race who defended long the mountains of Chili against the Spaniards. All these nations display in their physical type the characters above described; they differ in some particular respects. The nations belonging to the Peruvian branch are of the smallest stature; the Araucans are the most vigorous in form, and they are of fairer complexion than the rest.

1. *Of the Peruvian Branch of the Andian Family of Nations.*

These nations, as I have said, consist of four races of distinct language, the Quichua or Inca race, or rather the race of people who were the proper subjects and followers of the dynasty of Inca sovereigns, the Aymaras, the Atacama, and the Changos.

The Quichua or Inca Peruvians.—It was among the nations of this stock that nearly all the civilisation of South America existed. The Peruvians are well known to have inhabited cities; in their elevated plains, they had troops of domesticated animals, the llama and the alpaca; and they cultivated extensively the quinoa and the potato, a native plant of these mountains, which stood to them in place of the cereal gramina of the civilised nations of the Old World; in the hot plains, they planted maize and the occa, or oxalis. Their woollen manufacture was comparable to the finest fabrics of Europe. They worked the precious metals, and copper and lead, but were ignorant of the more valuable use of iron. Among the Peruvian nations, the dominant race were the Quichuas, or Incas, distinguished by their language, which is the Quichuan. The Quichuas are a people of considerable mental culture; in the opinion of M. d'Orbigny, they are by no means inferior in intelligence to the nations of the ancient world; they have a lively conception, and acquire knowledge with facility. The old Incas had calculated with accuracy the duration of the solar year; they had acquired the art of sculpture; they recorded the even's of history by symbolic signs and by quipus, or knotted cords; they had a code of laws, and a regularly organised government; Peruvian orators swayed in public harangues the passions of the multitude: they cultivated poetry and music. Their language was harmonious, graceful, and formed by the most artificial system of inflections and combinations. Their religion was, if we may apply such epithets to any uninspired faith, the mere result of the inward light of the untaught human mind, in the highest degree spiritual and sublime. They recognised in Pachacamac the invisible God, the creator of all things, supreme over all, who governed the motion of the heavenly bodies, and whom they worshipped without image or temple in the open air, while to the Sun, his visible creature, they erected temples, honoured him with costly gifts, and with rites performed by consecrated virgins. Like the Rajpúts of the Hindús, the royal dynasty of Incas were the offspring of the Sun: the nearest relative of the reigning Inca was the high-priest, who offered up the ripened fruits of the earth, and on stated occasions sacrificed llamas, the only bloody offerings of the Peruvians. In the milder character of their religion, and the greater softness and gentleness of their moral disposition, the Peruvians are strongly distinguished from the nations of Anahuac, and particularly from those of the Toltec and Aztec races.

The physical characters of the Quichua, or Inca race, have been carefully described by M. d'Orbigny. Their complexion, as he assures us, has no tinge of the red or copper colour which is assigned to the nations of South America, nor the deep yellow of those of the Brasilio-Guaranian race. It is the same mixture of brown olive that we discover in the Patagonians of the Pampas. Indeed the colour of the Quichuas is that of Mulattos, and their uniformity is very remarkable among all the men of a pure race. Ulloa, in his description of the Americans, often confounds these nations; he speaks as if they were but one stock, and, confounding them in his memory with the North Americans, calls them all red, which they are not. Nevertheless he attributed to the heat of the sun and the action of the air the deeper colour of the Peruvians, which M. de Humboldt correctly terms bronze.

"The stature of the Quichuas is low. We have never met with any who attained a greater height than five feet three inches. The great number of measurements that we have made authorise us to believe that their mean height is not above four feet nine inches, and often under that in many provinces, particularly in the elevated plateaux where the rarefication of the air is greatest; while those whom we had seen, who were of a higher stature, lived principally in the warm and humid valleys of the province of Ayupaya. The women are still less, and, perhaps, below the relative proportion which generally exists among white races."

The forms of the Quichuas are more robust than those of other mountain tribes; they may be described as characteristic of the race. The Quichuas have very large square shoulders, a broad chest, very voluminous, highly arched, and longer than usual, which increases the size of the trunk, while the normal relation, in respect to length, of the trunk to the extremities, does not appear to be the same among the Quichuas as among our European races; it differs equally from that of other American families; the extremities are, nevertheless, very muscular, and bespeak great strength; the head is larger than usual in proportion to the rest of the body; the hands and feet are always small. The women present the same characteristics; their necks are always large.

"It has been observed, that the trunk is longer in proportion than among other Americans; and that, for the same reason, the extremities are, on the contrary, shorter. We endeavoured at the same time to explain this fact by the greater development of the chest. It would appear that any given part of the body may take a greater extension from any adequate cause, while other parts follow the ordinary course. An evident proof of this fact may be found in the phenomena of imperfect conformation, in which a certain part of the body, in consequence of deformity, does not assume, in external appearance, its complete natural development, as we see in the trunk of a dwarf, while this defect does not prevent the extremities from acquiring those proportions that they would have had if the trunk had received its full growth. This accounts for the want of symmetry in the persons of dwarfs, and for that length of the upper or lower limbs so much out of proportion with the body. If we admit this fact, difficult to contest, why, in the case in question, may we not admit as well, that the chest, from a cause which we shall explain, having acquired a more than ordinary extension, might naturally lengthen the trunk without causing the extremities to lose their normal proportion, which would make it appear, as, indeed, it would be, longer than among other men, where no accident can have altered the form common to the race?

"Let us return to the causes which occasion in the Quichuas the great volume of chest which has been observed in them. Many considerations have led us to attribute this to the influence of the elevated regions in which they live, and to the modifications occasioned by the extreme expansion of the air. The plateaux which they inhabit are always comprised between the limits of 7500 to 15,000 feet above the level of the sea; there the air is so rarefied that a much greater quantity must be inhaled at each inspiration than at the level of the ocean. The lungs require in consequence of their great necessary volume and of their greater dilatation in breathing, a cavity larger than in lower regions. This cavity receives from infancy, and during the time of its growth, a great development entirely independent of that of other parts. We were desirous of determining whether, as we might suppose *à priori*, the lungs, in consequence of their great size, were not subject to extraordinary modifications. Inhabiting the city of La Paz, upwards of 11,000 feet above the level of the ocean, and being informed that in the hospital there were constantly Indians from the populous plateaux still more elevated, we had recourse to the kindness of our countryman, M. Burnier, physician to the hospital, and he permitted us to make a *post-mortem* examination of some of these Indians from the highest regions; in these we have, as we expected, found the lungs of an extraordinary dimension, which the external form of the chest clearly indicated. We remarked that the cells were much larger, and more in number, than in those of the lungs we had dissected in France; a condition very necesssry to increase the surface in contact with the ambient fluid. To conclude, we have discovered, 1st, that the cells were more dilated; 2dly, that their dilatation increases considerably the volume of the lungs; 3dly, that consequently they must have, to contain them, a larger cavity; 4thly, that, therefore, the chest has a capacity much larger than in the normal state; 5thly, lastly, that this great development of the chest elongates the trunk beyond its natural proportions, and places it almost out of harmony with the length of the extremities, this remaining the same as if the chest had preserved its natural dimensions.

"The features of the Quichuas are well characterised, and have no resemblance to those of the nations of the Mediterranean and Brasilio-Guarani races; theirs is a type entirely distinct, though approaching slightly to the Mexican. Their head is oblong before and behind, a little compressed at the sides; the forehead is slightly arched, short, and falling a little back; nevertheless, the skull is often voluminous, and announces a tolerably large development of brain; their face is generally broad, approaching to an oval form; their nose is remarkable, always prominent, long, and strongly aquiline, as if bent at its extremity over the upper lip; the nostrils are large, broad, and very open; the mouth is larger than common, and prominent, though the lips are not very thick; the teeth are always beautiful, even in old age: the chin is rather short, without receding, sometimes being even rather prominent: the cheeks are slightly raised, and only in advanced age; the eyes are of common size, and sometimes even small, always horizontal; they are never oblique, or raised at their exterior angle; the cornea is never white, it is invariably rather yellow; the eyebrows are long, arched, narrow, and scanty; the hair is always of a beautiful black, thick, long, very soft, and straight, and descending very low over the forehead and sides; the beard is reduced among all the Quichuas without exception, to some straight and scanty hairs, covering the upper lip, the sides of the mouth, and the middle of the chin. The Quichua nation is, perhaps, among the indigenous races, that one which has the least beard. The profile of the Quichuas forms a very obtuse angle, and little different from ours: only the maxillaries advance more than in the Caucasian race; the arches of the eyebrows are prominent; the base of the nose is very deep. Their physiognomy is, upon the whole, uniform, serious, reflective, even melancholy, without, however, shewing indifference: it denotes rather penetration without frankness. It might be said that they endeavour to hide their thoughts under the sameness that is remarked in their countenances, where emotions are rarely exhibited externally, and never with that vivacity that betrays the feelings of some races; their features altogether retain a mediocrity of expression. The women are seldom very handsome; their noses are not so prominent or curved as those of the men: the latter, although they have no beard, have a masculine expression, derived from their strongly marked features. An ancient vase, which represents with striking fidelity the features of the present race of Quichuas, convinces us that for four or five centuries their physiognomy has undergone no sensible alteration."

The outline annexed shews the form of a Peruvian skull in the Museum of the Royal College of Surgeons. It was brought from an ancient temple in Peru, and is supposed to have belonged to the Quichua race: in its general shape, it is very similar to many other crania from the same country, and to many of the figures given by Dr. Morton in his great work, "Crania Americana." The forehead in this skull is narrow, but the vertex elevated: these traits, and the shortness of the antero-posterior diameter, are the principal characters of the skull of the ancient Incas.

FIG. 95.

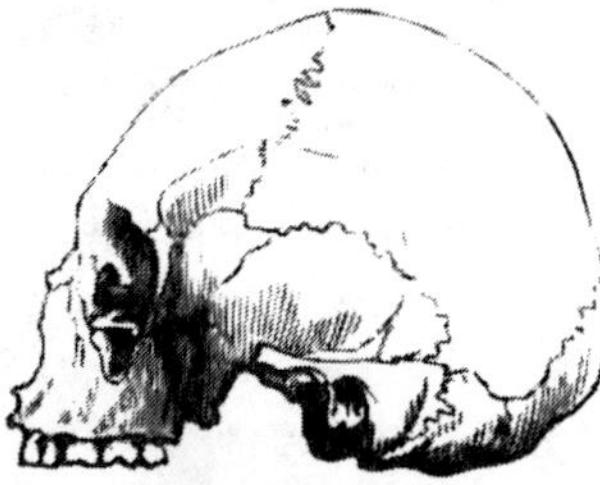

Skull of a Peruvian.

Of the Aymaras.—The second race belonging to the Peruvian branch of the Alpine family of nations in South America are the Aymaras, who greatly resemble the Incas or Quichuas in physical characters, but differ from them entirely in language. They were a more numerous, and extensively spread, and, as it is supposed, a more early civilised people. The Aymaras appear to be the descendants of that ancient race, who, in ages long past, inhabited the high plains covered by the singular monuments of Tiaguanaco, the most ancient city of South America, and the banks of the mountain lake of Titicaca, where Manco-Capac, founder of the late dynasty of the Incas, was believed to have risen from the bosom of the waves. The fourth of the Incas, who founded their empire at Cuzco, reduced under his sway Tiaguanaco, and conquered the country of the Aymaras. This event happened but two or three centuries before the arrival of Pizarro in Peru.

No written documents remain to record the ancient history of the Aymaras. That the solar worship of the Incas, their arts and civilisation, were derived from them, may be inferred from the position of the ancient temples, which turn precisely to the rising sun, and from the various allegorical sculptures on the sides of the monolithal porticos. On these is seen the figure of the sun surrounded by rays, and that of a man holding the sceptre, the emblems of a double, both secular and priestly, rule; while on each side are rows of crowned kings; and aloft the condor, the great vulture of the American Alps, supposed to be the messenger of the gods. It was from Tiaguanaco, according to the researches of M. d'Orbigny, that the arts and civilisation of Peru originated, whence they were conveyed by Manco-Capac and the Incas to the later city of Cuzco, the seat of regal and sacerdotal magnificence at the era of the Spanish Conquest.

The Aymaras resemble the Quichuas in one of their principal characteristics of organisation, which is the great length and breadth of the chest, a form which eminently adapts them, by the greater expansion which it allows to the pulmonary organs, to be the inhabitants of high mountain-tracts where the atmosphere is light and rare. They have also the same form of the head, which is often large, with a capacious cranium, oblong from back to front, and slightly compressed at the sides. The heads of the present Aymaras display no traces of that flatness which is so conspicuous in the skulls found around the lake of Titicaca, and in other parts of the Aymara country.

In their character, likewise, in their intellectual faculties, in manners, customs, private and social, in agriculture and manufactures, and dress, the Aymaras resemble in every respect the Quichuas, to whom they were subject. If we cast a rapid glance over the mode of architecture of their monuments, the origin of which is lost in the darkness of antiquity, we shall find a great difference between them and those of the Incas. We refer to the monuments of Tiaguanaco, situated in the centre of the country belonging to this nation, near to the lake of Titicaca, of which many ancient authors have spoken, and of which the origin was so completely unknown, that they were said, by a figurative expression, to have been built before the sun enlightened the earth. The monuments discovered in this country by M. d'Orbigny announce a civilisation more advanced than those which have been described in the ruins of Palenque. They consist of a tumulus raised more than 100 feet, surrounded with pillars; of temples, from 100 to 200 metres in length, placed precisely towards the east, and adorned with colossal angular columns; of porticos of one stone, which are covered with reliefs of skilful execution, although of rude design, displaying symbolical representations of the sun and the condor, his messenger; also a colossal statue of basalt loaded with bas-reliefs, in which the design of the carved head is half Egyptian; and lastly, the interior of a palace, formed of enormous blocks of rock completely hewn, whose dimensions are often seven metres in length and four metres in breadth and thickness. In the temples and palaces the portals are not inclined, as among those of the Incas, but perpendicular: and their vast dimensions, and the imposing masses of which they are composed, surpass in beauty and grandeur all that were afterwards built by the sovereigns of Cuzco. We know not the existence of sculpture, or of bas-reliefs, in the monuments of the Quichuas, while those of Tiaguanaco are all thus ornamented. "The presence of these remains of an ancient civilisation, upon the point from which the first Inca emerged, to found the empire of Cuzco, appears to offer an additional proof that from thence were transported with Manco-Capac the last memorials of the earlier grandeur of the Aymaras."

The tombs of the Aymaras are very different from those of the Quichuas; instead of being subterranean, sometimes they are great square buildings with a simple opening, through which the dead body was introduced. Corpses were arranged round a confined cavity, sitting in their clothes, and, in some instances, covered with a kind of cloth of straw; sometimes these tombs consist of small houses built of unburnt bricks of the same form, the top inclined, and the opening always directed towards the east; often they are square towers of several stories, containing each a body, as in the Isle of Quebaya and some others upon the lake of Titicaca; but these tombs, although of immense size, are always joined in groups, and appear often like large villages.

The fact that the peculiar form of the flattened skulls found at Titicaca and elsewhere is the result of artificial pressure, is so important in regard to the physical history of the race, and of mankind in general, that I shall incur the risk of being somewhat prolix in order to lay before my readers M. d'Orbigny's observations on this subject.

It is not difficult to furnish proofs of the artificial change in the aspect of the skulls themselves. "We observe," says M. d'Orbigny, "in the flattening of the frontal bone, in the projection that it forms over the parietal bones at the upper part, that there has evidently been compression before and behind, and which has forced the mass of the brain backwards, by pushing, as it were, the frontal bone over the parietals."

"The head of a young subject in my possession shows still more clearly by a longitudinal fold which exists at the upper medial part of the vertex, by a strong projection of frontal over the parietal bones, and by the prominence equally strong of the upper part of the occipital over these parietal bones, that the pressure has been employed in a circular manner from the earliest age of infancy by means of a large ligature. This supposition appears still more admissible when we observe from behind, that not only the mass of the brain has given a great size to the posterior parts, to the prejudice of the anterior, but also that the pressure, having greatly increased the convexity of the posterior lobes of the brain, the parietal bones have necessarily followed the same shape in being modelled upon them; the parietal bones, likewise, form always two latero-posterior convexities, slightly separated by an evident depression. We find again another proof of this pressure in the obliteration of the sutures, which is observable upon all the points affected by pressure, even in the heads of the youngest subjects."

M. d'Orbigny considers it as now fully proved, that the depressed or elongated form of these heads is not, as was supposed, the natural character of the skulls of the Aymaras, but is only an exception evidently owing to the intervention of art. It would be interesting to inquire into the antiquity of this custom of flattening the head, and the influence that it is likely to have exercised over the intelligence of the subjects among whom it is found most marked.

"As to the antiquity of the custom, we see by the profile of the head of a colossal statue before the era of the Incas, that they were not then depressed; for the ancient people, who always aimed to exaggerate existing characteristics, would not have failed to exhibit them. It is, therefore, probable that this custom was contemporaneous with the reign of the Incas. Even the lengthening of the ears of one of these compressed heads may lead us to determine very nearly the age in which the individual lived. It was found in the province of Caraugas to the west of Oruro. It is known that this province was only conquered under the reign of the seventh Inca, Yahuar Hucac, who, according to all probability, lived about the thirteenth century; thus, as the Incas only granted the honour of stretching the ears by a special grace, and to recompense a conquered nation for its prompt submission to their laws, and as this concession came necessarily at the end of the establishment of the customs of the conquerors, we may suppose that it was not generally in practice among the Aymaras till towards the fourteenth or fifteenth century. The statues show, besides, that the custom of lengthening the ears was unknown at the time of the first civilisation of the plateaux of the Andes.

"We have not been able to learn anything clearly with respect to the influence which this artificial deformity of the head had upon the intellectual faculties of the Aymaras, since the old historians give us no information; but there is reason to believe that there may be a displacement of the parts of the brain without any diminution of substance.

It will be admitted that, by the nature of their occupations, the chiefs of these nations had probably their intellectual faculties more expanded than their vassals. May we not from this fact draw an argument in favor of our opinion? for the most depressed heads that we have seen have been constantly found in tombs whose construction announces that they belong to the chiefs."

FIG. 96.

Skull of Titicacan.

Atacamas and Changos.—Two other nations of inferior numbers make up the Peruvian group: these are the Atacama, who occupy the western declivity of the Peruvian Andes, and the Changos spread along the coast of the Pacific. They resemble the Quichua in physical characters; but the Changos are of darker hue: their colour is a tawny approaching to black. We cannot fail to connect this circumstance with their local situation on the sea-coast, while in so many parallel observations are elsewhere to be found.

The entire mass of the Peruvian nations has embraced Christianity. The old Peruvians were pastors and agriculturists. Their collective number is stated at nearly two millions, of whom upwards of 1,300,000 are of the pure American blood. The example of the Peruvian nations is sufficient to solve the question, whether the American races are susceptible of civilisation and of Christianity.

2. *Antisian Branch of the Alpine Races of South America.*

It is from the Inca, Garcilaso de la Vega, learned in the history of his ancestors, which he has written in the Spanish language, that the name of Antisian is derived as the distinguishing term for the races who inhabit the eastern declivity of the Bolivian and Peruvian Andes extending from the 13° to the 17° of southern latitude. In this region we look in vain for those lofty and shadeless uplands, where cold mountains and grassy plains near the limits of perpetual snow enable the Quichua and Aymara herdsman to live peaceably on the produce of his tillage and of his flocks, amidst the ruins of ancient civilisation and monuments of his national glory. The territory held by the Antisian races appears at the first view unfit for human habitation. It consists of abrupt and precipitous mountains, on which, however, a vigorous and magnificent vegetation is everywhere displayed; of deep and gloomy valleys, where impetuous torrents rush over rocky beds. It is on the banks of mountain-streams, and amidst the darkness of lofty primeval forests, that the Antisian tribes have acquired those modifications of character, physical and moral, which distinguish them from the natives of the high and open regions before described.

The nations belonging to this branch are the Yuracarès, the Mocéténès, the Tacanas, the Maropas, and the Apolistas.

The people of these races, dwelling amid humid forests scarcely penetrated by the solar rays, are, in comparison with the Quichuas and Aymaras, almost white,* and those tribes are the fairest who dwell most under the dense and thickest woods. Their hue is a white, but slightly tawny or mixed with yellow. One remarkable trait, as yet but imperfectly described, is that many persons among these tribes have their skin spotted with large patches of a still paler hue. Collectively they are of much greater stature than the Peruvians of the higher region: their forms are vigorous and robust; their countenances differ from those of the mountaineers; their faces are more round; their features less elevated; their languages are peculiar; their manners barbarous and wild.

---

* The Yuracarès are so named by the Quichuas; the word *yurak* meaning "white," and *kari* "men," in their language. See The Physical History of Mankind, Vol. v. p. 476.—Ed.

[Some notices of the almost unknown tribes coming under this head, occur incidentally in Lieut. Herndon's work on the Amazon,* which river he reached by a land journey from Lima, over the Andes, and along the Huallaga and Ucayali rivers. The little information previously accessible may be estimated from the fact that Dr. Latham could obtain only an imperfect list of their names. The statements of Lieutenant Herndon relate chiefly to the tribes on the Ucayali; they are scanty, as he was merely on his way to the objects of his expedition, but they are given as the only notices obtainable.

The Conibos live in villages, cultivate the ground, weave cotton cloth, and make baskets: the weaving is mostly done by the women. All wear a long cotton gown, which is painted in various devices by the women. Lieutenant Herndon met one man whom he describes as the dandy of his tribe; he was painted with a broad stripe of red under each eye, three narrow stripes of blue were carried from one ear to the other, across the upper lip; the whole of the lower jaw was painted with a blue chain-work of Chinese-looking figures. A broad tight necklace of black and white beads was around his neck, and a breast-plate of the same hung down from it, partly hidden by the long gown. He had broad bracelets of white beads, and bands of lizards' skins, set round with monkeys' teeth, higher up the arm. He wore a little silver shield hanging from his nose, and a thin plate of silver, 2½ inches long, thrust through a hole in his lip, and hanging on his chin. He had his wife and two children with him, not described.

The Remos and Shipebos on the same river are painted and clothed much like the Conibos. "The Remos are low and small; the Shipebos taller." The Pirros are exactly like the Conibos, but they speak a different language. "They have no idea of a future state, and worship nothing. In fact, I think they have no ideas at all,

* Exploration of the Valley of the Amazon, by Lieut. Wm. Lewis Herndon, United States Navy. 8vo. Washington, 1854.

although they can make a bow or a canoe, and take a fish; and their women can weave a coarse cloth from cotton, and dye it." The Amajuacas are hunters; they live in the interior in villages, and seldom come down upon the rivers; the Pirros and Conibos sometimes make war upon them, and bring away captives.

"The Conibos, Shipebos, Setebos, Pirros, Remos, and Amajuacas, are the vagabonds of the Ucayali, wandering about from place to place, and settling where they take a fancy. They are great boatmen and fishermen... They have settlements on the banks of the river; but many of them live in their canoes, making huts of reeds and palms upon the beaches in bad weather. . . . . Many have two or three wives; they marry young, and have many children, but do not raise more than half of them. They seem docile and tractable, though lazy and faithless." In another place he says, "The Indians here [at Sarayacu], as elsewhere, are drunken and lazy. The women do most of the work; carry most of the burdens to and from the chacras [huts] and canoes; make the masato [an intoxicating drink made from the yucca], and the earthen vessels out of which it is drunk; spin the cotton and weave the cloth; cook, and take care of the children. And their reward is to be maltreated by their husbands, and, in their drunken frolics, to be cruelly beaten, and sometimes badly wounded."

The Sencis, above Sarayacu, on the right bank of the river, are said, on the authority of the Peruvian missionary governor, to be superior to the other tribes; to be numerous, bold, and warlike; to have names for the constellations, and to take an interest in the astronomical observations made by white men; and finally, to be so industrious "that they kill those who are idle, and indisposed to do their fair share of work." Lieut. Herndon, however, tells us that he saw some Sencis at Sarayacu, who seemed to be just like other Indians, and that he heard there of nothing peculiar about them.

The Campas, on the upper waters of the Ucayali, are the most numerous and warlike tribe, who have succeeded in prohibiting all strangers from entering their country. Lieut. Herndon believes that these are the warlike Chunchos who have been so often opposed to the whites, and who destroyed the missions of the Cerro de la Sal in 1742; and he has "little doubt that they are descendants of the Inca race." The Cashibos, or Callisecas, found on the Pachitea, an affluent of the Ucayali, are also warlike and exclusive; they have beards, and are said to be cannibals. A small tribe called Lorenzos occupy the upper part of the same river.

The inhabitants of Sarayacu are divided into the three tribes of Panos, Omaguas, and Yameos; the latter the whitest and handsomest tribe seen by Lieut. Herndon. They lived in separate parts of the town, and spoke different languages, but in their communication they used the Pano language.

Lower down the river, and along the south bank of the Amazon, are the Mayorunas, a warlike and exclusive tribe, of whom Lieut. Herndon could hear little more than that they wore beards, were whiter than the other Indians, and were naked. His boatmen were careful not to camp on their side of the river.

Lieut. Herndon also visited the Yaguas, a tribe on the northern frontier of Peru, where it joins the republic of Ecuador. He describes them as having a vacant and stupid expression, but being in their general appearance thoroughly savage. Their dress is composed of a girdle of bark around the loins, with bunches of a fibrous bark hanging down before and behind, and similar bunches hung round the neck and arms by a collar and bracelets of little beads. Long tail-feathers of the macaw were stuck in the armlets, reaching above the shoulders, and a chaplet of smaller white feathers was worn around the head. The dress of the women was a yard or two of cotton cloth rolled round the hips. Their houses are like a gigantic bee-hive, about thirty feet in diameter, composed of strong poles well wattled and thatched; on the inside, four or five small cabins of cane are built around the walls at intervals, in which separate families reside. The middle space is used in common; "it is never cleaned, nor even levelled, and is littered with all manner of abominations. The Yaguas are quiet and harmless, but the men are lazy, and much given to drunkenness. The patient, much-enduring women do all the work, including the preparation of drink for their lazy masters. They are fond of dancing, which they keep up with a vigour somewhat opposed to their alleged laziness, to the monotonous music of the drum.

Lieut. Herndon, speaking of these Indians generally, compares them to children, and thinks that good example, with a wholesome degree of discipline, may do much with so docile a race; but he continues, somewhat inconsistently, "I myself believe, and I think the case of the Indians in my own country bears me out in the belief, that any attempt to communicate with them ends in their destruction. They cannot bear the restraints of law, or the burden of sustained toil, and they retreat before the face of the white man, with his improvements, till they disappear" (p. 228).]

3. *The Araucanian Branch.*

The Araucanian branch of the Alpine family of South American nations comprehends the native inhabitants of all the southern regions of the Cordillera, and of its declivities on both sides, reaching from the 30° of south latitude to the extremity of the Land of Fire. It consists of two nations, the Araucans, a warlike and indomitable race, whose heroism is celebrated in the history of the Spanish conquerors of Peru, and the Pesherais, or Ichthyophagi of Tierra del Fuego, who inhabit the southern extremity of the long American mountain-chain separated from the continent by the Magellanic Straits. These two nations have, owing to their different local circumstances, very different manners; but they display, according to the observations of M. d'Orbigny, who lived among one of the two nations, similar physical characters. They exemplify, indeed, that physical type which is peculiar to the American mountaineers, and common to the nations of this and of the first branch of the Alpine group. One description is applicable to both nations: their heads are proportionably large; their face round, with projecting cheek-bones, large mouths, thick lips, short, flattened noses, with wide nostrils; their eyes are horizontally placed, and not inclined; otherwise their countenance would approximate greatly to that of the nomadic Tartars; they have little beard; their foreheads are narrow and falling back; their chins broad and short.

The Araucans are of the same colour as the Peruvian nations, but of a much lighter shade.* The Boroanos, one of these tribes, are, indeed, almost white. M. d'Orbigny discredits the positive statement of Molina, that the Araucans of the high province of Boroa have fair complexions, with blue eyes. The statement of Molina, that the Boroanos are very fair, is given and repeated in different passages. I find, in an extract given by Malte-Brun from an account of Chili, in the "Viagero Universal," translated from the Spanish in the "Annales des Voyages," the following account of the Araucans in general:—"Ils ont le teint brun-roux et plus clair que celui des autres Américains. Ceux de la tribu des Boroanos sont même blancs et blonds." An English traveller in Chili, Mr. Caldcleugh, gives some confirmation to this remark. He says that, among the lower classes in Chili, some surprisingly white men, with features different from those of the Spaniards, were pointed out to him, and were said to be the descendants of the White Araucans (see Plate 58).

There could be nothing very wonderful in the appearance of the xanthous complexion in the high tracts of

* The portrait of an Araucan, from the Atlas of Von Spix and Martius, exemplifies this description.

Araucanian Native of Chile.

South America beyond the tropics, when we consider that the same phenomenon displays itself in the inhabitants of the Rocky Mountains in the Northern hemisphere.

[A volume by Don Ignatius Domeyko, printed at Santiago in 1845, gives a rather different account of the physical characteristics of the Araucans. The following notice is extracted from a translation of part of the work taken out of a Report in a late number of the Literary Gazette. With regard to the remarks on their moral condition, it must be premised that the work of the reverend professor is upon the whole somewhat of a panegyric. "They are of swarthy complexion, less ruddy but clearer than that of the other indigenous Americans. The face is somewhat oblong, eyes large, lively, and expressive, with narrow, well-arched eyebrows. The countenance is more like the Caucasian than the Mongolian type. The nose is less broad and more prominent than that of the Indians of the North; in some it is aquiline: the lips are well formed, the lower one a little prominent: the hair black, harsh, and dense, but never curling. . . . . The Araucanian Indian's features are less Indian, and his complexion less coppery in colour, than the Indians of the Northern provinces of Chili. . . . . In domestic life they are sociable and liberal, but jealously preserve the rights of their homestead. No guest enters a house without the knowledge and permission of the owner. When guests have entered the house by invitation, the owner approaches, gives his hand to each, invites them to feel at ease, and, having conducted them to their appointed seats, sits down in front of them. He then with great seriousness makes a long and elaborate discourse of compliments, which may occupy a full half-hour. The guests silently evince respect, and are as solemn as if they were concerned in some religious act. While these ceremonials of etiquette are taking place, refreshment is being prepared in another room. The discourse ended, the features relax, the tone is changed, and general conversation on ordinary topics succeeds. It is customary, on the conclusion of the discourse, for the owner to rise from his seat, and, if the guests be worthy, to embrace each three times, placing his hand alternately to the right and to the left" (Literary Gazette, Nov. 26, 1853).]

The Pesherais, or Ichthyophagi of Tierra del Fuego.— The Pesherais are the inhabitants of Tierra del Fuego, referred by d'Orbigny to the Araucanian race. These people first received the name Péchérais from Bougainville; by it they have been since distinguished, and there seems to be no reason for changing this designation for the awkward one of Fuegian.

The affinity of the Pesherais to the Araucanos is as yet only a matter of conjecture; the supposition is founded on their proximity and mutual resemblance.

The Pesherais inhabit all the coast of Tierra del Fuego, and both borders of the Strait of Magellan, from the Island of Elizabeth and Port Famine towards the east, as far as the group of islands which spread to the northward and southward of the Strait; they are separated from the Patagonians by the sea, and by the chain of mountains which constitutes the isthmus, and joins the Peninsula of Brunswick to the continent. It is between these limits that navigators discovered the people whom they have described as Patagonians of small stature. The Pesherais may there communicate on one side with the Patagonians, to the east of the Port Famine, or with the tribe of the Araucans, of the Archipelago of Chonos, upon the western side of America; and this accounts for the Spanish words which Captain Weddell heard them pronounce. Their manner of life, and the ices of the mountainous country which they inhabit, confine them exclusively to the coast.

Their colour is olive, or tawny, and paler than that of the Peruvians and their neighbours the Araucanos.

Their figure has but little elegance, like that of almost all the Americans; they have huge forms and large chests, and are, notwithstanding, tolerably well made. The difference of opinion between travellers who saw them robust and with well-formed limbs, as Brak, Narborough, Degennes, Cook, and Weddell, and, on the other hand, Duclos Guyot, and Bougainville, who represent them as puny and meagre, arises, probably, from the season when they were seen, as the winter would naturally have great influence on the plentifulness of their nourishment. Their staggering gait depends, no doubt, upon the crookedness of their legs, which is caused by their way of sitting on the ground cross-legged, after the eastern fashion; this custom naturally turns the feet inwards. The women appear to have the same shape as the men; and it would be in vain to seek among them those proportions which are consecrated by European art.

Their features indicate relation to the Araucanos, whose neighbours they are; their head is rather large, and their face round; they have a short and rather broad nose, open nostrils, little eyes, black and horizontal; the mouth is wide, the lips thick, the teeth white, and well arranged; the ears are small, and the cheek-bones project but little. They appear to have very little beard, and pluck it out, as they do also their eyebrows. Their hair, like that of all the Americans, is black, long, and flat. With this assemblage of characteristics, we never find among them that fierce expression which marks some nations of hunters: on the contrary, they have a smile full of simplicity, and their character perfectly corresponds with their exterior. Mild and obliging as they are, no voyager has ever complained of them, and many have even described them with praise.

"As they are habitually a walking and wandering race, the manner of their existence does not permit them to form themselves into large societies. Living only by the chase and fishing, they are always advancing in small numbers from one place to another, as they exhaust the animals, and especially the shell-fish of the coasts. Since they inhabit a country cut up into a multitude of islands, they have become navigators, and in this differ completely from the nations who border upon them; for the Patagonians have never had a notion of making a raft to pass a river. The Pesherais traverse incessantly all the shores of the Land of Fire, and of the countries situated to the westward of the Strait: they are seen assembled in companies of two or three families, or sometimes four. They construct canoes with the bark of trees, sewn together with the tendons of animals, twelve or fifteen feet long, and three wide, and stop up the joints with rushes; within they support them with branches, and without smear them over with resin, with aid of no other tools than shells or pieces of flint: then they desert their cabins, which are conical, and made of branches of trees fixed in a circle in the ground, and joined at the top. They often live in dwellings some feet under ground, and covered with clay or the skin of the sea-wolf; and, near the middle, a fire burns, whose smoke can only escape by a single low aperture, which serves them for a door. Men, women, children, and a number of dogs, embark in the frail skiff; the women row, the men remain inactive, but always ready to pierce the fish which they see with a dart armed with a sharp stone at the end. Thus they arrive at another island; and then the women are charged with guarding the canoes, and fishing for shell-fish, while the men busy themselves in the chase with a sling and bow, with arrows headed with flint. Next they build a new cabin, and live there for some time; but, as the chase and fishing become less plentiful, re-embark and proceed to establish themselves elsewhere. Each family is thus constantly exposed to the perils of the sea, and to the rough weather of a climate almost always frosty, and that, so to say, without clothing. A piece of sea-wolf's skin scarcely covers the shoulders of the men, while the woman only has a little apron of the same material, or, in winter, some pieces of the skin of the guanaco. In the midst of this poverty, who would not be surprised to see a sort of refinement and coquetry among the Pesherais? They cover their neck, arms, and legs, with nick-nacks or shells; they paint their bodies, and still more often their faces, with different white, black, and red figures,—a custom common to the Patagonians; and the men sometimes adorn their heads with a bonnet and feathers. All of them carry a kind of buskins made of the skin of the sea-wolf."

As is customary among hunting people, they have often quarrels and petty wars among them, which last but a short time, but are often renewed.

Unfortunate in their climate and country, they live for the most part on shell-fish, roasted or raw; on fish, birds, and sea-wolves, whose fat they eat raw; sharing their food with their dogs, which accompany them wherever they go. Thus they pass the most rigorous season, not under ground, like the inhabitants of the extreme North, but without the temperature having the slightest influence on their manner of life. Among them, as among all other savage tribes, the women, whom civilisation spares from hard toil, are forced to engage in occupations the most fatiguing, besides the employments natural to their sex, and their duties as mothers: they row, fish, build cabins, and, even in the water, brave the extreme rigour of cold. In a word, the Pesherai women are, perhaps, of all the savage women of America, those whose lot is the hardest.

The religion of the Pesherais, according to the slight account that voyagers have given of it, appears to be that of the Patagonians; they believe, at any rate, in another life, and mark the instant of death by lamentation and superstitious ceremonies.

When sick, they have sorceries, like the Patagonians and Araucanos, practised by a woman: pressure of the stomach, suction of different parts of the body, magic words addressed to an invisible being; the physician-priest has his hair powdered and adorned with two white feathers, which is not seen among the Patagonians.

Though they have been referred to the race of black

men who occupy Van Diemen's Land, the Pesherais have certainly none of the characteristic traits of the nations of the Great Ocean; they evidently belong to the American family. So far as their features and stature are concerned, they have much resemblance to the Araucanos; their language approaches in sound to that of the Patagonians and Puelches, and in grammatical form to that of the Araucanos; their arms, religion, and their style of painting the face, are also those of the three neighbouring nations; but they are distinguished from them by their speech. Their physical characters seem, on the whole, to connect them with the branch of the Aucas, or Araucanos, of Chili.

CHAPTER XXXII.

MEDITERRANEAN GROUP OF SOUTH AMERICAN NATIONS.

I VENTURE to give this designation to the third great class of races in South America, inhabiting principally inland countries, intermediate between the Alpine nations of the Cordilleras, and the widely spread tribes of the Brasilian countries, or of the western region. The races included in this department are further divided into three subordinate groups or branches,—the Patagonian, the Chiquitian, and the Moxian. I shall first describe the Patagonian branch.

1. *Patagonian Branch.*

The Patagonian group comprehends, besides the proper Patagonians, several other nomadic tribes who resemble that people, and who live partly to the southward and in part to the northward of the Rio de la Plata. Those to the southward are all the wandering hordes of the Pampas, or level plains between the River of Silver and the Magellanic Straits. The northern tribes are people who resemble the

The last of the Charruas

Patagonians in physical characters, living between the river Paraguay and the lowest outskirts of the Cordillera, extending northward as far as the latitude of Potosi in 20° south latitude, and reaching over the great inland plain of Chaco. The Patagonian tribes are the nomadic nations of the New World. Ever erratic, since horses have been naturalised in South America these nations have become equestrian nomades, and wander over their arid plains, living under tents of skins, or in the forests of Chaco under huts of straw or bark. They are all fierce, untamable warriors, averse to agriculture and all the arts of civilisation; and have ever resisted, some to extermination, the arms of the Spaniards.

The complexion of these nations is darker than that of most other South Americans; it has nothing of the red or copper colour, but is an olive-brown. M. d'Orbigny compares it to the colour of Mulattos.* The natives of Chaco are all, according to that writer, equally dark with the Patagonians: the Charrua and the Puelche are of the deepest tint (see Plate 59). Among the tribes of this stock are the tallest, more powerful, and athletic forms. The Patagonians and the Abipones are celebrated in this point of view. The stature of the most southern of the stock is greatest; it diminishes as we go northward towards Chaco, in the middle part of the continent. In these tribes generally the trunk of the body is large and robust; the breast strongly arched; the limbs massive and round; but the hands and feet are small. The women are stout and vigorous, and without feminine grace or comeliness. The heads of the Patagonians are large; their face broad and flat; their cheek-bones prominent. These characters are tolerably well displayed in the following sketch.

* This description suits at least one nation of the stock, namely, the Charruas, who, however, are darker than Mulattos. A plate opposite to this page displays a tolerably good portrait of a small group of Charruas, who were exhibited some years ago in Paris, whither they had been brought at the time when the Charruan race was exterminated.

FIG. 97.

Patagonian.

In the nations of Chaco, the eyes are small, horizontal, but sometimes turned up slightly at the outer angle; the nose depressed, broad, with patulous nostrils; the mouth large; lips thick and prominent; chin short; eyebrows arched; beard scanty; hair lank and black; the expression of their countenance is cold, sullen, often fierce.* The languages of these nations have some characters in common, though they are distinct among themselves: they are harsh, and guttural, and difficult of utterance.

FIG. 98.

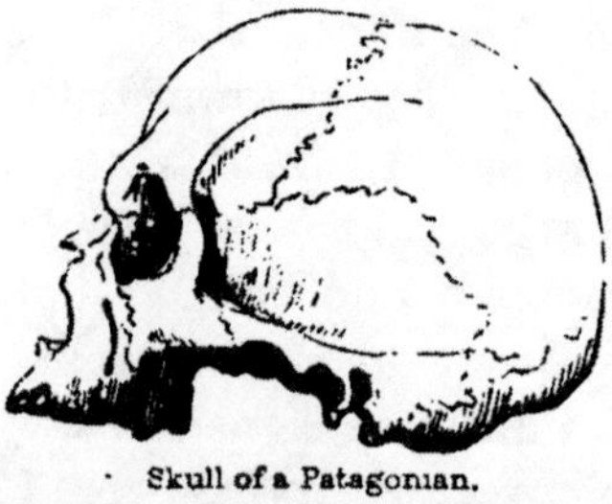

Skull of a Patagonian.

* There is a Patagonian skull in the Museum of the Royal College of Surgeons, from which the sketch that accompanies the text was taken. Its contour is large and round, the longitudinal diameter short: the breadth of the face, which cannot be estimated by the outline, is very considerable.

The particular nations comprehended under this group are the Téhuelche, or proper Patagonians; the Puelche, or tribes of the eastern Pampas to the southward of the Silver River; the Charruas, on the Uruguay; the Tobas or Mbocobi, who possess the greater part of Chaco; these are the most numerous nations of the whole group, their probable number amounting to 14,000 souls; the Mataguayos, likewise in Chaco; the Lenguas; and lastly, the celebrated Abipones of Azara and Dobrizhofer, the Centaurs of the New World.

Besides these nations, the Spanish authors give the names of forty others, inhabitants of Chaco and the countries to the westward of the Paraguay. Among them the Payaguas and the Mbayas are the most celebrated. In the opinion of M. d'Orbigny, their number has been greatly exaggerated. They appear to belong to this same group of nations, if arranged according to their physical characters.

The following account of Chaco and its inhabitants is taken from Dobrizhofer, who made a long abode in South America.

Chaco, according to this writer, is looked upon by the Spaniards as the theatre of their misery, and by the native people as their Paradise or Elysium. "Several tribes," he says, "formerly dwelt in Chaco, of whom the names alone, or very slender relics, now exist. Of this number were the Calchaquis, formerly very numerous, famous for military ferocity; at present a few survive in a corner of the territory of Santa Fe, the rest having long since fallen victims to war or to the small-pox. Nearly the same fate has swept away the equestrian tribes of the Malbalaes, Mataras, Palomos, Mogosnas, Oxejones, Aquilotes, Churumates, Ojotades, Tanos, Quamalcas, &c. The equestrian nations still subsisting in Chaco are the Abipones, Natekebits, Tobas, Amokebits, Mocobios, Yapetalacas, and Oekakakalots, Guaycurus or Lenguas. The Mbayas, dwelling on the eastern shore of the Paraguay, call themselves Epiguayegis; those on the western, Quetiadegodis. The pedestrian tribes are the Lules and the Ysistines, who speak the same language, viz. the Tonocote, and have been for the most part converted by us, and settled in towns; the Homoampas, Vilelas, Chunipies, Yooles, Ocoles, and Pazaines, who are in great part Christians; the Mataguayos, whom we have so often attempted to civilise, and who have always proved indocile; the Payaguas, the Guanas, and the Chiquitos. Other tribes, speaking various languages, in the woods, have been added by our order to the colonies of the Chiquitos, as the Zamucos, Caypotades, Ygaronos."

The particular characters of the southern tribes of this division, who inhabit the open plains called the Pampas, must be expected to differ considerably from those of the forests of Chaco.

The people of the Pampas, who are the Puelche, are described by the English missionary, Falkner, and by Don Felix de Azara. "At the arrival of the Spaniards," says Azara, "they wandered on the shores of the Great River, opposite to the Charruas, a nation of Paraguay, but without any intercourse, neither people possessing barks or canoes by which they might pass the stream. They made a vigorous resistance to the colonists who first settled at Buenos Ayres; but were obliged gradually to retire towards the south."

The people of the Pampas lived formerly by hunting sloths, hares, stags, and ostriches, which were very abundant in their country; but since horses and horned cattle have run wild, and spread in immense herds over the plains, they have fed on the flesh of these animals. Their language, according to Azara, is different from all others. They are not so taciturn as other nations in this part of America, and their voice is not so low and almost inaudible. "Leur taille," says the author above cited, "ne me parait pas inférieure à l'Espagnole, mais en général ils ont les membres plus forts, la tête plus ronde et plus grosse, les bras plus courts, la figure plus large, et plus sévère que nous et que les autres Indiens, et *la couleur moins foncée.*" The men go nearly naked. "Ils ne font point usage du barbote:" by this last circumstance they are distinguished from all the tribes of Paraguay. The women wear a *poncho*, or shirt, which covers their whole body. They wander about and dwell under tents formed of hides, which they easily remove. They are of milder disposition and less depraved than most of the nations of savages in this part of America.

Azara has likewise described the tribes inhabiting Chaco. He says that the Abipones in particular are well formed, and have handsome faces, much like those of Europeans, except in colour. "I observed that almost all of them had black, but rather small eyes; yet they see more acutely with them than we do with our larger ones." The common shape of their noses is aquiline; they are a very handsome people; have seldom or never any bodily defects. Almost all the Abipones are so tall that they might be enlisted among the Austrian Musketeers; they are destitute of beard, and have perfectly smooth chins, like all the other Indians. "If you see an Indian with a little beard, you may conclude, without hesitation, that one of his parents or more remote ancestors was an European." The same writer afterwards adds, "that they have a few straggling hairs, or down, on their chins, which are plucked out by the women, who act as barbers. All the Abipones have thick, raven-black locks." As to colour, he says "that none of the native Americans whom he has seen are as fair as the Germans or English; but many of them are fairer than many Spaniards, Portuguese, and Italians. They have whitish faces, but this whiteness, in some nations, approaches more to a pasty colour; in some it is darker,—a difference occasioned by diversity of climate, manner of living, or food. The women are fairer than the men, because they go out of doors less frequently." He informs us in the sequel to these observations, that the

Abipones, Mbocobis, and Tobas, and other tribes who live in Chaco, about ten degrees farther north, and, consequently, in a hotter climate, are yet of fairer colour than the Puelche and Aucas of the Magellanic region. Probably the different degrees of elevation above the level of the sea ought here to be taken into the account. The author of this remark contrasts the fact with the *more than moderate whiteness of the people of Tierra del Fuego.*

2 and 3. *Agricultural and Fishing Tribes of the Chiquitos and the Moxos.*

The inland and almost central provinces of South America, to the northward of Chaco, receive their Spanish names of Los Chiquitos and Los Moxos from two principal nations who inhabit them. These same nations are the types of two groups of American races who are found in the same regions. M. d'Orbigny makes them subordinate divisions of the class of nations described under the last head. They differ, however, in many important particulars from all the Patagonian tribes, and from those of Chaco. These differences may, indeed, be accounted for by referring to the local conditions of their respective countries. Unlike the wide plains of Chaco, which afford a proper abode to nomadic and equestrian tribes, the country of the Chiquitos, consisting of low hills covered with forests, and intersected by an infinity of small streams, confines the people to the places of their birth, where they live in small villages, and cultivate the soil. The Moxos, on the other hand, dwell in vast plains, subject to frequent inundations, and traversed by immense rivers, which they are obliged to navigate in boats. The Moxos are fishing tribes, ichthyophagi of the river-lands of the interior. The Chiquitos lived in small villages, each containing a family or clan: among them the men were naked; the females covered with a loose and gaily decorated garment. They buried their dead, and, like other savages, with them laid arms and provisions for their use in a future life. The Chiquitos are remarkable for the liveliness of their disposition, for their fondness for dancing and music, for their kindness on all occasions, their sociable temper, their hospitality, their freedom from jealousy as to their wives and daughters, for their perseverance, and the facility with which they became Christians. We must not, however, suppose that all the tribes proved themselves equally docile: the deaths of several Jesuits since the foundation of the missions would prove the contrary; but, once become Christians, they persevered, and at this time would not return to the woods under any consideration; and in this they differ from the people of the plains, who, so far from having ever submitted to the yoke, are to this day what they were at the era of their discovery. The nation of the Chiquitos were the most easy of reduction, and, without doubt, drew others by their example.

The features of the Chiquitos, according to M. d'Orbigny, differing from those of the nations of Chaco, might serve as the type of the races inhabiting the hilly tracts in the centre of America. They have a round head, larger than usual, almost always circular, and seldom compressed at the sides; a round and full face; cheek-bones projecting but little; a low and arched forehead; a nose always short, and but slightly flattened; and nostrils little open, compared with those of southern nations; the eyes, full of expression and vivacity, are small and horizontal; however, in the case of some individuals, they are slightly drawn out at the outer corner, which makes them seem a little elevated; but this is an exception. The lips are tolerably thin; the teeth good; the mouth small; the chin rounded and short; the eyebrows narrow and gracefully arched: they have a thin beard, and not curled, which only grows at an advanced age, and never covers more than the upper lip and under part of the chin; their hair is long, black, and sleek, and, in extreme old age, grows yellow, but never white. Their features, on the whole, do not approach to the European type.

The Moxos resemble the Chiquitos in their moral qualities, which are, with but little modification, the same in all these nations. Before the conquest, fixed by their religious customs, they were scattered among villages established on the banks of the rivers and lakes, as well as in the woods or in the midst of plains: they were everywhere fishermen, hunters, and principally cultivators of the land. The chase was only used by them as a recreation, but fishing was a necessary employment, and agriculture procured them provisions, and the materials necessary for a favourite liquor, which, as among the Chiquitians, was made in a common house where strangers were received, and where, on certain days, the inhabitants met to drink, sing, and dance; but their amusements had a character of gravity that was not found among the Chiquitos: their customs, also, were more barbarous. A Moxos would sacrifice his wife if she miscarried, through superstition, and his children if they were twins; while the mother, on her side, often got rid of her children when they troubled her. Marriage was a convention that might be dissolved at the wish of the parties, and polygamy was of ordinary occurrence. Their habit of being always in canoes caused them to explore the streams, which they were ever traversing, whether for hunting or fishing, or even for going to their habitations. They were all, more or less, warriors; but traditions and records have only preserved the memory of a single cannibal tribe who ate their prisoners; this was the Canichana, who, even to this day, are the terror of the other tribes. The manners of this nation have been modified by the discipline of the missions; but it has preserved many of its primitive customs.

Several particular nations are included under each of these divisions. The tribes coming into the same group with the Chiquitos are thus enumerated by M. d'Orbigny:—

Number of Individuals in each Nation.

Name of Nations.	Christians.	Heathens.	Total.
Chiquitos	14,925	—	14,925
Samucus	1,250	1000	2,250
Païconécas	610	300	910
Saravécas	350	—	350
Otukés	150	—	150
Curuminacas	150	—	150
Curavès	150	—	150
Covarécas	50	100	150
Corabécas	—	100	100
Tapiis	50	—	50
Curucanécas	50	—	50
Totals	17,735	1500	19,235

From this total, it is easy to judge of the number of the aborigines remaining in the territory of the province of Chiquitos. If we believe historians, the number must have been much greater, and entire nations, as well as many tribes of Chiquitos, must have been decimated in the expeditions of discovery made by those adventurers who left Paraguay in search of gold; in the incursions of the Mamelucos of San-Pablo, of Brazil, who hunted down the Indians to sell them; and, lastly, by a company of Spanish merchants of Santa Cruz, of the Sierra, who, following the example of the Portuguese, made for some time an infamous trade of the poor Chiquitos with the proprietors of the mines of Peru. Afterwards there were continued pestilences, the ravages of which were dreadful, from the era when the Jesuits arrived in the territory of the province, and continued to our time. All these causes of depopulation make it probable that at present not more than half the number of inhabitants who possessed the country at the time of its discovery, survive. It is easy to see, on casting an eye over our table, that the nation of Chiquitos forms, by itself, six-sevenths of the population of the country; while, of the rest, only the Samucus and Païconécas are of any importance: hence the propriety of taking the nation of the Chiquitos as the type of a group of nations, in which we recognise the following general characters :—

The colour is the same as that of the aborigines of Chaco, though a little less deep; that is to say, bronze, or more correctly, a pale brown, mixed with olive, and not with red or yellow. It has been observed that the Samucus are more deeply coloured than the other nations of the province; but this is in so slight a degree, that it is necessary to see many individuals together in order to recognise the difference.

The stature of the Chiquitos is smaller than that of the inhabitants of the plains of Chaco and of the south, and scarcely varies. The average is five feet one inch and a half, while the tallest are not more than five feet five to six inches. The women do not approach so nearly to the men in height as is common among the southern nations; they only preserve the relative proportions.

The form of the body, among the Chiquitos, differs but little from that of the Indians of Chaco: as in them the trunk is robust, the chest protruding, and the shoulders broad; but in general there is less of strength apparent in them. The body is compact; the limbs are full, exhibiting a well-rounded shape, without having any apparent muscles; otherwise the men are straight and well-set, and have an easy gait. The women are larger and heavier, and of the same diameter down the whole length of their body; accordingly, they exhibit much vigour, and present nothing of the ideal beauty of ancient forms.

The features of the Chiquitos are characteristic: the head is large and nearly round, not compressed at the sides; the face very full and rounded; the cheek-bones not projecting; the forehead low and arched; the nose, always short, is less flattened than that of the races of the plains; the eyes are sunk, lively, expressive, almost always horizontal; but, in the case of some individuals, the outer angle is drawn out, and shows a tendency to raise itself, as in the Guaranian race; the lips are tolerably thin; the mouth much smaller than among the nations of Chaco, and always ready to smile; the chin is rounded and short; the eyebrows thin and well-marked; the beard only covers the under part of the chin, and the moustache, which is constantly thin, is not curled; the countenance is open, and shows gaiety, frankness, and much vivacity. Notwithstanding, no one could say that they have elegant figures; most of them, on the contrary, are below mediocrity. The women have a still rounder face than the men, with an expression of much gaiety and simplicity. In general, the figure of the men has nothing masculine.

The Chiquitian languages are as numerous as the nations who speak them. Far from being as guttural as those of Chaco, most of them are even sweet and melodious, and present neither harsh sounds nor that redundance of consonants so common in the latter. The language of Chiquito, by its termination in *ch*, and that of the Morotocas, a section of the Samucus, by those in *od* and *ad*, offer a trait of resemblance to those of Chaco. The guttural sound of the Spanish *j* occurs in the languages of Saravéca, Curuminéca, Covaréca, and Païconéca; but in all the others it is wanting. The French *u*, pronounced in the nose, is to be found in the language of Chiquito, in the Otukéan, Curuminécan, Covarécan, and Païconécané. Several of them have the French *ch*, and the soft sound of the *z*. A singular anomaly occurs in the Chiquitian language, in which, for many things, men and women use different words; while, for others, the woman uses the same words as the men, contenting herself with changing the termination. Though those languages are very complicated, especially that of the Chiquitos, none of them has an extended system of numeration, which proves the existence of few relations, and an entire want of traffic.

The nations who resemble the Moxos are associated with that people under one division, as follows:—

Number of Individuals in each Nation.

Name of Nations.	Christians.	Heathens.	Total.
Moxos	12,620	1000	13,620
Chapacuras	1,050	300	1,350
Itonamas	4,815	—	4,815
Canichanas	1,939	—	1,939
Movimas	1,238	—	1,238
Cayuvavas	2,073	—	2,073
Pacaguarras	12	1000	1,012
Iténés	3	1197	1,200
Totals	23,750	3497	27,247

The colour of the Moxians is pale brown, mixed with olive; the Chapacuras, the Itonamas, and the Canichanas, appear to have absolutely the same tinge as the Chiquitians; while the Moxos and other nations of that group are a little less dark, having, perhaps, a little yellow mixed with the former shades; but this difference is so slight that it can only be discovered by close attention; otherwise, the general tinge, differing but little from that of the people of Chaco, is only a little paler or a little more yellow.

In the Moxian branch, the stature is generally greater than among the Chiquitians, and it nearly resembles that of the inhabitants of Chaco. The tallest attain a height of five feet six inches, and the average stature of the Movimas, Moxos, Canichanas, and Cayuvavas, is at most five feet two inches. The only nations who do not arrive at this size are the Chapacuras and Itonamas. This difference may be explained up to a certain point: among the first, by their neighbourhood to the mountains of Chiquitos. The women are generally in proportion with the men: nevertheless, those of the Canichanas appeared to us smaller; while among the Movimas, as we have already noticed among the tribes of the Pampas, the women are, on the contrary, nearly as tall as their husbands, or, at any rate, much above the usual relative proportion.

The figure of the Moxos resembles that of the Chiquitians and inhabitants of Chaco; at the same time that, among these latter, broad shoulders, a chest very much arched, and a stouter body, prove great strength,—with this difference notwithstanding, that the Moxos, generally still more vigorous than the Chiquitians, are apparently as strong as the natives of Chaco; yet they are distinguished from both by taller figures, bodies of better shape, and more slender waists. Their limbs, without projecting muscles, are generally fuller and more rounded. These characters present an exception to be remarked in the case of the Itonamas, who, though resembling in form the other nations, always have their limbs thin, and especially their legs. The Moxos are well-set, and walk straight, and with much ease. The greater number, especially of the Moxos, are subject to obesity. The women differ a little from those of the Chiquitian branch; they have large shoulders and hips; but their persons are less compact, and their waist is narrower, which indicates a tendency to the slight figure of European women. They are more agreeable, in general, than the Chiquitian women; they are yet robust, and have the bosom well formed, and of but moderate development, and their hands and feet are small.

The features of the Moxos are very different and easily distinguishable from those of the Chiquitians: the head is large, and a little elongated behind; the face is less full and broad than that of the Chiquitians, and is rather oblong; the cheek-bones are scarcely to be seen: the forehead is low and little arched; the nose short and flat, without being too large; the nostrils are expanded; the mouth small; the lips not thick; the eyes are in general small and horizontal; the ears small; the eyebrows narrow and arched; the chin rounded; the beard black, with little hair, and slow of growth; it is only seen on the upper lip and chin, and is never curled; the hair is black, long, thick, and sleek. Such are the general characters remarked in almost all these nations, yet with some exceptions.*

* For further details I must refer to M. d'Orbigny, from whose work these observations have been abstracted.

CHAPTER XXXIII.

THE BRASILIO-GUARANI, OR EASTERN NATIONS OF SOUTH AMERICA.

THE vast region of South America which lies to the eastward of the river Paraguay, and is cut off from the remainder of the continent by that stream, and by a line reaching northward from its sources to the mouth of the Orinoco in the Gulf of Mexico, was inhabited by a great number of aboriginal tribes, who were at one time supposed to speak as many distinct languages, and to constitute separate nations. Later information has considerably diminished their number. Two great families of nations exist within this region, viz. the Guarani, spread through Paraguay, and known to be allied to the Tupi tribes of Brazil;* and, secondly, the races who belong to the stock of the Caríbí, Galibi, or Caribbees, in the countries bordering on the Gulf of Mexico. They have a certain resemblance in feature and complexion, and are, according to d'Orbigny, referable to one physical type, of which the following is the characteristic description:—

"Complexion yellowish; statue middle; forehead not so much arched as in other races; eyes obliquely placed, and raised at the outer angle." These traits, which belong to the great nomadic races of South America, approximate to

* An interesting discussion upon the diffusion of the Tupi-Guarani languages, by Dr. R. G. Latham, will be found in the Appendix to Wallace's "Travels on the Amazon and Rio Negro," London, 1853. See p. 530 *et seq.* Dr. Latham confirms the statements of Hervas, who includes the Omagua in this class of languages, as stated by the author in this chapter, and carries it down so far to the south as Buenos Ayres. He shows also that the Mundrucu tongue, spoken by a large and warlike nation dwelling between the Tapajos and Madeira Rivers, is allied to the same class. The Mundrucus number from fifteen to twenty thousand warriors, and are the terror of all the other tribes who dwell on the right bank of the Amazons. See Lieut. W. L. Herndon's "Exploration of the Valley of the Amazon," Washington, 8vo. 1854, p. 314.—ED.

those of the nomades of High Asia. The complexion is nearly the same, for these nations do not generally belong to the Red Men of the New World: the face is round, the nose short, but the nostrils are not so wide or patulous nor do the cheek-bones project so much as in the Asiatic races. Von Spix and Martius thought the Caríbí strikingly similar to the Chinese.

The Guarani nation is one of the most interesting South American races, owing to the fact that they showed themselves particularly susceptible of civilisation and of instruction in the Christian religion, which they embraced in great numbers through the instructions of the Jesuit missionaries. We have many interesting accounts of the achievements of these zealous promoters of social improvement among the inhabitants of the wildernesses of South America, chiefly in the writings of ecclesiastics, before the evil hour when the king of Spain, yielding to the advice of the enemies of religion and of monarchy, ordered their expulsion from Paraguay, and left 120,000 new converts from one single aboriginal nation destitute of the advice and guidance of their spiritual and temporal instructors.

1. *Southern Guarani of Paraguay.*—The southern Guarani are those of Paraguay, either reduced now under the missions above mentioned, or still wandering in a state of liberty in the forests of that great province. Besides the Guarani, commonly so termed, who are converted to the Catholic religion, and inhabit thirty-two large towns on the shores of the Paraná, Paraguay, and Uruguay, there are other tribes of the same race still hidden in the forests, who have assumed different names from the neighbouring rivers or mountains, but still speak the Guarani language. Among these are the Tapes, Tobatinguas, and Cayuguas.

2. *Western Guarani.*—The western Guarani are the people described by Hervas under the names of Guarayi, Chiriguani, and Cirionos. The Guarayi were civilised by the Jesuits, and reduced under the celebrated missions of the Chiquitos. In the woods between the Chiquitos and

the Moxos, there are still some tribes of savage Guarayi. Dobrizhofer says, "Their language is a dialect of the Guarani, very little corrupted;" though, according to some traditions, they inhabited this country in the time of the Inca Yupangui. The Pagan Chiriguanos are formidable to all their neighbours. According to Abbot Gilii, the Guarani language is spoken with purity by the natives of 160 villages between the great river of Chaco and that of Mapayo of Santa Cruz, in the valleys of the Andes. To the northward of Santa Cruz are the barbarous Cirionos, who speak a dialect of the Chiriguano, and consequently of the Guarani language.

3. *Eastern Guarani of Brazil.*—The Eastern Guarani are the Tupi, or native inhabitants of the Brazils. "The general language of Brazil," says Hervas, "called Tupi, from the name of the first Indians who were converted to the holy faith, is not more different from the Guarani, viz. of Paraguay, than the Portuguese from the Spanish." The same writer enumerates, from information derived from ecclesiastics, the following tribes who speak the Tupi, with little variety of dialect, viz. the Cariyi, southward of the Tupi proper, reaching as far towards the south as the Rio Grande del Sud, or S. Pietro, the Samoyi, Tupinaqui, Timmiminos, Tobayari, Tupinambi, Apanti, Tapigoas, and several other tribes, occupying all the maritime countries as far northward as the river Marañon.

4. *Tribes Related to this Race on the Marañon.*—According to Hervas, the Omagua, and other dialects allied to it, spoken in the kingdom of Quito, are also branches of the great Guarani language. This implies a still further extension of the same race. Azara, as we have seen, supposed it to reach even as far northward as Guiana.

The Omagua, with the tribes nearly connected with them, form one of the most extensive nations in the northern parts of South America. They possessed the banks and islands of the Marañon, or river of Amazons, 200 leagues from the mouth of the Napo river, and probably formed a great part of those numerous tribes found by Orellana in this region.

[Wallace's Narrative of his Travels on the Amazon River may be consulted for many interesting details on the character of the aborigines who frequent its shores : out of these the following brief notices are selected. There is a general character among the whole of the Amazon Indians from which particular tribes vary but very slightly. "The skin is of a coppery or brown colour of various shades, often nearly the tint of smooth Honduras mahogany; jet-black straight hair, thick, and never curled, black eyes, and very little or no beard..... In some, the whole face is wide and rather flattened, but I could never discern an unusual obliquity of the eyes, or projection of the cheek-bones : in many of both sexes, the most perfect regularity of features exists, and there are numbers who in colour alone differ from a good-looking European. Their figures are generally superb..... the development of the chest is such as I believe never exists in the best-formed European, exhibiting a splendid series of convex undulations, without a hollow in any part of it."

"High up the rivers Tocantíns and Araguáya, there are numerous tribes of tall well-formed Indians..... most of them have enormously elongated ears hanging down on their shoulders, produced probably by weights suspended from the lobe in youth..... Commencing near Santarem, and extending among all the half-civilised Indians of the Amazon, Rio Negro, and other rivers, the Lingoa Geral,* or general Indian language, is spoken.

* In his Notes to Wallace's Narrative, p. 529, 531, Dr. Latham observes that the basis of the Lingoa Geral is Guarani, or Tupi; that the races in the Portuguese colony of Brazil who speak it are Tupis, while the allied populations of Entre Rios, Corrientes, Monte Video, and Paraguay, all settled by Spaniards, are known as Guarani. "This gave us a Tupi-Guarani class of languages, in which it was not very incorrect to say that the Tupi were the Guarani of Brazil, and the Guarani the Tupi of Paraguay. The *chief* difference was a verbal and nominal one" (p. 531).

Near the more populous towns and villages, it is used indiscriminately with the Portuguese; a little further it is often the only language known; and far up in the interior it exists in common with the native language of the tribe to which the inhabitants belong. It is now spread over all the interior of Brazil, and even extends into Peru and Venezuela, as well as Bolivia and Paraguay..... It is a simple and euphonious language, and is often preferred by Europeans who get thoroughly used to it."

Mr. Wallace informs us (p. 481) that he was best acquainted with the tribes on the Uacaiarí, an equatorial river which falls into the Rio Negro, between 67° and 68° W. Long. He enumerates in this region thirty tribes, of whom fourteen are upon the main stream; all have their distinct names, but they are collectively known as the Uaupés, which name is applied to the river itself on our maps. They are generally tall, very stout, and well formed. The men do not cut their hair, but tie it behind with a cord, and let it hang down below the middle of the back, invariably decorating the head with a comb, which is stuck in at the top; the women cut theirs to a moderate length, and it falls loose over the neck and back; they wear no comb. The men have little beard, which they carefully pull out, and they, as well as the women, pull out the hair of the eye-brows. The colour of the skin is a light, uniform, glossy, reddish brown.

They cultivate the soil, manufacture many useful articles, and have permanent houses; all their dwellings are built on one plan, which is a parallelogram having a semicircle at one end. They are always built of a size to contain several families, sometimes a whole tribe. One measured was 115 feet long by 75 broad, and about 30 in height, which held a dozen families, of near 100 persons. The roof is supported by cylindrical columns, beautifully straight and smooth, formed of trunks of trees; there is a clear opening in the centre 25 feet in width, and on the sides partitions of palm-leaves divide the area into distinct habitations for the separate families; the walls are made of the same material, so thickly bound together that they are proof against arrow and bullet. There is a large door at the square end 6 feet wide, and 8 or 10 in height, for the tribe generally, and a smaller one at the semicircular end for the chief, who has exclusive possession of that part of the house. The whole is carefully and strongly built, and all the parts "are bound together with split creepers, in a manner that a sailor would admire." Their hammocks, cooking utensils, and baskets, of which they have great quantities, are kept in the private apartments; the huge ovens and pans for making cashirí [mandioc beer] are placed in the sides of the central space, leaving room for the sports of the children and dances of the tribe in the middle.

The men wear a small piece of cloth as the only dress, the women none whatever; but all paint their bodies with red, black, and yellow colours, in regular patterns, as an equivalent. The men alone have any ornaments; and this circumstance, together with the never absent comb, gives them a feminine look, which Mr. Wallace thinks is the source of the tales of Amazons found by the early navigators on these rivers.

Their agriculture extends to a great variety of products, and is chiefly carried on by women, while the men are much engaged in hunting and fishing. We refer to the book for details on their modes of cultivation, the preparation of the produce, and various modes of catching fish.

Among the weapons of these tribes one is the gravatana, which is precisely the sampitan of the Malays,—a blowpipe, used, like the sampitan, with small poisoned arrows, and for the same purpose,—an evidence of the little ethnological value of similar analogies.

One tribe, the Cobeus, are cannibals; they eat the people of other tribes, and even make war for the purpose of procuring the means of gratifying their unnatural propensity. When they have more than they can consume at once, they smoke-dry the flesh over the fire, and preserve it for food a long time.

The work from which the above is taken, contains a good deal more about these and other tribes: but our limits compel us to confine ourselves to the concluding paragraphs :—"The main feature in the personal character of the Indians of this part of South America is a degree of diffidence, bashfulness, or coldness, which affects all their actions..... It is the same peculiarity which causes the men never to exhibit any feeling on meeting after a separation; though they have, and show, a great affection for their children, whom they never part with, nor can they be induced to do so, even for a short time. They scarcely ever quarrel among themselves, work hard, and submit willingly to authority. They are ingenious and skilful workmen, and readily adopt any customs of civilised life that may be introduced among them; and they seem capable of being formed, by education and good government, into a peaceable and civilised community.

"This change, however, will perhaps never take place: they are exposed to the influence of the refuse of Brazilian society, and will probably, before many years, be reduced to the condition of the other half-civilised Indians of the country, who seem to have lost the good qualities of savage life, and gained only the vices of civilisation."]

Of the Caríbian Race.

The Caríbian race, who, as we have seen, are supposed by M. d'Orbigny to be connected in language and other proofs of affinity with the Guarani, are of themselves one of the most extensively spread families of nations of South America.* The people who give name to this group are

* M. d'Orbigny has omitted these nations in his description of the South American tribes. From M. de Humboldt we derive the greater part of our information respecting them. The other nations of the Brazils, whose affinity to the Caríbí and the Guarani can only be con-

the celebrated race of Caraibs, or Caríbís. In the sixteenth century, this race was found spread over all the shores and islands of America, from the mouth of the river of Amazons, or from the borders of Brazil, to the Orinoco and the neighbourhood of Porto Rico. The lesser Antilles received from this nation the name of Caribbean Islands.* The Tamanacs, who belong to the same family, live on the right bank of the Orinoco: they were formerly powerful, but are now reduced to a small number.† The Arawacs live near Surinam and Berbice: on the upper part of the river of the last name they border on the Caribbees.‡ The Guäraünas inhabit the two islands in the delta of the Orinoco, where they build their houses upon trees.§ The Guaiquerías inhabit the Island of Margarette and the Peninsula of Araya.|| The Cumanagotos live to the westward of Cumana, in the mission of Piritoo.¶ The Pariagotos are the inhabitants of the Peninsula of Paria. Lastly, the Chayma, a race whose relations have been discovered by the Baron Von Humboldt, live to the westward of the Guäraünas, along the high mountains of the Cocollar and the Guacharo, in the missions of the Arragonese Capuchins of Cumana.

The Chaymas are inhabitants of a country distant more than 100 leagues from that of the Tamanacs. The dialect of the other nations mentioned above are associated either with the Tamanac or with the Caribbee, and more generally with the former. The idiom of the insular Caribbees, in the Antilles, differs somewhat from that spoken on the Continent; but these tribes are evidently branches of one stock.

Von Humboldt has given us a more particular account

---

jectured from a general resemblance, are best described in the works of Von Spix and Martius.

* "Mithridates," p. 674.

† Von Humboldt's "Personal Narrative," Vol. iii. p. 254.

‡ Quandt's "Nachricht von Suriname und seinen Einwohnern."

§ Von Humboldt's "Personal Narrative," p. 277.

|| Ibid. p. 288.

¶ Ibid. p. 281.

of the Chaymas, who are a people less known than the Caribbees. He describes their countenance and features as follows:—"The countenance of the Chaymas, without being hard and stern, has something sedate and gloomy; the forehead is small, and but little prominent. The eyes of the Chaymas are black, sunk, and very long; but they are neither so obliquely placed nor so small as in the people of the Mongolian race. The corner of the eye is, however, sensibly raised up towards the temples; the eyebrows are black, or dark brown, slender, and a little arched; the eyelids are furnished with very long eyelashes, and the habit of casting them down, as if they were lowered by lassitude, softens the look of the women, and makes the eye, thus veiled, less than it really is."

We are informed by the same author, that the complexion of the Chaymas is the same as that of the other American tribes who are nearly in the same latitude. It is not a copper colour. "The denomination of *rouge-cuivrés*, or copper-coloured, could never have originated in equinoctial America, in the description of the native inhabitants."* He remarks, also, that the old accounts of the earliest voyagers to these regions represent some of the inhabitants, as those of Paria, to be of a much fairer colour than that now prevalent among the generality of the inhabitants. The climate of Paria is remarkable for the great coolness of the mornings. The inhabitants of Paria, according to Ferdinand Columbus, "were better made, more civilised, and whiter than the people whom the discoverer of America had till then seen." But many other writers are more particular in their account. If we may believe these writers, the old inhabitants of Paria were clothed, though the races now existing on the coast are naked: they were nearly white, when not exposed to the sun's rays, and had long flowing hair, of a yellow or auburn colour.†

* Von Humboldt's "Personal Narrative," p. 221.

† "Pariæ incolæ albi, capillis oblongis, protensis, flavis." "Utriusque

Juri

Botocudos

*The Botocudos.**

The Botocudos are well known as one of the most barbarous nations of the world. Their country, in the sixteenth century, was the Capitanerias of Ilheos, as far as Porto Seguro, where they carried on a dangerous and destructive warfare against the Portuguese colonists of the Brazils. They are now confined to the inland country, from the Rio Doce to the Rio Pardo, that is, from the 18° to the 20° of south latitude.

M. d'Orbigny says that the complexion of the Botocudos is very similar to that of the Guarani, but somewhat lighter,—the result, as he supposes, of their inhabiting shady forests: it approaches to the colour of the Guarayos. A native Botocudo described by this traveller resembled the Guarani in stature, form, and proportions, and likewise in features, with this exception, that the cheek-bones were a little more prominent, the nose somewhat shorter, the mouth larger, the countenance more savage, the beard still less, and the eyes smaller and more oblique at the outer angle, which give them a greater resemblance to the Mongoles. The Botocudos are likewise of a yellower colour than the Guarani and other nations of South America. (See the right hand figure of Plate 60.)

The Botocudos are said to have been cannibals, and the most savage of all the American nations. They wore for

sexûs indigenæ albi velut nostrates, præter eos qui sub sole versantur."—*Peter Martyr*. Gomara and Garcia are cited nearly to the same effect by Von Humboldt.—*Personal Narrative*, Vol. iii. p. 288, English translation.

For the Caribs and kindred races, see Latham's "Varieties of Man," p. 446—448. Dr. Latham is of opinion that a part of the Caribs conquered their way from South to North, rather than in the opposite direction, as some writers have supposed from very unsatisfactory reasons. —Sir R. Schomburgk's valuable papers in the Transactions of several learned societies contain much information on the tribes in British Guiana. Dalton's "History of British Guiana," London, 1855, affords the most recent notices of these tribes.—Ed.

* The best accounts of the Botocudos are to be found in the voyages of MM. Spix and Martius, of M. Auguste de St.-Hilaire, and Prince Maximilian of Neuwied.

ornaments collars or strings of human teeth.* Of late, attempts have been made to introduce among them civilisation and Christianity. The following account of these efforts is to be found in the papers of the Society for the Protection of Aborigines :—

"In contrast with these violations of human right, perpetrated, upon the confines of the Brasilian empire, upon the aborigines of Guiana, it is gratifying to be able to report the peculiarly pleasing and encouraging change which has taken place nearer to the seat of the imperial government, and under the auspices of the young emperor. The Botocudo Indians, who inhabit the country watered by Rio Doce and its tributaries, have been described as amongst the lowest of the human race on the continent of South America. Wandering, savage, and all but naked, they rendered their repulsive countenances more ugly by the insertion of billets of wood in their perforated lips and ears, and cannibalism is said to have been practised among them. By the exertions of Guido Marliere, to whom communications were made on the part of this Society, almost at the commencement, Guido Pocrane, a Botocudo Indian of great native talent, was introduced to the blessings of civilisation and Christianity, and his new acquirements were directed to the amelioration of his countrymen. His exertions have been crowned with signal success, and four sections of the barbarous tribes have been brought under the influence of civilisation, and taught to cultivate their soil, from which they have raised not only enough for their own support, but a surplus, which has been the means of rescuing even a portion of the white Brasilians from famine and starvation. Useful laws have been introduced among them, and Guido Pocrane, in the criminal code which he has established, has set an example which legislators, the hereditary professors of Christianity, would do well to imitate, in the total exclusion of capital punishment."

* In the first volume of Sir. W. Ouseley's Travels, there is a portrait of a Botocudo woman ornamented in the way described.

The various nations of the Brasilian countries, whose languages have never been adequately investigated and compared, but are generally regarded as distinct from each other, bear a resemblance in physical characters to the Guarani. They are supposed by M. d'Orbigny to belong to the same race or family of nations. This opinion is founded on the various portraits furnished by the works of MM. Spix and Martius, Prince Maximilian of Neuwied, and MM. Rugendas and Debret, of the Bogres of the province of San Paolo, the Cumacans, the Juris,* the Coroados, and the Cordopos. The same observation applies also to a variety of tribes less known, and of whom we have but imperfect descriptions, such as the Macuani, the Penhams of Minas-Geraes, the Machacali, the Capoxos, the Cataxos, the Comanaxos of the frontiers of Porto Seguro and of Bahia, the Carivi, the Sabúcas, the Murus, the Mundrucus.†

All these tribes, and many others described by the travellers above mentioned, resemble in the general type of organisation the Brasilio-Guarani races.

* See the left hand figure on Plate from the Atlas of Spix and Martius. Wallace, in his "Travels on the Amazon and Rio Negro," London, 8vo. 1853, says, "The Jurís.... are remarkable for a custom of tattooing in a circle (not in a square, as in a plate in Dr. Prichard's work) round the mouth, so as to resemble the little black-mouthed squirrel-monkeys (Callithrix sciureus)" (p. 510).—Ed.

† See note in p. 632, *suprà*.

BOOK III.

CONCLUSIONS.

CHAPTER I.

GENERAL OBSERVATIONS DEDUCED FROM THE PRECEDING SURVEY OF HUMAN RACES.

In the ethnographical outline which I have now concluded, the facts have been very briefly stated, and it would be difficult to recapitulate them in a shorter compass. I shall merely point out some of the most obvious inferences.

The different races of men are not distinguished from each other by strongly marked, uniform, and permanent distinctions, as are the several species belonging to any given tribe of animals. All the diversities which exist are variable, and pass into each other by insensible gradations; and there is, moreover, scarcely an instance in which the actual transition cannot be proved to have taken place.

Thus, if we consider the varieties of figure which are generally looked upon as the most important, and begin with those of the skeleton and the skull as their foundation, we shall find every particular type undergoing deviations and passing into other forms. We have seen that, in many races who have, generally and originally, as far as we can go back towards their origin, heads of the pyramidal figure, with broad faces, or the Mongolian type, the oval or European shape, with European features, displays itself in individuals, and often becomes the characteristic of tribes. We must refer the reader to the account given in the preceding pages of the five great nomadic races, to the description of the Chinese, Japanese, Koreans, and Indo-Chinese nations.

Again, the shape of the head in the black races varies in like manner. The Sudanian nations have a black complexion and crisp hair, with a form of the head different from that of the Negro; and the type varies in particular tribes, and even in the same tribe. Towards the south, the black and crisp-haired Africans display, in the highland of the Kafirs, a form resembling the European; and, in the country of the nomadic Hottentots, make a signal approximation to the physical character prevalent among the nomades of High Asia. Among the aboriginal races of the New World, similar varieties and similar deviations occur. We have seen that the nations of America are not, as it has been represented, reducible to one physical type,—that their skulls display many different leading forms; and although the ethnology of the Western Continent is as yet, owing to obvious causes, much less complete than that of Asia and Europe, we have, notwithstanding this circumstance, found instances in which the most strongly marked deviations are displayed within the limits of one and the same great family of American nations.

Individual varieties have been pointed out as affording a similar evidence. In the plates at the early part of this volume, which contain figures of three skulls in one view (p. 111), the reader may see an example of striking resemblance in heads taken from the most dissimilar and widely separated races of mankind. Many similar examples might easily be found, and, perhaps, some still more precisely to the purpose. The three figures above mentioned were taken casually from skulls now in my own collection.

With respect to colour, it is still more easy to trace the greatest variations within the limits of one race. There is, perhaps, not one great family of nations, having its branches spread through different climates, which does not display in this particular the most strongly marked varieties. It is true that among European colonists settled in hot climates such varieties are not so perceptible within a few generations; but in many well-known instances of earlier colonisation they are very clearly manifested. We have traced them in the instances of the Jews and Arabs, in the tribes of Hindús, or rather of the Indian race, spread through India, compared with those of the Himálayan countries. We might add innumerable facts tending to bring out the same result. Under this head, it would be quite fair to take the whole Indo-European family of nations as one example, since from one identical stock must have sprung the Gothic, the Iranian races, and the Arian stem of India, including the xanthous Siah-Posh of Kafiristan, the yellow-haired and blue-eyed villagers of Jumnotri and Gangotri, and the black Hindús of Anu-gangam.

It has often been said that the native tribes of America present an exception to the general observation deduced from a survey of the nations of the Old World, and that the complexion of the Americans displays no relation to climate. We have proved, on the contrary, that tribes alike belonging to the American stock manifest the influence of external agencies not less distinctly than do the white inhabitants of Europe compared with the black races of Africa. Witness the comparison of the white Americans of the north-west coast with the black Californians.

If any one should call in question the assertion that the colour of human races has any relation to the climates of different countries, we have only need to appeal to the most general and broadly marked facts which the history of mankind presents.

Thus it is obvious that the intertropical region of the earth is the principal seat of the black races of men, and the region remote from the tropics that of the white races, and that the climates approaching to the tropics are generally inhabited by nations which are neither of the darkest nor of the fairest complexion, but of an intermediate one. To this observation it may be added that high mountains, and countries of great elevation, are generally inhabited by people of lighter colour than those where the level is low, such as sandy or swampy plains on the sea-coast. Thus, if we begin with Africa, we shall find a great number of distinct races, as far as a total diversity of languages can be thought to distinguish men into separate races, spread over that great continent; and it may be observed that those whose abode is between the tropics, though differing from each other in many peculiarities, agree in the darkness of their complexion. In fact, if we divide Africa into three portions, we may define by the tropics the extent of the black complexion in its inhabitants.

The nature of the hair is, perhaps, one of the most permanent characteristics of different races. The hair of the Negro has been termed woolly: it is not wool, and only differs from the hair of other races in less important respects. This subject has been discussed in the early part of my work, and I shall not repeat what has there been said. It may be seen that the texture of the hair affords in the animal kingdom no specific characters. In mankind, we find it in every gradation of variety; and if we take the African nations, I mean the black tribes who are apparently of genuine native origin, as one body, we shall discover among them every possible gradation in the texture of the hair, from the short close curls of the Kafir to the crisp but bushy locks of the Berberine, and, again, to the flowing hair of the black Tuarík, or Tibbo. In some instances, indeed, it appears that the change from one to the other may be shown in actual transition.

I have now gone as far as the prescribed limits of this work admit, in the investigation of anatomical and external bodily characters, as they vary in different tribes of men and deviate from a common type: it now remains for me to advert in a summary manner to two other questions which were proposed for discussion in the outset. I allude to physiological varieties, or differences between races in regard to the laws of the animal economy; and, secondly, to psychological varieties, or diversities in the mental powers and habits, or in the intellectual and moral character of nations.

CHAPTER II.

PHYSIOLOGICAL COMPARISON OF HUMAN RACES.

I HAVE observed, in the former part of this work, that a criterion of distinctness of species, or of common origin, may be obtained by comparing the physiological history of any two or more given races in the animal kingdom. Such a criterion must be founded on the general observation that tribes of one kind resemble each other in regard to the great laws of the animal economy, while, in respect to all the leading principles of organisation, animals of different species, though proximate and so analogous as to be referred by naturalists to one genus or tribe, are uniformly found to differ. I must now proceed to apply this remark to the comparison of human races, with a view to determine on this ground, which affords a somewhat distinct field of inquiry from that hitherto surveyed, the principal point which I have undertaken to discuss.

The laws of the animal economy determine all the principal facts connected with reproduction, as the times and frequency of breeding, in mammalia the period of gestation, in birds that of sitting on eggs, the number of progeny brought forth at a time, and the period of suckling or watching over the offspring. The progress of physical development and decay is likewise ordained by Nature to take place in each species, though with some variety as regards individuals, according to a definite rule. The periods at which individuals arrive at adult growth, the different changes which the constitution undergoes at particular ages, the periods of greatest vigour and decline, and the total duration of life, are given, though with individual exceptions and varieties to every species of animals.

A remark must be made in the outset of this inquiry which will considerably modify the result. Although it is obvious, on a cursory view of the subject, that greater uniformity prevails in the several tribes of the animal kingdom in regard to these fundamental laws and in the physiological constitution, than in the outward aspect or colour and the nature of the integument, still there is a considerable range of variation, even in the internal functions. We have already adverted to the change produced in cows, or to an hereditary peculiarity produced by habit and by human interference in the breeds, and changing the length of time of giving milk. It seems from this, and from other facts which have been related, that when domesticated animals have been brought to undergo a particular modification of their natural state, and to obey a new law for some generations, the habit becomes, as it were, their second nature, and that their hereditary constitution is changed. Facts of a similar kind may be collected from the history of human tribes. We have seen that the nations who have inhabited for centuries the heights of the South American Andes have a longer or more capacious chest, and lungs of a greater volume, than other races,—a structure of body eminently useful to men who breathe a rare atmosphere, —a peculiarity, moreover, which the conditions of their existence have an obvious tendency to produce by their mechanical efforts. Here, then, since the Quichuas and the Aymaras are but branches of the American family of nations, and not a distinct and peculiar race, such as any one might assume to have been created on the spot, with a physical adaptation to its local conditions,—here we find an instance of long-continued habit, and the result of external agencies, modifying the structure of body, and with it the state of the most important functions of life, in such a manner as to constitute and bring forth, *de novo*, an adaptation to the surrounding agencies. This may furnish an idea of the modification which various races undergo, and have undergone, in different regions,—modifications which have brought them into relation with the physical conditions prevalent in such regions. Many parallel facts are obvious to those who look for them. If we compare the light and muscular, though lean and agile, Arab, whose daily allowance of food is five dates and a little water, with the fat, blubber-eating Esquimaux, what a vast difference do we perceive in the external appearance! bespeaking an equally great one in the internal constitution of these two nations. These peculiarities are the result of external circumstances: we perceive the actual presence of external conditions which have a natural tendency to call them forth. In other instances, when we cannot perceive how these agencies operate, we may infer a similar causation, and this particularly in those cases where an adaptation is to be discovered of the peculiar organic type to the local conditions of existence.

It is, doubtless, on a similar principle that the constitution of races becomes so formed as to bear without inconvenience particular climates, which are unwholesome and destructive to other races. Thus the natives of Sierra Leone sustain comparatively little inconvenience from their climate, though it is destructive to Europeans. That this is not owing to original organisation we collect from the fact, of which we are assured by an intelligent physician long resident in the colony, that the free Negroes who were brought from Nova Scotia, and whose ancestors had been generally resident for some generations in a very different climate from that of Sierra Leone, are subject to the same diseases as Europeans. In my "Researches into the Physical History of Mankind," I have collected a great number of examples of similar acclimatisation, or of a change brought about in races of men who have been removed to a new climate. It is there proved, if I am not mistaken, by abundant evidence, that this process generally requires many generations to bring it about, and that, when once produced, the new characters are hereditary, and impressed upon the race.

If due allowances are made for such modifications, which are changes taking place according to a law of adaptation, we shall find all human races remarkably uniform with respect to all the principal laws, or leading phenomena, of the animal economy.

1. The average duration of human life is nearly the same in the different races of men. But in order to estimate the facts which bear upon this subject, an account must be taken of the vast influence which climate alone exercises on the rate of mortality. It is well known that the proportional number of individuals who attain a given age differs in different countries; and that the warmer the climate, other circumstances being equal, so much the shorter is the average duration of human life. Even within the limits of Europe the difference is very great.

In some instances, according to the calculations of M. Moreau de Jonnès, the rate of mortality, and inversely the duration of life, differ by nearly one-half from the proportions discovered in other examples. The following is a brief extract from a table presented to the Institute by this celebrated calculator. The table comprehends returns belonging to different periods, illustrative of the effect produced by political changes and improvements in the state of society on the duration of human life. I have omitted this part, and have only abstracted that which illustrates the influence of climate:—

Table exhibiting the Annual Mortality in different Countries in Europe.

In		from	to		1 death in
In Sweden	from	1821	to 1825	......	1 death in 45
Denmark	..	1819 ..	—	....	45
Germany	..	1825 ..	—	....	45
Prussia	..	1821 ..	1824	....	39
Austrian Empire	..	1825 ..	1830	....	43
Holland	..	1824 ..	—	....	40
England	..	1821 ..	—	....	58*
Great Britain	..	1800 ..	1804	....	47
France	..	1825 ..	1827	....	39·5
Canton de Vaud	..	1824 ..	—	....	47
Lombardy	..	1827 ..	1828	....	31
Roman States	..	1827 ..	—	....	28
Scotland	..	1821 ..	—	....	50

The difference of twenty-eight and fifty is very considerable: but even the latter rate of mortality is considerably greater than that which the data collected by M. Moreau de Jonnès attribute to Iceland, Norway, and the northern parts of Scotland.

No adequate data have yet been collected for estimating the comparative longevity of different races of men, after making suitable allowances for the influence of climates; but facts are easily to be found which prove that no great difference exists in this respect between the most dissimilar tribes. It was calculated by Buffon, with reference principally to white men, that a third part of the human race die before the age of ten years; one-half before that of thirty-five; two-thirds before fifty-two; and three-fourths before sixty-one years of age. A very different computation has been made by later writers: according to Hufeland's estimate, out of a hundred individuals born, fifty die before their tenth year, and six only live to be above the age of sixty.†

Many instances of longevity in Europeans have been collected by Mr. Easton, from whose work I have taken the

* There must be a mistake in this number. According to Porter and Rickman, the number of annual deaths in England, from 1821 to 1831, is 1 in 51.

† Hist. Nat. du Genre-Humain, par M. Virey, Paris, 1824.

first of the following tables. He has discovered the following numbers of persons who have reached the ages below stated :—

From 100 to 110, both inclusive	....	1310
..	110 .. 120	277
..	120 .. 130	84
..	130 .. 140	26
..	140 .. 150	7
..	150 .. 160	3
..	160 .. 170	2
..	170 .. 180	3

Instances of Longevity in Negroes.

Mallum Dando, king of Rabbah	115
Robert Lynch, Jamaica	160
Catherine Lopez, Jamaica	134
Margaret Darby, Jamaica	130
Mulatto at Fredericktown, North America, in 1797	180
Mary Goodrall, Jamaica	120
Statera ——, St. John's, Antigua	130
Rebecca Tury, Falmouth, Jamaica	140
Tom, a slave of Mrs. Bacon, South Carolina	130
Francis Peat, Kingston	130
Jane Morgan, Jamaica	120
Juan Moroygota	138
Joseph Ban, Jamaica	146
Catherine Hiatt, Jamaica	150
Frances Johnson, a Sambo woman	107

Particular notices respecting these individuals may be seen in the first volume of my "Researches into the Physical History of Mankind," where the reader who wishes to pursue the inquiry will find evidence that a similar degree of longevity belongs to other races of men, both in the Old and New Continents.

The general conclusion to which we are brought by all the facts that can be collected in relation to the period imposed by nature on human longevity, and the general duration of human life, is that there is no ascertained difference in this particular between the various races which constitute the human family. It would appear that the same law, as to the duration of life, has been imposed by Providence on all nations of men. In this point of view they appear as one species. Even in different climates the *tendency to exist* for a given time is the same: the duration of life varies only from the circumstance, that the external causes which bring about an accidental and premature catastrophe, or which wear out the health and impair the bodily frame, are more rife or more potent in one climate than in another.

Of the Progress of Physical Development and the Periodical Changes of the Constitution: Natural and Vital Functions of different Races.

The specific temperature of the body is the same, or nearly so, in all the races of men. This subject has been investigated, and the above-stated fact established by the researches of Dr. Davy.

There is no remarkable difference in the frequency of the pulse, or any of the other vital functions, between different tribes, except such occasional, and temporary, and individual variations as are easily explained by the results of immediate external agencies.

There is one subject connected with this department of physiology which has not yet been fully explored, or, at least, on which naturalists and physicians have not arrived at an unanimous sentiment. It has been a very general and long-established opinion, that the period appointed by nature for marriage, and the commencement of relations between the sexes, varies in different climates; that women begin to bear children, or to be capable of bearing them, at a very much earlier period in warm countries than in cold ones, and that they become old at an age when the females of Europe are still in their prime. This notion has been universally prevalent among physiologists: it was established by the authority of the celebrated Haller, and until lately has never been called in question. It was laid hold of by Montesquieu as a fact which tended to explain some of the great moral diversities which distinguish the Oriental from the Western nations. "Women in hot climates," says this philosopher, "are marriageable at eight, nine, or ten years of age. Thus, in these countries, infancy and marriage almost always coincide. They are old at twenty; their reason, therefore, never accompanies their beauty. When beauty demands the empire, the want of reason forbids the claim; when reason is obtained, beauty is no more. The women ought, then, to be in a state of dependence, for reason cannot procure in old age that empire which even youth and beauty could not give. It is, therefore, extremely natural that in these places a man, where no law opposes it, should leave one wife to take another, and that polygamy should be introduced."

A very exaggerated idea has prevailed in Europe, founded on the assertions of travellers who wanted data for accurate conclusions, as to the periods of physical development, particularly in Arabia and Palestine, and it is to these countries that Montesquieu chiefly referred. Very different conclusions might be deduced from passages in the Old Testament as to the inhabitants of Palestine; and, with respect to the women of Arabia, the question seems to have been settled by a reference to authority which on this point few will venture to dispute; I mean that of Mohammed and the commentators on the Koran. In the fourth chapter of the Koran, "On Woman," there is this command in reference to the duty of a guardian:—"Examine the orphans (in religious matters) until they attain the age of marriage." "The age of marriage," says Mr. Sale, "or of maturity, is reckoned to be fifteen,—a decision supported by a tradition of the Prophet, although Abu Hanifah thinks eighteen the proper age." In the regulations touching divorce, in the chapter of the "Cow," precautions are laid down against dismissing a wife under any uncertainty as to her being pregnant at the time. Sale adds, "that in the case of women who are too young—such premature marriages being sanctioned or tolerated in Arabia, a custom which is probably the real foundation for the mistaken notion to which I advert—as well as in those who are too old to have children, it is the rule to wait only three months. The age at which they are reckoned too old is that of *fifty-five lunar or fifty-three solar years.*" We thus find that the periods of life at which the principal physical changes take place are just the same among the natives of Arabia as in Europe; and the plea or excuse, founded on this supposed premature development and decay of the female sex, in favour of the depraved morality of the Oriental nations, is just as groundless as was the position long maintained, but refuted by the inquiries of Carsten Niebuhr, that the proportionate numbers of the sexes are different in Arabia and in Europe.

The whole subject of the periodical changes in physical life with respect to the female sex has been of late years investigated afresh by a very able writer, who has collected much new and valuable information regarding it. To his papers, which have elucidated a very important part of physiology, and are calculated to remove much prejudice and misconception, I must refer my readers who wish to pursue the inquiry. The general conclusion which he has in my opinion fully established, is, that the difference of climate occasions very little, if any, important diversity as to the periods of life and the physical changes to which the human constitution is subject; and that in all these great regulations of the animal economy, if we may use such an expression, mankind, whether white or black, are placed by nature nearly on an equal footing. As the duration of life and the age of adult growth are known to be nearly the same, it would be contrary to all probability should any material difference be found to prevail in respect to any one particular function or set of functions; yet the contrary opinion was universally prevalent from the time of Haller till it was refuted by Mr. Roberton.*

* Mr. Roberton's memoir, which deserves to be much better known than it has hitherto been, was published in the "Edinburgh Medical and

CHAPTER III.

COMPARISON OF HUMAN RACES WITH RESPECT TO MENTAL ENDOWMENTS.

THERE is one point of view in which it still remains for us to compare the different tribes of the human family; that is, with regard to mental endowments.

Psychology is, with respect to mankind, the history of the mental faculties; it comprehends, likewise, an account of those properties in the different races of animals which most nearly resemble the mental endowments of man. It has been observed, in the preliminary part of this work, that the instincts of one tribe of animals are not those of another; that no two separate species resemble each other precisely in their habits of life, tendencies to action, manner of existence, or in the internal principles of feeling, appetency, and aversion, of which the actions and habits are the outward signs and manifestations. If now it should appear, on inquiry, that one common mind, or psychical nature, belongs to the whole human family, a very strong argument would thence arise, on the ground of analogy, for their community of species and origin.

But can it be maintained that such is really the fact? On first adverting to this inquiry, most persons would be likely to adopt the negative side of the question; for what greater contrasts can be imagined than those which present themselves when we compare in their actual state the different races of mankind? Let us imagine, for a moment, a stranger from another planet to visit our globe, and to contemplate and compare the manners of its inhabitants, and let him first witness some brilliant spectacle in one of the highly civilised countries of Europe,—the coronation of a monarch, the installation of St. Louis on the throne of

Surgical Journal," Vol. xxxviii. 1832. The same writer has lately published an additional memoir, with a continuation of his researches in reference to the Negro race, in No. 152 of the same Journal.

his ancestors, surrounded by an august assembly of peers, and barons, and mitred abbots, anointed from the cruse of sacred oil brought by an angel to ratify the divine privilege of kings,—let the same person be carried into a hamlet in Negroland, in the hour when the sable race recreate themselves with dancing and barbarous music,—let him then be transported to the saline plains over which bald and tawny Mongoles roam, differing but little in hue from the yellow soil of their steppes, brightened by the saffron flowers of the iris and tulip,—let him be placed near the solitary den of the Bushman, where the lean and hungry savage crouches in silence like a beast of prey, watching with fixed eyes the birds which enter his pitfall, or the insects and reptiles which chance brings within his grasp, —let the traveller be carried into the midst of an Australian forest, where the squalid companions of kangaroos may be seen crawling in procession in imitation of quadrupeds,—can it be supposed that such a person would conclude the various groups of beings whom he had surveyed to be of one nature, one tribe, or the offspring of the same original stock? It is much more probable that he would arrive at an opposite conclusion.

It is only by tracing the history of the diversified human races from ancient times, and by comparing the former with the present state, we are made aware of the great changes which time and circumstances have effected in the condition of particular nations, and are brought to admit the probability of the opinion that beings apparently so different in their whole manner of existence can be in any way allied. It is this inquiry that brings within our observation, in the first instance, one of the great distinctions between the nature of mankind and that of animals. I allude to the uniformity of habits in successive generations which prevails through all the tribes belonging to the lower departments of the living world, and the variations which take place in human races, and their tendency to improve, or to alternate periods of improvement, with reverses and retrograde changes. The Numidian lion and the satyr of the desert, the monarchies of bees and the republics of African termites, are precisely to-day what they were in the age of Æsop and in the kingdom of Juba; while the descendants of the tribes who are described by Tacitus as living in squalid misery in solitary dens, amid the morasses of the Vistula, have built St. Petersburg and Moscow; and the posterity of cannibals and phthirophagi now feed on pillaus and wheaten bread. When we consider that the habits of men are so changed, in some races whose past and present state comes within the sphere of history, we cannot presume to determine that such differences as those to which we have before adverted may not have been the result of circumstances favouring the progressive improvement of our race, and, in other instances, preventing it, or forcing a tribe already civilised to return to the brutality of savage life.

It would appear that, in all that belongs to the sustenance of life and the supply of bodily wants, the habits of men are liable to indefinite variations. In the external aspect of human actions and human society, the most complete changes that can be imagined have actually taken place, and in these things there is nothing stable or permanent. In order to discover fixed principles of human action, which, by reason of their constancy, may be regarded as typical of the whole family of mankind, or of some particular department of it, and thus furnish a topic of comparison with the uniform and specific instincts of the brute creation, we must look somewhat more deeply into the subject, and contemplate the inward principles of human nature, the sentiments, feelings, sympathies, internal consciousness, as well as the external habits of life and action, which thence result. There are, indeed, certain habits of mankind which, from their prevalence, may be regarded as universal characters. The use of conventional speech has been regarded as one of the most remarkable characteristics of humanity: its universal existence among men is not less remarkable than its total absence among the inferior tribes. The use of fire, of artificial clothing, of arms, the art of domesticating animals, are, some of them at least, characters not less general. But all these arts, as well as that of conventional language, are only certain outward manifestations of that internal agency which is the really distinctive attribute of human nature. It is this principle, and its most essential and characteristic phenomena, if we can discover them, that we must take as the subject of comparison with the psychical nature of the lower animals. If, now, we inquire more intimately into the relations of this faculty of man with that which corresponds with it in brutes, we shall find great and important relations to subsist between them. Both, for example, are principles of action bestowed on the respective orders of creatures to promote the well-being and conservation of individuals and of tribes. The desire of present pleasure, or to secure for the future happiness and prosperity, is the end or aim and the leading principle of action in all animated beings, and this is the great source of active energy in mankind and in the lower tribes. But, in the nature of this principle, some philosophers insist on drawing a strong distinction between mankind and the inferior orders, and they found it on the circumstance, taken for granted rather than proved, that all the acts of the lower animals are performed without consciousness of the end. "Deus est anima brutorum," said the metaphysicians of the middle ages, who maintained that the lower species are merely mechanical agents. The assertion had no other groundwork than a mere conjecture: it was incapable of proof; for who can demonstrate that birds, in building their nests, are not aware that they are making provision for their young; that the ant constructs her heap without caution of her future wants; that the working bees which surround their queen feel nothing like a loyal devotion to the monarch of the hive; or that the termites, who drag their vanquished enemies into captivity, and force them to guard their young, do not lord it over their vassals with the same domineering pride with which the Persian despot trod on the neck of a Roman emperor?

The changeless uniformity which prevails in the habits of one class of beings, contrasted with the variation, equally remarkable when one generation is compared with another, in the higher class, is a more really characteristic difference between the life of instinctive and that of rational agents. This is the distinction most obvious, and the only one that is obvious, to a superficial and casual observer. But those who look more closely into the nature of actions, and into the more recondite history of feelings and sentiments, which are the prime movers and secret springs of actions, are enabled to discover a more important distinction; and this is to be found in the very different scope towards which the active energies of instinct and of reason are directed. The energies of all the lower animals, the whole sum of their activities, excited into action by the stimulus of desire or aversion, according to different laws impressed on each species, are directed towards the present safety and immediate well-being of the individual or of his tribe. But if we survey the whole sphere of human actions, in the vast field of observation which the entire history of mankind presents, we shall find the same remark can here be applied but in a very limited degree. On the contrary, there is nothing more remarkable in the habitudes of mankind, and in their manner of existence in various parts of the world, than a reference, which is everywhere more or less distinctly perceptible, to a state of existence to which they feel themselves to be destined after the termination of their visible career, and to the influence which both civilised and barbarous men believe to be exercised over their condition, present and future, by unseen agents, differing in attributes according to the sentiments of different nations, but everywhere acknowledged to exist, and regarded with sentiments of awe and apprehension. The rites everywhere performed for the dead, the various ceremonies of sepulture, of embalming, of cremation, funereal processions and pomps following the deceased, in every age and nation during countless ages,—tombs raised over their remains, innumerable tumuli scattered over all the regions of the world, the only memorials of races long extinct,—the morais, or houses of the dead, and the gigantic monuments of the Polynesians,—the magnificent pyramids of Egypt and of Anahuac,—the prayers and litanies set up in behalf of the living and of the dead in the churches of Christendom, in the mosques and pagodas of the East, as heretofore in the temples of the Pagan world,—the power of sacerdotal and consecrated orders, who have caused themselves to be revered as the interpreters of destiny, and as mediators between gods and men,—pontiffs, vicegerents of the Deity, on the banks of the Tiber, of the Brahmaputra, and the Arabian Gulf,—sacred wars, desolating empires through zeal for some metaphysical dogma, which the mass of those who fought and perished never understood,—toilsome pilgrimages performed every year, during long successive centuries, through every region of the earth, by thousands, of black and of white men, seeking atonement for guilt at the tombs of prophets and saints,—immolations of the old and the young, voluntary deaths of the aged, and sacrifices of children by their parents,—the slaughter of animals for the typical or piacular averting of contracted guilt,—all these, and other similar phenomena in the history of all the barbarous and civilised nations of the world, would lead us to believe that all mankind sympathise in deeply impressed feelings and sentiments, which are as mysterious in their nature as in their origin. These are certainly among the most remarkable of the psychological phenomena which are peculiar to human beings, and which serve to distinguish the habits of men, not in their external aspect, but in their inward nature and originating principles of action, from the whole life and agency of the lower orders of the creation.

If it should appear, after a full investigation of these

phenomena, that there are leading principles in the psychology of human races which, in their most important relations, stand in correspondence with the diversified instincts of the lower species, and, moreover, that these leading principles are common to all human races, a strong argument, as we have before observed, is plainly deducible in favour of the common origin of mankind.

I shall now endeavour to pursue this line of inquiry, and to illustrate the psychological history of the most widely separated races of men. This object may be attained by collecting, in the first place, the most striking and characteristic particulars relating to the moral and intellectual state of such tribes, of their original superstitions or religious dogmas in times when they were as yet cut off from participation in the common acquirements of the civilised and Christianised world; and, secondly, by showing how far such races have been found capable of receiving and appropriating the blessings of civilisation and Christianity when they were introduced among them.

It would occupy too much time and space to go through this problem in relation to all the different tribes of men, and it will be sufficient to survey two or three of the most diversified races. The nations of the New World, taken as an aggregate, may claim the first place in this inquiry. I shall collect facts which may tend to throw some light on the inquiry, as it regards the American nations from the Polar regions to Cape Horn; secondly, I shall advert to the woolly-haired races of Africa. A comparison of these with the nations of Europe and Asia will furnish a sufficient ground for resolving all doubts, or for confirming them.

CHAPTER IV.

PSYCHOLOGICAL VIEW OF THE NATIVE RACES OF AMERICA.

If there is any department of the human family which may be said, with an appearance of truth, to differ in its psychological character from the rest of mankind, it will be allowed to be the aboriginal stock of people in the New World. A celebrated writer, Dr. Von Martius, who has enjoyed great opportunities of research into the natural history of the Portuguese territory in America, and is well known to have directed his attention to the ethnography of its inhabitants, has represented in a very strong—and, as it appears to me, in an exaggerated—manner the moral as well as the physical peculiarities of these people. In order to avoid the risk of misrepresenting his opinions, I shall cite some passages from one of his works which has appeared in an English translation.

"The indigenous race of the New World," he observes, "is distinguished from all the other nations of the earth, externally, by peculiarities of make, but still more, internally, by their state of mind and intellect. The aboriginal American is at once in the incapacity of infancy and unpliancy of old age,—he unites the opposite poles of intellectual life. This strange and inexplicable condition has hitherto frustrated almost every attempt to reconcile him completely with the European, to whom he gives way, so as to make him a cheerful and happy member of the community: and it is this his double nature which presents the greatest difficulty to science when she endeavours to investigate his origin, and those earlier epochs of history in which he has for thousands of years moved, indeed, but made no improvement in his condition. But this is far removed from that natural state of child-like security which marked (as an inward voice declares to us, and as the most ancient written documents affirm) the first and foremost period of the history of mankind. The men of the red race, on the contrary, it must be confessed, do not appear to feel the blessing of a Divine descent, but to have been led, by merely animal instinct and tardy steps, through a dark Past to their actual cheerless Present. Much, therefore, seems to indicate that the native Americans are not in the first stage of that simple, we might say physical (*naturhistorischen*) development, — that they are in a secondary regenerated state.

"Besides the traces of a primeval, and, in like manner, ante-historic culture of the human race in America, as well as a very early influence on the productions of nature, we may also adduce as a ground for these views the basis of the present state of natural and civil rights among the aboriginal Americans,—I mean precisely, as before observed, that enigmatical subdivision of the natives into an almost countless multitude of greater and smaller groups, and that almost entire exclusion and excommunication with regard to each other, in which mankind presents its different families to us in America, like fragments of a vast ruin. The history of the other nations inhabiting the earth furnishes nothing which has any analogy to this.

"Long-continued migrations of single nations and tribes have doubtless taken place from a very early period throughout the whole continent of America, and they may have been especially the causes of dismemberment and corruption in the languages, and of a corresponding demoralisation of the people. By assuming that only a few leading nations were at first, as was the case with the Tupí people, dispersed like so many rays of light, mingled together, and dissolved, as it were, into each other by mutual collision, and that these migrations, divisions, and subsequent combinations, have been continued for countless ages, the present state of mankind in America may assuredly be accounted for; but the cause of this singular mis-development remains, no less on that account, unknown and enigmatical.

"Can it be conjectured that some extensive convulsion of nature—some earthquake rending asunder sea and land, such as is reported to have swallowed up the far-famed Island of Atlantis—has there swept away the inhabitants in its vortex? Has such a calamity filled the survivors with a terror so monstrous, as, handed down from race to race, must have darkened and perplexed their intellects, hardened their hearts, and driven them, as if flying at random, from each other, far from the blessings of social life? Have, perchance, burning and destructive suns, or overwhelming floods, threatened the man of the red race with a horrible death by famine, and armed him with a rude and unholy hostility, so that, maddened against himself by atrocious and bloody acts of cannibalism, he has fallen from the godlike dignity for which he was designed, to his present degraded state of darkness? Or is this inhumanising (*Ent-menschung*) the consequence of deeply-rooted preternatural vices, inflicted by the Genius of our race (with a severity which, to the eye of a short-sighted observer, appears throughout all nature like cruelty) on the innocent as well as on the guilty?"

Thus far Dr. Von Martius. His various works contain many developments of the same series of observations.* He is a writer highly imaginative, and his mind was forcibly struck with the singular aspect of human existence which he discovered in the western parts of South America. Had he taken a more extensive survey of the nations of the whole Continent, his opinion might have been somewhat modified.

That the American nations are not, in a psychological point of view, removed at so great a distance from the rest of mankind as these observations would lead us to suspect, will appear, if I am not mistaken, from the following considerations:—

1. The religious sentiments and impressions which prevailed of old among the nations of the New World, the dogmas that were universally received among them, their expectations as to a future state of existence, the religious rites and practices which they performed, their superstitious

* "Von dem Rechts-Zustande unter den Ur-Einwohnern Braziliens, Eine Abhandlung," von Dr. C. F. Ph. Von Martius. München, 1832. 4to. Translated in the second volume of the "Journal of the Royal Geographical Society."—"Reise in Brazilien," von Dr. Von Spix und Martius, ex. Th. 4to.—"Ueber die Zukunft und Vergangenheit der Amerikanischen Volkstamm," von Dr. Martius. München.

persuasions, the modes in which their credulity displayed itself, the juggleries and impostures by which they practised on each other, and excited the opinion of preternatural powers, of the possession of magical skill,—all these, and other exhibitions of the internal feelings, were, as they appear among the American races, precisely in harmony with what we discover in other departments of mankind.

I shall take the account which Loskiel, an excellent old writer, who resided many years among the Delaware Indians, has given of their native religion and superstition.

"The prevailing opinion of all these nations," says Loskiel, "is that there is one God, or, as they call him, one Great and Good Spirit." It seems, from the testimony of this writer, which is supported by the evidence of all those who have conversed with the aboriginal nations of North America, that the conceptions of these nations respecting the Deity are much more complete and philosophical than those of most savage people in the Old Continent. They suppose him literally to be the Creator of heaven and earth, of men and all other creatures; they represent him as all-mighty, and able to do as much good as he pleases; "nor do they doubt that he is kindly disposed towards men, because he imparts power to plants to grow, causes rain and sunshine, and gives fish and venison to man for his support;"—these gifts, however, to the Indians exclusively. "They are convinced that God requires of them to do good and to eschew evil." We may observe that, in these particulars, the Americans resemble the Northern Asiatics. We are assured by the late traveller, M. Erman, on the authority of the metropolitan Philopheï, who lived among the Ostiaks on the Oby, that these people had, before Christian missionaries ever came among them, a belief in the existence of a Supreme Deity, of whose nature they had pure and exalted ideas, and to whom they affirmed that they never made offerings, nor had they represented his form; while, to inferior gods, and particularly to Oertidk, who was a sort of mediator, and whose name, as it was preserved among the Magyars, Oerdig, was used by the monks as a designation for the devil, they made divers gifts: they performed before his image dances, which Erman, who visited the Kolushians on the Sitcka, declares to be precisely similar to the war-dances of those Americans. Some of the American people make images of the Manitos.

Besides the Supreme Deity, the American nations believe in a number of inferior spirits, whom the Delaware Indians term Manitos: they are both good and evil. "From the accounts of the oldest Indians," says Loskiel, "it appears that when war was in contemplation, they used to admonish each other to hearken to the good and not to evil spirits, the former always recommending peace." They had formerly no notion of a devil, or evil being, in the Christian and Eastern sense of the term, but readily adopted, according to Loskiel, such a belief from the white people. They have among them preachers who pretend to have received revelations, and who dispute and teach different opinions. Some pretend to have travelled near to the dwelling of God, or near enough to hear the cocks crow, and see the smoke of the chimneys in heaven; others declare that no one ever knew the dwelling-place of God, but that the abode of the Good Spirit is above the blue sky, and that the road to it is the milky way,—a notion, by the way, which Beausobre and others have traced in the remains of the Manicheans, and other Eastern philosophers.

The Americans believe in the existence of souls distinct from bodies, and many of them in the transmigration of souls. According to Loskiel, they declare "that Indians cannot die eternally; for even Indian corn is vivified, and rises again." The general opinion among them is that the souls of the good alone go to a place abounding in all earthly pleasures, while the wicked wander about dejected and melancholy.

Like other nations, they had sacrifices. "Sacrifices," says Loskiel, "made with a view to pacify God and the subordinate deities, are of very ancient date among them, and considered in so sacred a light, that unless they are performed in a time and manner acceptable, illness, misfortune, and death, would befall them and their families." They offer on these occasions hares, bear's flesh, and Indian corn. Many nations have, besides other stated times of sacrifice, one principal festival in two years, when they sacrifice an animal, and make a point of eating the whole. "A small quantity of melted fat is poured by the oldest men into the fire, and in this the main part of the offering consists. The offerings are made to Manitos. The Manitos are precisely the Fetisses of the African nations and of the Northern Asiatics; they are tutelar beings, often in visible forms. Every Indian has a guardian Manito: one has the sun for his Manito, one the moon; one has a dream that he must make his Manito an owl, one a buffalo. The Delawares had five festivals in the year, one in honour of Fire, supposed to have been the parent of all the Indian nations."

Like other nations, these people believed in the necessity of purification from guilt by fasting and bodily mortification. Some underwent for this end the pain of being beaten with sticks from the soles of their feet to their head. "Some give the poor people vomits as the most expeditious mode."

Like the Northern Asiatics, the American nations had, instead of a regular priesthood, jugglers or sorcerers, who pretended to have supernatural power and knowledge. They appear to conform in every respect to the Shamans of the Siberians, and the Fetiss-seers of the African nations. Mr. Catlin's work contains numerous anecdotes illustrative of this part; and of other likewise of the superstitions of the native Americans.

As for their susceptibility of civilisation and of Christianity, enough has been said in the preceding chapters of this work to prove that those who deny it to the nations of America are under the influence of a mere prejudice. Whole tribes in North America have embraced Christianity, and live under its influence, and are addicted to agriculture and improving in arts. How far their reputed conversion goes must be a matter of personal inquiry, and can only be known from those who have had intercourse with the people themselves. I have been assured by Mr. Schoolcraft, a most intelligent and enlightened man, long employed by the government of the United States as a public agent in the affairs of the Cherokees, who has had most extensive opportunities of becoming intimately acquainted with the Indians in various parts, that he has known many persons of that race whose minds were thoroughly imbued with the principles and sentiments of the Christian religion, and who lived and died in that faith, who were in the full sense of the expression pious and devout Christians.* The following account, given by

---

* The closing sentences of the eloquent preface to the great work of Schoolcraft on the "Indian Tribes of the United States" contain the most recent views of this profound and philosophical observer.

"We perceive in them many noble and disinterested traits. The simplicity of their eloquence has challenged admiration. Higher principles of devotion to what they believe to be cardinal virtues, no people ever evinced. Faith has furnished the Christian martyr with motives to sustain him at the stake: but the North American Indian has endured the keenest torments of fire without the consolations of the Gospel. Civilised nations are cheered on their way to face the cannon's mouth by inspiring music; but the warrior of the forest requires no roll of the drum to animate his steps.

"Mistaken in his belief in a system of gods of the elements—misconceiving the whole plan of industrial prosperity and happiness—wrong in his conceptions of the social duties of life, and doubly wrong in his notions of death and eternity, he yet approves himself to the best sensibilities of the human heart by the strong exhibition of those ties which bind a father to his children, and link whole forest communities in the indissoluble bonds of brotherhood. He lingers with affection, but with helpless ignorance, around the dying couch of his relatives; and his long memory of the dead ceases but with life itself. No costly tomb or cenotaph marks his place of burial; but he visits that spot with the silent majesty of grief. God has

Loskiel, of the congregation of converted Indians belonging to the Moravian or Herrnhuter's settlement at New Salem, will be read by many persons with interest :—

"This mission," he says, "has now stood forty-five years. From a register of the congregation, dated 1772, we learn that, from the beginning of the mission to that year, 720 Indians had been added to the Church of Christ by holy baptism, most of whom had departed this life rejoicing in God their Saviour. I would willingly add the number of those converted to the Lord since that period; but as the church books and other writings of the missionaries were burnt when they were taken prisoners in the Muskingum, in 1781, I cannot speak with certainty. Supposing even that from 1772 to 1787 the number of new converts was the same, yet, considering the long standing of the mission, and the great pains and sufferings of the missionaries, the flock collected was very small. The reason of this may be found partly in the peculiar character of the Indian nations, but chiefly in this, that the missionaries did not so much endeavour to gather a large number of baptised heathen, as to lead souls to Christ who should truly believe on and live unto Him."

I shall conclude these remarks on the psychological history of the American nations with a short survey of the Esquimaux. This race belongs, as we have seen, to the class of nations who, by their peculiar culture of language, as well as by local circumstances, are separated from the rest of mankind and form the original stock of the New World. I term them aboriginal, because the era of their isolation goes back beyond the reach of history. If, in

planted in his heart affections and feelings which only require to be moulded, and directed to noble aims. That impress seals him as a brother,—erring, indeed, and benighted in his ways, but still a brother.

"To reclaim such a race to the paths of virtue and truth; to enlighten the mind which has been so long in darkness; and to give it new and solid foundations for its hopes, is a duty alike of high civilisation and warm benevolence."

Dec. 3, 1850.

this race, so widely distinguished from other human tribes, we can prove the existence of a similar intellectual and moral nature, it may well be assumed that in no other human tribe will similar principles be found wanting. "The habits of the Hyperborean people," says M. Lesson, "are nearly the same wherever they have been carefully observed. Living on tracts of the earth where living nature seems to be expiring, buried under the eternal ices of the pole, their industry is directed towards fishing and the chase, which are their only resources for support, and in which they have acquired great skill. The rigour of the climate during long winters has obliged them to dig for themselves subterraneous abodes and storehouses for the provisions which they lay up against the season when they can no longer fish or hunt. During the long polar nights which the aurora borealis feebly illuminates, the Esquimaux, buried under the ice and snow in yourtes excavated deeply in the soil, feed upon dried fish or the flesh of whales, and drink with delight the oil which they have laid up in bladders. They sew with nerves their winter garments, made of the skins of seals, the hair of which serves the purposes of fur; and make their summer dress of the intestine of the largest whales, which resembles varnished stuffs.

"The Esquimaux is skilful in the chase of foxes and sables, whose skin serves him for clothing and for an object of barter in the traffic of the Arctic people. He boldly harpoons the cetacea: his darts, made of bone and pointed stones, are surmounted with inflated bladders, the resistance of which upon the water wears out the strength of the whale, who speedily rises and exposes himself to fresh attacks."

"Superstitious to excess," says the same writer, "the Polar race, with some slight shades of difference, displays the same religious sentiments prevalent among all its tribes. Their loose morality renders the men addicted to polygamy, and causes them to prostitute without shame their wives and daughters, whom they regard as creatures of an inferior order, to be disposed of according to their pleasure.

"In Greenland and in Labrador, missionaries of the United Brethren have long ago settled among the native people, who are of the same race which is elsewhere spread along the shores of the Polar seas. We have obtained much more accurate information respecting the habits of the people from these missionaries than from any other quarter. The following particulars, which I extract from their accounts, relate chiefly to the Esquimaux of Greenland, from whom, however, it is well known that the western tribes of the same race differ but in accidental circumstances.

"The voyagers who first described the natives of Greenland formed very erroneous opinions respecting them. It was reported that they worshipped the sun, and sacrificed to the devil. Sailors, who had observed them look intently on the heavens on rising in the morning, hence derived the first of these notions; the second arose from the discovery of flat square stones, strewn with cinders and bones: it was concluded that these were places of sacrifice, and to whom should they sacrifice but to the devil? When the Moravian missionaries learned their language, and were able to converse with them, they found these notions to be quite erroneous."

The Greenlanders, like other nations, believed in the existence of supernatural powers exercising control over the destinies of men. It appears, however, as we might *à priori* imagine, that they had in general no clear idea of a Creator or a creation. "They knew not, and, perhaps, the generality of them never considered, whether things were always as they are or not." Yet, if we may believe the Moravian missionaries, whose good faith seems above suspicion, there were some philosophers among these Pagan seal-catchers who speculated on the doctrine of final causes. An Esquimaux told one of the missionaries that he had often reflected that a kadjak, with all its tackle and implements, does not grow of itself into existence, but must be made with labour and contrivance; but a bird, he added, is constructed with greater skill than the best kadjak, and no man can make a bird. "I bethought me," said the Greenlander, "that he proceeded from his parents, and they from their parents: but there must have been some first parents—whence did they come? Certainly, I concluded, there must be a being able to make them and all other things: a being infinitely more mighty and knowing than the wisest man."

The Greenlanders believed in the existence of spirits, good and evil, besides the souls of men. The angekoks, or diviners, who pretended to have visited frequently the realm of souls, describe them as pale and soft, not to be felt if anyone should attempt to grasp them. They believed in a future existence, which was to be without end. This Elysium was generally placed by them in the abysses of the ocean, to which the deep cavities of rocks are avenues. There dwells the great spirit, Torngarsuk, and his mother, under a joyous and perpetual summer, where a shining sun is obscured by no night: there is a fine limpid stream abounding with fine seals, fish, and fowls, easy to be caught, and even to be found boiling alive in a great kettle. But these seats of the gods can be approached only by those who have displayed great courage and address, who have mastered many seals, and who have undergone hardships, have been drowned in the sea, or by women who have died in child-bed. Here is obviously the persuasion that virtue, bravery at least, is rewarded in the future life. Before the disembodied soul enters Torngarsuk's realm, it undergoes a sort of purgation by sliding, five days or longer, down a rugged rock, which is thereby full of blood and gore. Unfortunate souls who perish in cold winter, or boisterous weather, incur a risk of being utterly destroyed on the road. Annihilation is regarded by the Greenlanders, as by other nations, with peculiar horror; and to prevent it, the survivors abstain for five days from certain meats and from all noisy work. The fictions of this people are not so definite as to admit of no variations in the site and description of Elysium; some fancy it to be the sky, and say that the northern lights are the dances of sportive souls; others maintain this state of agitation in the air to be the destiny of worthless souls, who will there be half starved and tormented by ravens. It seems, on the whole, that the future state of the old Pagan Esquimaux, or Greenlanders, was in a great measure a state of retribution of rewards and punishments. Happiness and misery were at least not dispensed with indifference to merit and demerit.

The chief of the spirits is named Torngarsuk, who dwells in his happy subterranean mansion. His mother, or wife, is a mischievous being. This Proserpine of the north lives in a great house under the ocean, where, by magic spells, she can detain all the animals of the sea. In the oil-jar under her lamps sea-birds swim about. Her throne is guarded by rampant seals, or defended by a great dog, who never sleeps but the twinkling of an eye. So many curious traits occur in the description of this infernal goddess and her abode which recall the Proserpine of classical mythology, the Patala of the Hindús, and the subterranean scenes of enchantment among the Arabs, that we might well be inclined to derive these fables from a common source, if the resemblance between them was not better accounted for by referring it to the common laws of the human mind, and to the tendency of the imagination to create similar fictions with reference to particular subjects, and under the influence of corresponding feeling and impressions. But this brings out so much the stronger proof that the mind is the same in different countries and in different races of men.

The Greenlanders likewise believe that the souls of the dead are sometimes seen near the places of burial. The sun and moon have their tutelary genii; water, air, and fire, mountains and caves, are the abodes of Nereids and salamandrine spirits; giants and pigmies, and monsters with dogs' heads, find their place in this as in so many other mythologies.

The natives of Greenland were strongly imbued with the notions so prevalent among mankind in different regions, that there must be a particular class of men fitted to mediate between the people and the supernatural powers. These persons were termed *angekoks*, that is, sorcerers and diviners. Many families living together, according to Crantz, keep an angekok as their counsellor on particular occasions; and if they cannot get one, they are despised and pitied as miserable wretches. In order to become an angekok, it is necessary to abandon for a long time the intercourse of men, to macerate the body by long fasting and by strenuous intensity of thought, and, like the Indian sanyasis performing pujah, to distract the mind almost into madness. When a torngak, or familiar spirit, is obtained by these efforts, the individual becomes an angekok, and thenceforward is possessed of the powers of sorcerers and magicians. On all occasions of distress or sickness the angekoks are applied to for relief. It is believed that they can take diseases off or lay them on; that they can enchant, and dissolve the spell of the enchanted arrow; that they can call blessings down or chase spectres away. If they have to do with a sick patient, they must mutter something over him, and blow upon him, to cure him; or they must fetch and implant a healthy soul in him, or perhaps only predict if he will recover or die. By other enchantments, they discover if an absent man is living or dead. They cite the soul of a man to appear before them; and if they wound such a soul with a spear, the man must die a lingering death. The witches of Greenland are exactly parallel to the witches of England, according to the belief of our ancestors.

The account of the conversion of the Esquimaux to Christianity and to civilisation, as given by Crantz from the simple and unaffected narrative of the Moravian missionaries, cannot be read without a lively interest. In the long and painful struggle, almost leading to despair of ultimate success, and in the event which rewarded their labours, the history of these missions affords a specimen of what has taken place in almost every similar instance, where the promulgators of Christianity have been sincerely devoted to their undertaking, and have been endowed with sufficient zeal and perseverance, and with other requisite qualifications. Among the Greenlanders, as elsewhere, many years of patient labour were toiled through, and many a prediction had been heard of utter failure in so vain and impracticable an undertaking, before a more encouraging prospect was opened, or any perceptible effect was produced upon the minds of the ignorant savages. In the resistance long made by these people to Christianity, as well as in the circumstances which attended its ultimate reception, we perceive the workings of the same mind which has often displayed itself in other races of men. It was in 1721 that Egede, the apostle of Greenland, established the first Danish mission in that country. He was followed by missionaries belonging to the Unitas Fratrum. After an interval of fifteen years, we find Crantz, the historian of this community, thus confessing the total want of any apparent result of their long and painful exertions. "Hitherto," he says, "they had not seen the trace of any permanent impression from the truths they had held forth. The Greenlanders who came from a distance were stupid, ignorant, and devoid of reflection; and the little that could be told them in a short visit, even if it was heard with attention, died away in their perpetual wanderings. Those who lived constantly in the immediate neighbourhood of the missionaries, and had been instructed so many years, were not grown better, but most of them worse; they were disgusted, tired, and hardened against the truth." When pressed to give a serious attention to the doctrines of Christianity, they either showed their dislike openly, or excused themselves in terms like the following:—"Show us the God whom you describe," said they; "then we will believe in him and serve him. You represent him too sublime and incomprehensible; how shall we come at him? Neither will he trouble himself about us. We have invoked him when we have nothing to eat, or when we have been sick, but it is as if he would not hear us. We think what you say of him is not true; for if you know him better than we, then do you by your prayers obtain for us sufficient food, a healthy body, and dry house, and that is all we desire or want. Our soul is healthy already, and nothing is wanting if we have but a sound body and enough to eat. You are another sort of folk than we: in your country, people may, perhaps, have diseased souls; and, indeed, we see proofs enough in those who come here that they are good for nothing; they may stand in need of a Saviour and of a Physician for the soul. Your heaven, and your spiritual joys and felicities, may be good enough for you, but would be too tiresome for us. We must have seals, fishes, and birds; for our soul can no more subsist without them than our bodies. We should not find these in your heaven; therefore we will leave your heaven to you and the worthless part of the Greenlanders; but as for us, we will go down to Torngarsuk; there we shall find an exuberance of everything without any trouble."

The first individual of this nation who became a convert was a man of extraordinary mental powers in such a state of society, and one whom the missionaries always mention as altogether a most remarkable person. His name was Kajarnak. They describe him as "a man whom they cannot but wonder at, when they consider the great supineness and stupidity of the Greenlanders in general, and that they can comprehend nothing except what they are daily conversant with. But this man," they continue, "scarcely hears a thing twice before he understands it and retains it in his mind and heart. At the same time, he shows an uncommon love to us, and a constant desire to be better instructed; so that he seems to catch every word out of our mouths, which we have never perceived in any

Greenlander before." Kajarnak had come from a remote part of Greenland; he was a stranger to the missionaries, and was immediately interested with their representations of the Christian religion, and impressed with the narrative, which in a simple and emphatic manner they delivered, of the most striking events of the evangelical history.*

* I have no doubt that some of my readers will be interested with the account which the missionaries transmitted of the manner in which doctrines so remote from their habit of thought penetrated the minds of the first converts among the Esquimaux. The following is an extract from Crantz's work:—

"In the summer of 1728, many natives of the southern country visited the settlement. One day, when a missionary named John Beck was employed in copying part of a translation of the Gospels, he read a portion of it to these savages, and took an opportunity of explaining it to them. 'The Holy Spirit,' say the missionaries, 'prompted this brother to describe the agonies and death of Christ with more and more energy, and he exhorted them with a warm heart to think seriously how much it had cost our Saviour to redeem us, and that on that account thay should by no means withhold their hearts from Him, which He had earned at so dear a price; for He had been wounded, and shed His blood, and died to purchase them, and had endured such anguish of soul that it made Him sweat blood. At the same time he read, out of the New Testament, the history of our Saviour's agony on the Mount of Olives, and of His bloody sweat. Then the Lord opened the heart of one of the Pagans, whose name was Kajarnak, and he stepped up to the table, and said with a loud, earnest, and affecting voice, 'How was that? tell me that once more, for I fain would be saved too.' 'These words,' says the missionary, 'penetrated my very soul, and kindled in me such an ardour, that I gave the Greenlanders a full account of our Saviour's life and death, and of the counsel of God for our salvation, while tears ran down my cheeks.' From that time Kajarnak became a disciple of the missionaries, and was a willing and able instrument in propagating the Christian doctrine among his countrymen."

In a further account of the state of the new converts, written a few years after the transaction above related, we find the following reflections:—

"Though the woful state of the heathen still grieved the brethren, yet the fruits of grace which they discerned in Kajarnak and the rest of the catechumens rejoiced them more and more. They evinced plain signs not only of a true consciousness of a Divine Being, and a profound reverence for Him, not only joy that Christ will raise the dead, and that believers will be happy in another world, but *principally* a real sense of their own misery, a joy in the love of God manifested to the fallen

Kajarnak became a zealous convert and disciple of the missionaries, and was a willing and able instrument in propagating the doctrine which he had embraced among his countrymen. A few of them soon followed his example, and a small community of proselytes was formed, which in a few years increased to a considerable number.

When such a commencement had once been made, the conversion of the Esquimaux of Greenland to Christianity seems to have proceeded rapidly. In the year 1744, it was evident that a considerable effect had been produced upon the minds of the people generally; great numbers were interested in the subjects which the missionaries set before them. In 1748, not less than 230 converts resided at New Herrnhut, thirty-five of whom had been baptised during the year. "Though these people are not without imperfections," says the historian of these missions, "it is yet evident that they are advancing. Their intercourse with one another is become more and more characterised by mutual kindness and the proofs of real conversion." A few years afterwards, it was observed that, though nearly 200 persons baptised by the missionaries had finished their earthly career, the congregation now consisted of 400 persons. "Since 1742, when the first general awakening of the natives commenced, the increase has been considerable, in proportion to the population of the country. Several

human race in the atonement of Christ, and a growing desire after the word of life. It was plainly to be seen that the work of grace had taken deep root in their hearts, by a change of life, by a voluntary abstinence from heathenish vanities, and by cheerfully enduring the reproach of their infidel countrymen, by whom they were forsaken, hated, and despised. Kajarnak, after his country people had been catechised by the missionaries, used to subjoin an exhortation, that, having been so long ignorant, they should now embrace the truth with a willing and thankful heart, and let it effect a true change; or he would sometimes conclude with a short but fervent prayer. And here let it be observed, that this was not a thing he was ordered or led to do, but of his own free impulse. He had, at the same time, a clear head, helped his teachers to the words they wanted in the language of the Greenlanders, and often corrected them because he pretty well understood their meaning."

new colonies have now been established by the Danes, provided with missionaries from the Royal College at Copenhagen. These were stationed in different parts of the country. Two additional settlements were founded by the United Brethren in 1758 and 1774, at Lichtenfels and at Lichtenau, near Cape Farewell, when there was soon a congregation of 205 baptised Greenlanders. In the conclusion of the history, drawn up a few years ago, it is observed that, since the commencement of the mission, a very remarkable moral change has taken place in the state of the country and the character of the natives. "Along the whole extent of the western coast, the barbarities of savage life, and the enormities ever attending Paganism when it is dominant, are now rarely to be met with; and the state of the country, compared with what it was eighty or but fifty years ago, may be termed civilised. The nature and climate of this dreary region, and the methods by which the natives procure their subsistence, necessarily preclude the introduction of many arts of civilised society. The people can neither till the land nor employ themselves in manufactures; a Greenlander can neither live in the European manner, nor clothe himself like an European, dwelling as he does on sterile rocks, and under the rigours of a Polar sky. Yet it may be said with truth that the converted Greenlanders, by the habits of industry which they have acquired since the introduction of Christianity among them, by their contentment amidst privations and hardships, and by the charity of the more affluent towards their needy brethren, strikingly exemplify the doctrine that in every circumstance of life, and in every station, a religious life is great gain, having the promise of reward in this world, and in that which is to come."*

The particulars which I have collected relating to the superstitious opinions and impressions of the Greenlanders

* "Historical Sketches," p. 62. "From the accounts recently published, it appears that a fourth mission has been established, and that the number of Christian Greenlanders belonging to the Moravian Church,

in their primitive state, and especially the facts connected with their conversion to Christianity and civilised habits, are sufficient, if I am not mistaken, to prove that the mind of the Esquimaux has the same moral and intellectual constitution as that of other human beings. They have the same elements of moral feeling, the same sympathies and susceptibilities of affection, the same conscience, or internal conviction of accountableness, more or less obscurely or clearly impressed, the same sentiments of guilt and self-condemnation, the same desires of expiation which are common to so many other nations in almost every degree of mental culture. The most elevated of these principles are only recognised in the natural or Pagan state of these men as mere rudiments of higher and better understanding, or as scintillations now and then shooting forth. When those doctrines and representations are opened to them which have been found, in so many other parts of the world, congenial to the human mind, and, as such, have been received by the most polished as well as by the most barbarous nations, they have produced their wonted effects upon the Esquimaux. The minds of these people appear to be, as to all essential principles of feeling and understanding, in harmony and in strict analogy with those of other men. Such a mind can hardly be supposed common to different species of organised beings.

---

which excludes those under Danish Lutheran ministers, is 1808. In this last account, we are informed that the effects of Christianity upon the moral and social state of the Greenlanders has been in every respect cheering and most beneficial. The national superstitions have almost everywhere entirely disappeared; the practice of sorcery is almost unknown upon the coast; cruelty and licentiousness, with a whole train of attendant vices, have, through the influence of Christianity, given way to brotherly kindness, good order, decorum, and such a measure of civilisation as is compatible with peculiar circumstances. The mind of the Greenlander has been cultivated, and his heart softened and purified, though his mode of life is still rude, and his habits greatly at variance with European ideas of comfort and civilisation."

CHAPTER V.

PSYCHOLOGICAL HISTORY OF THE AFRICAN NATIONS.

I SHALL divide what is to be said on the mental history of the African nations into two heads: first, the history of the Hottentot race; secondly, that of the Negro nations of Western Africa.

1. *Of the Hottentot and Bushman Race.*

Writers on the history of mankind seem to be nearly agreed in considering the Bushmen, or Bosjesmen, of South Africa as the most degraded and miserable of all nations, and the lowest in the scale of humanity. M. Bory de St. Vincent describes them in his usual manner, as differing most widely from what he terms the Japetic species of men, and as forming the transition from the genus *homo* to the genera of orangs and gibbons: he even finds analogies between them and the macacos.

"Of all species of men, this race, approaching as it does in its form most nearly to the second genus of bimanous animals, is still more closely allied to the orangs through the inferiority of its intellectual faculties. Happily for themselves," he continues, "these people are so brutish, lazy, and stupid, that the idea of reducing them to slavery has been abandoned." "A peine peuvent-ils former un raisonnement, et leur langage, aussi stérile que leurs idées, se réduit à une sorte de gloussement qui n'a presque plus rien de semblable à notre voix. D'une malpropreté révoltante qui les rend infects, toujours frottés de suif, ou arrosés de leur propre urine, se faisant des ornemens de boyeaux d'animaux qu'ils laissent se dessécher en bracelets ou en bandelettes sur leur peau huileux, se remplissant les cheveux de graisse et de terre, vêtus de peaux de bête sans préparation, se nourissant de racines sauvages ou de panses d'animaux et d'entrailles qu'ils ne lavent même pas, passant leur vie assoupis ou accroupis et fumant, par fois ils errent avec quelques troupeaux qui leur fournissent du lait. Isolés, taciturnes, fugitifs, se rétirant dans les cavernes, ou dans les bois, à peine font-ils usage du feu, si ce n'est pour allumer leur pipes, qu'ils ne quittent point. Le foyer domestique leur est à-peu-près inconnu, et ils ne bâtissent pas de villages, ainsi que les Cafres, leur voisins, qui regardent ces misérables comme une sorte de gibier, leur donnent la chasse, et exterminent tous ceux qu'ils rencontrent. On les a dit bons parce qu'ils sont apathiques, tranquilles parce qu'ils sont paresseux, et doux parce qu'ils se montrent lâches en toute occasion."

No picture of human degradation and wretchedness can be drawn which exceeds the real abasement and misery of the Bushmen, as we find it displayed by the most accurate writers who describe this people. Without houses, or even huts, living in caves and holes in the earth, these naked and half-starved savages wander through forests, in small companies or separate families, hardly supporting their comfortless existence, by collecting wild roots, by a toilsome search for the eggs of ants, and by devouring, whenever they can catch them, lizards, snakes, and the most loathsome insects. It is no matter of surprise that those writers who search for approximations between mankind and the inferior orders of creation fix upon the Bushmen as their favourite theme.

But accurate observers, who cannot be suspected of undue prepossession towards opposite sentiments and representations of human nature, have drawn a less unfavourable picture of the moral and intellectual character of the Bushmen. Mr. Burchell, who sought and obtained opportunities of conversing with them, and observing their manner of existence, though he found them in the most destitute and miserable state, yet discovered among them traits of kind and social feelings, and all the essential attributes of humanity.

It must not be forgotten that the Bushmen are not a distinct race, but a branch or subdivision of the once extensive nation of Hottentots. This was at one time denied. Lichtenstein, who was followed by other writers, asserted that the Bosjesmen are a peculiar family of men: he regarded them as entirely distinct from all the other inhabitants of Southern Africa. A careful comparison of their language with that of the Korah and other Hottentots convinced Professor Vater that there is an essential affinity between them; and in recent times this conclusion has been fully established by local inquiries, and no diversity of opinion at present exists upon the subject. We are assured by one of the latest and best writers on South Africa, that the Bushmen are the remains of Hottentot hordes, who subsisted originally, like all the tribes of Southern Africa, chiefly by rearing sheep and cattle, but who have been driven by the gradual encroachments of European colonists, and by internal wars with other tribes, to seek for refuge among the inaccessible deserts and rocks of the interior. "Most of the hordes," says the same writer, "known by the name of the Bushmen, are entirely destitute of flocks and herds, and subsist partly by hunting, partly on the wild roots of the wilderness, on reptiles, locusts, and the larvæ of ants, or by plundering their hereditary oppressors, the colonists of the frontier. Having descended from the pastoral to the state of robbers and hunters, the Bushmen, as we are assured, have necessarily acquired, with their increased perils and privations, a more resolute and ferocious character: from a mild, confiding, and unenterprising race of shepherds, they have been gradually transformed into wandering hordes of fierce, suspicious, and vindictive savages; by their fellow-men they have been treated as wild beasts, until they have become assimilated to wild beasts in their habits and dispositions."

Difficult as it may be to imagine a change from the state of herdsmen to that of the miserable Bushmen, the transition has been actually observed and described. Among the Hottentot tribes, the Koranas are well known to be the most advanced in all the possessions and improvements which belong to the pastoral life. A late traveller in Africa, whose narrative is replete with good sense and the marks of accurate knowledge, has traced from observation the process by which hordes even of the Korah race have been reduced from the life of peaceful herdsmen to the condition of hunters and predatory savages. The Koranas, as visited by Mr. Thomson on the Hartebeest river, had actually undergone this transition; having been plundered by their neighbours, and driven out into the wilderness to subsist upon wild fruits, they had adopted the habits of the Bushmen, and had become assimilated in every essential particular to that miserable tribe.

Considering the pastoral Hottentots and the Bushmen as one race, I shall make some remarks on their mental character in general, in order to furnish the ground for a comparison between this and other families of men.

We must attempt to estimate the character of the Hottentot race, not from their present degraded condition, after the cruelty and oppression, which they have endured from European colonists during so many generations, have broken their spirit and reduced them to bondage or exile, but from the accounts left by older writers of the condition of these tribes soon after the first settlement of the Dutch colony.

The voyager Kolben has given us a full and circumstantial account of the Hottentots at this time, and many of his statements are singularly at variance with the description which late writers have drawn. The original Hottentots were a numerous people, divided into many tribes under the patriarchal government of chiefs or elders: they wandered about with flocks and herds, associated in companies of three or four hundred persons, living in kraals, or movable villages of huts, constructed of poles or boughs covered with rush-mats, which were taken down and carried on pack-oxen. A mantle of sewn sheep-skins was their clothing; their arms were a bow with poisoned arrows, and a light javelin, or assagai. They were bold and active in the chase; and, although mild in their disposition, were courageous in warfare, as their European invaders frequently experienced.

Kolben extols the good moral qualities of the Hottentots. "They are, perhaps, the most faithful servants in the world. Though infinitely fond of wine, brandy, and tobacco, they are safely intrusted with them, and will neither themselves take, nor suffer others to diminish, any such articles when committed to their trust. To this quality they add the greatest humanity and good nature. Their chastity is remarkable, and adultery, when known among them, is punished with death. They are dirty in their habits, slothful and indolent; and, though they can think," as he says, "to the purpose, they hate the trouble of thought." Kolben considered their intellect as by no means deficient. He declares that "he has known many of them who understood Dutch, French, and Portuguese, to a degree of perfection; one particularly, who learned English and Portuguese in a very short time, and having conquered the habits of pronunciation contracted from his native language, was said by good judges to understand and speak them with surprising readiness and propriety. They are even employed by Europeans in affairs that require judgment and capacity; a Hottentot, named Cloos, was entrusted by Van der Stel, the late Governor of the Cape, with the business of carrying on a trade of barter for cattle with the tribes at a great distance, and he generally returned, after executing his commission, with great success."

The internal character of the mind is best known by discovering the religious ideas and impressions. It has often been said that the Hottentots are destitute of all belief in a Deity or a future state. Enslaved and separated from their fellows, and scarcely able, without constant toil, to support life, some may have lost the power and habit of reflection and all traces of sentiment; but Kolben assures us that the Hottentots of his time had a firm belief in a supreme power, which they termed "Gounya Tekquoa," or the god of all gods, saying that he lived beyond the moon. They paid him no adoration; but they worshipped the moon at the full and change, by sacrifices of cattle, with distorted faces and postures, shouting, swearing, singing, jumping, stamping, dancing, and making numerous prostrations, repeating an unintelligible jargon of words. "They also pay singular veneration to a peculiar kind of beetle, the appearance of which is supposed to be particularly fortunate. They have an evil deity, called Toutouka, whom they represent as a little crabbed, ill-natured being, a great enemy to the Hottentots, and the author of all the mischief in the world. They offer sacrifices to him in order to soften his temper; all sudden pain, accidents, or sicknesses, are attributed to witchcraft. Charms and amulets are in high esteem among them." Kolben thinks they have not the least notion of rewards and punishments; "yet," says he, "that they believe in the immortality of the soul, seems evident from these particulars: first, that they offer up prayers to saints, or good Hottentots departed; secondly, that they are apprehensive of the return of the departed spirits to molest them; for which reason, on the death of any person, they remove their kraal, believing that the departed souls remain about the places which they formerly inhabited; thirdly, they believe it is in the power of the witches or wizards to lay these spirits."

A faithful and correct account of the conversion of this people to Christianity would not fail to display in striking points of view many traits in their moral and intellectual history. The early endeavours that were made to induce them to receive the truths of Christianity were met with the same obstinate resistance of which we hear so much in almost every similar instance; and one writer has given us as the summing up of his observations, that "the Hottentots, in short, seem born with a natural antipathy to all customs, and every religion but their own." This remark is exemplified by the account of a Hottentot boy who was bred up by the Governor Van der Stel in the habits and religion of the Dutch; and, having learned several languages, and discovering a promising genius, was sent to India, and employed in public business. After his return to the Cape, he stripped off his European dress, clothed himself in sheep-skin, and, presenting himself to the Governor, emphatically renounced the society of civilised men and the Christian religion, declaring that he would live and die in the customs and religion of his forefathers.* In this we trace one characteristic trait of human nature as it exists in other races of men. A sort of instinctive and blind attachment to the earliest impressions made upon the mind is one of our strongest intellectual propensities. In the example above cited it appears to have been equally powerful in the mind of the Hottentot as it is known to be in more cultivated nations; yet this has not prevented the spread of Christianity in the same race of people, when introduced among them under different circumstances.†

* Kolben's "Voyages, and Natural History of the Cape of Good Hope."

† Similar instances may be cited of other races of men. The case of Bennilong, the Australian native, who returned to savage life after a residence of considerable duration in London, will be remembered by our older colonists. Mallat records the narrative of a Philippine Negrito, who was taken young, educated at a regular theological seminary, and actually received into the Catholic church as a priest in full orders, but who, after a long interval, returned to his original tribe and habits as a genuine Negrito. A recent account of a Caffre woman educated in an English family at the Cape may be also cited. The advocates of the notion that the savage is the natural state of man, usually adduce such cases in proof of their position, and are inclined to doubt that similar instances of a voluntary return to the original condition are to be found so decidedly pronounced among the more highly civilised races. The fact, however, seems to be that they are exhibited in all races, but are more striking in the cases noticed. The return of a European to society after years of sojourn among Algonquins would hardly be recorded as very extraordinary. But, even admitting that the lowest tribes exhibit this yearning after their old habits more frequently or more strongly than the higher races, it may fairly be attributed to the wider interval they are suddenly required to step over. In the instances of white children brought up from early youth by savages, the families from whom the children were taken have usually been

Of the Introduction of Christianity among the Hottentots.

It is indeed surprising, after all we have heard of the sloth and brutish sensuality of the Hottentots, to learn that no other uncivilised race has given a more willing ear to the preaching of Christianity, and that none has been more strikingly and speedily improved by its reception, not only in moral character and conduct, but also in outward condition and prosperity. So rapid has been the spread of civilisation around the settlements of the United Brethren, by whom the task of introducing the Christian religion among the Hottentots was undertaken, as to have given rise to a general notion that the missionaries of that church direct their endeavours, in the first place, to the diffusion of industry and social arts, and make religion a secondary object of attention. This, however, they uniformly deny. It is the unvarying statement of these missionaries, deduced from the experience of a hundred years of patient service and laborious exertions among the rudest and most abject tribes of human beings, that the moral nature of man must be in the first instance quickened, the conscience awakened, and the better feelings of the heart aroused by the motives which Christianity brings with it, before any improvement can be hoped for in the outward behaviour and social state; that the rudest savages have sufficient understanding to be susceptible of such a change; and that when it has once taken place, all the blessings of civilisation follow as a necessary result.

The first attempt made to spread Christianity among the Hottentots was by a missionary named Schmidt, a man of great zeal and courage, who undertook this task in the early period of the Moravian Church. He arrived in South Africa in 1737; and, having settled at some dis-

long residents in the neighbourhood of these tribes, and have probably acquired instincts approaching those of their neighbours. White families, moreover, make strenuous efforts to recover their children; there are also social difficulties in the way of a white man's return to his place in society, which would scarcely exist in the opposite case.—ED.

tance from the Cape, soon collected a small congregation of Hottentots, by whom he was much beloved. Being obliged to sail to Holland, his return was prevented by adversaries under pretence of zeal for the purity of doctrine and peace of the Church. The undertaking was suspended during nearly fifty years. It was renewed under more favourable auspices in 1792. The new missionaries sought out the ruins of Schmidt's abode; they found some aged Hottentots, who still revered his memory, and laid the foundations of the settlement of Bavian's Kloof, since Gnadenthal.

The school established by the missionaries was soon attended by many Hottentots, both children and adults; and the religious instructions by reading the Bible, and expositions, were frequented by many attentive hearers. The historians of the mission say, "The reverential stillness with which the Hottentots attended these meetings, the eagerness with which they listened to the discourses, and the emotion visible on their countenances, astonished the missionaries, who had been told that they would find it impossible to fix the attention of their hearers, even to the shortest address of a serious nature." The number of scholars increased, and soon amounted to 200, who were instructed in the open air. Many Hottentots came from a considerable distance, bringing their families and their cattle with them, and associated themselves to the settlement. The colonial boors became alarmed at the idea of being deprived of the service of their Hottentots, and on many occasions threatened, and even attempted, the destruction of the settlement; but these menaces were averted, and it became at length apparent, even to this class of the inhabitants, that the Hottentots, who had become Christianised under the instruction of the missionaries, were far more useful and trustworthy servants than the sensual and degraded pagans whom they had previously been obliged to employ.

In the course of a few years the Hottentots began to

resort from all parts of the colony, and increased the population of Bavian's Kloof. The missionaries were slow and cautious in baptising converts, until they thought that evidences were perceptible of repentance and faith. There were, however, in 1799, 238 Hottentot houses; the number of inhabitants amounted to 1234, of whom 304 were actual members of the congregation, 84 of them having been baptised during the year.

When the Cape colony came under the power of the English, the beneficial results of instruction imparted to the Hottentots by the missionaries of the United Brethren were so manifest in the improvement of manners and industry, that the missions obtained the steady and uniform protection and favour of government. Gnadenthal had now grown into a populous settlement, displaying the best effects of human culture, and occupied by numerous and thriving families of husbandmen, who obtained a rich produce from the soil over which their ancestors had wandered for ages without attempting to improve it. In addition to this settlement, another tract, called Groene kloof, was given by the government to the United Brethren. In the course of a year, from being a wilderness it was made to bear a plentiful crop. The missionaries reported that in conducting their temporal concerns "the Hottentots gave evidence that they were under the influence of Christian motives; they went diligently to work in building their huts and cultivating their grounds, and God blessed the labour of their hands." Some of the Dutch farmers expressed their surprise at the change which they witnessed in this people. "They were astonished," say the missionaries, "in seeing how the wretched drunken Hottentots, when they get to Gnadenthal and hear the Word of God, truly receive grace, and *become quite a different* sort of people."

Perhaps nothing in this account is more remarkable than the fact that so strong a sensation was produced among the whole Hottentot nation, and even among the neighbouring tribes of different people, by the improved and happy condition of the Christian Hottentots, as to excite a desire for similar advantages. Whole families of Hottentots, and even of Bushmen, set out for the borders of Kafirland, and even performed journeys of many weeks, in order to settle at Gnadenthal. Individuals of the Tambúki nation, and some from the Damaras beyond Great Namáqualand, resorted to Groene kloof, and there took up their abode. It is a singular fact in the history of these barbarous races of men, that the savage Bushmen, of their own accord, solicited from the colonial government, when negotiations were opened with them with the view of putting an end to a long and bloody contest, that teachers might be sent among them, such as those who had dwelt among the tame Hottentots at Gnadenthal. "History," says the historian of the mission, "probably furnishes few parallel examples of a savage people, in treaty with a Christian power, making one of the conditions of peace, that missionaries should be sent to instruct them in Christianity."

I have not room to add further details from this account. The facts which I have extracted have an important bearing on the psychical history of a curious and interesting race of human beings, and could not be omitted in connection with the inquiry in which I am engaged. Those who will candidly consider them, and give them their due weight, will allow that they prove the existence of the same principle of action, and of the same internal nature, in the Hottentot race, as are recognised in other divisions of mankind; and this conviction will be increased by a careful perusal of all the details which the missionaries have afforded of the progress of the work, and of the moral changes which accompanied it.

CHAPTER VI.

PSYCHOLOGICAL TRAITS OF THE NEGRO NATIONS IN WESTERN AFRICA.

It is a common impression that the native religion, if I may use that expression, or the belief of old prevalent, before the dawning of history and the introduction either of Christianity or of Islám among the nations of Western Africa, is nothing but the superstition of fetisses, or spells. This notion, however, is not perfectly correct. The superstition of charms, or spells, holds a principal place in the minds of the idolatrous Negroes; but this does not preclude a very general prevalence, in their belief, of the first principles of natural religion. It may be observed, that among nations enjoying a much higher degree of mental culture, the prevalence of superstitions and practices more or less resembling the fetishism of Africa, may be recognised: such are a belief in destiny, or fatality, astrology, necromancy, charms, spells, omens, lucky and unlucky days, fortune, and the good and evil genius of individuals.

"The word *fetisso*," says Barbot, in his description of Guinea, "is a Portuguese word, signifying charm or spell."* It is not a native African term, though used by the Negroes of the Gold Coast after the Portuguese. These Negroes term their idols Bossum, or Bossefoe. Father Godfrey Loyer, apostolical prefect of the Jacobites, who made a voyage to the kingdom of Issini, and studied the temper, manners, and religion of the natives, says that it is a great mistake to suppose that fetisses are the gods of the Negroes. He declares that they have a belief in one universally powerful being, and to him the people of the countries visited by Father Loyer addressed prayers.

"Every morning," he says, "after they rise, they go to the river-side to wash, and throwing a handful of water on their head, or pouring sand with it to express their humility, they join their hands, and then open them,

* The Portuguese word is *feitiço*, of which the primary signification is "artificial."—Ed.

whisper softly the word "Eksuvair:" then, lifting up their eyes to heaven, they make this prayer:—'Anghiûme mamé maro, mamé rice, mamé shike e okkori, mamé akaka, mamé bremlic, mamé unquan e aconsan;' that is, My God, give me this day rice and yams, give me gold and aigris, give me slaves and riches, give me health, and grant that I may be active and swift."

The excellent missionary Oldendorp, who appears to have had rare opportunities, and to have taken great pains to become accurately acquainted with the mental history and character of the Negroes, assures us that he recognised among them an universal belief in the "existence of a God," whom they represent as very powerful and beneficent. "He is the maker of the world and of men: he it is who thunders in the air, as he punishes the wicked with his bolts. He regards beneficent actions with complacency, and rewards them with long life. To him the Negroes ascribe their own personal gifts, the fruits of the earth, and all good things; from him the rain descends upon the earth. They believe that he is pleased when men offer prayers to him in all their wants, and that he succours them in dangers, in diseases, and in seasons of drought. This is the chief god who lives far from them on high; he is supreme over all other gods."

"Among all the black nations," says Oldendorp, "with whom I have become acquainted, even among the utterly ignorant and rude, there is none that did not believe in a God, which had not learned to give him a name, which did not regard him as the maker of the world, and ascribe to him, more or less clearly, all the attributes which I have briefly summed up. As, however, the Negroes always designate God and the heaven by the same term, it is doubtful whether they do not regard heaven itself as the Deity: but, perhaps, their notions are not so clear as to have led them even to contemplate this distinction.

"Besides this supreme beneficent divinity, whom all the various nations worship in some way or other, they believe in many gods of inferior dignity, who are subject to the chief Deity, and are mediators between him and mankind. Such are the powers which they reverence in serpents, tigers, wolves, rivers, trees, hills, and large stones. The more stupid of the Negroes certainly imagine the serpent, the tiger, and the stones, to be themselves gods,—that the tree understands them, and the tiger gives them rain: on the other hand, the more intelligent look upon these objects as representations of the inferior gods, and imagine that local deities dwell unseen under certain trees or on particular hills. This appears from the fiction which the priests of Akkran have respecting the subordination of the tutelar gods under the supreme divinity, and from the notion that these gods absent themselves during a certain season of the year while the visible objects remain."

The objects of their worship are neither national nor domestic. Thus the Fida, besides the great serpent which is adored by the whole nation, have each their particular smaller serpents, which are worshipped as household gods, but are not esteemed so powerful by far as the great one to whom the smaller serpents are subjected. Where the latter are unable to assist, their worshippers have recourse to the great serpent. The national deity of the Kanga is an elephant's tooth, and that of the tribe of the Wawa, a tiger. The Sember have wooden gods in human form, which they call Zioo. The Loango also have similar carved idols of both sexes, some clothed, some naked and painted, as well in their dwellings as in sacred buildings. They are served by priests, who are said to be inspired by them, and give out the answers of the gods as oracles. Some of the Amina call the Creator of the world and of their nation Borriborri, and imagine that he has a wife, who is called Sankomaago, by whom he has a son called Sankombúm, who is the mediator between man and the superior deity.

It is the opinion of these people that the inferior gods are appointed by the chief deity as tutelar gods over certain countries, men, animals, plants, rivers, &c., and must yearly give an account of their conduct. This is done in a general assembly of all the gods at the court of the chief divinity. He who has given satisfaction is confirmed by the great god in his tutelar office of a protecting spirit for a year, and is marked with a red-hot iron: but those who have permitted the evil spirit to disseminate unjust wars among the nations, or have wilfully allowed pestilence or fires, and such evils, in the territory entrusted to them, are deposed from their office, expelled from the rank of gods, and made mortals. From despair and malice such deposed gods are accustomed to embrace the party in opposition to the divinity, and become maleficent spirits. "I have taken this account," says Oldendorp, "of the relation of the inferior gods to the higher deity, from the Journal of Christian Protten,* a native African, who had been for a long time in the community of the brethren."

The fetisses of the Negroes, which hold so prominent a part in their superstition, are of the same nature as the spells and charms of the northern nations, and as the amulets and talismans of the East.

"Fetisses, or schambas," says Oldendorp, "as they are called by the Wawa, are sacred things which have received a peculiar power from God, as well to drive away the evil spirits, as to succour in all sorts of diseases and dangers, especially against enchantment. They have not the dignity of gods; although it might be supposed, from the peculiar veneration of the Negroes for these fetisses, that they were the objects of their national worship, as indeed many ignorant people say. They ornament, not only themselves, but also their idols, with these fetisses, which descend by inheritance from parents to children, who preserve them with the greatest care. Others are preserved in particular houses, over which overseers are appointed. The Mandongo willingly receive for their fetisses anything that has been struck by thunder. Thus we perceive that the Ne-

* The author of a Grammar of the Accra Language, printed at Copenhagen in the year 1764.—Ed.

groes only venerate their fetisses because they believe that something divine has been united to them; and how could this take place more manifestly than in the instance of thunder, which they look upon as the peculiar attribute of the Deity, and proceeding immediately from him?

"The Negroes employ these fetisses especially as a means of protection against everything which they esteem evil or hurtful. Thus the Ibo, when they go to war, bind fetisses with cords round the bodies, to protect them from wounds; and the Amina expect the same advantages from a consecrated cow's tail. They make use of them particularly to preserve them from the evil spirit and his hostile attempts. They believe that he is the origin of all evil; he is the enemy of the good God; he seeks to mislead men, to injure them, destroy them, and after death to get their souls into his power. They never consider themselves secure from his snares.

"No African nation makes this malevolent demon an object of worship, or calls upon him for assistance; but they are universally afraid of this powerful agent, and seek to appease him with favours. Thus, for example, the priests of Amina, before they bury their dead, place some costly things upon a place cleansed for this purpose for the evil spirit, whom they term *Didi*. They call him, and give him to understand that these gifts are for him, and that he must be contented with them, and leave the dead alone. When they wish ill to anyone, they curse him by the Didi, Kaltiampemba, or by whatever name they address the evil spirit."

Religious Practices of these Nations.

We have seen that the Negro nations have agreed with other races of men in the belief that supernatural powers exist to whose control all things are subject, and that they differ not materially from other nations in their conceptions of the nature, attributes, and relations of the gods to each other. It seems that they further agree with European and Asiatic nations in the methods by which they endeavour to conciliate the favour of the unseen beings to whose power they hold themselves to be subject. The principal of these have been everywhere prayers and sacrifices. "The Negroes," says Oldendorp, "profess their dependence upon the Deity in different ways, especially by prayers and offerings. They pray at different times, in different places, and, as the Amina Negroes told me, in every time of need. They pray at the rising and setting of the sun, on eating and drinking, and when they go to war. Even in the midst of the contest, the Amina sing songs to their god, whom they seek to move to their assistance by appealing to his paternal duty. The daily prayer of a Watja Negress was, 'O God, I know thee not, but thou knowest me; thy assistance is necessary to me.' At meals they say, 'O God, thou hast given us this, thou hast made it grow;' and when they work, 'O God, thou hast caused that I should have strength to do this.' The Sember pray in the morning, 'O God, help us; we do not know whether we shall live to-morrow; we are in thy hand.' The Mandongo pray also for their deceased friends. They pray in the presence of their idols and fetisses. The solemn prayers which are made by a tribe or nation are accompanied by dancing to the sound of instruments, and are pronounced with terrific cries. The Akkran frequently interrupt their dances by kneeling down.

"The requests which they make to God refer to their bodies, health, good weather, rich harvests, victory over their enemies, and such things. In a continued dry season, the Wawa assemble in a melancholy procession, whilst they bind leaves upon their bodies and heads, before the schambeo-house, in which a tiger is worshipped as a god. With howling and lamentation they represent to him their necessity, and pray that he will cause it to rain, since they must all otherwise die of hunger. Among the Loango, upon a similar occasion, an offering of cattle is brought. When this is accomplished with the customary ceremonies, the priest, who is as well an enchanter, desires the people to hasten home, and not to be surprised by rain. Among the Koromanti Negroes the women go in procession to their priest, whom they call *belum*, bring him all sorts of fruits, and beg him to procure them rain. The Watja beseech the new moon to give them strength for labour, and the Amina even request their god to pay their debts.

"The sacrifices, which are always performed in sacred places by consecrated persons, constitute the most important part of their worship. The sacred places are those where one of their divinities dwells, visibly or invisibly, particularly buildings, or hills, or trees, remarkable for their age, height, and strength. They have also sacred groves, which are the abodes of a deity, which no Negro ventures to enter, except the priests.

"The oblations of the Negroes consist of oxen, cows, sheep, goats, fowls, palm-oil, brandy, yams, &c. Human sacrifices are offered by some nations. On joyful occasions they offer white, and on sorrowful, black animals. The sacrifices take place partly at appointed seasons, and partly occasionally; the intention of them is to gain the favour of the deity, to procure help in sickness or in war, and rain in dry seasons, or to manifest their gratitude for benefits received. Oblations are also brought for the dead.

"When the young men of Temba go to war, the old, who remain at home, seek to gain for them the protection and assistance of Sioo, their divinity, by prayers and offerings. They fall before the image upon their knees, offer him sheep and fowls, pour out the blood and entrails before him; but they dress the flesh for a meal for themselves. If the design of the sacrifices is not obtained, and the expedition does not succeed well, the fault is not laid upon Sioo: they do not doubt his willingness to assist; he has been unable for this time to prevail against the powerful god of the enemy. In order to obtain rain, the Amina sacrifice many sheep and fowls, and beseech the Tankoubum to cause rain to flow as plentifully from heaven as their blood has flowed for him. Many oblations are made for the sick, and many presents are given to the priests, that they may assist in restoring him to health. If the sick person dies, the priests are persuaded that the gods wished for his soul; against this no presents could be of service. If he recovers, his friends prepare a great feast, and offer for a testimony of gratitude white sheep and fowls."

Obsequies—Public Celebrations—Pilgrimages.

"Even the dead are not buried without sacrifices. A white hen is slain by the priest before the corpse comes to the grave, and the bier whereon the body lies is sprinkled with its blood. This custom was introduced by the nation of the Kangrent. These people offer to the deity a tame animal when they till the ground, and vow another of the same kind if God will bless their produce. Human sacrifices are very rare among the Negroes, but not entirely unknown. In Old Kalabar a child of ten months old was hanged upon a tree with a living fowl for the recovery of the king, which M. Seelgrave relates as an eye-witness. Thus the king of Dahomeh sacrificed to his god, out of gratitude for the victory granted to him, 4000 captive Fidans, and caused their heads to be cut off, and piled together in a heap.

"At the annual harvest-feast, which nearly all the nations of Guinea solemnise, thank-offerings are brought to the deity. These festivals are days of rejoicing which the Negroes pass with feasting and dancing, and they prove their gratitude to their divinities by pouring out before them and offering to them a portion of their prepared food. They likewise give back to their gods, in gratitude, a part of everything they earn. The Karabari have the peculiar custom on such feast-days of hunting the evil spirit out of their villages before they celebrate their harvest-feast. The Watja assemble at harvest upon a pleasant plain, when they thank God thrice upon their knees, under the direction of a priest, for the good harvest, and pray to him for further blessings. When they have risen, the whole assembly testify their gratitude to God and their rejoicing by clapping their hands. After this divine service a joyful feast follows, for which each family kills and prepares white sheep and fowls.

"Among the annual festivals is the pilgrimage of the nation of Fida to the great serpent. The people collected before the house of the serpent, lying upon their faces, worship this supposed divinity, without daring to look upon him. Except the priests, the king alone has this favour once. In the same manner the Wawa hold an annual service in honour of a tiger, whom they look upon as a god, and whom a priestess serves. They do not only then solemnly worship him, but bring him oblations of maize, fowls, sheep, and such things. These are first set before the tiger, who is ornamented at this solemnity with schambos or fetisses, and what he leaves is made into a sacrificial repast, which is accompanied with dances and other amusements. A Negro also annually solemnises the day on which he first shed the blood of a human being."

Of their orders of Priests, their Offices and Power.

Like all the nations of antiquity, the Pagan Negroes ascribe to a particular class of men the office of mediators between mankind and the gods. The priests in Africa, as elsewhere, are the only individuals who can offer acceptable sacrifices to the divinity,—they alone are interpreters of the divine will. To this function they join that of diviners, or magicians, masters of spells and amulets. It is really wonderful to discover so extensive an analogy in the opinions of men and of races separated from each other from immemorial time, not only in the general principles of natural religion which conscience and the internal feelings impress upon the understanding and belief, but in all the various phases and modifications of superstition, and in the modes by which crafty and designing men have availed themselves of the weakness and credulity of the people.

"The priests and priestesses are the sacred persons

upon whom the divine service of the Negroes depends, and who, as they suppose, have confidential intercourse with the gods, and interpret their will. They alone understand by what means the wrath of the deity may be appeased. To them it belongs to present the offerings to the gods, and to be the intercessors between them and the people. They convey the questions of the people to the gods, who reply by the mouth of the priests. It is not, therefore, to be wondered at that they are held in the greatest esteem by the people, and exercise almost boundless authority over them. No Negro will transgress the priest's commands. Even after death, in the performance of sacred ceremonies at the burial of the body, the assistance of the priest is necessary, for he alone understands how to prevent the evil spirit from getting the soul into his power.

"At times of sickness, warlike expeditions, and in other important affairs, the Negroes desire to be assured of the issue by a divine answer. In such cases, the Amina bring a sheep, either entirely white or black, to the priest, who sacrifices it, and with its blood sprinkles a large vessel; whereupon he receives an answer to the question laid before him. If a Fida Negro is sick, he causes the serpent to be interrogated through the priest, whether his disease proceeds from God or from enchantment. Together with the answer which he receives, a remedy is shown him, by means of which he may recover. But if the disease is fatal, he receives the melancholy intelligence that he can be cured by no possible means. In this case, the priest, or priestess, takes no reward for their trouble, which is required in all other instances. The great snake, unasked, reveals impending wars to the priestess, who does not fail to give intelligence of it to the king. She tells him the name of the enemy, appoints the time of the invasion, and the fortunate or unfortunate issue of the affair. In the latter case, she gives him the prudent advice to save himself by a speedy flight. She also foretells to the king the time when ships will arrive. The priests likewise foretell death and sterility, as the effect of the anger of the gods, who, however, may be appeased by presents and sacrifices. Nothing is so concealed that the priests cannot foretell it: even the fate of souls after death is known to them, and from them it can be learned whether each individual is gone to God or to the evil spirit.

"The priests of the Negroes are also the physicians, as were the priests of Apollo and Æsculapius. The notions which the Negroes entertain of the causes of diseases are very different. The Watje attribute them to evil spirits, whom they call Dobbo. When these are very numerous, they ask of their sacred cotton-tree permission to hunt them out. Hereupon a chase is appointed, and they do not cease following the demons with arms and great cries until they have chased them beyond their boundaries. This chase of the spirits of disease is very customary among many nations of Guinea, who universally believe that many diseases arise from enchantment, and others by the direction of the Deity."

Ingenious Figments by which these Pretensions are Maintained: Auguries or Omens by Birds.

"It is not in consequence of the unskilfulness of physicians that their remedies are of little use during the rainy season, but, as they say, on account of the absence of their gods, who are obliged to appear at this dangerous season at the court of their superior Deity. Consequently, the priests cannot get advice from them, and they can do nothing effectually without instructions. During the absence of the protecting spirits, which lasts six weeks, the sacred drum is not beaten, no holydays are held, and the dead are interred without noise or songs, and without being bewailed. Among the Fida, those who have received no help in their sickness from small snakes or household gods, turn to the great serpent, who discovers through the priests a remedy, or reproves them for not having sufficiently honoured or entirely obeyed the inferior gods; and, to regain their favour, he advises them to offer fowls and the like, to appoint a feast in honour of the gods, and to invite an assembly to sing, play, dance, and make merry. In this way the inferior gods will become favourable to them and heal them. When the Mokko, by the instruction of the priests, have brought an offering for a sick person, they leave a portion of the sacrificial meat for the birds, and decide upon the cure or death of the person according to the deportment of the birds to the food. Some of the sacrificial blood is sprinkled upon the medicaments which the sick person is to take."

Holy Water.

"The priests of the Akripons take of the holy water, which flows from the hole in the rock in which their god Kinka dwells, and give it to the patients, who are to wash themselves with it, and be cured of their infirmities. Some Kassenti offer for a sick person a hen at a sacred tree, which they worship on their knees, and they pour a thick pap of maize over it before the tree, part of which they take to anoint the patient.

"Of the Bliakefa, the priests of Karabani and of Sokko, it is remarkable that they give some instruction to the people concerning the divinity and prayer. The Negroes come to them for this purpose, either singly or in companies, when they pray with them on their knees that God, whom they call Tschukka, will protect them from war, captivity, and the like.

"They promise to their priests that they will use their slaves mildly, and give them two days in each week for their own concerns. Some priests are likewise sorcerers; but among several nations, the Sokko and Watje for example, the latter office is distinguished from the former."

Immortality of the Soul.

"There is scarcely any nation of Guinea which does not believe in the immortality of the soul, and that it continues to live after its separation from the body, has certain necessities, performs actions, and is especially capable of the enjoyment of happiness or misery. The Amina call the soul and the shadow by the same name; and some of the Watje nation told me that they consider the soul to be of as subtile a nature as is the shadow."

State of Retribution.

"The Negroes believe, almost universally, that the souls of good men, after their separation from the body, go to God, and the wicked to the evil spirit; whence, at the death of their chiefs, they make use of the expression, 'God has taken their souls.' The Loango imagine the abode of the blessed to be where Sambeau Pungo, that is, God, dwells, but hell to be above in the air, which others, on the contrary, suppose to be deep in the earth. They believe that the souls which go to the evil spirit become ghosts, and reappear; and because they preserve their inclination to do evil, torment those whom they dislike in sleep; and, besides, flutter about in the air, and make noises and disturbances in the bushes. If anyone, therefore, is said to appear on the third day after his death, it is a proof that he is not gone to God. The body of a Negro of whom a wicked neighbour pretends to have seen the spirit is not buried with honour, among the Amina. The Negroes imagine, also, that even the good souls are often compelled to pass by the evil spirit before they go to God, when this wicked spirit endeavours to bring them into his power. Hence arises a custom which the Amina observe: survivors satisfy the claims of the Dide, as it has been before observed. The Mokko affirm that they free themselves from the claims of the evil spirit, by proving that they belong to God by the marks which they have upon their bodies, to which nothing can be objected. The Ibo say that each soul is accompanied upon the way to its appointed place by two spirits, a good and evil one, and has to pass a dangerous part (a wall) by which the road is divided. The good spirit helps a pious soul happily by: on the other hand, a wicked one knocks his head against it. After this, the road opens (a narrow one), by which the good soul is led by his benevolent director to God, and one broad, by which the wicked soul, under the guidance of the malevolent spirit, is conducted to a darker place. The representations which these ignorant people give of the situation of the blessed are very similar to their other ideas. Their conduct towards the deceased gives us to understand that they suppose the future condition to be little different from the present life, and they believe them to be affected with the same wants which they have here; on which account they not only place for some time food upon their graves, but give them likewise their wives, servants, and slaves, in the other world."

Metempsychosis.

The Karabari, and several other black tribes, believe in the doctrine of the transmigration of the soul from one body to another, and imagine that the soul of a dead person revives in the body of the next child born after his death. It is fully established, by the assurances of the Negroes, that they believe in the transmigration of a human soul into the body of a bird, fish, or other creature. This belief in metempsychosis has a very injurious effect upon many Negroes. If their slavery is too severe in the West Indies, they destroy themselves, with the prospect that their souls will wander to their country, and there revive in the body of a child. Some fully believe that they will rise alive in Guinea. Murderers and such criminals are shut out from the privilege of commencing a second happier course of life in a strange body. Abarre, the evil spirit, will ordain that, as a punishment, they fly about as ghosts, and by inclination torment men by frightful appearances.

I could cite other writers on the history of the African nations who confirm the statements given by Oldendorp, though none of them have written so clearly and distinctly, and apparently from such full and satisfactory sources of information. Many similar observations occur in the accounts obtained by Fathers Loyer, Labat, and by Bosman. From the last-mentioned writer I shall cite some further particulars.

Bosman mentions their superstitious fear of ghosts and apparitions. He says "they steadfastly believe the apparitions of spirits and ghosts, and that they disturb and terrify some people. If any considerable person dies, they are perplexed with horrid fears, fancying that he appears for several nights successively before his late dwelling."

"They have long been acquainted with the division of time into weeks, and each day of the seven has its proper name in their language. Their sabbath falls on our Tuesday, except at Ante, where, like that of the Mohammedans, it is on Friday. No person is then permitted to fish, which is the only difference."

In their belief of lucky and unlucky days, oracles, omens, and the like, the Negro tribes might be supposed to form their opinions on the model of the Greeks and other nations of antiquity. "The inland Negroes," says Bosman, "divide time into lucky and unlucky days. The great period of good fortune lasts in some countries nineteen, and the lesser seven days: between these there are seven unfortunate days. During the unlucky days, they neither travel, till the land, nor undertake any affair of consequence, but remain altogether idle. The Aquambo people will not even willingly receive any presents made to them on these days. The inhabitants of some countries differ from those of others as to the particular days which they hold to be lucky and unlucky."

Of the Conversion of the Negroes to Christianity.

We have seen that the Negroes of Africa display in their original and primitive state of mind, untaught by foreign instructors, at least within the reach of history, the same tendencies to superstitious belief, as well as the same moral impressions, as the rest of the human family. It only remains, to fill up this part of the mental history of the Negro race, to remark that they have given a ready reception to foreign religions, both true and false. Mohammedanism is well known to have spread in Africa. Sudan sends its yearly pilgrims to venerate the sacred stone; and the sable Hadji is as highly revered on the Niger and the Western Nile as the Syrian pilgrims among the Moslems of Damascus. But I have not room for tracing the progress of Islàm, and it will probably be more satisfactory to my readers to observe the result of endeavours which have been made by European teachers to bring Negroes to the Christian religion. Of these, we have some of the most successful examples in the efforts of the missionaries sent out by the Church of the United Brethren. An interesting account of the proceedings of these well-meaning and devoted persons is to be found in the undisguised and simple narrative of Oldendorp. I shall extract from it a brief statement of such particulars as are necessary, in order to point out the way in which the rudiments of true and uncorrupted religion found their way into the minds of the Africans, and to show how far the process of their conversion indicates an agreement of feeling and sentiment between them and other divisions of mankind.

The first attempts to convert the slaves of the Caribbean Islands to Christianity had their occasion in a meeting of some followers of Count Zinzendorf with one Anthony, a Negro from the Island of St. Thomas, who had been baptised at Copenhagen. This man represented in so strong colours the wretchedness and ignorance of his countrymen and relatives, and urged so zealously his entreaties on the brethren to undertake their conversion, that the congregation at Herrnhut, before whom he had been induced to appear, were disposed to make the attempt. The difficulties of the enterprise were great, and they were not lessened by Anthony, who affirmed that, in order to promote the conversion of slaves, the missionary must himself consent to become a slave. Even under these conditions, several of the brethren were willing to devote themselves to the task. The names of the heroical men who voluntarily offered themselves, believing themselves called to the undertaking, were Leonard Dobel and Tobias Leupold. Leupold did not go, the lot having determined otherwise, and David Nitschmann was substituted for him, who entered on the voyage with similar expectations.

The business was commenced under the most unfavourable circumstances. The work proceeded slowly at first, and amidst great opposition; yet a small number of hearers were soon collected, some of whom gave signs of sincere conversion, and of disgust at their former courses of life. Circumstances required the return of the missionaries to Europe, and an interval ensued, during which the mission was suspended. It was renewed in 1734, on the arrival of Martin, a zealous preacher, and a man of great energy, whose exhortations were followed with so much effect, that when Bishop Spangenberg visited the mission, in 1736, he found in not less than 200 Blacks who attended the services of the brethren a great desire to be instructed in the Christian religion, and three individuals who, on a careful examination, were judged to be in a fit state to receive baptism. It is impossible to read the narrative of Oldendorp without being convinced of the perfect sincerity of the writer and the truth of his account. It proves that no other means were used to influence the Negroes, that no other motives were put in operation to affect their minds, than those of which the promulgators of Christianity availed themselves in the first ages of the Church. "Full of ardour for the salvation of men," says Oldendorp, "Martin declared to the poor slaves the infinite kindness and condescension of the Saviour; what for their sakes He had done and suffered; and how worthy He was of their gratitude and love." "If he once received concerning any individual the impression that a change had been commenced in his mind, he never lost sight of such a person, but with the greatest constancy followed up his work till he gained him over to the cause of religion. By the constant exhortations of the brethren, a perceptible change was produced in the minds and characters of the Negroes; and notwithstanding the unfavourable circumstances and the bad examples by which they were surrounded, it became manifest, not only that the number of professed converts increased, but that motives and influences were in operation capable of effecting a moral revolution in their minds and character; and so deep was the impression which had been produced, that when the colonial government, jealous of innovation, threw the missionaries into prison, baptised Negroes were found ready to carry on the work of exhortation, and contribute greatly to increase the number of converts. When, in the following year, 1739, Count Zinzendorf visited the island, he was filled with astonishment at the greatness of the work which had been accomplished. It seems that at this time the number of Negroes who regularly attended the preaching of the Gospel amounted to 800."

The other Danish islands, St. Croix and St. Jan, were afterwards visited by the Moravian missionaries, whose exertions were attended with like success. I shall not attempt to follow the steps of their progress, which are described by the writer so frequently cited. In his conclusion, he gives the summary of its results, from which it appears that in the year 1768 the number of Negroes who had been baptised in the three islands by the missionaries during thirty-four years amounted to 4711.

In this very general statement of the facts connected with the conversion of the Negroes in these islands, the principal evidence is yet wanting by which it may be proved that the minds of Negroes are not otherwise than those of Europeans capable of receiving all the impressions implied in conversion to Christianity. This evidence can only be fully appreciated by those who read in detail the biographical notices and other particulars detailed by the historians of the community to which Oldendorp, as well as Crantz, belonged. But no part of this evidence is more conclusive than the selection of short homilies composed by Negro preachers or assistants, and addressed by them to congregations of their countrymen. Some of these, though they do not rival in strength of expression the reflections of Pascal and Fénélon, breathe the same spirit, and were evidently written under the influence of the same sentiments. A selection of these addresses has been appended by Oldendorp to his work, which I have so often cited.

CONCLUSION.

It would not greatly strengthen the conclusion which I am entitled to draw from the evidence already afforded, if the limits of this work allowed me to survey the history of every particular branch of the human family. The woolly-haired races of Africa, compared with the native tribes of the New World, and with the anciently civilised inhabitants of the Old Continent, furnish a sufficiently ample field for induction on this subject, since among them are comprised these human races who differ most widely from each other in structure of body and in all their physical attributes, and who have been represented as displaying the most decided contrasts in their moral and intellectual endowments. It would, indeed, be very easy to extend this research, with similar results, to all the other tribes of whose character we have yet any sufficient knowledge. Thus the nations of the great Southern Ocean might be shown to have had among themselves, long before their discovery by Europeans, traits of a very similar kind. They had social institutions resembling those of the rest of mankind; they had universally the belief in a future life, in the protection and government of the world by Providence, in the influence of good and evil genii on human affairs, in the duty of worshipping the gods, in the efficiency of sacrifices and obsequies, or rites performed in behalf of the dead, in the influence of priests, or human mediators. Similar observations may be made with respect to all the barbarous nations of Northern Asia. The history of the conversion of these nations to Christianity, and of the adoption among them of the ideas and practices of civilised nations, would furnish chapters equally striking and remarkable as those to which our attention has already been directed, in the history of the human mind. The Australians as yet remain of all nations the least known, since scarcely any one has yet been able to converse with them, or to understand the expression of their thoughts. But fresh evidence is every day collected tending to raise the low estimate which had been formed, and long maintained, of their extreme mental degradation. Degraded they doubtless are: the tribes with whom the colonists have principally had intercourse are, in their external condition, perhaps the most miserable of the human family, being destitute of the arts which could alone enable them to live with any degree of comfort in the region which they inhabit, or even to support, unless scattered in small wandering bands over a wide space, their physical existence. But there is reason to believe that we have as yet seen only the most destitute of the whole nation; and that there are tribes farther to the northward, perhaps in the inland countries of the great Austral land, who are by no means so miserable or so savage as the people near the southern shores. But even with respect to these, the opinion of the extreme stupidity of the race has been shown to be unfounded, and the latest and most authentic statements enable us to recognise among them the same principles of a moral and intellectual nature, which, in more cultivated tribes, constitute the highest endowments of humanity.

We contemplate among all the diversified tribes who are

endowed with reason and speech, the same internal feelings, appetences, aversions; the same inward convictions, the same sentiments of subjection to invisible powers, and, more or less fully developed, of accountableness or responsibility to unseen avengers of wrong and agents of retributive justice, from whose tribunal men cannot even by death escape. We find everywhere the same susceptibility, though not always in the same degree of forwardness or ripeness of improvement, of admitting the cultivation of these universal endowments, of opening the eyes of the mind to the more clear and luminous views which Christianity unfolds, of becoming moulded to the institutions of religion and of civilised life: in a word, the same inward and mental nature is to recognised in all the races of men. When we compare this fact with the observations which have been heretofore fully established as to the specific instincts and separate psychical endowments of all the distinct tribes of sentient beings in the universe, we are entitled to draw confidently the conclusion that all human races are of one species and one family.

INDEX.

C.

D.

E.

F.

G.

THE END.